AF660984

CRIME

Law & Advice

Everyday Guide to
Criminal Law Problems

The daring publisher, Universal Law Publishing Company, among the foremost in the law publishing field and progressive in venturing to bring out rare legal literature of avant garde *character has rightly enriched the* corpus juris *of India*

Justice V R Krishna Iyer
Random Reflections, page 14

CRIME
Law & Advice

Everyday Guide to Criminal Law Problems

Sudershan Goel
Advocate (Attorney-at-Law)
International Visiting Scholar
School of Law, University of North Carolina
at Chapel Hill NC, USA

Ravi Sodhi
Advocate
Punjab & Haryana High Court
Addl. Standing Counsel, Chandigarh Administration
(Former Addl., Advocate General, Punjab)

Foreword by

Justice M. Jeyapaul
Judge, Punjab & Haryana High Court

Universal
Law Publishing Co. Pvt. Ltd.
NEW DELHI - INDIA

2013 Edition

ISBN: 978-93-5035-343-1

© Publishers

No part of this publication can be reproduced or transmitted in any form or by any means, without prior permission of the Publishers.

Published by
UNIVERSAL LAW PUBLISHING CO. PVT. LTD.
C-FF-1A, Dilkhush Industrial Estate,
(Near Azadpur Metro Station) G.T. Karnal Road,
Delhi-110 033
Tel.: 011-47082254, 27438103, 27215334
Fax : 011-27458529
E-mail *(For sales inquiries)* : unilaw@vsnl.com
(For editorial inquiries) : edit@unilawbooks.com
Website : www.unilawbooks.com
Join us on Facebook
www.facebook.com/unilawbooks

Recommended citation: Sudershan Goel & Ravi Sodhi, *Crime, Law & Advice Everyday Guide to Criminal Law Problems* (New Delhi: Universal Law Publishing Co. Pvt. Ltd., 2013).

This publication is being sold on the condition and understanding that the information, comments, and views it contains are merely for guidance and reference and must not be taken as having the authority of, or being binding in any way on, the author, editors, publishers, and sellers, who do not owe any responsibility whatsoever for any loss, damage, or distress to any person, whether or not a purchaser of this publication, on account of any action taken or not taken on the basis of this publication. Despite all the care taken, errors or omissions may have crept inadvertently into this publication. The publishers shall be obliged if any such error or omission is brought to their notice for possible correction in a future edition. In the case of binding defect, misprint, missing pages, etc., the publishers' liability is limited to replacement of the defective copy within one month of its purchase by a copy of the same edition or reprint. All disputes are subject to the jurisdiction of competent courts in Delhi.

Computer Typeset at Aesthetic and *Printed* at Glorious Printers, New Delhi.

M. JEYAPAUL
Judge
Punjab and Haryana High Court

Kothi No. 31, Sector 4,
Chandigarh
Tel.: 0172-2744333 (Resi.)

सत्यमेव जयते

FOREWORD

Crime, justice and criminal laws have occupied a front row in today's society characterized by turbulence. Criminal Law Tablets is an efficacious potion for infusing awareness about criminal laws of India. The book is punctuated with the legal position on multi-dimensional aspects. It has also references to the practices in UK, USA, Germany, Japan and Canada and the relevance of International charters. The book is well researched and updated with the laws enunciated by the Supreme Court of India.

The book is quite readable and fascinating. The exceptional topics under treatment in this Book are relevant to wide ranging sections of society. It would be equally useful to the common man, the law students, the lawyers, the jurists, the judges and the social scientists. It is heartening to note that practicing lawyers still participate in academics and legal research of this high order. The authors have proven credentials in the legal field in India and the United States. Their contribution to legal field is noteworthy and commendable.

The book covers a broad spectrum of topics on jurisdictional issues, heinous crimes of rape, murder, mercy killing, white collar crimes, child abuse, investigating methods and their legal value, law on bails, hostile and child witness, perjury and the like.

I am sure that this book will have a unique place in the most coveted libraries and it would be a worthy reference book in highest juristic circles. A book in this excellent format was long due and the authors have aptly filled the vacuum. I congratulate them for the scholarly authorship and wish them all success in their academic and professional endeavor.

Sd/-

Justice M. Jeyapaul

PREFACE

Rampant crime has become an integral part of modern life. In a developing country like ours, the impact of criminal activities is profound and far reaching. As lawyers, this area of criminal justice has always held a special interest for us with a dormant desire to make our limited contribution in this oft neglected sphere by our law makers and enforcement agencies. This book is a manifestation of this latent desire. It is surprising as to how many laws need to be updated and fine tuned to the present day realities of Indian life. Our sensitivity to human suffering could not allow us, any longer, to remain silent spectators to the pain and suffering which accompanies the commission of an offence. We derive our inspiration for this book from **Emersons' recipe for success:**

> *"To laugh often and much; to win the respect of intelligent people and the affection of children; to earn the appreciation of honest critics and endure to find the best in others; to leave the world a bit better, whether by the healthy child, a garden patch or a redeemed social condition; to know even one life has breathed easier because you have lived. This is to have succeeded".*

This book would have served its purpose even if one single human finds recourse in alleviating his or her suffering due to any criminal activity being mitigated by finding an answer in this work.

This book is a potion in tablet form of our three-decades long experience as practicing lawyers and academicians at various national and international fora. We have painted with a big brush on the wide canvas of criminal law and have dwelled on wide ranging topics covering perjury, corruption, domestic violence, bails, evidence, criminal procedures, medical jurisprudence, ballistics, forensic science and criminology.

The format of this book is in easy simple language for laymen, students, lawyers, Judges and the jurists. It is in question and answer form and covers several hundred Judgments of the Indian Supreme Court punctuated with foreign law. We have dealt with many life threatening situations faced by common men in a clear and lucid manner. We derive our motivations from **Benjamin Franklin's** sentiments, thus:

> *"If you would not be forgotten,*
> *As soon as you are dead and rotten,*
> *Either write things worth reading,*
> *Or do things worth writing."*

ACKNOWLEDGEMENTS

Our heart-felt acknowledgement to our close family members and associates, Shri J.K. Bahri, Mrs Monica Sodhi, Miss Seema Chettri, Mr. Eeeshan Sodhi and Miss Aditi Goel, who not only encouraged us but also provided full support.

We are grateful to the Universal team, more particularly Dr Manish Arora, Shri Sanjeev Arora and Shri Vaibhav Arora for their support and encouragement to complete this project. Our colleagues S/Shri V.C. Mahajan, (Sr. Advocate), Shri B. C. Rajput [former Member, Punjab Human Rights Commission], Mr. P. N. Puri, Advocate Supreme Court, S. Sunder Singh, Advocate [IPS retd and former Addl DGP West Bengal), Mr. R.N. Singal, former District & Sessions Judge, Mr. Balwan Singh, Advocate and IAS (Retd), and Mr. Ramesh Goyat, Advocate, Shashi Bhushan Goel, who provided their valuable suggestions. Shri Suresh Chand, Shri Suresh Sharma, Daya Kishan and Rajesh in our office team were of valuable assistance. We acknowledge in advance our readers and request them to support us with their suggestions which may be incorporated in next edition.

CONTENTS

SECTION I

SECTION II

CHAPTER 9
WITNESS PROTECTION AND SUPPORT
[A] CANCELLATION OF BAIL ON THE PRAYER OF THE VICTIM/COMPLAINANT

[B] TRANSFER OF CASE ON THE PRAYER OF THE VICTIM/COMPLAINANT

CHAPTER 10
WILD LIFE (PROTECTION) ACT, 1972 – POWER OF FORFEITURE

CHAPTER 11
DNA FINGERPRINTING – ESTABLISHMENT OF IDENTITY OF DEAD BODY

CHAPTER 12
MERCY KILLING – LAW OF EUTHANASIA AND RIGHT OF SUICIDE

CHAPTER 13
ELECTRONIC EVIDENCE

CHAPTER 14
MAINTENANCE

CHAPTER 15
THE LAW OF SENTENCING – MITIGATING FACTORS FOR DEATH PENALTY

CHAPTER 16
A DIVORCED MUSLIM WIFE'S MAINTENANCE RIGHTS UNDER MUSLIM WOMEN (PROTECTION OF RIGHTS ON DIVORCE) ACT, 1986 READ WITH SECTION 125 CR PC

CHAPTER 17

CIVIL REMEDIES AVAILABLE/ CIVIL PROCEEDINGS PENDING

CHAPTER 18

PUBLIC TRIAL – SHIFTING OF COURT SITTING TO JAIL PREMISES

CHAPTER 19

LAW PLACING BURDEN OF PROOF ON THE ACCUSED VALIDATED BEING NECESSARY TO MEET WITH THE MENACE OF LIQUOR ADULTERATION

CHAPTER 20

LEGAL MEANING OF "CONSENT" AND VALUE OF VICTIM'S STATEMENT IN RAPE CASES

TABLE OF CASES

C

S

SECTION I

SECTION I

- Indian Penal Code
- Criminal Procedure Code
- Probation of Offenders Act
- Insecticides Act

1. Jurisdiction Regarding FIR Against NRIs

Q.1. After marrying an NRI, a lady joined her husband at Dubai where she was tormented for dowry. Forced to return to India, the husband's intimidations continued on phone. Can the accused be prosecuted in India?

Ans. Section 3 IPC prescribes punishment of offences committed beyond, India, but which by law may be tried within India. It provides, "Any person liable, by any Indian law, to be tried for an offence committed beyond India shall be dealt with according to the provisions of this Code for any act committed beyond India in the same manner as if such act had been committed within India."

Section 4 IPC extends the provisions of IPC to extra-territorial offences in the following words:

"Extension of Code to extra-territorial offences.—The provisions of this Code apply also to any offence committed by—

(1) any citizen of India in any place without and beyond India;

(2) any person on any ship or aircraft registered in India wherever it may be.

Explanation.—In this section the word "offence" includes every act committed outside India which, if committed in India, would be punishable under this Code.

> *Illustration*—A, who is a citizen of India, commits a Murder in Uganda. He can be tried and convicted of murder in any place in India in which he may be found."

Section 188 of Criminal Procedure Code reads:

> **"Offence committed outside India.**—When an offence is committed outside India—
>
> (a) by a citizen of India, whether on the high seas or elsewhere; or
>
> (b) by a person, not being such citizen, on any ship or aircraft registered in India,
>
> he may be dealt with in respect of such offence as if it had been committed at any place within India at which he may be found:
>
> Provided that, notwithstanding anything in any of the preceding sections of this Chapter, no such offence shall be inquired into or tried in India except with the previous sanction of the Central Government".

The offence alleged is covered within the definition of "continuing offence". The term "continuing offence" has been explained in Halsbury's Law of England, third edition, vol. 10, page 327, paras 602 and 603 thus:

> "602. - A criminal enterprise may consist of continuing act which is done in more places than one or of a series of acts which are done in several places. In such cases, though there is one criminal enterprise, there may be several crimes, and a crime is committed in each place where a complete criminal act is performed although the act may be only a part of the enterprise".
>
> "603. - What constitutes a complete criminal act is determined by the nature of the crime. Thus, as regards continuing acts, in the case of sending by post or otherwise a libellous or threatening letter, or a letter to provoke a breach of the peace, a crime is committed, both where the letter is posted or otherwise sent, and also where it is received, and the venue may be laid in either place."

Thus there is no impediment for the police to register an FIR against the accused under section 498A and 506 of Indian Penal Code. In *Vijayha Saradhi Vaijja* v. *Devi Sriroopa Madapati,* 2007 (3) RCR (Cri) 151, the High Court of Andhra Pradesh, following a Supreme Court judgment in *Ajay Aggarwal* v. *Union of India,* (1993) 3 SCC 609: AIR 1993 SC 1637: (1993) 3 SCR 543, held that resulting effect of section 188 Criminal Procedure Code is that an offence committed by an Indian citizen outside the country is deemed to have been committed in India. However, even though sanction of Central Government is required for the court to proceed further with the trial after filing of charge-sheet, there is no bar for the police to investigate the crime and file a charge-sheet.

Q.2. A girl, married at Delhi, was forced to reside at her parents house at Ambala due to dowry-demands by her in-laws. Could a case be registered at Ambala for return of dowry?

Ans. The courts at Ambala will also have the territorial jurisdiction to try the offence punishable under sections 406 of the Indian Penal Code. In

Shiv Dayal Arora v. *Renu Arora,* 2007 (3) RCR Criminal 10, the Punjab and Haryana High Court ruled that as per section 181(4) of the Criminal Procedure Code the offence of criminal breach of trust may be enquired into or tried by a court within whose jurisdiction any part of the property, which is subject of the offence, was required to be returned or accounted for by the person.

The wife, living at Ambala, can thus validly ask for return of dowry articles there. The High Court held, "... at the most it would amount to an irregularity under section 462 of the Code of Criminal Procedure as the petitioners had failed to show whether any prejudice had been caused to them due to the investigation or enquiry conducted by the police of Police Station...."

The court referred to the law laid down in *Mandeep Singh* v. *State of Punjab,* 1997 (2) RCR (Cri) 154 wherein it was held that in matrimonial cases, the Court at the bride's residence had the jurisdiction to try the offence under sections 406 and 498A, IPC, as the effect of physical cruelty in the shape of mental cruelty travelled to the said place. The following passage was quoted with approval:

> "The debtor must find its creditor is the basic law. Assuming for the sake of argument that this principle of contractual liability is not applicable to the matrimonial cases, still it is the husband who is to account for the dowry articles of his wife which were given in the shape of *Istridhan*. The case of the complainant is that right from the very beginning the family of the accused was not satisfied with the dowry articles. They made a demand of Rs. Five lacs for the installation of a factory. The husband made false representation to the wife, so much so, threat was given to the wife for her liquidation and finally like a prudent lady, the complainant was left with no option but to say to her in-laws, the petitioner, her husband and her sister-in-law to return the dowry articles and this demand was made at Amritsar and once the demand has been made, it becomes obligatory on the part of the accused to account for those articles, and by not doing so, they *prima facie* committed an offence giving territorial jurisdiction to the Amritsar Courts and thus the finding of this Court is in consonance with the provisions of section 181(4) of the Code of Criminal Procedure, which lays down that any offence of criminal misappropriation or of criminal breach of trust may be inquired into or tried by a Court within whose local jurisdiction the offence was committed or any part of the property which is the subject to the offence was received or retained, or was required or accounted for by the accused person. The accused were bound to return the dowry articles/ *Istridhan* of the complainant at Amritsar irrespective of the fact that they were residing outside Amritsar."

Thus in matrimonial cases, the matrimonial courts at the bride's residence have the jurisdiction to try the offences both under sections 406 and 498A Indian Penal Code.

2. Abetment to Commit Suicide

Q.3. On resistance of marriage by girl's parents, the boy committed suicide implicating them in his suicide note. The girl and her parents were

booked for abetment of suicide under sections 306/34 of the Indian Penal Code. Please guide.

Ans. From the above facts and circumstances, it cannot be said that the girl or her parents instigated the victim to take the extreme step. Refusal and resistance of marriage by the girl and her parents does not tantamount to abetment of suicide. Therefore, the FIR is liable to be quashed in view of Punjab and Haryana High Court judgment in *Jaikab Pal* v. *State of Punjab*, 2006 (3) RCR Criminal 84.

Q.4. *'A'* lent Rs. 50,000 to B for one year. *'B'* did not return the money for two years. *A's* asking for return shamed *B* and he committed suicide leaving behind a suicide note implicating *A*. Please guide.

Ans. To prove the offence of abetment, three ingredients are necessary:

(i) The person who committed suicide should be instigated by the accused to take his own life.

(ii) The accused should be involved in the conspiracy whereby the deceased committed suicide.

(iii) The accused should have provided intentional criminal aids to the deceased either by act or by omission for doing such act.

In this case the ingredients of the offence are not *prima facie* made out. In *Vishnu Parshad* v. *State of Madhya Pradesh*, 2005 (3) RCR Criminal 777 MP, followed by Punjab and Haryana High Court in *Amarjit Singh* v. *State of Punjab*, Criminal Misc. No. M-16407 of 2007, decided on 2-2-2009 it was held:

> "When present case is examined in view of the abovesaid background then certainly not a single ingredient of the offence is made out on the basis of entire papers of the charge-sheet. For the sake of argument if story of prosecution is relied as it is then it speaks that there was some loan transaction in between Chintu @ Vivek and deceased and also in between the deceased and present applicant and there was a regular demand of repayment of loan amount and even an altercation took place in between the accused and the deceased and the loan was not repaid by the applicant to the deceased then deceased was having only cause of action to recover this amount through prescribed procedure of law, but it does not mean that if the payment has not been made and some altercation took place in between them and deceased committed suicide only on the ground of non-payment of loan amount. It appears that incident took place because of breach of contract between them but it does not give any indication in respect of criminal offence and in the totality of the facts and circumstances and scenario of case does not reflect any circumstances in which the alleged charges could have been framed and can be sustained."

Q.5. A landlady asked her tenant to vacate her house. The tenant refused. The land-lady committed suicide leaving a suicide note stating refusal to vacate her house by the tenant as a reason. The tenant stands booked under section 306 IPC. Please guide.

Ans. For the offence of abetment of suicide punishable by 306 Indian Penal Code, the presence of *mens rea* is a *sine qua non*. Further, cogent proof that the accused instigated, goaded and provoked the commission of suicide is essential. Merely, because the landlady committed suicide due to non-vacation of her house by the tenant and simply because she named him in her suicide note would not be sufficient to charge the tenant with the offence of abetment to suicide. [Ref: *Ramesh Chander Sibbal* v. *State of (Govt. of NCT of Delhi)*, 2010 (1) RCR (Cri) 673 (Del HC)].

Q.6. A servant committed theft of gold and cash. Despite employer's threat, he did not return the stolen goods and instead committed suicide. The employer was booked under section 306 Indian Penal Code (abetment to suicide). Please guide.

Ans. In order to bring home an offence punishable under section 306 of Indian Penal Code, there has to be a clear *'mens rea'* to commit the offence. It also requires a direct act which leads the deceased to commit suicide. This act must have been intended to push the victim into such a position that he was forced to take such an extreme step. The Supreme Court in *Chitresh Kumar Chopra* v. *State (Govt. of NCT of Delhi)*, 2009 (4) RCR (Cri) 196, has held that there should be intention to provoke, incite or encourage the doing of an act by the latter and each person's suicidal tendency is different from the others as each person has own idea of self-esteem and self-respect.

> "....in order to prove that the accused abetted commission of suicide by a person, it has to be established that: (i) the accused kept on irritating or annoying the deceased by words, deeds or wilful omission or conduct which may even be a wilful silence until the deceased reacted or pushed or forced the deceased by his deeds, words or wilful omission or conduct to make the deceased move forward more quickly in a forward direction; and (ii) that the accused had the intention to provoke, urge or encourage the deceased to commit suicide while acting in the manner noted above. Undoubtedly, presence of *mens rea* is the necessary concomitant of instigation."

In a similar situation, the Supreme Court ruled in *Gangula Mohan Reddy* v. *State of Andhra Pradesh*, 2010 (1) RCR (Cri) 603 thus: "The intention of the Legislature and the ratio of the cases decided by this court is clear that in order to convict a person under section 306 IPC there has to be a clear *mens rea* to commit the offence. It also requires an active act or direct act which led the deceased to commit suicide seeing no option and this act must have been intended to push the deceased into such a position that he committed suicide."

3. Rash and Negligent Act

Q.7. A farmer had laid naked electric wires in his field to avoid entry of stray animals. A person, who entered the area, died due to electrocution. The police booked the farmer under section 304A of the Indian Penal Code. Please guide.

Ans. Section 304A of the Indian Penal Code reads:

> "304A. Whoever causes the death of any person by doing any rash or negligent act not amounting to culpable homicide shall be punished with imprisonment of either description for a term which may extend to two years, or with fine, or with both."

In *Chembin Gregory* v. *State of Bihar*, AIR 1964 SC 205: (1964) 4 SCR 199: 1963 Cur LJ (SC) 123, the Supreme Court ruled: "The voltage of the current passing through the naked wire being high enough to be lethal, there could be no dispute that charging it with current of that voltage was a 'rash act' done in reckless disregard of the serious consequences to people coming in contact with it. .... It is, no doubt true that the trespasser enters the property at his own risk and the occupier owes no duty to take any reasonable care for his protection, but at the same time the occupier is not entitled to do willfully acts such as set a trap or set a naked live wire with the deliberate intention of causing harm to trespassers or in reckless disregard of the presence of the trespassers. As we pointed out earlier, the voltage of the current fed into the wire precludes any contention that it was merely a reasonable precaution for the protection of private property." This judgement has been followed by the Punjab and Haryana High Court in *Rattan Chand* v. *State of Punjab*, 2007 (2) RCR Criminal 622 (P&H).

4. Right of Private Defence

Q.8. If an advocate did not take the specific plea of self-defence during cross-examination or statement of accused recorded under section 313 Criminal Procedure Code, whether self-defence can be pleaded at the stage of arguments?

Ans. Even if the plea of private defence is not specifically taken by the accused in their statements under section 313, Code of Criminal Procedure and even if the accused who was injured in the incident did not enter in the witness box, a plea of private defence can still be raised during arguments. In view of law laid down by the Supreme Court *Kashi Ram* v. *State of Madhya Pradesh*, (2002) 1 SCC 71: AIR 2001 SC 2902: 2001 AIR SCW 4350 such plea can be considered by the courts if made out from the evidence on record. The Supreme Court ruled: "A plea of self defence can be taken by introducing such plea in the cross-examination of prosecution witnesses or in the statement of the accused persons recorded under section 313, Cr. P.C. or by adducing defence evidence. And, even if the plea is not introduced in any one of these three modes still it can be raised during the course of submissions by relying on the probabilities and circumstances obtaining in the case. ..... It is basic criminal jurisprudence that an accused cannot be compelled to be examined as a witness and no adverse inference can be drawn against the defence merely because an accused person has chosen to abstain from the witness box."

Q.9. Whether the right of Private Defence can be weighed in golden scales?

Ans. Private defence, being essentially a defensive right as opposed to acts of reprisal, postulates infliction of injury commensurate with perceived threat.

All the same, it is neither pragmatic nor possible to expect the person exercising this right in good faith to carry weights in his pocket for measuring with golden scale the amount of physical force necessary. *Bona fide* action is the *sine qua non*. In *Subramani* v. *State of Tamil Nadu*, (2002) 7 SCC 210: AIR 2002 SC 2980: 2002 Cr LJ 4102 the Supreme Court held that in exercise of the right of private defence only such force may be used as may be necessary but it is equally well-settled that at a time when a person is faced with immediate peril of life and limb of himself or other, he is not expected to weigh in golden scales the precise force needed to repel the danger.

Q.10. To what extent is use of force justified by a person under threat to life?

Ans. Section 99 of Indian Penal Code reads:

"Section 99. Act against which there is no right of private defence.—There is no right of private defence against an act which does not reasonably cause the apprehension of death or of grievous hurt, if done, or attempted to be done, by a public servant acting in good faith under colour of his office, though that act, may not be strictly justifiable by law.

There is no right of private defence against an act which does not reasonable cause the apprehension of death or of grievous hurt, if done, or attempted to be done, by the direction of a public servant acting in good faith under colour of his office, though that direction may not be strictly justifiable by law.

"There is no right of private defence in cases in which there is time to have recourse to the protection of the public authorities.

Extent to which the right may be exercised - **The right to private defence in no case extends to the inflicting of more harm that it is necessary to inflict for the purpose of defence.**

Explanation 1.—A person is not deprived of the right of private defence against an act done, or attempted to be done, by a public servant, as such, unless he knows or has reason to believe, that the person doing the act is such public servant.

Explanation 2.—A person is not deprived of the right of private defence against an act done, or attempted to be done, by the direction of a public servant, unless he knows, or has reason to believe, that the person doing the act is acting by such direction, or unless such person states the authority under which he acts, or if he has authority in writing, unless he produces such authority, if demanded."

In *Darshan Singh* v. *State of Punjab*, (2010) 2 SCC 333 (334): AIR 2010 SC 1212: 2010 AIR SCW 832, the Supreme Court ruled that "when a person is exercising his right of private defence, it is not possible to weigh the force with which the right is exercised. The principle is common to all civilized jurisprudence. In *Robert B. Brown* v. *United States of America*, (1921) 256 US 335: 6 Law Ed 961, it is observed that a person in fear of his life in not expected to modulate his defence step by step or tier by tier. Justice Holmes in the aforementioned case aptly observed "detached reflection cannot be demanded in the presence of an uplifted knife"

The following principles have been laid down by the Supreme Court in Para 58:—

(i) Self-preservation is the basic human instinct and is duly recognized by the criminal jurisprudence of all civilized countries. All free, democratic and civilized countries recognize the right of private defence within certain reasonable limits.

(ii) The right of private defence is available only to one who is suddenly confronted with the necessity of averting an impending danger and not of self-creation.

(iii) A mere reasonable apprehension is enough to put the right of self defence into operation. In other words, it is not necessary that there should be an actual commission of the offence in order to give rise to the right of private defence. It is enough if the accused apprehended that such an offence is contemplated and it is likely to be committed if the right of private defence is not exercised.

(iv) The right of private defence commences as soon as a reasonable apprehension arises and it is co- terminus with the duration of such apprehension.

(v) It is unrealistic to expect a person under assault to modulate his defence step by step with any arithmetical exactitude.

(vi) In private defence the force used by the accused ought not to be wholly disproportionate or much greater than necessary for protection of the person or property.

(vii) It is well settled that even if the accused does not plead self-defence, it is open to consider such a plea if the same arises from the material on record.

(viii) The accused need not prove the existence of the right of private defence beyond reasonable doubt.

(ix) The Indian Penal Code confers the right of private defence only when that unlawful or wrongful act is an offence.

(x) A person who is in imminent and reasonable danger of losing his life or limb may in exercise of self defence inflict any harm even extending to death on his assailant either when the assault is attempted or directly threatened.

5. Teachers' Right of Corporal Punishment

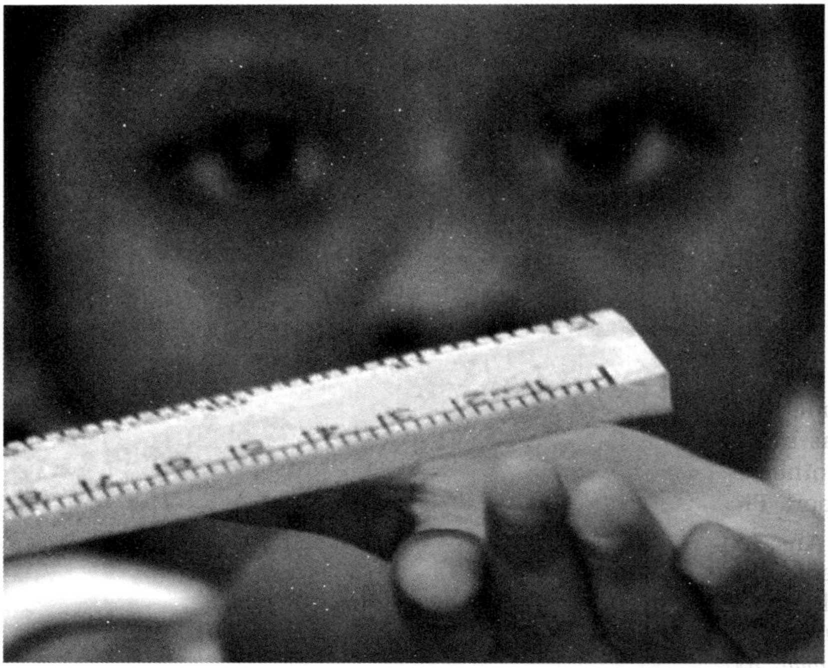

Q.11. A student aged nine years was caught stealing in class. He sustained injuries at the hand of the teacher. What is the master's liability?

Ans. When a child is sent by his parents to a school, the parent must be said to have given an implied consent to his being under the discipline and control of the school authorities and to the infliction of such reasonable punishment as may be necessary for the purpose of school discipline or for correcting him. Sections 88 and 89 of the Indian Penal Code deals with such a situation. Whether the benefit of exception under sections 88 and 89 of Indian Penal Code will be extended to a teacher or not will depend upon the particular nature, extent, and severity of the punishment inflicted and where a teacher exceeds the authority and inflicts more harm to the student as may be considered to be unreasonable and excessive, he could lose the benefit of exceptions as provided under sections 88 and 89 of Indian Penal Code. In *Abdul Valid* v. *State of Kerala*, 2005 (2) RCR (Criminal) 374, the Kerala High Court held that no offence under sections 323/324 Indian Penal Code is made out against a teacher who gave beating to a student with a cane to maintain discipline with no intention to cause harm, as it was done with *bona fide* intentions. The action of the teacher in administering corporal punishment would be covered by section 88 of the Indian Penal Code.

6. Medical Negligence/Opinion

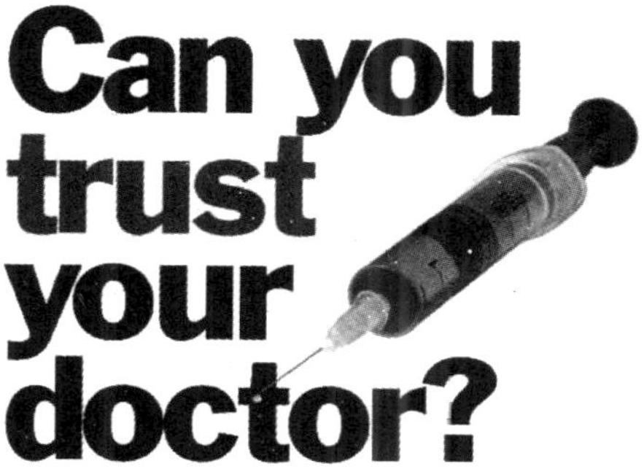

Q.12. During trial of offence under sections 326/324 of the Indian Penal Code for causing injuries to a person, the doctor, who conducted the X-ray, was not produced. The accused was convicted on the basis of statement of another doctor who had declared the injury as grievous in the medico-legal report. Please guide.

Ans. In the absence of the radiologist, the opinion of the doctor who did the medico legal report declaring a particular injury as grievous is of no value as held by a Division Bench of Punjab and Haryana High Court in *State of Haryana* v. *Prem Singh*, 2007 (2) RCR (Cri) 537 and in *Naib Singh* v. *State of Punjab*, 2007 (3) RCR (Cri) 14. The court altered the conviction to section 324 of the Indian Penal Code. It is thus settled that if an X-ray report has not been proved by its author, the same is liable to be excluded from consideration.

Q.13. What is the criminal liability of a doctor when a patient dies despite his best efforts?

Ans. A doctor is not criminally liable unless negligence is reckless and gross and as such, he cannot be punished under section 304A, Indian Penal Code. All the same, he can be sued for damages in civil law. However, his criminal liability under section 304A of Indian Penal Code arises only in cases of reckless negligence endangering human life. A bald statement by the complainant will not suffice. The Doctor's culpability should be substantiated by expert medical evidence.

In *Jacob Mathew* v. *State of Punjab,* (2005) 6 SCC 1: AIR 2005 SC 3180: 2005 Cr LJ 3710, the Supreme Court ruled: "Statutory Rules or Executive Instructions incorporating certain guidelines need to be framed and issued by the Government of India and/or the State Governments in consultation with the Medical Council of India. So long as it is not done, we propose to lay down certain guidelines for the future which should govern the prosecution of doctors for offences of which criminal rashness or criminal negligence is an ingredient. A private complaint may not be entertained unless the complainant has produced *prima facie* evidence before the Court in the form of a credible opinion given by another competent doctor to support the charge of rashness or negligence on the part of the accused doctor. The investigating officer should, before proceeding against the doctor accused of rash or negligent act or omission, obtain an independent and competent medical opinion preferably from a doctor in government service qualified in that branch of medical practice who can normally be expected to give an impartial and unbiased opinion applying Bolam's test to the facts collected in the investigation. A doctor accused of rashness or negligence, may not be arrested in a routine manner (simply because a charge has been levelled against him). Unless his arrest is necessary for furthering the investigation or for collecting evidence or unless the investigation officer feels satisfied that the doctor proceeded against would not make himself available to face the prosecution unless arrested, the arrest may be withheld."

The Court agreed with some of the conclusions arrived at by the learned authors of "Errors, Medicine and the Law" (pp. 241-248), (recorded at the end of the book in the chapter titled 'Conclusion') highlighting the link between moral fault, blame and justice in reference to medical profession and negligence. These are—

"(i) The social efficacy of blame and related sanctions in particular cases of deliberate wrongdoings may be a matter of dispute, but their necessity in principle from a moral point of view, has been accepted. Distasteful as punishment may be, the social, and possibly moral, need to punish people for wrongdoing, occasionally in a severe fashion, cannot be escaped. A society in which blame is overemphasized may become paralysed. This is not only because such a society will inevitably be backward-looking, but also because fear of blame inhibits the uncluttered exercise of judgment in relations between persons. If we are constantly concerned about whether our actions will be the subject of complaint, and that such complaint is likely to lead to legal action or disciplinary proceedings, a relationship of suspicious formality between persons is inevitable. (*ibid.*, pp. 242-243)

(ii) Culpability may attach to the consequence of an error in circumstances where substandard antecedent conduct has been deliberate, and has contributed to the generation of the error or to its outcome. In case of errors, the only failure is a failure defined in terms of the normative standard of what should have been done. There is a tendency to confuse the reasonable person with the error-free person. While nobody can avoid errors on the basis of simply choosing not to make them, people can choose not to commit violations. A violation is culpable. (*ibid.*, p. 245).

(iii) Before the court is faced with deciding the cases of professional negligence there are two sets of interests which are at stake : the interests of the plaintiff and the interests of the defendant. A correct balance of these two sets of interests should ensure that tort liability is restricted to those cases where there is a real failure to behave as a reasonably competent practitioner would have behaved. An inappropriate raising of the standard of care threatens this balance. (*ibid.*, p.246). A consequence of encouraging litigation for loss is to persuade the public that all loss encountered in a medical context is the result of the failure of somebody in the system to provide the level of care to which the patient is entitled. The effect of this on the doctor-patient relationship is distorting and will not be to the benefit of the patient in the long run. It is also unjustified to impose on those engaged in medical treatment an undue degree of additional stress and anxiety in the conduct of their profession. Equally, it would be wrong to impose such stress and anxiety on any other person performing a demanding function in society. (*ibid.*, p.247). While expectations from the professionals must be realistic and the expected standards attainable, this implies recognition of the nature of ordinary human error and human limitations in the performance of complex tasks. (*ibid.*, p. 247).

(iv) Conviction for any substantial criminal offence requires that the accused person should have acted with a morally blameworthy state of mind. Recklessness and deliberate wrongdoing, are morally blameworthy, but any conduct falling short of that should not be the subject of criminal liability. Common-law systems have traditionally only made negligence the subject of criminal sanction when the level of negligence has been high a standard traditionally described as gross negligence. In fact, negligence at that level is likely to be indistinguishable from recklessness. (*ibid.*, p.248).

(v) Blame is a powerful weapon. Its inappropriate use distorts tolerant and constructive relations between people. Distinguishing between (a) accidents which are life's misfortune for which nobody is morally responsible, (b) wrongs amounting to culpable conduct and constituting grounds for compensation, and (c) those (*i.e.* wrongs) calling for punishment on account of being gross or of a very high degree requires and calls for careful, morally sensitive and scientifically informed analysis; else there would be injustice to the larger interest of the society. (*ibid.*, p. 248)."

Further the Supreme Court held, "Indiscriminate prosecution of medical professionals for criminal negligence is counter-productive and does no service or good to the society." The Court summed up its conclusions as under:

"(1) Negligence is the breach of a duty caused by omission to do something which a reasonable man guided by those considerations which ordinarily regulate the conduct of human affairs would do, or doing something which a prudent and reasonable man would not do. The definition of negligence as given in Law of Torts, Ratanlal & Dhirajlal (edited by Justice G.P. Singh), referred to hereinabove, holds good. Negligence becomes actionable on account of injury resulting from the act or omission amounting to negligence attributable to the person sued. The essential components of negligence are three: 'duty', 'breach' and 'resulting damage'.

(2) Negligence in the context of medical profession necessarily calls for a treatment with a difference. To infer rashness or negligence on the part of a professional, in particular a doctor, additional considerations apply. A case of occupational negligence is different from one of professional negligence. A simple lack of care, an error of judgment or an accident, is not proof of negligence on the part of a medical professional. So long as a doctor

follows a practice acceptable to the medical profession of that day, he cannot be held liable for negligence merely because a better alternative course or method of treatment was also available or simply because a more skilled doctor would not have chosen to follow or resort to that practice or procedure which the accused followed. When it comes to the failure of taking precautions what has to be seen is whether those precautions were taken which the ordinary experience of men has found to be sufficient; a failure to use special or extraordinary precautions which might have prevented the particular happening cannot be the standard for judging the alleged negligence. So also, the standard of care, while assessing the practice as adopted, is judged in the light of knowledge available at the time of the incident, and not at the date of trial. Similarly, when the charge of negligence arises out of failure to use some particular equipment, the charge would fail if the equipment was not generally available at that particular time (that is, the time of the incident) at which it is suggested it should have been used.

(3) A professional may be held liable for negligence on one of the two findings: either he was not possessed of the requisite skill which he professed to have possessed, or, he did not exercise, with reasonable competence in the given case, the skill which he did possess. The standard to be applied for judging, whether the person charged has been negligent or not, would be that of an ordinary competent person exercising ordinary skill in that profession. It is not possible for every professional to possess the highest level of expertise or skills in that branch which he practices. A highly skilled professional may be possessed of better qualities, but that cannot be made the basis or the yardstick for judging the performance of the professional proceeded against on indictment of negligence.

(4) The test for determining medical negligence as laid down in *Bolam's* case, [1957] 1 WLR 582 (586) holds good in its applicability in India.

(5) The jurisprudential concept of negligence differs in civil and criminal law. What may be negligence in civil law may not necessarily be negligence in criminal law. For negligence to amount to an offence, the element of *mens rea* must be shown to exist. For an act to amount to criminal negligence, the degree of negligence should be much higher *i.e.* gross or of a very high degree. Negligence which is neither gross nor of a higher degree may provide a ground for action in civil law but cannot form the basis for prosecution.

(6) The word 'gross' has not been used in section 304A of IPC, yet it is settled that in criminal law negligence or recklessness, to be so held, must be of such a high degree as to be 'gross'. The expression 'rash or negligent act' as occurring in section 304A of the IPC has to be read as qualified by the word 'grossly'.

(7) To prosecute a medical professional for negligence under criminal law it must be shown that the accused did something or failed to do something which in the given facts and circumstances no medical professional in his

ordinary senses and prudence would have done or failed to do. The hazard taken by the accused doctor should be of such a nature that the injury which resulted was most likely imminent.

(8) *Res ipsa loquitur* is only a rule of evidence and operates in the domain of civil law specially in cases of torts and helps in determining the onus of proof in actions relating to negligence. It cannot be pressed in service for determining per se the liability for negligence within the domain of criminal law. *Res ipsa loquitur* has, if at all, a limited application in trial on a charge of criminal negligence."

Q.14. Can a woman, who delivered a child despite sterilization, claim compensation from the doctor who sterilized her?

Ans. The surgeon cannot be held liable for compensation unless his negligence is established. Merely because a woman underwent a sterilization operation but subsequently became pregnant and delivered a child will not be sufficient to fasten liability upon the doctor. It was held by the Supreme Court in *State of Punjab* v. *Shiv Ram,* AIR 2005 SC 3280: 2005 AIR SCW 4108: (2005) 7 SCC 1 (Para 25) that, "We are, therefore, clearly of the opinion that merely because a woman having undergone a sterilization operation became pregnant and delivered a child, the operating surgeon or his employer cannot be held liable for compensation on account of unwanted pregnancy or unwanted child. The claim in tort can be sustained only if there was negligence on the part of the surgeon in performing the surgery. The proof of negligence shall have to satisfy Bolam's test. So also, the surgeon cannot be held liable in contract unless the plaintiff alleges and proves that the surgeon had assured 100% exclusion of pregnancy after the surgery and was only on the basis of such assurance that the plaintiff was persuaded to undergo surgery."

Q.15. A lady died during delivery. Her husband alleged negligence and claimed compensation which was rejected by the Consumer Forum for lack of expert medical evidence. Please advise?

Ans. In *Kusum Sharma* v. *Batra Hospital,* AIR 2010 SC 1050: 2010 AIR SCW 1315: (2010) 3 SCC 480, the Supreme Court has held that in cases where medical negligence is alleged, and medical expert opinion is required, then at the outset a Medical Board shall be constituted by the courts. Dismissing appeal filed by Kusum Sharma claiming damages from Batra Hospital, the Supreme Court has recently held that: "It would not be conducive to the efficiency of the medical profession if a doctor is to administer medicine with a halter around his neck".

7. Rape by Women

Q.16. A lady was booked for the offence of gang-rape on the allegation of facilitating her husband in committing rape. Please advise?

Ans. A woman cannot be booked for the offence of rape. In *State of Rajasthan* v. *Hem Raj*, (2009) 12 SCC 403, the Supreme Court has observed that, "A bare reading of section 375 makes the position clear that rape can be committed only by a man. The section itself provides as to when a man can be said to have committed rape. Section 376(2) makes certain categories of serious cases of rape as enumerated therein attracting more severe punishment. One of them relates to "gang rape". The language of sub-section (2)(g) provides that "whoever commits gang-rape" shall be punished etc. The *Explanation* only clarifies that when a woman is raped by one or more in a group of persons acting in furtherance of their common intention each such person shall be deemed to have committed gang-rape within sub-section (2). That cannot make a woman guilty of committing rape. This is conceptually inconceivable."

8. Rape – Abortion – Gay Sex

Q.17. A lady developed physical relations with a married man who was separated from his wife. They married. Later, they fell apart. Can the lady sue him for bigamy and sexual abuse?

Ans. No, the husband is not liable. Under section 494 of IPC, an offence of 'bigamy' is committed when a man marries again during the subsistence of his earlier marriage. The lady, not being the first wife and being admittedly a consenting party, has no locus to file a complaint. A complaint of 'bigamy' can be made only by an 'aggrieved person'. In a similar case involving an offence of 'defamation', where the complaint can be filed only by the person aggrieved, it was held by the Supreme Court in *G. Narasimhan* v. *T.V. Chokkappa,* AIR 1972 SC 2609: 1973 Mad LW (Cri) 59: (1973) 2 SCR 40 that "..... no magistrate shall take cognizance of an offence falling *inter alia* under Chapter XXI of the Penal Code (that is, ssections 499 to 502) except upon a complaint made by some persons aggrieved of such offence. Sec. 198, thus, lays down an exception to the general rule that a complaint 'can be filed by anybody whether he is an aggrieved person or not and modifies that rule by permitting only an aggrieved person to move a magistrate in cases of defamation. The section is mandatory, so that if a magistrate were to take cognizance of the offence of defamation on a complaint filed by one who is not an aggrieved person, the trial and conviction of an accused in such a case by the magistrate would be void and illegal."

Q.18. A man was in love with a girl aged 22 and promised to marry her. A child was born out of their physical relationship. On the pretext of family pressure, the man refused to marry. Whether in these circumstances, he is guilty of rape?

Ans. The man is not guilty of rape. It is a breach of promise and not a case of false promise. In *Jayanti Rani Panda* v. *State of West Bengal,* 1983 (2) Cal HN 290: 1984 Cr LJ 1535 Cal (DB), a Division Bench of the Calcutta High Court held that, "... If a full grown girl consents to the act of sexual intercourse on a promise of marriage and continues to indulge in such activity until she becomes pregnant it is an act of promiscuity on her part and not an act induced by misconception of fact." This view has been approved by the Supreme Court in *Dalip Singh* v. *State of Bihar,* (2004) 1 SCC 88. The Supreme Court in Dalip cited with approval its earlier view in *Uday* v. *State of Karnataka,* (2003) 2 SCALE 329: AIR 2003 SC 1639: 2003 AIR SCW 1035 "It therefore appears that the consensus of judicial opinion is in favour of the view that the consent given by the prosecutrix to sexual intercourse with a person with whom she is deeply in love on a promise that he would marry her on a later date, cannot be said to be given under a misconception of fact. A false promise is not a fact within the meaning of the Code. We are inclined to agree with this view, but we must add that there is no strait jacket formula for determining whether consent given by the prosecutrix to sexual intercourse is voluntary, or whether it is given under a misconception of fact. In the ultimate analysis, the tests laid down by the Courts provide at best guidance to the judicial mind while considering a question of consent, but the Court must, in each case, consider the evidence before it and the surrounding circumstances, before reaching a conclusion, because each case has its own peculiar facts which may have a bearing on the question whether the consent was voluntary, or was given under a misconception of fact. It must also weigh the evidence keeping in view the fact that the burden is on the prosecution to prove each and every ingredient of the offence, absence of consent being one of them."

The Court added in *Dalip Singh's* case: "The first two sentences in the above passage need some explanation. While we reiterate that a promise to marry without anything more will not give rise to 'misconception of fact' within the meaning of section 90, it needs to be clarified that a representation deliberately made by the accused with a view to elicit the assent of the victim without having the intention or inclination to marry her, will vitiate the consent. If on the facts it is established that at the very inception of the making of promise, the accused did not really entertain the intention of marrying her and the promise to marry held out by him was a mere hoax, the consent ostensibly given by the victim will be of no avail to the accused to exculpate him from the ambit of section 375 Clause secondly." However, the Supreme Court decided to compensate the victim holding the accused accountable for damages under civil law.

Q.19. A doctor forced his wife to undergo abortion against her wishes. Her protest invited maltreatment, cruelty and dowry demand by the husband. Please guide.

Ans. The husband is *prima facie* guilty *of* cruelty punishable under section 498A, IPC as well as for forceful abortion punishable under section 313, IPC. The lady may lodge a criminal complaint against her husband. [Reference may be made to: *Pranab Kanti Sen* v. *State of West Bengal*, 2010 (2) Rec CR (Cri) 75 WB].

Q.20. A lady committed suicide within one month of marriage. Her parents alleged 'dowry death' without furnishing any evidence. Can a 'dowry death' be presumed?

Ans. Section 113B of Indian Evidence Act reads as under:

> *113B. Presumption as to dowry death.*—When the question is whether a person has committed the dowry death of a woman and it is shown that soon before her death such woman had been subjected by such person to cruelty or harassment for, or in connection with, any demand for dowry; the court shall presume that such person had caused the dowry death.
>
> *Explanation.*—For the purposes of this section, "dowry death" shall have the same meaning as in section 304B of the Indian Penal Code (45 of 1860).

Relevant portion of section 304B of the Indian Penal Code, (45 of 1860), is reproduced below:

> *304B. Dowry death.*—(1) Where the death of a woman is caused by any burn or bodily injury or occurs otherwise than normal circumstances within seven years of her marriage and it is shown that soon before her death she was subjected to cruelty or harassment by her husband or any relative of her husband for, or in connection with any demand for dowry, such death shall be called "dowry death".

In *Kans Raj* v. *State of Punjab*, (2000) 5 SCC 207: AIR 2000 SC 2324: 2000 AIR SCW 2093 the Supreme Court held, "The law as it exists now provides that where the death of a woman is caused by any burns or bodily injury or occurs otherwise than under normal circumstances within 7 years of marriage and it is shown that soon before her death she was subjected to cruelty or harassment by her husband or any relative for or in connection with any demand of dowry such death shall be punishable under section 304B. In order to seek a conviction against a person for the offence of dowry death, the prosecution is obliged to prove that:

(a) the death of a woman was caused by burns or bodily injury or had occurred otherwise than under normal circumstances;
(b) such death should have occurred within 7 years of her marriage;
(c) the deceased was subjected to cruelty or harassment by her husband or by any relative of her husband;
(d) such cruelty or harassment should be for or in connection with the demand of dowry; and
(e) to such cruelty or harassment the deceased should have been subjected to soon before her death.

No presumption under section 113B of the Evidence Act would be drawn against the accused if it is shown that after the alleged demand, cruelty or harassment the dispute stood resolved and there was no evidence of cruelty, and harassment thereafter. Mere lapse of some time by itself would not provide to an accused a defence, if the course of conduct relating to cruelty or harassment in connection with the dowry demand is shown to have existed earlier in time not too late and not too stale before the date of death of the woman.

The Supreme Court has deprecated the tendency of roping in all the relations of the husband in dowry cases by holding, "for the fault of the husband, the in-laws or the other relations cannot, in all cases, be held to be involved in the demand of dowry. In cases where such accusations are made, the overt acts attributed to persons other than husband are required to be proved beyond reasonable doubt. By mere conjectures and implications such relations cannot be held guilty for the offence relating to dowry deaths. A tendency has, however, developed for roping in all relations of the in-laws of the deceased wives in the matters of dowry deaths which, if not discouraged, is likely to affect the case of the prosecution even against the real culprits. In their over enthusiasm and anxiety to seek conviction for maximum people, the parents of the deceased have been found to be making efforts for involving other relations which ultimately weaken the case of the prosecution even against the real accused as appears to have happened in the instant case."

Q.21. What is the legal position with regard to Gay sex?

Ans. A Division Bench of Delhi High Court in *NAZ Foundation* v. *Government of NCT of Delhi*, 2009 (3) Rec CR (Cri) 523, has held that Gay Sex is legal between consenting adults who are above eighteen. It has been held that section 377 IPC, in so far as it criminalizes consensual sex between two adults in private is violative of articles 21, 14, and 15 of the Constitution of India.

The Court ruled: "If there is one constitutional tenet that can be said to be underlying theme of the Indian Constitution, it is that of 'inclusiveness'. This Court believes that Indian Constitution reflects this value deeply ingrained in Indian society, nurtured over several generations. The inclusiveness that Indian society traditionally displayed, literally in every aspect of life, is manifest in recognising a role in society for everyone. Those perceived by the majority as "deviants' or 'different' are not on that score excluded or ostracised.

> "Where society can display inclusiveness and understanding, such persons can be assured of a life of dignity and non- discrimination. This was the 'spirit behind the Resolution' of which Nehru spoke so passionately. In our view, Indian Constitutional law does not permit the statutory criminal law to be held captive by the popular misconceptions of who the LGBTs are. It cannot be forgotten that discrimination is anti- thesis of equality and that it is the recognition of equality which will foster the dignity of every individual.
>
> "We declare that section 377 IPC, insofar it criminalises consensual sexual acts of adults in private, is violative of Articles 21, 14 and 15 of the Constitution. The provisions of section 377 IPC will continue to govern non-consensual penile non-vaginal sex and penile non-vaginal sex involving minors. By 'adult' we mean everyone who is 18 years of age and above. A person below 18 would be presumed not to be able to consent to a sexual act. This clarification will hold till, of course, Parliament chooses to amend the law to effectuate the recommendation of the Law Commission of India in its 172nd Report which we believe removes a great deal of confusion."

9. Fake Currency

Q.22. In a wedding, some gifted currency notes turned out to be fake. The police insisted on hair-splitting technicality to identity the guest who gifted the currency. Please advise?

Ans. Sections 489B and 489C of I.P.C. read as under:

"*489B. Using as genuine, forged or counterfeit currency-notes or bank-notes.*—Whoever sells to, or buys or receives from, any other person or otherwise traffics in or uses as genuine, any forged or counterfeit currency-note or bank-note, knowing or having reason to believe the same to be forged or counterfeit, shall be punished with [imprisonment for life], or with imprisonment of either description for a term which may extend to ten years, and shall also be liable to fine.

489C. Possession of forged or counterfeit currency notes or bank-notes.—Whoever has in his possession any forged or counterfeit currency-note or bank-note, knowing or having reason to believe the same to be forged or counterfeit and intending to use the same as genuine or that it may be used as genuine, shall be punished with imprisonment of either description for a term which may extend to seven years, or with fine, or with both."

In *Uma Shanker* v. *State of Chattisgarh*, reported as (2001) 9 SCC 642: AIR 2001 SC 3074: 2001 Cr LJ 4696 the Supreme Court has held that in such cases '*mens rea*' or guilty mind is essential to constitute the offence. Merely because the currency notes were found fake, no presumption of '*mens rea*' can be raised." The Supreme Court has further held that unwary possessors or users cannot be prosecuted. The Court ruled: "sections 489A to 489E deal with various economic offences in respect of forged or counterfeit currency-note or bank-notes. The object of Legislature in enacting these provisions is not only to protect the economy of the country but also to provide adequate protection to currency-notes and bank-notes. The currency-notes are, inspite of growing accustomedness to the credit cards system, still the backbone of the commercial transactions by multitudes in our country. But these provisions are not meant to punish unwary possessors or users. A perusal of the provisions, extracted above, shows that *mens rea* of offences under sections 489B and 489C is, "knowing or having reason to believe the currency-notes or bank-notes are forged or counterfeit". Without the afore-mentioned *mens rea* selling, buying or receiving from another person or otherwise trafficking in or using as genuine forged or counterfeit currency-notes or bank-notes, is not enough to constitute offence under section 489B of I.P.C. So also possessing or even intending to use any forged or counterfeit currency-notes or bank-notes is not sufficient to make out a case under section 489C in the absence of the *mens rea*, noted above."

Similarly, the Kerala High Court has held in *Kuttan Nadar Wilson* v. *State*, 2002 (4) RCR Cri 687, that attempt to use the currency note as genuine will not make out an offence under section 489C of the Indian Penal Code as the prosecution has to establish that accused has done so with the knowledge or having reason to believe that the currency note was counterfeit. Similarly, the Karnataka High Court [in *Bimal Kanti Ghosh Dastidar* v. *Sri Sukhen Roy*, 2004 (3) RCR Cri 123] has held that mere possession of counterfeit notes is not enough and it must be established by the prosecution that the accused knew or had reason to believe about the notes being forged, and that he had intended to use them as genuine; the burden is on the prosecution to prove the knowledge and intention; the burden does not shift even because of recovery of large number of such currency notes.

10. Destruction of Evidence

Q.23. A person was charged with murder of his wife and disposing of her corpse. He has been acquitted of murder but convicted under section 201, Indian Penal Code. Please advise?

Ans. Section 201 in The Indian Penal Code, 1860

"201. *Causing disappearance of evidence of offence, or giving false information to screen offender*.—Whoever, knowing or having reason to believe that an offence has been committed, causes any evidence of the commission of that offence to disappear, with the intention of screening the offender from legal punishment, or with that intention gives any information respecting the offence which he knows or believes to be false, if a capital offence; if a capital offence – shall, if the offence which he knows or believes to have been committed is punishable with death, be punished with imprisonment of either description for a term which may extend to seven years, and shall also be liable to fine; if punishable with imprisonment for life; if punishable with imprisonment for life – and if the offence is punishable with imprisonment for life, or with imprisonment which may extend to ten years, shall be punished with imprisonment of either description for a term which may extend to three years, and shall also be liable to fine; if punishable with less than ten years' imprisonment. if punishable with less than ten years' imprisonment – and if the offence is punishable with imprisonment for any term not extending to ten years, shall be punished with imprisonment of the description provided for the offence, for a term which may extend to one-fourth part of the longest term of the imprisonment provided for the offence, or with fine, or with both.

Illustration A, knowing that B has murdered Z, assists B to hide the body with the intention of screening B from punishment. A is liable to imprisonment of either description for seven years, and also to fine."

Although the accused has been acquitted for murder, nevertheless he can be convicted under section 201 of the Indian Penal Code for causing disappearance of evidence. As such, the order is legally sustainable in view of Supreme Court judgment in *V.L. Teresa* v. *State of Kerala*, (2001) 3 SCC 549.

11. Embezzlement

Q.24. A village Sarpanch, on being charged with misappropriation of funds, returned the amount with interest. Please advise regarding quashing of F.I.R.?

Ans. Even though the accused has deposited the Panchayat amount with interest, the offence of temporary embezzlement punishable under section 409 of the Indian Penal Code is still made out against him and as such FIR cannot be quashed by the High Court on this ground. However, in case of conviction by the Trial Court, he can get the benefit of lenient view for a concession in the sentence. [Reference: *Chandgi Ram* v. *State of Haryana*, 2006 (3) RCR (Cri) (P&H) 880].

12. Mercy Killing

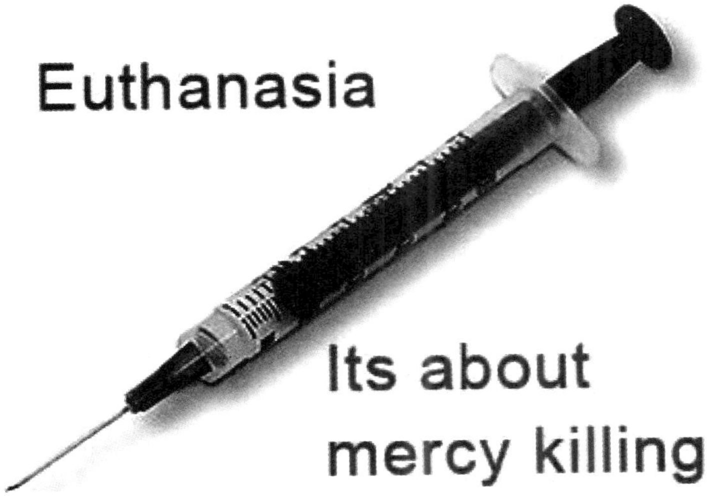

Q.25. In some countries, mercy killing is permissible under the law. What is legal position in our country?

Ans. In India, mercy killing is not permissible. The Supreme Court, in the case of *Smt. Gian Kaur* v. *State of Punjab*, (1996) 2 SCC 648: AIR 1996 SC 946: 1996 Cr LJ 1660 held: "Whatever may be the philosophy of permitting a person to extinguish his life by committing suicide, we find it difficult to construe article 21 of the Constitution to include within it the right to die as a part of the fundamental right guaranteed therein. Right to life is a natural right embodied in article 21 but suicide is an unnatural termination of or extinction of life and therefore incompatiable and inconsistent with the concept of right to life."

Similar view was taken by the Karnataka High Court in the case of *A.S. Rawat* v. *State of Karnataka* reported as 2001 (3) RCR Cri 326 holding that right to life does not include right to die and as such a person who is seriously ill cannot take his own life.

In *Aruna Ramachandra Shanbaug* v. *Union of India*, (2011) 4 SCC 454, the Supreme Court dismissed a plea for mercy killing on behalf of a 60 year old nurse, living in a vegetative state for the last 37 years in a Mumbai hospital after a brutal sexual assault. The petition filed by activist Pinki Virani on Shanbaug's behalf contended that she cannot see or speak properly and keeping her alive violates her right to live with dignity. The court, while dismissing the plea filed on behalf of KEM hospital nurse, held that while active euthanasia (mercy killing) was illegal, yet "passive euthanasia" can be permissible in exceptional circumstances. The Supreme Court has laid down the law in following terms:—

> "There is no statutory provision in our country as to the legal procedure for withdrawing life support to a person in PVS or who is otherwise incompetent to take a decision in this connection. We agree with Mr. Andhyarujina that passive euthanasia should be permitted in our country in certain situations, and we disagree with the learned Attorney General that it should never be permitted. Hence, following the technique used in *Vishakha's* case (supra), we are laying down the law in this connection which will continue to be the law until Parliament makes a law on the subject.
>
> (i) A decision has to be taken to discontinue life support either by the parents or the spouse or other close relatives, or in the absence of any of them, such a decision can be taken even by a person or a body of persons acting as a next friend. It can also be taken by the doctors attending the patient. However, the decision should be taken *bona fide* in the best interest of the patient. ..
>
> (ii) Hence, even if a decision is taken by the near relatives or doctors or next friend to withdraw life support, such a decision requires approval from the High Court concerned as laid down in *Airedale's* case (*supra*). In our opinion, this is even more necessary in our country as we cannot rule out the possibility of mischief being done by relatives or others for inheriting the property of the patient.

"In our opinion, if we leave it solely to the patient's relatives or to the doctors or next friend to decide whether to withdraw the life support of an incompetent person there is always a risk in our country that this may be misused by some unscrupulous persons who wish to inherit or otherwise grab the property of the patient. Considering the low ethical levels prevailing in our society today and the rampant commercialization and corruption, we cannot rule out the possibility that unscrupulous persons with the help of some unscrupulous doctors may fabricate material to show that it is a terminal case with no chance of recovery. There are doctors and doctors. While many doctors are upright, there are others who can do anything for money (see George Bernard Shaw's play `The Doctors Dilemma'). The commercialization of our society has crossed all limits. Hence we have to guard against the potential of misuse (see Robin Cook's novel `Coma'). In our opinion, while giving great weight to the wishes of the parents, spouse, or other close relatives or next friend of the incompetent patient and also giving due weight to the opinion of the attending doctors, we cannot leave it entirely to their discretion whether to discontinue the life support or not. We agree with the decision of the Lord Keith in Airedale's case (supra) that the approval of the High Court should be taken in this connection. This is in the interest of the protection of the patient, protection of the doctors, relative and next friend, and for reassurance of the patient's family as well as the public. This is also in consonance with the doctrine of *parens patriae* which is a well known principle of law."

Procedure to be adopted by the High Court when such an application is filed

(1) When such an application is filed the Chief Justice of the High Court should forthwith constitute a Bench of at least two Judges who should decide to grant approval or not. Before doing so the Bench should seek the opinion of a committee of three reputed doctors to be nominated by the Bench after consulting such medical authorities/medical practitioners as it may deem fit. Preferably one of the three doctors should be a neurologist, one should be a psychiatrist, and the third a physician. For this purpose a panel of doctors in every city may be prepared by the High Court in consultation with the State Government/Union Territory and their fees for this purpose may be fixed.

(2) The committee of three doctors nominated by the Bench should carefully examine the patient and also consult the record of the patient as well as taking the views of the hospital staff and submit its report to the High Court Bench.

(3) Simultaneously with appointing the committee of doctors, the High Court Bench shall also issue notice to the State and close relatives *e.g.* parents, spouse, brothers/sisters etc. of the patient, and in their absence his/her next friend, and supply a copy of the report of the doctor's committee to them as soon as it is available. After hearing them, the High Court bench should give its verdict. The above procedure should be followed all over India until Parliament makes legislation on this subject.

(4) The High Court should give its decision speedily at the earliest, since delay in the matter may result in causing great mental agony to the relatives and persons close to the patient.

(5) The High Court should give its decision assigning specific reasons in accordance with the principle of 'best interest of the patient' laid down by the House of Lords in *Airedale's* case (supra). The views of the near relatives and committee of doctors should be given due weight by the High Court before pronouncing a final verdict which shall not be summary in nature.

13. Additional Evidence

Q.26. After conclusion of trial and hearing of arguments, when a case was posted for pronouncement of orders, the court allowed prosecution's application under section 311 of Cr. P. C. to lead additional evidence. Please advise.

Ans. A trial is terminated by the pronouncement of a judgment. The power provided to the courts under section 311 of the Criminal Procedure Code is intended to be very wide. When a court finds that for a just decision of the case, a witness has to be examined, the court is duty bound to exercise the power for the purpose of arriving at the truth. So in these circumstances, the order of trial court is legal and covered by a judgment of the Supreme Court in *Jamatraj* v. *State of Maharashtra*, reported as AIR 1968 SC 178: (1967) 2 SCWR 996: 1968 Cr LJ 231, where it was held, "..... in our criminal jurisdiction, statutory law confers a power in absolute terms to be exercised at any stage of the trial to summon a witness or examine one present in court or to recall a witness already examined, and makes this the duty and obligation of the court provided the just decision of the case demands it. In other words, where the court exercises the power under the second part, the inquiry cannot be whether the accused has brought anything suddenly or unexpectedly but whether the court is right in thinking that the new evidence is needed by it for a just decision of the case."

The said judgement has been followed by the Supreme Court in *Mohan Lal Sham Ji* v. *Union of India* AIR 1991 SC 1346: 1991 Cr LJ 1521: 1991 Supp (1) SCC 271 and by Kerala HC in *Sree Venkateswara Enterprises* v. *G. Rajasekharan Nair,* 2006 (4) RCR Cri 993 (DB).

Q.27. After being declared hostile, a witness applied for re-examination on the ground of not being able to testify the truth due to an earlier threat from accused's brother who later died. The court permitted re-examination. Please advise.

Ans. Under section 311 of Cr.P.C. wide powers are vested with the Trial Court to summon and examine or recall and re-examine any person, who appears to be essential for just decision of the case at any stage of any inquiry, trial or other proceedings. Section 311 reads as under:

> "311. Power to summon material witness, or examine person present. - Any Court may, at any stage of any inquiry, trial or other proceeding under this Code, summon any person as a witness or examine any person in attendance, though not summoned as a witness or recall and re-examine any person already examined, and the Court shall summon and examine or

recall and re-examine any such person if his evidence appears to it to be essential to the just decision of the case."

The object of this provision is to have the best available evidence and to find out the truth and render a just decision. The object of justice delivery system is to meet out justice and to convict the guilty. In *Zahira Habibulla H. Seikh* v. *State of Gujarat*, (2004) 4 SCC 158: AIR 2004 SC 3114: 2004 Cr LJ 2050 and again in (2006) 3 SCC 374 (between the same parties), also commonly known as BEST BAKERY CASE, the Supreme Court observed that the section is manifestly in two parts. Whereas the word used in the first part is "may", the second part uses "shall". In consequences, the first part gives purely discretionary authority to a Criminal Court and enables it at any stage of an enquiry, trial or proceeding under the Code (a) to summon any one as a witness, or (b) to examine any person present in Court, or (c) to recall and re-examine any person whose evidence has already been recorded. On the other hand, the second part is mandatory and compels the Court to take any of the aforementioned steps if the new evidence appears to it essential to the just decision of the case. This is a supplementary provision enabling, and in certain circumstances imposing on the Court the duty of examining a material witness who would not be otherwise brought before it. It is couched in the widest possible terms and calls for no limitation, either with regard to the stage at which the powers of the Court should be exercised, or with regard to the manner in which it should be exercised. It is not only the prerogative but also the plain duty of a Court to examine such of those witnesses as it considers absolutely necessary for doing justice between the State and the subject. There is a duty cast upon the Court to arrive at the truth by all lawful means and one of such means is the examination of witnesses of its own accord when for certain obvious reasons either party is not prepared to call witnesses who are known to be in a position to speak important relevant facts. The court observed:

> "The object underlying section 311 of the Code is that there may not be failure of justice on account of mistake of either party in bringing the valuable evidence on record or leaving ambiguity in the statements of the witnesses examined from either side. The determinative factor is whether it is essential to the just decision of the case. The section is not limited only for the benefit of the accused, and it will not be an improper exercise of the powers of the Court to summon a witness under the section merely because the evidence supports the case for the prosecution and not that of the accused. The section is a general section which applies to all proceedings, enquiries and trials under the Code and empowers Magistrate to issue summons to any witness at any stage of such proceedings, trial or enquiry. In section 311 the significant expression that occurs is "at any stage of inquiry or trial or other proceeding under this Code".

Q.28. After an eye-witness has been examined by the prosecution, can the same person be summoned and examined as a defence witness?

Ans. Under section 233(3) of Code of Criminal Procedure the defence is forbidden to summon and examine eye-witnesses who have already been examined by the prosecution. They cannot be turned into defence witnesses. In *Yakub Ismail Bhal Patel* v. *State of Gujarat,* (2004) 12 SCC 229, it was held by the Supreme Court that, "Once the witness is examined as a prosecution witness, he cannot be allowed to perjure himself by resiling from the testimony given in court on oath."

Again, in *State of Madhya Pradesh* v. *Badri Yadav,* (2006) 9 SCC 549: AIR 2006 SC 1769: 2006 Cr LJ 2128, the Supreme Court held that, "The power to summon any person as a witness or recall and re-examine any person already examined is the discretionary power of the court in case such evidence appears to it to be essential for a just decision of the case. Under section 233 of Cr.P.C. the accused can enter upon defence and he can apply for the issue of any process for compelling the attendance of any witness in his defence. The provisions of sub-section (3) of section 233 cannot be understood as compelling the attendance of any prosecution witness examined, cross-examined and discharged to be juxtaposed as DWs."

The court further observed that when such frivolous and vexatious applications are filed, a Judge is not powerless. He should use his discretionary power and reject the application having been filed for the purpose of vexation or delay or for defeating the ends of justice.

Q.29. After a case is posted for final orders, can an application be allowed by trial court under section 311 of Cr.P.C. for producing record not earlier summoned. Please advise.

Ans. The powers under section 311 of the Code of Criminal Procedure are discretionary and have to be exercised with great care and caution. No general rule can be made as to when and under what circumstances discretion to summon the witness ought to be exercised; the paramount consideration is to do justice. Thus, if a court comes to the conclusion that, for the sake of arriving at a just verdict, permission to produce certain evidence is essential, then merely because final arguments have been heard and the case is fixed for order stage, is no ground to limit his scope to pass such an order allowing additional evidence. Provisions of section 311, Cr.P.C. cannot be interpreted so as to limit the powers of the court to examine the witnesses or any other document only before the conclusion of the arguments. Simply because the application for additional evidence has been moved at a later stage, it cannot be rejected on the ground of delay.

14. Summoning of Persons not Named in Police Report

Q.30. Can a married woman residing separate from her parents family, be summoned as accused in a case of dowry death of her brother's wife after the police found her innocent and challaned other persons. Please advise?

Ans. Section 319, Cr.P.C. empowers the trial court to summon any person as an accused if it comes to the conclusion that such person appears to have committed the offence, even though the person is not named in the police report under section 173, Cr.P.C. However, power under section 319, Cr.P.C. is to be exercised only after there is sufficient evidence on record that the person appears to have committed the offence.

In *Ram Singh* v. *Ram Niwas*, (2009) 14 SCC 25: (2009 (2) KLT SN 72, the Supreme Court has held that the court should summon a person as an additional accused only when the court is satisfied that evidence against him would lead to conviction and that the court should use their power under section 319, Criminal Procedure Code sparingly and not as a matter of course. The court observed: "What is, therefore, necessary for the court is to arrive at a satisfaction that the evidence adduced on behalf of the prosecution, if unrebutted, would lead to conviction of the persons sought to be added as accused in the case."

15. Bail/Anticipatory Bail

Q.31. Is it necessary for a person apprehending his arrest in a non-bailable offence to first approach the court of Sessions before approaching the High Court? Is a direct application by such a person for anticipatory bail under section 438, Cr.P.C. before the High Court maintainable?

Ans. The statute confers concurrent jurisdiction upon both the Sessions as well as the High Courts, as is amply clear by the language of section 438(1) Cr.P.C.: "When any person has reason to believe that he may be arrested on an accusation of having committed a non-bailable offence, he may apply to the High Court or the court of Session for direction under this section; and that court may, if it thinks fit, direct that in the event of such arrest, he shall be released on bail."

It has been held by several High Courts that discretion to choose the forum is with the person apprehending his arrest. Reference may be made to a DB Judgement of Kerala High Court in *Balan* v. *State of Kerala* reported as 2003 (4) RCR Cri 733 (DB) relying upon Himachal Pradesh High Court Judgment in *Mohan Lal* v. *Prem Chand*, AIR 1980 HP 36 (FB): ILR (1980) HP 117: 1980 Sim LC 241; and Allahabad High Court in *Onkar Nath* v. *State of Himachal Pradesh*, 1976 Cr LJ 1142 (FB): 1976 All WC 81: 1976 All LJ 223.

However, for reasons of practical expediency, to keep the option of both forums open, it is advisable to first approach the Sessions Court in point of time.

Q.32. After refusal of anticipatory bail by the Sessions Judge on the ground that police has submitted challan, can the accused still approach the High Court?

Ans. Yes, an application for anticipatory bail can be made to the High Court. Even otherwise, the order of Sessions Court is not legally sustainable in view of law laid down by the Supreme Court in *Revindra Saxena* v. *State of Rajasthan*, (2010) 1 SCC 684. It was held that, "the provision with regard to the grant of anticipatory bail was introduced on the recommendations of the Law Commission of India in his 41st Report dated 24-09-1969. The recommendations were considered by this court in a Constitution Bench decision in the case of *Gurbaksh Singh Sibia* v. *State of Punjab*, (1980) 2 SCC 565: (1980) Cr LJ 1125: AIR 1980 SC 1632. Upon consideration of the entire issue this court laid down certain salutary principles to be followed in exercise of the power under section 438, Cr.P.C. by the Sessions Court and the High Court. It is clearly held that the anticipatory bail can be granted at any time so long as the applicant has not been arrested. When the application is made to the High Court or Court of Sessions it must apply its own mind on the question and decide when the case is made out for granting such relief. In our opinion, the High Court ought not to have left the matter to the Magistrate only on the ground that the challan has now been presented. There is also no reason to deny anticipatory bail merely because the allegation in this case pertains to cheating or forgery of a valuable security. The merits of these issues shall have to be assessed at the time of the trial of the accused persons and denial of anticipatory bail only on the ground that the challan has been presented would not satisfy the requirements of sections 437 and 438 Cr.P.C."

Q.33. In a criminal case under section 306, Indian Penal Code, the police filed the challan after 65 days, *i.e.* beyond the statutory requirement of sixty days. The Magistrate refused to exercise power under section 167(2)(a)(ii), Cr.P.C. and refused bail on the ground that statutory right of bail is lost after challan is filed. Please advise?

Ans. The Magistrate has rightly refused bail after filing of challan as the trial court has no power to invoke section 167(2), Cr.P.C. after filing of charge-sheet. The law is well settled that the statutory right of bail under section 167(2) is extinguished by filing of charge-sheet. An accused may be entitled to bail after the expiry of period of 60 days until the filing of charge-sheet. It has been also held by the Orissa High Court in *Rakesh Swain* v. *State*, 2005 (2) RCR Cri 677: 2005 Cr LJ 1451 (Ori): 2005 All MR (Cri) 193 (Ori), relying upon earlier decisions of Supreme Court. In *Uday Mohanlal Acharya* v. *State of Maharashtra*, (2001) 5 SCC 453: AIR 2001 SC 1910: 2001 AIR SCW 1500 the Supreme Court held that, "A Constitution Bench of this court in the case of *Sanjay Dutt* v. *State through CBI Bombay (II)*, (1994) 5 SCC 410: 1994 AIR SCW 3857: 1994 Cr LJ 477, while considering correctness of Division Bench decision of this court in the case of *Hitendra Vishnu Thakur* v. *State of Maharashtra*, (1994)

4 SCC 602: 1995 Cr LJ 517: AIR 1994 SC 2623, laid down the law thus ... it would be clear that the Constitution Bench considered and in unequivocal terms disapproved the ratio of decision in the case of Hitendra Vishnu Thakur wherein it was laid down by a Division Bench of this court that if for any reason the right of the accused to be released on bail under proviso to section 167(2) of the Code has been denied then it can be exercised at a later stage even if challan is filed after expiry of the statutory period prescribed. The Constitution Bench in the aforesaid judgment has clearly laid down that the indefeasible right of the accused is enforceable only prior to the filing of the challan and it does not survive or remain enforceable on the challan being filed, if not already availed of. It has further laid down that custody of the accused after challan has been filed is not governed by the provisions of section 167 of the Code, but different provisions of the Code. The right of the accused cannot be enforced after the challan is filed "since it is extinguished the moment challan is filed."

Q.34. An incomplete challan, without the FSL report, was submitted by the police within ninety days to frustrate right of statutory bail. Later, FSL report was submitted with supplementary challan after 90 days. Is the accused entitled to bail under section 167 Cr. P.C.?

Ans. A Full Bench of the Punjab and Haryana High Court, in *State of Haryana* v. *Mehal Singh*, AIR 1979 P&H 341: 1978 Cr LJ 1810: (1978) 5 Cri LT 146, held that the investigation of an offence is not incomplete or inconclusive for the reason that the report of expert was not appended along with the challan. This Full Bench has been recently followed in *Dr. Ravdeep Kaur* v. *State of Punjab*, 2006 (4) RCR (Cri) 328: ILR (1985) 1 P&H 343 where the High Court held that, "the filing of supplementary challan would not render the first challan incomplete. As a legal and valid challan stood presented much before the expiry of ninety days, the right to be released on bail under section 167(2) of Cr.P.C. was not available to the petitioner."

16. Cancellation Report by Police

Q.35. The police submitted cancellation report after investigation. The complainant filed protest petition. Please guide about powers of the Magistrate in this situation?

Ans. After receipt of cancellation report, courses open to a Magistrate are: (1) agree with the cancellation report; or (2) disagree with the police report and (a) order further investigation; or (b) hold that the evidence is sufficient to justify the forwarding of the accused to the Magistrate and take cognizance of the offence complained of. In *Manoj Narain Agrawal* v. *Shashi Agrawal*, (2009) 6 SCC 385: 2009 AIR SCW 3812: AIR 2009 SC (Supp) 1711, the Supreme Court observed, ".....Now what are the courses open to the Magistrate in such a situation? He may, as held by this court in *Abhinandan Jha* v. *Dinesh Mishra*, (1967) 3 SCR 668: AIR 1968 SC 117: 1968 Cr LJ 97, (1) agree with the report of the police and file the proceedings, or (2) not agree with the police report and (a) order further investigation, or (b) hold that the evidence is sufficient to justify the forwarding of the accused to the Magistrate and take cognizance of the offence complained of."

Q.36. Whether an application for further investigation is maintainable after acceptance of a final police report by the Magistrate?

Ans. Yes, the powers of police to further investigate the offence are not precluded by acceptance of earlier cancellation report in view of section 173(8) of Cr.P.C. However, the only riders are: (a) there should be some additional material available with the police; and (b) a formal permission of the court is sought. Thus after filing of final report, further investigation can be conducted by the same investigating agency after seeking 'formal permission' of the court as held in *Ram Lal Narang* v. *State (Delhi Administration)*, (1979) 2 SCC 322: AIR 1979 SC 1791: 1979 Cr LJ 1346, wherein it was held, "In our view, notwithstanding that a Magistrate had taken cognizance of the offence upon a police report submitted under section 173 of the 1898 Code, the right of the police to further investigate was not exhausted and the police could exercise such right as often as necessary when fresh information came to light. Where the police desired to make a further investigation, the police could express their regard and respect for the court by seeking its formal permission to make further investigation." This judgement has been cited with approval in *State of A.P.* v. *A.S. Peter*, (2008) 2 SCC 383: AIR 2008 SC 1052: 2008 AIR SCW 637.

Further, it is not necessary to hear the accused before granting such permission as held by the Kerala High Court in *Yeshodharan* v. *State of Kerala*, 2004 (3) RCR (Cri) 557.

Q.37. After acceptance of cancellation report submitted by the police, the complainant filed a criminal complaint on the same allegations. Whether such complaint is maintainable in law?

Ans. The fact that the Magistrate has accepted the police report does not affect the powers of Magistrate to take cognizance thereafter on the basis of a private complaint. The Supreme Court held in *Mukesh Chand* v. *B. Janardhan Reddy*, (2003) 1 SCC 734: 2002 AIR SCW 5385: AIR 2003 SC 702 that, "It is settled law that there is no statutory bar in filing a second complaint on the same facts. In a case where a previous complaint is dismissed without assigning any reasons, the Magistrate under section 204, Cr.P.C. may take cognizance of an offence and issue process if there is sufficient ground for proceeding. As held in *Pramatha Nath Talukdar,* AIR 1962 SC 876: 1962 1 Cri LJ 770: 1962 Supp (2) SCR 297 case second complaint could be dismissed after a decision has been given against the complainant in previous matter upon a full consideration of his case. Further, second complaint on the same facts could be entertained only in exceptional circumstances, namely, where the previous order was passed on an incomplete record or on a misunderstanding of the nature of complaint or it was manifestly absurd, unjust or where new facts which could not, with reasonable diligence, have been brought on record in the previous proceedings, have been adduced. In the facts and circumstances of this case, the matter, therefore, should have been remitted back to the learned Magistrate for the purpose of arriving at a finding as to whether any case for cognizance of the alleged offence had been made out or not."

Again, in *Kishore Kumar* v. *G.D. Mehrotra,* 2003 (2) RCR (Cri) 594 (SC), it was held by the Supreme Court that, "It is too well settled that when police after investigation files a final form under section 173 of the Code, the Magistrate may disagree with the conclusion arrived at by the police and take cognizance in exercise of power under section 190 of the Code. The Magistrate may not take cognizance and direct further investigation in the matter under section 156 of the Code. Where the Magistrate accepts the final form submitted by the police, the right of the complainant to file a regular complaint is not taken away and in fact on such a complaint being filed, the Magistrate follows the procedure under section 201 of the Code and takes cognizance if the materials produced by the complainant make out an offence."

Q.38. The Magistrate after accepting the report under section 173, Cr. P.C., discharged two persons and took cognizance against the remaining two accused. Subsequently, the complainant applied for further investigation of the case which was also accepted by the Magistrate and further investigation was ordered. Please guide?

Ans. The order of the Magistrate is legally sustainable. The jurisdiction of Magistrate after taking cognizance of the offence on the basis of police report is not precluded and he is empowered to order further investigation of the case on the basis of application of the complainant though he can pass such an order if requested by the prosecution under section 173(8) of Cr. P. C.

The Supreme Court in *Reeta Neg* v. *State of West Bengal,* (2009) 9 SCC 129: AIR 2010 SC (Supp) 401, para 25 at page 134, held that, "What emerges from the above-mentioned decisions of this court is that once a charge-sheet is filed under section 173(2), Cr.P.C. and either charge is framed or the accused are discharged, the Magistrate may, on the basis of a protest petition, take cognizance of the offence complained of or on the application made by the investigating authorities permit further investigation under section 173(8). The Magistrate cannot *suo moto* direct a further investigation under section 173(8), Cr.P.C. or direct a re-investigation into a case on account of the bar of section 167(2) of the Code."

17. Dog Track Evidence

Q.39. In a murder case, whether an accused can be convicted solely on the sniffer dog evidence tracing the scent from the place of occurrence?

Ans. In a catena of judgments the Supreme Court has held that dog-track evidence, even though admissible, is inherently weak and cannot be the sole basis for a conviction. In *Gade Lakshmi Mangraju* v. *State of A.P.*, (2001) 6 SCC 205 the Supreme Court observed that, "The weakness of the evidence based on tracker dogs has been dealt with in a article "Police and Security Dogs". .... from a scientific point of view, there is little knowledge and much uncertainty as to the precise faculties which enable police dogs to track and identify criminals. Police dogs engage in these actions by virtue of instincts and also by the training imparted to them." Further, the Supreme Court cited with approval *Abdul Razak Murtaza Dafadar* v. *State of Maharashtra,* AIR 1970 SC 283: (1969) 2 SCJ 870: (1970) 1 SCR 551 in which it was held that, "..... In the present state of scientific knowledge evidence of dog tracking, even if admissible, is not ordinarily of much weight."

Again, in *State of Maharashtra* v. *Mangi Lal,* (2009) 15 SCC 418, the Supreme Court observed that, "The police dog traced the scent from the place of incident to the house of the accused is really no evidence in the eye of law."

18. D.N.A. Test

Q.40. A maid servant levelled allegation of repeated rape against her employer resulting in pregnancy. The police obtained DNA sample. What is the evidentiary value of such report?

Ans. Section 45 of Indian Evidence Act, reads: "When the court has to form an opinion upon a point of foreign law, or of science, or art, or as to identity of hand-writing or finger-impressions, the opinions upon that point of persons specially skilled in such foreign law, science or art, or in questions as to identity of handwriting or finger impressions, are relevant facts. Such person are called experts." Thus DNA report by an expert can be accepted as a corroborative piece of evidence since it would be a relevant fact to determine the facts in issue. In *Kamti Devi* v. *Poshi Ram*, (2001) 5 SCC 311: AIR 2001 SC 2226: 2001 AIR SCW 2100, the Supreme Court observed that "... The result of a genuine DNA test is said to be scientifically accurate. If DNA report is negative, it would conclusively exonerate the accused from the charge." Again, in *Prem Ji Bhai Bachubhai Khasiya* v. *State of Gujarat*, 2009 (4) RCR (Cri) 186, a Division Bench of Gujarat High Court held that the science of DNA is at developing stage and cannot be considered as conclusive proof of paternity. However, positive report of DNA test is of immense significance where there is other supporting evidence. In every case one has to put the DNA evidence in the context of the rest of the evidence and decide whether taken as a whole it does amount to a *prima facie* case.

Further held that since 'the science of DNA is at developing stage and when the Random Occurrence Ratio is not available for Indian Society, it would be risky to act solely on a positive DNA report, because only if the DNA profile of the accused matches with the foetus, it cannot be considered as a conclusive proof of paternity. Contrarily, if it is solitary piece of evidence with negative result, it would conclusively exclude the possibility of involvement of the accused in the offence.'

Q.41. A doctor deposed in a murder case on nature of injuries which was not acceptable to the accused. Please guide regarding the authenticity and efficacy of the doctor's expert opinion?

Ans. The doctor's expert opinion is generally accepted unless it suffers from the fallacy of inherent weaknesses. This was so held in *Sahebrao Mohan Berad* v. *State of Maharashtra*, (2011) 4 SCC 249: In our opinion, the doctor who examined the deceased and conducted the post-mortem is the only competent person to opine the nature of injuries and the cause of death. It is only in a case, where the opinion is inherently defective, the court will discard its evidence. Reference in this connection can be made to a decision of this court in *Mafabhai Nagarbhai Raval* v. *State of Gujarat*, (1992) 4 SCC 69: AIR 1992 SC 2186: 1992 AIR SCW 2592 in which it has been held as follows: "3......... *It is needless to say that the doctor who has examined the deceased and conducted the postmortem is the only competent witness to speak about the nature of injuries and the cause of death. Unless there is something inherently defective the court cannot substitute its opinion for that of the doctor.*"

Q.42. Whether the court can force a rape accused to undergo DNA test?

Ans. Yes. DNA is an acid in the chromosomes in centre of cells of living things. It determines the structure and function of each cell. DNA is an abbreviation for 'DEOXYRIBONUCLEIC ACID'. The police can get the accused medically examined under section 53 of Cr.P.C. for any test which may include

DNA test also. In *Smt. Selvi* v. *State of Karnataka*, (2010) 7 SCC 263: AIR 2010 SC 1974: 2010 AIR SCW 3011, it was held by the Supreme Court that "... taking and retention of DNA samples which are in the nature of physical evidence does not face the Constitutional hurdles in the Indian context".

Q.43. Is there any difference between DNA test and DNA profiling?

Ans. Yes, the two concepts are different as laid down by the Supreme Court in *Smt. Selvi* v. *State of Karnataka*, (2010) 7 SCC 263: AIR 2010 SC 1974: 2010 AIR SCW 3011: "A `DNA profile' is different from a DNA sample which can be obtained from bodily substances. A DNA profile is a record created on the basis of DNA samples made available to forensic experts. Creating and maintaining DNA profiles of offenders and suspects are useful practices since newly obtained DNA samples can be readily matched with existing profiles that are already in the possession of law-enforcement agencies. The matching of DNA samples is emerging as a vital tool for linking suspects to specific criminal acts."

19. Lie-detector Tests

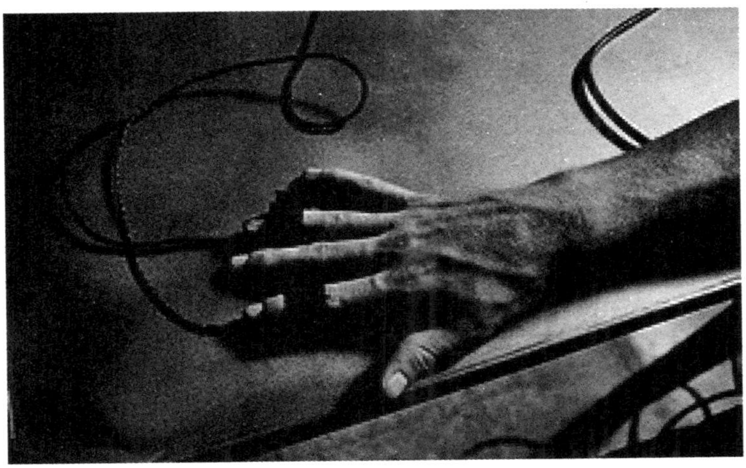

Q.44. What are the modalities of a Lie-detector test?

Ans. The origins of polygraph examination (lie-detector) have been traced back to the efforts of Lombroso, a criminologist who experimented with a machine that measured blood pressure and pulse to assess the honesty of persons suspected of criminal conduct. His device was called a hydrosphygmograph. A similar device was used by psychologist William Marston during World War I in espionage cases, which proved to be a precursor to its use in the criminal justice system. In 1921, John Larson incorporated the measurement of respiration rate and by 1939 Leonard Keeler added skin conductance and an amplifier to the parameters examined by a polygraph machine.

The theory behind polygraph tests is that when a subject is lying in response to a question, he/she will produce physiological responses that are different from those that arise in the normal course. During the polygraph examination, several instruments are attached to the subject for measuring and recording the physiological responses. The examiner then reads these results, analyzes them and proceeds to gauge the credibility of the subject's answers. Instruments such as cardiographs, pneumographs, cardio-cuffs and sensitive electrodes are used in the course of polygraph examinations. [Reference: *Smt. Selvi* v. *State of Karnataka,* (2010) 7 SCC 263: AIR 2010 SC 1974: 2010 AIR SCW 3011].

Q.45. What is 'brain electrical activation profile' (BEAP) test?

Ans. The 'Brain Electrical Activation Profile test' is also known as the "P300Waves test'. It is a process of detecting whether an individual is familiar with certain information by way of measuring activity in the brain that is triggered by exposure to selected stimuli. This test consists of examining and measuring 'event-related potentials' (ERP) *i.e.,* electrical wave forms emitted by the brain after it has absorbed an external event. An ERP measurement is the recognition of specific patterns of electrical brain activity in a subject that are indicative of certain cognitive mental activities that occur when a person is exposed to a stimulus in the form of an image or a concept expressed in words. The measurement of the cognitive brain activity allows the examiner to ascertain whether the subject recognised stimuli to which he/she was exposed. [Cited from: Andre A Moenssens, 'Brain Fingerprinting - Can it be used to detect the innocence of persons charged with a crime?' University of Missouri at Kansas City Law Review 891-920 (Summer 2002) at p. 893] – cited by the Supreme Court in *Selvi* v. *State of Karnataka,* (2010) 7 SCC 263 (para 71 at page 309).

Q.46. What is Narco-Analysis test and how is it administered?

Ans. This test involves the intravenous administration of a drug that causes the subject to enter into a hypnotic trance and become less inhibited. The drug-induced hypnotic stage is useful for investigators since it makes the subject more likely to divulge information. The drug used for this test is sodium pentothal, higher quantities of which are routinely used for inducing general anaesthesia in surgical procedures. This drug is also used in the field of psychiatry since the revelations can enable the diagnosis of mental disorders. The use of 'truth-serums' and hypnosis is not a recent development. Earlier versions of the narco-analysis technique utilised substances such as scopolamine and sodium amytal. In recent years, the debate over the use of 'truth-serums' has been revived with demands for their use on persons suspected of involvement in terrorist activities. Coming to the test procedure, when the drug (sodium pentothal) is administered intravenously, the subject ordinarily descends into anaesthesia in four stages, namely:—

(i) Awake stage

(ii) Hypnotic stage

(iii) Sedative stage

(iv) Anaesthetic stage.

[Reference: *Smt. Selvi* v. *State of Karnataka,* (2010) 7 SCC 263: AIR 2010 SC 1974: 2010 AIR SCW 3011 (para 71 at page 309).

Q.47. What is the authenticity of the Narco-Analysis test?

Ans. The 'narco-analysis' technique suffers from certain limitations. It does not have an absolute success rate and there is always the possibility that the subject will not reveal any relevant information. Some studies have shown that most of the drug-induced revelations are not related to the relevant facts and they are more likely to be in the nature of inconsequential information about the subjects' personal lives. It takes great skill on part of the interrogators to extract and identify information which could eventually prove to be useful. While some persons are able to retain their ability to deceive even in the hypnotic state, others can become extremely suggestible to questioning. This is especially worrying, since investigators who are under pressure to deliver results could frame questions in a manner that prompts incriminatory responses. Subjects could also concoct fanciful stories in the course of the 'hypnotic stage'. Since the responses of different individuals are bound to vary, there is no uniform criteria for evaluating the efficacy of the 'narco-analysis' technique. [Reference: *Selvi* v. *State of Karnataka,* (2010) 7 SCC 263].

Q.48. Whether a murder accused can refuse to undergo polygraph-test and Narco-analysis during police investigation? Whether involuntary administration of the above techniques would be legal?

Ans. In *Selvi* v. *State of Karnataka,* (2010) 7 SCC 263, the Supreme Court held that the above mentioned tests do not fall within the purview of section 53, 53A and 54 of Cr.P.C. as these tests are violative of article 20(3) of Constitution of India. It was held that "no individual should be forcibly subjected to any of the techniques in question, whether in the context of investigation in criminal cases or otherwise. Doing so would amount to an unwarranted intrusion into personal liberty. However, we do leave room for the voluntary administration of the impugned techniques in the context of criminal justice, provided that certain safeguards are in place. Even when the subject has given consent to undergo any of these tests, the test results by themselves cannot be admitted as evidence because the subject does not exercise conscious control over the responses during the administration of the test. However, any information or material that is subsequently discovered with the help of voluntary administered test results can be admitted, in accordance with section 27 of the Evidence Act, 1872.

"The National Human Rights Commission had published 'Guidelines for the Administration of Polygraph Test (Lie Detector Test) on an Accused' in 2000. These guidelines should be strictly adhered to and similar safeguards should be adopted for conducting the 'Narcoanalysis technique' and the 'Brain Electrical Activation Profile' test. The text of these guidelines has been reproduced below:

(i) No Lie Detector Test should be administered except on the basis of consent of the accused. An option should be given to the accused whether he wishes to avail such test.

(ii) If the accused volunteers for a Lie Detector Test, he should be given access to a lawyer and the physical, emotional and legal implication of such a test should be explained to him by the police and his lawyer.

(iii) The consent should be recorded before a Judicial Magistrate.

(iv) During the hearing before the Magistrate, the person alleged to have agreed should be duly represented by a lawyer.

(v) At the hearing, the person in question should also be told in clear terms that the statement that is made shall not be a 'confessional' statement to the Magistrate but will have the status of a statement made to the police.

(vi) The Magistrate shall consider all factors relating to the detention including the length of detention and the nature of the interrogation.

(vii) The actual recording of the Lie Detector Test shall be done by an independent agency (such as a hospital) and conducted in the presence of a lawyer.

(viii) A full medical and factual narration of the manner of the information received must be taken on record."

Q.49. In an application under section 125 of Cr.P.C. claiming maintenance by the wife against her husband, can a court direct a child's blood test to determine paternity?

Ans. Section 125, Cr.P.C. provides a summary procedure in which the courts are not justified to doubt chastity of the lady merely on the asking of her husband. Section 125, Cr.P.C. provides a swift remedy against the husband who, despite sufficient means, neglects or refuses to maintain his wife and her children. In case the husband wants to challenge the paternity of the child he can always file a civil suit in the appropriate civil court for such declaration. In proceeding under section 125, Cr.P.C., the Magistrate is not justified in directing blood test of the child. Section 112 of Indian Evidence Act, deals with legitimacy of a child in these terms: "The fact that any person was born during the continuance of a valid marriage between his mother and any man, or within two hundred and eighty days after its dissolution, the mother remaining unmarried, shall be conclusive proof that he is the legitimate son of that man, unless it can be shown that the parties to the marriage had no access to each other at any time when he could have been begotten."

In *Gautam Kundu* v. *State of West Bengal*, AIR 1993 SC 2295: 1993 AIR SCW 2325: 1993 Cr LJ 3233, the Supreme Court concluded that:

"(1) courts in India cannot order blood test as matter of course;

(2) wherever applications are made for such requests in order to have a roving inquiry, the request for blood test cannot be entertained;

(3) There must be a strong *prima facie* case in that the husband must establish non-access in order to dispel the presumption arising under section 112 of the Evidence Act;

(4) The court must carefully examine as to what would be the consequence of ordering the blood test; whether it will have the effect of branding a child as a bastard and the mother as an unchaste woman;

(5) No one can be compelled to give sample of blood for analysis."

Q.50. In a father-son property dispute of ancestral property, the son applied for DNA test to establish the relationship. The court directed DNA test of both. Please advise?

Ans. Paternity can be presumed in situations enumerated in section 112 of the Indian Evidence Act. In *Banarsi Dass* v. *Mrs. Teeku Dutta,* (2005) 4 SCC 449: JT 2005 (4) SC 627 the Supreme Court held that: "We may remember that section 112 of the Evidence Act, was enacted at a time when scientific advancements with deoxyribonucleic acid (DNA) as well as ribonucleic acid (RNA) tests were not even in contemplation of the legislature. The result of a genuine DNA test is said to be scientifically accurate. But even that is not enough to escape from the conclusiveness of section 112 of the Act *e.g.* if a husband and wife were living together during the time of conception but the DNA test revealed that the child was not born to the husband, the conclusiveness in law would remain irrebuttable. This may look hard from the point of view of the husband who would be compelled to bear the fatherhood of a child of which he may be innocent. But even in such a case the law leans in favour of the innocent child from being branded a bastard if his mother and her spouse were living together during the time of conception. Hence the question regarding the degree of proof of non-access for rebutting the conclusiveness must be answered in the light of what is meant by access or non-access as delineated above. ... DNA test is not to be directed as a matter of routine and only in deserving cases such a direction can be given...

The court cannot compel a person to undergo a DNA test as it will be interfering with his personal liberty. At the most, an adverse inference can be drawn against the person who refuses at the final conclusion."

Q.51. After the court has received report from one Laboratory, can the court direct a party in adultery case to provide fresh samples for a second DNA test from some other laboratory?

Ans. A trial court cannot order a second DNA test after report of first DNA test has been produced in court. In *Sakthivel* v. *Karpagam,* 2005 (4) RCR (Cri) 422, the Madras High Court upheld a decision of subordinate court where an application for second DNA test was dismissed. The court observed that, "DNA test report is only a piece of evidence (though of course a strong piece of evidence) in determining the paternity of a child. It supplements the oral evidence. The opinion evidence/expert evidence is only to assist the court in determining the paternity. The DNA test report is to be analysed alongwith the facts and other evidence to be adduced by the parties. The DNA test report is only a supporting evidence in favour of either party. During the trial, it is for the husband to establish that the earlier DNA test is exposed to reasonable degree of suspicion. But the petitioner cannot demand another DNA examination."

20. F.I.R.

Q.52. Can a telephonic message be treated as a First Information Report (FIR) and can the police register a case on such information?

Ans. The police cannot register a case on the basis of information received on telephone. Section 154 Cr.P.C. requires that, information disclosing commission of an offence must be reduced into writing and signed by the informant.

Section 154(1) reads: "Every information relating to the commission of a cognizable offence, if given orally to an officer in charge of a police station, shall be reduced to writing by him or under his direction, and be read over to the informant; and every such information, whether given in writing or reduced to writing as aforesaid, shall be signed by the person giving it, and the substance thereof shall be entered in a book to be kept by such officer in such form as the State Government may prescribe in this behalf."

It was held by the Supreme Court in *Mundrika Mahto* v. *State of Bihar*, (2002) 9 SCC 183: AIR 2002 SC 2042: 2002 AIR SCW 2093 that, ".....telephonic conversation could not be treated as FIR as it was cryptic information that was received and recorded in the daily dairy regarding the commission of offence."

Q.53. Whether the police is bound to register an FIR after receipt of a written complaint disclosing commission of a cognizable offence?

Ans. Though there is a mandate under section 154 Cr.P.C. to register an FIR, yet the power of the competent officer to make a preliminary enquiry is retained as laid down by the Supreme Court in *Rajinder Singh Katoch* v. *Chandigarh Administration*, (2007) 10 SCC 69: AIR 2008 SC 178: 2008 Cr LJ 356 "Although the officer in charge of a police station is legally bound to register a first information report in terms of section 154 of the Code of Criminal Procedure, if the allegations made by them gives rise to an offence which can be investigated without obtaining any permission from the Magistrate concerned; the same by itself, however, does not take away the right of the competent officer to make a preliminary enquiry, in a given case, in order to find out as to whether the first information sought to be lodged had any substance or not."

21. Defective Investigation

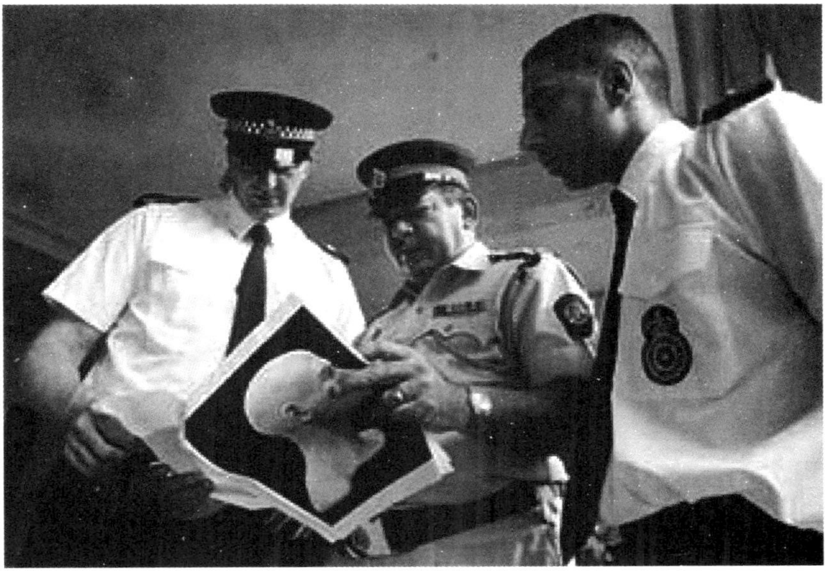

Q.54. In a murder case, the police failed to send the recovered fire arm, cartridges and blood-stained clothes to the Ballistic Expert and Chemical Examiner respectively. Whether the accused can get benefit of such lapses in investigation?

Ans. No mileage can be gained by the accused on account of defects in investigation, which can at times be deliberate due to an unholy nexus between the investigating officer and the accused. Every faulty investigation on the part of the police/investigation officer cannot by itself lead to total demolition of the prosecution case if it can otherwise stand ignoring these fallacies. In *Amar Singh* v. *Balwinder,* (2003) 2 SCC 518: AIR 2003 SC 1164: 2003 Cr LJ 1282 it was held by the Supreme Court that in case of defective investigation the court has to be circumspect in evaluating the evidence but it would not be right to acquit the accused on account of the defect as it would tantamount to playing into the hands of the investigating officer if the investigation is designedly defective. The Court observed, "It would have been certainly better if the investigating agency had sent the fire arms and the empties to the Forensic Science Laboratory for comparison. However, the report of the Ballistic Expert would in any case be in the nature of an expert opinion and the same is not conclusive. The failure of the investigating officer in sending the fire arms and the empties for comparison cannot completely throw out the prosecution case when the same is fully established from the testimony of eye-witnesses whose presence on the spot cannot be doubted as they all received gun-shot injuries in the incident." In *Chaju* v. *State of Himachal Pradesh,* (2010) 2 SCC 445: 2010 Cr LJ 1655: 2010 AIR SCW 1396 the Supreme Court has held that non-sending of blood-stained clothes to the Chemical Examiner in a rape case is hardly any ground to discredit the testimony of the victim because the victim had no control over the investigating agency and the negligence, if any, of the investigating officer could not alter the credibility of her statement. In the language of the Court: "It was contended by the learned counsel for the appellant that the blood-stained clothes which were said to have been handed over to the Officer-in-Charge at the Police Station by the husband of the victim were not sent for chemical examination and, therefore, the corroboration with which such evidence could offer was absent. In our view, the failure of the investigating agency cannot be a ground to discredit the testimony of the victim. The victim had no control over the investigating agency and the negligence, if any, of the investigating officer could not affect the credibility of the statement of PW-1 - the victim. Having regard to the facts and circumstances of this case, we are satisfied that on the basis of the evidence on record, the conviction of the appellant can be sustained."

22. Handwriting Expert

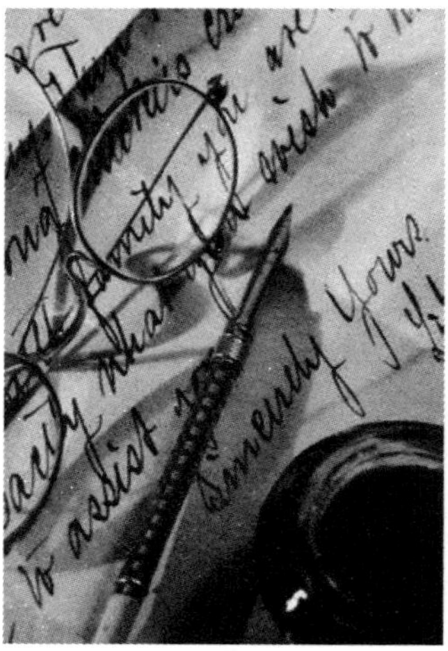

Q.55. In a dispute regarding the hand-writing in love-letters, on an application for comparison, the court itself compared the writing. Is it legally tenable?

Ans. Section 73 of the Indian Evidence Act provides: "Comparison of signature, writing or seal with others admitted or proved. - In order to ascertain whether a signature, writing or seal is that of the person by whom it purports to have been written or made, any signature, writing or seal admitted or proved to the satisfaction of the Court to have been written or made by that person may be compared with the one which is to be proved, although that signature, writing or seal has not been produced or proved for any other purpose. The Court may direct any person present in Court to write any words or figures for the purpose of enabling the Court to compare the words or figures so written with any words or figures alleged to have been written by such person." Thus the Court is empowered to make a comparison of disputed writing with the original writing of the author. There is no legal bar for a

Judge to examine a document with his naked eyes. However, in a case of disputed writing, the court should prefer opinion of hand-writing experts.

In *Sunil Kumar* v. *State of Haryana,* 2006 (2) RCR (Cri) 15, a Division Bench of the Punjab and Haryana High Court held that, "No doubt, there is no legal bar to the Judge using his eyes, but he (Judge) should hesitate to base his finding with regard to the identity of handwriting solely on comparison made by him, more so when the quality of relevant evidence and evidence in respect of specimen/admitted writings is not of high standard. It is well settled that as a matter of extreme caution and judicial sobriety, the Court should not normally take upon itself the responsibility of comparing the disputed signatures with that of admitted signatures or handwritings and in the event of slightest doubt, leave the matter to the wisdom of experts."

23. Benefit of Doubt

Q.56. What is the difference between "honourable acquittal" and acquittal by giving the 'benefit of doubt'.

Ans. Mere use of the words 'benefit of doubt' or 'not proved beyond reasonable doubt' by the court do not convert an acquittal on the ground of 'no evidence' to something less. The concept of "honourable acquittal" is unknown to the Criminal Procedure Code, 1973. It was held by a Division Bench of the Punjab and Haryana High Court, in *Bhag Singh* v. *Punjab and Sind Bank*, 2005 (3) PLR 861: "In our opinion, the mere use of the expression "benefit of doubt" or "not proved beyond reasonable doubt" by the trial Court or the appellate court, cannot be permitted to convert an acquittal on the ground of no evidence, to something less than that. The concepts of "Honourable Acquittal", "fully exonerated" or "acquitted of blame" are all unknown to the Criminal Procedure Code, 1973. Therefore, the term "benefit of doubt" cannot detract from the impact of the acquittal." Similar view has been expressed by a Division Bench of the Madras High Court in *Union of India* v. *Jayaram*, AIR 1960 Mad 325: ILR (1960) Mad 392: (1959) 2 Lab LJ 212.

24. Identification of Accused in Court

Q.57. In a dacoity case, the accused were produced with muffled faces before the Magistrate and the police sought their identification parade but they refused to join. The stolen ornaments were also recovered. During trial, the complainant identified the accused in the court. The court acquitted the accused on the ground that identification for the first time in the court was of no significance. Please guide.

Ans. Identification of the accused for the first time in the Trial Court by the eye-witnesses in absence of any prior test identification parade is not of much significance. Yet, in this case since the accused refused to join the identification parade earlier and the prosecution also produced them in muffled faces, there would be presumption that they were involved in the said crime as the accused cannot take advantage of their own lapse. Moreover, some of the stolen ornaments were also recovered from their possession, which is another factor against them.

In *State of Haryana* v. *Surender*, (2007) 11 SCC 281: AIR 2007 SC 2312: 2007 AIR SCW 4009, it was held by the Supreme Court: "There is no embargo on the appellate Court reviewing the evidence upon which an order of acquittal is based. Generally, the order of acquittal shall not be interfered with because the presumption of innocence of the accused is further strengthened by acquittal. The golden thread which runs through the web of administration of justice in criminal cases is that if two views are possible on the evidence adduced in the case, one pointing to the guilt of the accused and the other to his innocence, the view which is favorable to the accused should be adopted. The paramount consideration of the Court is to ensure that miscarriage of justice is prevented. A miscarriage of justice which may arise from acquittal of the guilty is no less than from the conviction of an innocent. In a case where admissible evidence is ignored, a duty is cast upon the appellate Court to re-appreciate the evidence where the accused has been acquitted, for the purpose of ascertaining as to whether any of the accused really committed any offence or not. [See *Bhagwan Singh* v. *State of Madhya Pradesh*, 2002 (2) Supreme 567: AIR 2002 SC 1621: 2002 AIR SCW 1532]. The principle to be followed by appellate Court considering the appeal against the judgment of acquittal is to interfere only when there are compelling and substantial reasons for doing so. If the impugned judgment is clearly unreasonable and relevant and convincing materials have been unjustifiably eliminated in the process, it is a compelling reason for interference."

25. Investigation

Q.58. In a theft case the Magistrate remanded the accused to police custody for total initial period of fifteen days. The police recovered a part of the stolen amount. The gold and jewellery involved in another case confessed by the accused could not be recovered. The police sought further remand beyond the initial fifteen days remand. Please advise?

Ans. In a new case the Magistrate is empowered to grant fresh remand beyond the stipulated fifteen days period. In *State of Haryana* v. *Zafar Ali,* 2007 (3) RCR (Cri) 856, the Punjab and Haryana High Court, while distinguishing judgment of Supreme Court in *CBI* v. *Anupam Kulkarni,* (1992) 3 SCC 141: AIR 1992 SC 1768: 1992 Cr LJ 2768] has held that the provisions of section 167(2), Cr.P.C. do not indicate that the accused could not be remanded to police custody after the initial period of 15 days is over. Section 167(2) reads thus:

> "2) The Magistrate to whom all accused person is forwarded under this section may, whether he has or not jurisdiction to try the case, from time to time, authorise the detention of the accused in such custody as such Magistrate thinks fit, a term not exceeding fifteen days in the whole; and if he has no jurisdiction to try the case or commit it for trial, and considers further detention unnecessary, he may order the accused to be forwarded to a Magistrate having such jurisdiction:
>
> Provided that—
>
> [(a) The Magistrate may authorize the detention of the accused person, otherwise than in the custody of the police, beyond the period of fifteen days, if he is satisfied that adequate grounds exist for doing so, but no Magistrate shall authorise the detention of the accused person in custody under this paragraph for a total period exceeding—
>
> (i) Ninety days, where the investigation relates to an offence punishable with death, imprisonment for life or imprisonment for a term of not less than ten years;
>
> (ii) Sixty days, where the investigation relates to any other offence,
>
> And, on the expiry of the said period of ninety days, or sixty days, as the case may be, the accused person shall be released on bail if he is prepared to and does furnish bail, and every person released on bail under this sub-section shall be deemed to be to released under the provisions of Chapter XXXIII for the purposes of that Chapter;]
>
> (b) No Magistrate shall authorize detention in any custody under this section unless the accused is produced before him;
>
> (c) No Magistrate of the second class, not specially empowered in this behalf by the high Court, shall authorize detention in the custody of the police.
>
> [*Explanation I.* For the avoidance of doubts, it is hereby declared that, notwithstanding the expiry of the period specified in paragraph (a), the accused shall be detained in Custody so long as he does not furnish bail.]
>
> [*Explanation II*]. If any question arises whether an accused person was produced before the Magistrate as required under paragraph (b), the production of the accused person may be proved by his signature on the order authorizing detention."

In *Dinesh Dalmia* v. *C.B.I.*, (2007) 8 SCC 770 (Para 27): 2007 AIR SCW 6112: AIR 2008 SC 78, the Supreme Court ruled: "The object of enactment of such proviso in section 167 Cr. P.C. is to have control over a lethargic, delayed investigation, especially keeping a person in custody. It is a specific direction to the police to collect material without any delay. If sufficient incriminating materials are not collected against the accused with the crime alleged, it safeguards the interest of such accused person. If materials are collected and reported to the Magistrate within the period stipulated by filing charge-sheet, then the scope of proviso to section 167 extinguishes and an accused can claim bail only on merit."

The Supreme Court further approved the following passage from *State Through CBI* v. *Dawood Ibrahim Kaskar,* (2000) 10 SCC 438: AIR 1997 SC 2494: 1997 AIR SCW 2434: "There cannot be any manner of doubt that the remand and the custody referred to in the first proviso to the above sub-section are different from detention in custody under section 167. While remand under the former relates to a stage after cognizance and can only be to judicial custody, detention under the latter relates to the stage of investigation and can initially be either in police custody or judicial custody. Since, however, even after cognizance is taken of an offence the police has a power to investigate into it further, which can be exercised only in accordance with Chapter XII, we see no reason whatsoever why the provisions of section 167 thereof would not apply to a person who comes to be later arrested by the police in course of such investigation. If section 309(2) is to be interpreted - as has been interpreted by the Bombay High Court in Mansuri (supra) - to mean that after the Court takes cognizance of an offence it cannot exercise its power of detention in police custody under section 167 of the Code, the Investigating Agency would be deprived of an opportunity to interrogate a person arrested during further investigation, even if it can on production of sufficient materials, convince the Court that his detention in its (police) custody was essential for that purpose. We are therefore of the opinion that the words "accused if in custody" appearing in section 309(2) refer and relate to an accused who was before the Court when cognizance was taken or when enquiry or trial was being held in respect of him and not to an accused who is subsequently arrested in course of further investigation. So far as the accused in the first category is concerned he can be remanded to judicial custody only in view of section 309(2), but he who comes under the second category will be governed by section 167 so long as further investigation continues. That necessarily means that in respect of the latter the Court which had taken cognizance of the offence may exercise its power to detain him in police custody, subject to the fulfilment of the requirements and the limitation of section 167."

Q.59. Two persons facing a murder trial under sections 302/34 of the Indian Penal Code moved an application requesting for supply of copies of notes made by the supervisory officer who verified the investigations conducted by the investigating officer by visiting the place of occurrence. Can the complainant oppose this application?

Ans. The documents in terms of sections 207 and 208 of Code of Criminal Procedure are supplied to the accused to make him aware of the materials, which are sought to be utilised against him. But the copies of supervision notes being part of case diaries cannot be supplied, since these are not a part of papers supplied to the accused in view of bar of section 172, Cr.P.C. In *Shakila Abdul Gafar Khan* v. *Vasant Raghunath Dhobles*, (2003) 7 SCC 749: 2003 Cr LJ 4548: AIR 2003 SC 4567, the Supreme Court held,"section 208 of the Code deals with the requirements of furnishing documents to the accused. Of course, it has rightly been submitted by Mr. Sanyal that mere non-supply of documents may not be considered prejudicial but the court has to give a definite finding about the prejudice or otherwise."

The Supreme Court approved its previous judgment in *Noor Khan* v. *State of Rajasthan,* (1964) 4 SCR 521: AIR 1964 SC 286: 1964 (1) Cr LJ 167 in which it was held: "The object of sections 162, 173(4) and 207A(3) is to enable the accused to obtain a clear picture of the case against him before the commencement of the inquiry. The sections impose an obligation upon the investigating officer to supply before the commencement of the inquiry, copies of the statements of witnesses who are intended to be examined at the trial so that the accused may utilize those statements for cross-examining the witnesses to establish such defence as he desires to put up, and also to shake their testimony. Section 161(3) does not require a police-officer to record in writing the statements of witnesses examined by him in the course of the investigation, but if he does record in writing any such statements, he is obliged to make copies of those statements available to the accused before the commencement of proceedings in the court so that the accused may know the details and particulars of the case against him and how the case is intended to be proved. The object of the provision is manifestly to give the accused the fullest information in the possession of the prosecution, on which the case of the State is based, and the statements made against him. But failure to furnish statements of witnesses recorded in the course of investigation may not vitiate the trial. It does not affect the jurisdiction of the court to try a case, nor is the failure by itself a ground which affects the power of the court to record a conviction, if the evidence warrants such a course."

Q.60. What are the powers of Investigating Officer to recover the SIM card and records of a mobile phone suspected to be used in the crime?

Ans. Under section 91 of the Criminal Procedure Code, a police officer is empowered to call upon any person who is believed to be in possession of any material required for investigation of an offence and to direct him to attend and produce the same for the purpose of investigation. If such person refuses to produce the required material, he can be booked under section 175 of IPC for disobeying the directions issued under section 91 of the Cr.P.C.

Q.61. Whether the attached property of a proclaimed offender, whose case has been amicably settled, can be released?

Ans. The provisions of sections 82, 83 and 85 of Cr.P.C. were enacted to secure the presence of the accused and once the purpose is achieved, the property attached should be restored to its owner. Provisions of the Criminal Procedure Code do not warrant sale of the property when the absconding accused surrenders in court and obtains bail. Once he surrenders before the court and the standing warrants are cancelled, he is no longer an absconder and the purpose of attaching the property comes to an end.

In *Vimlaben Ajitbhai Patel* v. *Vatslaben Ashokbhai Patel*, (2008) 4 SCC 649: AIR 2008 SC 2675: 2008 AIR SCW 4475, the Supreme Court held (in Para 32) that, "The provisions contained in section 82 of the Code of Criminal Procedure were put on the statute book for certain purpose. It was enacted to secure the presence of the accused. Once the said purpose is achieved, the attachment shall be withdrawn. Even the property which was attached, should be restored. The provisions of the Code of Criminal Procedure do not warrant sale of the property despite the fact that the absconding accused had surrendered and obtained bail. Once he surrenders before the Court and the Standing Warrants cancelled, he is no longer an absconder. The purpose of attaching the property comes to an end. It is to be released subject to the provisions of the Code. Securing the attendance of an absconding accused, is a matter between the State and the accused. Complainant should not ordinarily derive any benefit therefrom. If the property is to be sold, it vests with the State subject to any order passed under section 85 of the Code. It cannot be a subject matter of execution of a decree, far less for executing the decree of a third party, who had no right, title or interest thereon."

Q.62. Despite a written complaint specifying offences under sections 326/325/34 of IPC, the police did not register an FIR. Please guide.

Ans. In *Sakiri Vasu* v. *State of Uttar Pradesh*, (2008) 2 SCC 409: AIR 2008 SC 907: 2008 AIR SCW 30, the Supreme Court has held that, "if a person has a grievance that the police station is not registering his FIR under section 154, Cr.P.C., then he can approach the Superintendent of Police under section 154(3) Cr.P.C. by an application in writing. Even if that does not yield any satisfactory result in the sense that either the FIR is still not registered, or that even after registering it no proper investigation is held, it is open to the aggrieved person to file an application under section 156(3), Cr.P.C. before the learned Magistrate concerned. If such an application under section 156(3) is filed before the Magistrate, the Magistrate can direct the FIR to be registered and also can direct a proper investigation to be made, in a case where, according to the aggrieved person, no proper investigation was made. The Magistrate can also under the same provision monitor the investigation to ensure a proper investigation." The Supreme Court has further held that the Magistrate can also order reopening of investigation even after the police had submitted final report.

Q.63. A lady died under suspicious circumstances at her in-laws house within two years of her marriage. Her in-laws hurriedly buried the body without getting any post-mortem conducted. Whether the police can dig out her body and get autopsy done?

Ans. A body, which is formally buried, can be disinterred only on the orders of a Magistrate under section 176(3) of the Cr.P.C. In such cases, the SHO should apply to the area Magistrate. The body can be disinterred in the presence of the Magistrate or in presence of two or more respectable members of the locality. Thereafter, formal investigation under section 174 of Cr.P.C. is required. Of course, the identity of the body shall be ascertained prior to the proceedings.

Q.64. After lodging a protest petition against cancellation report filed by the police, the complainant sought CBI investigation which was turned down by the Magistrate. Please advise.

Ans. The Magistrate is not empowered to direct the CBI or any other agency, except the local police under his jurisdiction, for investigating an offence. In *CBI* v. *State of Rajasthan,* (2001) 3 SCC 333: AIR 2001 SC 668: 2001 AIR SCW 305, the Supreme Court set aside Magistrate's order directing the CBI to conduct investigation, holding that, "the magisterial power cannot be stretched under the said sub-section beyond directing the officer in charge of a police station to conduct the investigation." A similar view has been taken by the Andhra Pradesh High Court in *Gun-Rock Enclave Co-op Housing Society Ltd.* v. *P. Ranganaya Kamma*, 2006 (1) RCR (Cri) 665. However, in appropriate cases, the High Court has powers to order CBI investigation.

Q.65. In an opium matter under NDPS Act, the police did not conduct investigation at the place of recovery, and rather completed the formality of sample collection and memo preparation at a nearby police post. Whether this procedure is legally permissible?

Ans. Generally, the entire investigation work is done by the investigating officer at the spot *i.e.,* at the place where the accused is apprehended and where the contraband article is recovered. The Supreme Court considered this issue in *Khet Singh* v. *Union of India,* 2002 SCC (Cri) 806: AIR 2002 SC 1450: 2002 AIR SCW 1308 and held that, "It is true that when a contraband article is seized during investigation or search, a seizure mahazar should be prepared at the spot in accordance with law. There may, however, be circumstances in which it would not have been possible for the officer to prepare the mahazar at the spot, as it may be a chance recovery and the officer may not have the facility to prepare a seizure mahazar at the spot itself. If the seizure is effected at the place where there are no witnesses and there is no facility for weighing the contraband article or other requisite facilities are lacking, the officer can prepare the seizure mahazar at a later stage as and when the facilities are available, provided there are justifiable and reasonable grounds to do so. In that event, where the seizure mahazar is prepared at a later stage, the officer should indicate his reasons as to why he had not prepared the mahazar at the spot of recovery ..... Law on the point is very clear that even if there is any sort of procedural illegality in conducting the search and seizure, the evidence collected thereby will not become inadmissible and the court would consider all the circumstances and find out whether any serious prejudice had been caused to the accused. If the search and seizure was in complete defiance of the law and procedure and there was any possibility of the evidence collected likely to have been tampered with or interpolated during the course of such search or seizure, then, it could be said that the evidence is not liable to be admissible in evidence."

Q.66. Whether signatures on statements under section 161 of Cr.P.C. recorded by the police are admissible in evidence?

Ans. The law on the point was explained by Kerala High Court in *V.A. Abraham* v. *Superintendent of Police,* 1988 Cr LJ 1144: 1988 (1) Ker LJ 176: 1988 (1) Ker LT 379, in these terms: "Section 162, Cr.P.C. contains a prohibition against obtaining the signature of witness whose statement is recorded during investigation. The policy underlying the rule is that at the trial the witnesses should be free to make statements which they wish to make even if they are in favour of the accused, unhampered by anything which they might have been made to say to the police. The signature may tie them to the statement or at least give them an impression that they are not free to make a different statement. But section 162 does not provide that evidence of a witness given in court becomes inadmissible for the mere reason that his statement obtained during investigation was signed by him. The signature does not render the evidence inadmissible. It merely puts the court on caution and may necessitate indepth scrutiny of the evidence, that is all."

Q.67. What is the effect of not producing the Investigating Officer by the prosecution despite several opportunities granted by the court in a motor accident case?

Ans. Failure to examine the Investigating Officer is not fatal to the prosecution unless it is shown as to what prejudice has been caused to the accused by such non-examination. In the case of accident, since the Investigating Officer is a formal witness, his examination is not fatal. As such one cannot derive any benefit on this ground. In *Jarnail Singh* v. *State of Haryana,* 2004 (4) RCR (Cri) 588, the Punjab and Haryana High Court held, "If the Investigating Officer was not examined, the same would be of no consequence considering that the eye witnesses who had witnessed the accident had appeared in witness box and had categorically stated about the manner in which the accident took place and with regard to the rash and negligent driving of the bus in question by the accused-petitioner".

Q.68. Is there any difference between the admissibility of a rough site plan (i) prepared by the investigating officer himself, (ii) prepared when pointed out by eye-witnesses, and (iii) prepared by a draftsman?

Ans. The Supreme Court in *Sat Kumar* v. *State* AIR 1974 SC 294: 1974 Cr LJ 345: (1974) 3 SCC 643, has held that when the investigating officer prepares the site plan as told by witnesses, it would be inadmissible in evidence and no reliance can be placed on the place of occurrence as shown in the site plan.

(ii) In *Rameshwar Dayal* v. *State* AIR 1978 SC 1558: (1978) 2 SCC 518: 1978 All LJ 1011, the Supreme Court has held that, "Documents like the Inquest report, seizure lists or the site plans consists of two parts, one of which is admissible and the other is inadmissible. That part of such documents which is based on the actual observation of the witness at the spot being direct evidence in the case, is clearly admissible, under section 60 of the Evidence Act, whereas the other part which is based on information given to the Investigating Officer, or on the statement recorded by him inadmissible under section 162, Cr.P.C., except for the limited purpose mentioned in that section".

(iii) In *Santa Singh* v. *State,* AIR 1956 SC 526: 1955 Cr LJ 930 the Supreme Court has held that the map of place of occurrence prepared by the draftsman after ascertaining from the witnesses is admissible as evidence. The Court observed: "If the draftsman is asked to prepare a sketch map of the place of the occurrence, and if after ascertaining from the witnesses where exactly the assailant and the victim stood at the time of the commission of the offence and the draftsman measures the distance between the two places thus shown to him and puts it down on the plan, and further, if the witnesses corroborate his statement that they showed him the places, it is somewhat difficult to see how this is not legal evidence and why it is inadmissible."

Q.69. The police submitted challan under section 18 of NDPS Act showing recovery of contraband by the ASI who had conducted investigation of the case. The sample was sent to FSL after a delay of 7 days. Please advise.

Ans. If the police officer who is the complainant also conducts the investigation of the case and it is not proved that any prejudice has been caused to the accused, the accused cannot be acquitted on this ground alone. [Reliance: (i) *S. Jeevanantham* v. *State of Tamil Nadu,* (2004) 5 SCC 230: AIR 2004 SC 4608: 2004 AIR SCW 4203; (ii) *Nande Lal* v. *State of Haryana,* 2009 (4) RCR (Cri) 694 (P&H)].

Secondly, delay of seven days in sending the sample would not be fatal to the prosecution case if it is proved that the sealed sample remained untampered until the same reached the FSL.

26. Limitation

Q.70. As in civil matters, is there any limitation in criminal cases where cognizance of the offences is involved?

Ans. The law of limitation operates in criminal cases also. Section 468 of Criminal Procedure Code which provides limitation for taking cognizance of certain offences reads:

"(1) Except as otherwise provided elsewhere in this Code, no court shall take cognizance of an offence of the category specified in sub-section (2), after the expiry of the period of limitation.

(2) The period of limitation shall be—

(a) six months, if the offence is punishable with fine only;

(b) one year, if the offence is punishable with imprisonment for a term not exceeding one year;

(c) three years, if the offence is punishable with imprisonment for a term exceeding one year but not exceeding three years."

Q.71. How and when is the starting point of limitation in criminal law?

Ans. Chapter XXXVI of the Cr.P.C. deals with limitation for taking cognizance for certain categories of offences enumerated in section 468. The commencement of limitation period is provided in section 469 of Cr.P.C. which reads: (1) The period of limitation, in relation to an offender, shall commence,—

(a) on the date of the offence; or

(b) where the commission of the offence was not known to the person aggrieved by the offence or to any police officer, the first day on which such offence comes to the knowledge of such person or to any police officer, whichever is earlier; or

(c) where it is not known by whom the offence was committed, the first day on which the identity of the offender is known to the person aggrieved by the offence or to the police officer making investigation into the offence, whichever is earlier.

(2) In computing the said period, the day from which such period is to be computed shall be excluded.

Q.72. Is there any provision for extending limitation in criminal law?

Ans. The court has the power to take cognizance of an offence even after expiry of limitation period in view of section 473 of Cr.P.C. which reads: "Notwithstanding anything contained in the foregoing provisions of this Chapter, any court may take cognizance of an offence after the expiry of the period of limitation, if it is satisfied on the facts and in the circumstances of the case that the delay has been properly explained or that it is necessary so to do in the interests of justice."

Further, section 472 provides for a continuing offence which reads thus: "In the case of a continuing offence, a fresh period of limitation shall begin to run at every moment of the time during which the offence continues."

Q.73. In a case of theft which took place on April 10, 2004, the police submitted challan on April 15, 2006 under section 379/411 of the IPC. Thereafter, the accused absented but was re-arrested on May 20, 2007. At the time of framing charges, the defense counsel took the plea that limitation being three years, the court could not take cognizance. What is the legal position?

Ans. Section 468(1) provides that, "Except as otherwise provided elsewhere in this Code, no court shall take cognizance of an offence of the category specified in sub-section (2), after the expiry of the period of limitation."

As per section 468(2) of Cr.P.C., the limitation is three years, if the offence is punishable with imprisonment for a term exceeding one year but not exceeding three years. The offence under section 411, IPC is punishable for three years. Therefore, *per se*, the defence plea seems to be plausible. However, the relevant date for starting point of limitation is the date of initiating criminal proceedings and not the date for framing of charge. Even otherwise, section 473 of Cr.P.C. provides that a court may take cognizance of an offence even after expiry of limitation period.

In *Japani Sahoo* v. *Chander Sekhar Mohanty,* (2007) 7 SCC 394: AIR 2007 SC 2762: 2007 Cr LJ 4068, the Supreme Court held, "Section 469 declares as to when the period of limitation would commence. Sections 470-471 provide for exclusion of period of limitation in certain cases. Section 472 deals with 'continuing' offences. Section 473 is an overriding provision and enables courts to condone delay where such delay has been properly explained or where the interest of justice demands extension of period of limitation. The general rule of criminal justice is that "a crime never dies". The principle is reflected in the well-known maxim *nullum tempus aut locus occurrit regi* (lapse of time is no bar to Crown in proceeding against offenders). The Limitation Act, 1963 does not apply to criminal proceedings unless there are express and specific provisions to that effect, for instance, articles 114, 115, 131 and 132 of the Act. It is settled law that a criminal offence is considered as a wrong against the State and the society, even though it has been committed against an individual. Normally, in serious offences, prosecution is launched by the State. A court of law has no power to throw away prosecution solely on the ground of delay. Mere delay in approaching a court of Law would not by itself afford a ground for dismissing the case, though it may be a relevant circumstance in reaching a final verdict."

Q.74. A criminal complaint was filed in the Magistrate's court within the period of limitation. The Magistrate returned the complaint being defective. The complaint was re-filed after the period of limitation had expired. The court refused to entertain the complaint being time-barred. Please advise.

Ans. The complaint cannot be said to be time-barred as it was filed within limitation at the first instance and the 'bar' under section 468, Cr.P.C. would thus not be applicable. The Kerala High Court, in *Labour Enforcement Officer, Cochin* v. *C.V Avarachan,* 2004 (3) RCR (Cri) 415: 2004 Cr LJ 2582 (Ker): 2004 (4) All Cri LR 13 relying upon *Zain Sait* v. *Intex Painter, Interior Decorators,* 1993 Cr LJ 2213: 1993 (1) Ker LJ 468: 1993 (1) Ker LT 532 and *Bharat Damodar Kale* v. *State of Andhra Pradesh,* (2003) 8 SCC 559: AIR 2003 SC 4560: 2003 Cr LJ 4543, held that "The date of filing of the complaint and not the later date on which the Court may have for its own reasons, chosen to issue summons after taking cognizance, is the crucial date for the purpose of deciding limitation." The Supreme Court, in *Bharat Damodar Kale* v. *State of Andhra Pradesh,* (2003) 8 SCC 559: AIR 2003 SC 4560: 2003 Cr LJ 4543, held, "A complaint filed within the period of limitation under the Code cannot be made infructuous by an act of court. The legal phrase *"actus curiae neminem gravabit"* which means an act of the court shall prejudice no man, or by a delay on the part of the court neither party should suffer, also supports the view that the legislature could not have intended to put a period of limitation on the act of the court of taking cognizance of an offence so as to defeat the case of the complainant."

Q.75. Can the time spent in obtaining sanction be excluded while computing limitation period for prosecution of a public servant?

In *Bharat Damodar Kale* v. *State of A.P.*, (2003) 8 SCC 559, the Supreme Court held, "Section 470 indicates that while computing the period of limitation, time taken during which the case was being diligently prosecuted in another court or in appeal or in revision against the offender should be excluded. The said section also provides in the Explanation that in computing the time required for obtaining the consent or sanction of the Government or any other authority should be excluded. Similarly, the period during which the court was closed will also have to be excluded. All these provisions indicate that the court taking cognizance can take cognizance of an offence the complaint of which is filed before it within the period of limitation prescribed and if need be after excluding such time which is legally excludable."

27. Public Prosecutor

Q.76. During raid, the tax authorities in Haryana seized some incriminating documents from a dealer on the basis of which evasion of tax was detected. The dealer filed a complaint in criminal court. The court summoned the concerned officer. Whether the State can provide services of Public Prosecutor or a private lawyer on Government expenses for defending the Officer?

Ans. As per chapter 12 of Haryana Law Department Manual, the government will ordinarily meet the reasonable expenses of the defence of a government servant in criminal cases brought against him for acts arising out of performance of his public duties provided that they are satisfied that he acted in good faith and that the complaint has been brought against him with the object of deterring him from or harassing him in the performance of his public duty.

However, it is not desirable that the Public Prosecutor shall be deputed for the defence of a criminal case in which an official is an accused. In a similar situation, the Supreme Court in *Sunil Kumar Pal* v. *Phota Seikh*, (1984) 4 SCC 533: AIR 1984 SC 1591: 1984 Cri LR (SC) 374 held that a Public Prosecutor should not appear on behalf of an accused. The Court ruled,"It is difficult to understand how consistently with ethics of the legal profession and fair play in the administration of justice, the Public Prosecutor of Nadia could appear on behalf of respondent Nos. 1 to 9. The appearance of the Public Prosecutor, Nadia on behalf of the defence does lent support to the allegation of the appellant that respondent Nos. 1 to 9 were supported by the Communist Party of India (Marxist) which was at the material time the ruling party in the State of West Bengal and this would naturally give rise to apprehension in the minds of the witnesses that in giving evidence against respondent Nos. 1 to 9, they would be not only incurring the displeasure of the government but would also be fighting against it."

However, the services of an advocate can be provided at government expense to defend the officer.

28. Quashing of F.I.R.

Q.77. A 22-year-old fell in love with a 17-year-old Muslim girl. They eloped. The girl's family lodged an FIR under section 363 and 366A of the

Indian Penal Code (IPC) against the boy. After a year, they were found in Mumbai. The police filed a challan on the ground that when the boy eloped with the girl, she was below 18 years. Can the FIR be quashed?

Ans. As explained by Mulla in his 'Principles of Mohammedan Law', a girl who has attained the age of puberty can marry without the consent of her parents. As per Mulla, puberty can be presumed at the age of 15. Similarly, according to article 27 of Tyabji Muslim Law, a girl reaching the age of puberty can marry without the consent of her guardian. Further article 268 of Mulla's Principles of Mohammedan Laws says that the marriage will be presumed in the absence of direct proof by mere fact of acceptance of a woman by the man as his wife. Similarly, article 90 of Tyabji Muslim Laws says that a marriage is to be presumed on the acknowledgement of either party to the marriage. The accused may seek quashing of FIR. In *Rukshana* v. *Govt. of NCT of Delhi*, 2007 (3) RCR (Cri) 542, the Delhi High Court quoted with approval the following passage from a Text Book of Mohammedan Law by Aqil Ahmad, "Puberty and majority are in the Muslim law one and the same. The presumption is that a person attains majority at the age of 15 years. It should be noted that marriage of a minor without the consent of the guardian is invalid unless it is ratified after the attainment of majority. A boy or girl who has attained puberty is at liberty to marry any one he or she likes and the guardian has no right to interfere if the match be equal." It was held, "the girl who is now more than 15 years of age has the option under the Muslim law to ratify or enter into the contract of marriage afresh." Therefore, the accused persons can approach the High Court for quashing of FIR.

Q.78. A criminal complaint under sections 419, 467, 468, 471 of the Indian Penal Code was filed alleging forgery of a Will. In a civil suit the same Will was held valid. Can the criminal proceedings be dropped?

Ans. After the court has upheld validity of the Will, the criminal proceedings can be dropped. The Trial Court may be requested to drop the proceedings in view of law laid down in *Manohar Lal* v. *Ram Chander*, 2003 (3) RCR (Cri) 786 (P&H) *and Amar Nath* v. *Atma Ram*, 2007 (2) RCR (Cri) 942 (PH).

29. Refreshing Memory

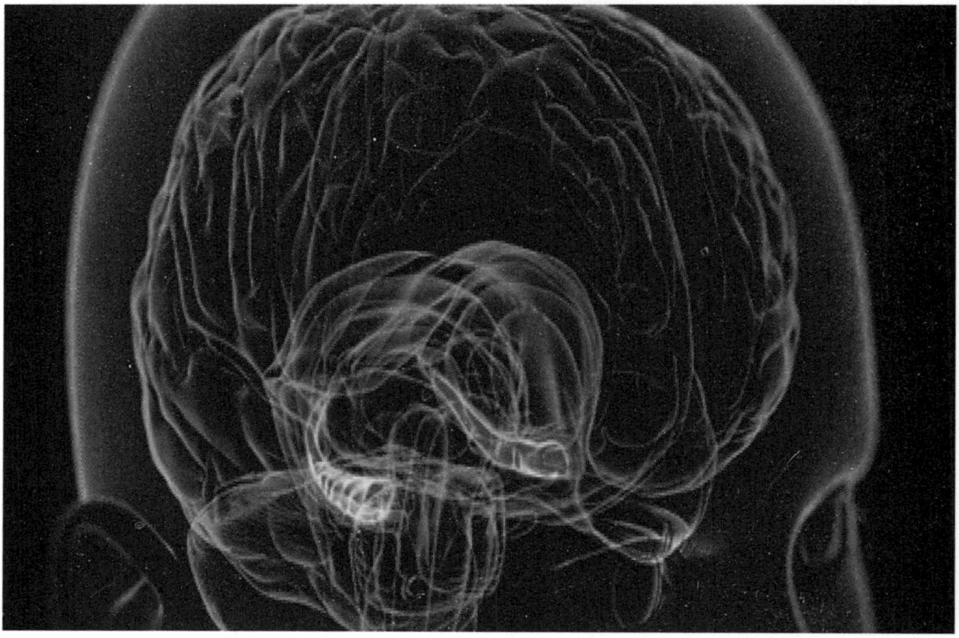

Q.79. In a murder trial, the Investigating Officer perused the court file before his deposition in examination-in-chief. The court rejected objections raised by the defence. What are the remedies available to the accused?

Ans. As per sections 159 and 160 of the Cr. P. C an Investigating Officer can refresh his memory from the case file. Considering the nature of a policeman's day-to-day duties during the investigation period, it is not to be expected of him to remember the contents of documents he prepared during the investigation. Thus, statement of the Investigating Officer, made after refreshing his memory, is not contrary to sections 159 and 160 of Cr.P.C. as held by Rajasthan High Court in *Harchanda* v. *State of Rajasthan,* 2004 (3) RCR 132. The Court observed: "it would be extremely difficulty to expect that any one of the police offices having regard to nature of their duties from day to day during the investigation period could positively remember orally the precise contents of the documents prepared by them during the investigation. Thus the statement of the I.O. by refreshing the memory in no way is found contrary to the provisions of law and the learned trial Judge rightly granted the permission to refresh the memory."

30. Sanction for Prosecution

Q.80. A challan under the Prevention of Corruption Act, 1988 was submitted against a government servant after his retirement without obtaining sanction for prosecution. Can the Trial Court take cognizance?

Ans. No sanction for prosecution under section 19 of the Prevention of Corruption Act, 1988 is required in case of a public servant who is no more in government service on the date of filing the charge-sheet.

In *Kalicharan Mahapatra* v. *State of Orissa,* (1998) 6 SCC 411: AIR 1998 SC 2595: 1998 AIR SCW 2629, the Supreme Court observed, "in spite of bringing such a significant change to section 197 of the Code in 1973, the Parliament was circumspect enough not to change the wording in section 19 of the Act which deals with sanction. The reason is obvious. The sanction contemplated in section 197 of the Code concerns a public servant who "is accused of any offence alleged to have been committed by him while acting or purporting to act in the discharge of his official duty", whereas the offences contemplated in the P.C. Act are those which cannot be treated as acts either directly or even purportedly done in the discharge of his official duties. Parliament must have desired to maintain the distinction and hence the wording in the corresponding provision in the former P.C. Act was materially imported in the new P.C. Act, 1988 without any change in spite of the change made in section 197 of the Code.

The result of the above discussion is thus: A public servant who committed an offence mentioned in the Act, while he was a public servant when the court takes cognizance of the offence. But if he ceases to be a public servant by that time the court can take cognizance of offence without any such sanction. In other words, the public servant who committed the offence while he was public servant is liable to be prosecuted whether he continues in office or not at the time of trial or during the pendency of the prosecution. "

The Supreme Court, in *State of Kerala* v. *M.M Manikantan Nair,* 2001 (2) RCR (Cri) 657: AIR 2001 SC 2145: 2001 Cr LJ 2346, held thus: "Section 19 of the Prevention of Corruption Act, *inter alia,* provides for previous sanction for prosecution and such sanction is necessary if a person is employed in connection with the affairs of the Union/State. This section came up for consideration by this court and in *State of Kerala* v. *V. Padmanabhan,* (1999) 5 SCC 690 this court held that a person who ceased to be a public servant on the date when the court took cognizance, no sanction under the above section is required." [Followed by Punjab and Haryana High Court in *Surinder Kumar Bansal* v. *State of Punjab,* 2006 Cr LJ 1329: 2006 (3) AIR Bom R 483 NOC: 2006 (1) Rec Cri R 743].

Q.81. Can an order granting sanction be challenged in a court of law?

Ans. The grounds for challenging sanction are limited. The court may set aside an order of sanction only in limited situations, for example, if it is based on 'no material' or suffers from complete 'non-application of mind'. In *State (Anti Corruption)* v. *Dr. R.C. Anand,* (2004) 4 SCC 615: 2004 AIR SCW 3659: AIR 2004 SC 3693, the Supreme Court held that, "The validity of the sanction would, therefore, depend upon the material placed before the sanctioning authority and the fact that all the relevant facts, material and evidence including the transcript of the tape record have been considered by the sanctioning authority. Consideration implies application of mind. The order of sanction must *ex facie* disclose that the sanctioning authority had considered the evidence and other material placed before it. This fact can also be established by extrinsic evidence by placing the relevant files before the court to show that all relevant facts were considered by the sanctioning authority." [See *Jaswant Singh* v. *State of Punjab,* AIR 1958 SC 124: AIR 1958 SC 124: 1958 SCR 762 and *State of Bihar* v. *P.P. Sharma,* 1992 Supp (1) SCC 222: 1991 Cr LJ 1438: AIR 1991 SC 1260].

Q.82. Whether grant of sanction is a mere formality and the sanctioning authority can grant sanction based upon report received from the police?

Ans. The sanctioning authority cannot grant sanction in a casual and routine manner merely on the basis of a report received from the police. In *State of Karnataka* v. *Ameerjan,* (2007) 11 SCC 273: AIR 2008 SC 108: 2008 Cr LJ 347, the Supreme Court held that, "application of mind on the part of the sanctioning authority is imperative. The order granting sanction must be demonstrative of the fact that there had been proper application of mind on the part of the sanctioning authority. ..... Ordinarily, before passing an order of sanction, the entire records containing the materials collected against the accused should be placed before the sanctioning authority. In the event, the order of sanction does not indicate application of mind as (sic to) the materials placed before the said authority before the order of sanction was passed, the same may be produced before the court to show that such materials had in fact been produced."

Q.83. Can an order refusing sanction be reviewed by the competent authority without any fresh material? Whether such a sanction is valid?

Ans. In the absence of any fresh material before the subsequent sanctioning authority, review of order passed under section 19 of the Prevention of Corruption Act, is not permissible. In *State of Punjab* v. *Mohammed Iqbal,* 2009 (3) RCR (Cri) 861: 2010 Cr LJ 1436: 2010 AIR SCW 1186 (SC), the Supreme Court considered a similar question in these terms: "....whether the State has any power of review in the matter of grant of sanction in terms of section 197 of the Code of Criminal Procedure, 1973?" The Supreme Court found that no fresh material was produced and no reasons were available for 'reconsideration' of earlier order refusing sanction. The court found, "Application of mind is also absent to show the necessity for reconsideration or review of the earlier order on the basis of the materials placed before the sanctioning authority or otherwise." Thus, the High Court quashed the sanctioning order while the Supreme Court dismissed the State appeal.

Q.84. Whether an order granting sanction can be challenged at the initial stage?

Ans. The courts are empowered to review and examine an order of sanction to arrive at a conclusion if such an order is valid. The Supreme Court has held in *State of Punjab* v. *Mohammed Iqbal Bhatti,* (2009) 17 SCC 92: JT 2009 (13) SC 180: 2010 AIR SCW 1186 that, "It is, however, beyond any cavil that while passing an order for grant of sanction, serious application of mind on the part of the concerned authority is imperative. The legality and/or validity of the order granting sanction would be subject to review by the criminal courts. An order refusing to grant sanction may attract judicial review by the Superior Courts. Validity of an order of sanction would depend upon application of mind on the part of the authority concerned and the material placed before it. All such material facts and material evidences must be considered by it. The sanctioning authority must apply its mind on such material facts and evidences collected during the investigation. Even when such application of mind does not appear from the order of sanction, extrinsic evidences may be placed before the court in that behalf. While granting sanction, the authority cannot take into consideration an irrelevant fact nor can it pass an order on extraneous consideration not germane for passing a statutory order. It is also well settled that the Superior Courts cannot direct the sanctioning authority either to grant sanction or not to do so. The source of power of an authority passing an order of sanction must also be considered. [See *Mansukhlal Vithaldas Chauhan* v. *State of Gujarat,* (1997) 7 SCC 622: AIR 1997 SC 3400: 1997 AIR SCW 3478]"

Q.85. In a case registered against an employee under the Prevention of Corruption Act, after holding a departmental enquiry, the authorities refused to accord sanction for prosecution. Can the complainant challenge this order?

Ans. In *Mansukhlal Vithaldas Chauhan* v. *State of Gujarat,* (1997) 7 SCC 622: AIR 1997 SC 3400: 1997 AIR SCW 3478 the Supreme Court has observed that the courts cannot order the sanctioning authority to accord sanction for prosecution under section 19(1) of the Prevention of Corruption Act, 1988.

The Court observed: "The question is whether the High Court could issue a mandamus of their and whether the order of Sanction, in these circumstances, is valid. Mandamus which is a discretionary remedy under Article 226 of the Constitution is requested to be issued, *inter alia,* to compel performance of public duties which may be administrative, ministerial or statutory in nature. Statutory duty may be either directory or mandatory. Statutory duties, if they are intended to be mandatory in character, are indicated by the use of the words "shall" or "must". But this is not conclusive as "shall" and "must" have, sometimes, been interpreted as "may". What is determinative of the nature of duty, whether it is obligatory, mandatory or directory, is the scheme of the Statute in which the 'duty" has been set out. Even if the "Duty" is not set out clearly and specially in the Statute, it may be implied as co-relative to a "Right". In the performance of this duty, if the authority in whom the discretion is vested under the Statute, does not act independently and passes an order under the instructions and orders of another authority, the Court would intervene in the matter, quash the orders and issue a mandamus to that authority to exercise its own discretion. The sanctioning authority, in the instant case, was left with no choice except to sanction the prosecution and in passing the order of sanction, it acted mechanically in obedience to the mandamus issued by the High Court by putting the signature on a pro forma drawn up by the office."

Q.86. If sanction for prosecution of an employee, booked under section 1 of Prevention of Corruption Act, 1988, is not granted for lack of evidence an more details are sought, can the authorities grant sanction on a fres evidence adduced by the police?

Ans. Since the sanctioning authority had not refused sanction but onl sought more details, the authority may consider grant of sanction on the basi of fresh evidence. [*Dharamveer Singh* v. *CBI,* 2005 (3) RCR (Cri) 198 (Del)].

Q.87. In the case of a public servant facing trial under section 13(1)(e) o the Prevention of Corruption Act, 1988 (disproportionate assets), sanction fo prosecution under section 19 was granted by an authority other than th competent authority. Whether the sanction order can be challenged?

Ans. Order of sanction, passed by an authority not competent to pass suc order, is a nullity. The prosecution cannot proceed with the case on the basi of a defective sanction. In *State Inspector of Police Vishakhapatnam* v. *Sury Sankaram Karri,* (2006) 7 SCC 172: AIR 2007 SC (Supp) 1860: 2006 AIR SCV 4576, the Supreme Court concluded that "when a sanction is granted by person not authorized in law, the same being without jurisdiction, would be nullity." In *State of Karnataka through CBI* v. *C. Nagarajaswamy,* (2005) 8 SC 370, it was held: "Grant of proper sanction by a competent authority is a *sin qua non* for taking cognizance of the offence. It is desirable that the question a regard sanction may be determined at an early stage."

Q.88. The competent authority refused to grant sanction of a governmen servant who was booked under sections 7 and 13 of the Prevention o Corruption Act, 1988. Can the court take cognizance of a challan filed by th police without an order of sanction?

Ans. The provisions of section 19 of the Prevention of Corruption Act, 198 are very much clear and a valid sanction is a condition precedent for takin cognizance of an offence. The Prevention of Corruption Act, is a special statut and as such the provisions of section 19 of the P.C. Act will have a overriding effect over the general provisions contained in section 197 Cr.P.C There is an express bar against any Court taking cognizance of an offenc punishable under sections 7, 10, 11, 13 and 15 of the Act alleged to have bee committed by a public servant except with the previous sanction of th concerned Government or the competent authority. [*Dilawar Singh* v. *Parvinde Singh,* 2006 (1) SCC (Cri) 722: (2005) 12 SCC 709: 2005 AIR SCW 6021; *Asho Mehta* v. *Ram Ashray Singh,* (2004) 13 SCC 705: 2006 (2) RCR (Cri) 329 (SC)].

Q.89. Without examining the sanctioning authority under the Prevention o Corruption Act, 1988, can the public prosecutor tender the sanction order during trial? Whether the sanction order can be read in evidence?

Ans. The court can take judicial notice of the signatures of the sanctioning authority and the law does not require that the sanctioning authority must depose before the court to prove the sanctioned order. Generally, a junior official, well conversant with signatures of the sanctioning authority, is included in the list of witnesses who prove the signatures of the officer concerned. As such, the court can take into consideration the sanction order even if the concerned officer who accorded sanction does not appear in the witness box. In *CBI Hyderabad* v. *Edwin Devasahaya*, (2007) 12 SCC 139, the Supreme Court approved the principles relating to alleged defect in sanction as laid down in *Central Bureau of Investigation* v. *V.K. Sehgal*, (1999) 8 SCC 501 and *Shankerbhai Laljibhai Rot* v. *State of Gujarat*, (2004) 13 SCC 487.

Q.90. What are the powers of Appellate/Revisionary Court while adjudicating a finding on the issue of sanction?

Ans. Section 465 of the Cr.P.C. reads:

> "465. Finding or sentence when reversible by reason of error, omission or irregularity.—(1) Subject to the provisions hereinbefore contained, no finding, sentence or order passed by a Court of competent jurisdiction shall be reversed or altered by a Court of appeal, confirmation or revision on account of any error, omission or irregularity; in the complaint, summons, warrant, proclamation, order, judgment or other proceedings before or during trial or in any inquiry or other proceedings under this Code, or any error, or irregularity in any sanction for the prosecution, unless in the opinion of that Court, a failure of justice has in fact been occasioned thereby.
>
> (2) In determining whether any error, omission or irregularity in any proceeding under this Code, or any error, or irregularity in any sanction for the prosecution has occasioned a failure of justice, the Court shall have regard to the fact whether the objection could and should have been raised at an earlier stage in the proceedings."

A Court of appeal or revision is debarred from reversing a finding (or even an order of conviction and sentence) on account of any error or irregularity in the sanction for the prosecution, unless failure of justice had been occasioned on account of such error or irregularity. For determining whether want of valid sanction had in fact occasioned failure of justice the aforesaid Sub-section (2) enjoins on the Court a duty to consider whether the accused had raised any objection on that score at the trial stage. Even if he had raised any such objection at the early stage it is hardly sufficient to conclude that there was failure of justice. It has to be determined on the facts of each case. But an accused who did not raise it at the trial stage cannot possibly sustain such a plea made for the first time in the appellate Court.

In *Kalpnath Rai* v. *State through CBI*, JT 1997 (9) SC 18 this Court has observed in paragraph 29 thus:

> "Sub-section (2) of section 465 of the Code is not a carte blanche for rendering all trials vitiated on the ground of the irregularity of sanction if objection thereto was raised at the first instance itself. The sub-section only says that 'the Court shall have regard to the fact' that objection has been raised at the earlier stage in the proceedings. It is only one of the considerations to be weighed but it does not mean that if objection was raised at the earlier stage, for that very reason the irregularity in the sanction would spoil the prosecution and transmute the proceedings into a void trial."

In a case where the accused failed to raise the question of a valid sanction the trial would normally proceed to its logical conclusion by making judicial scrutiny of the entire material. If that case concludes in a conviction, there is no question of failure of justice on the mere premise that no valid sanction was accorded for prosecuting the public servant. The very purpose of providing such a filtering check is to safeguard public servants from frivolous or *mala fide* prosecution. But once the judicial filtering process is over, then on completion of the trial, the purpose of providing for the initial sanction would bog down the PROCESS. This could be the reason for providing a bridle upon the appellate and revisional forums as envisaged in section 465 of the Cr.P.C.

Q.91. Can a person be summoned under section 319 Cr.P.C. to face trial for an offence under Prevention of Corruption Act without sanction of competent authority?

Ans. It was held by the Supreme Court in *Dilawar Singh* v. *Parvinder Singh* 2006 (1) SCC (Cri) 722 that "the Prevention of Corruption Act is a special statute and as the preamble shows this Act has been enacted to consolidate and amend the law relating to the prevention of corruption and for matters connected therewith. Here, the principle expressed in the maxim Generalia specialibus non derogant would apply which means that if a special provision has been made on a certain matter, that matter is excluded from the general provisions. (See *Venkateshwar Rao* v. *Govt. of Andhra Pradesh,* AIR 1966 SC 828: 1966 (2) SCJ 270: (1966) 2 SCR 172; *State of Bihar* v. *Yogendra Singh,* AIR 1982 SC 882: (1982) 1 SCC 664: 1982 BLJR 447 and *Maharashtra State Board of Secondary Education* v. *Paritosh Bhupesh Kumar Sheth,* AIR 1984 SC 1543: (1984) 4 SCC 27: 1984 86 Bom LR 428. Therefore the provisions of section 19 of the Act will have an overriding effect over the general provisions contained in section 190 or 319 Cr.P.C. A Special Judge while trying an offence under the Prevention of Corruption Act, 1988, cannot summon another person and proceed against him in the purported exercise of power under section 319 Cr.P.C. if no sanction has been granted by the appropriate authority for prosecution of such a person as the existence of a sanction is sine qua non for taking cognizance of the offence qua that person."

Q. 92. Can want of sanction be challenged in appeal against conviction?

Ans. In *Central Bureau of Investigation* v. *V.K. Sehgal,* (1999) 8 SCC 501: AIR 1999 SC 3706: 1999 Cr LJ 4593, the Supreme Court held in Para 18: "Thus the legal position to be followed, while dealing with the appeal filed against the conviction and sentence of any offence mentioned in 1947 Act, is that no such conviction and sentence shall be altered or reversed merely on the ground of absence of sanction, much less on the ground of want of competency of the authority who granted the sanction."

31. Charge/Dowry Death

Q.93. A person was booked for murder of his wife. The court convicted him for the offence punishable under section 306 IPC for abetment of suicide for which he was not charged. Is the order of the trial Court legally sustainable?

Ans. The two offences punishable under sections 302 and 306 of the IPC are of distinct and different categories. The basic constituent of offence under section 302 is homicidal death and that under section 306 is suicidal death and its abetment. In *Dalbir Singh* v. *State of Uttar Pradesh,* (2004) 5 SCC 334: AIR 2004 SC 1990: 2004 AIR SCW 2119, the Supreme Court had taken a view that the accused who is acquitted under section 302 of the IPC can be convicted under section 306 although this charge was not framed. In this case, the earlier view of Supreme Court taken in the case of *Sangaraboina Sreenu* v. *State of Andhra Pradesh,* AIR 1997 SC 3233: 1997 Cr LJ 3955: 1997 AIR SCW 3290 (a two-Judges Bench decision) was not approved.

The Court ruled: "In view of conflict of opinion in two decisions of this Court rendered in *Lakhjit Singh* v. *State of Punjab,* 1994 Supp (1) SCC 173: 1993 AIR SCW 2938 and *Sangarabonia Sreenu* v. *State of A.P.,* (1997) 5 SCC 348: AIR 1997 SC 3233: 1997 Cr LJ 3955 these appeals have been directed to be placed for hearing before a three-Judge Bench. ....Therefore, in view of section 464 Cr.P.C., it is possible for the appellate or revisional Court to convict an accused for an offence for which no charge was framed unless the Court is of the opinion that a failure of justice would in fact occasion. In order to judge whether a failure of justice has been occasioned, it will be relevant to examine whether the accused was aware of the basic ingredients of the offence for which he is being convicted and whether the main facts sought to be established against him were explained to him clearly and whether he got a fair chance to defend himself. We are, therefore, of the opinion that *Sangarabonia Sreenu* (supra) was not correctly decided as it purports to lay down as a principle of law that where the accused is charged under section

302 IPC, he cannot be convicted for the offence under section 306 IPC. Again in *Annareddy Sambasiva Reddy* v. *State of Andhra Pradesh*, (2009) 12 SCC 546: AIR 2009 SC 2661: 2009 AIR SCW 4091 the Supreme Court had occasion to deal with the same question and referred to section 464 of Cr.P.C. In paragraph 55 at page 567 of the report, the Court came to the conclusion that if the ingredients of the section charged with are obvious and implicit, conviction under such head can be sustained irrespective of the fact whether the said section has been mentioned or not in the charge. The basic question was one of prejudice.

Q.94. A persons convicted of murdering his wife was sentenced to life imprisonment. After having spent 22 years in prison, can he be released?

Ans. Section 57 of Indian Penal Code reads as follows:—

> "57. Fractions of terms of punishment. — In calculating fractions of terms of punishment, imprisonment for life shall be reckoned as equivalent to imprisonment for twenty years."

The above section is applicable for the purpose of remission when the matter is considered by the government under the appropriate provisions. The Judicial Committee of the Privy Council in *Kishori Lal* v. *Emperor*, AIR (32) 1945 PC 64: (1945) 46 Cr LJ 626 held, "Assuming that the sentence is to be regarded as one of 20 years, and subject to remission for good conduct, he had not earned remission sufficient to entitle him to discharge at the time of his application and it was therefore rightly dismissed but, in saying this, their Lordships are not to be taken as meaning that a life sentence must and in all cases be treated as one of not more than 20 years or that the convict is necessarily entitled to remission."

Life imprisonment means imprisonment for whole of the remaining period of the convict's natural life and as such the convict has no right of release even after 20 years. An accused cannot be released merely because he has spent 22 years in prison. Therefore, his detention is not illegal in any manner. In *Gopal Godse's* case, (1961) 3 SCR 440: AIR 1961 SC 600: (1961) 1 Cr LJ 736, a Constitution Bench of the Supreme Court held: "If transportation for a term, has been equated to rigorous imprisonment for the same term, by necessary implication, the sentence of 'transportation for life', now substituted by 'imprisonment for life', which is awardable for more serious, or more grave or more heinous crimes must mean rigorous imprisonment for life."

In *Naib Singh* v. *State of Punjab*, (1983) 2 SCC 454: AIR 1983 SC 855: 1983 Cr LJ 1345, the Supreme Court ruled: "In the first place, a distinction between 'imprisonment for life' and "imprisonment for a term" has been maintained in the Penal Code in several of its provisions Secondly, by its very terms section 60 is applicable to a case where "an offender is punishable with imprisonment which may be of either description" and it is only in such case that it is competent for the court to direct that "such imprisonment shall be either wholly rigorous or wholly simple or that any part of such imprisonment shall be rigorous and the rest simple." And it is clear that whenever an offender is punishable with "imprisonment for life" he is not punishable with "imprisonment which may be of either description", in other words section 60 would be inapplicable.

This position of law has been reiterated by the Supreme Court in *Munna* v. *Union of India*, (2005) 7 SCC 417: 2005 AIR SCW 4524: AIR 2005 SC 3440. However, the accused may move the State Government for remission of his remaining sentence.

Q.95. Whether in the absence of any specific charges under section 34, IPC (regarding common intention) in a murder case, the accused can be convicted for the offence of murder (302 IPC) read with section 34 IPC?

Ans. The Supreme Court, in *Ramji Singh* v. *State of Bihar* reported as (2001) 9 SCC 528: 2002 SCC (Cri) 760: AIR 2001 SC 3853 has held as under: "Legal position as to whether in the absence of charge under section 34 conviction could be maintained under section 34 was cleared by the Constitution Bench in *Wille Slaney* v. *State of Madhya Pradesh*, AIR 1956 SC 116: 1956 SCJ 182: (1955) 2 SCR 1140, where this Court observed in para 86:

> "Sections 34, 114 and 149 of the Indian Penal Code provide for criminal liability viewed from different angles as regards actual participants, accessories and men actuated by a common object or a common intention; and the charge is a rolled-up one involving the direct liability and the constructive liability without specifying who are directly liable and who are sought to be made constructively liable.
>
> In such a situation, the absence of a charge under one or other of the various head of criminal liability for the offence cannot be said to be fatal by itself, and before a conviction for the substantive offence, without a charge, can be set aside, prejudice will have to be made out. In most of the cases of this kind, evidence is normally given from the outset as to who was primarily responsible for the act which brought about the offence and such evidence is of course relevant.
>
> This was reiterated by the Supreme Court a number of times. We may refer to *Dhanna* v. *State of Madhya Pradesh*, AIR 1996 SC 2478: 1996 Cr LJ 3516: 1996 AIR SCW 3066, where this position is reiterated after referring to the other cases. It held: It is, therefore, open to the Court to take recourse to section 34 of IPC even if the said section was not specifically mentioned in the charge and instead section 149, IPC has been included. Of course a finding that the assailant concerned had a common intention with the other accused is necessary for resorting to such a course. This view was followed by this Court in later decisions also. *Amar Singh* v. *State of Haryana*, AIR 1973 SC 2221: 1973 Cr LJ 1409: 1973 SCC (Cri) 789; *Bhoor Singh* v. *State of Punjab*, AIR 1974 SC 1256: 1974 Cr LJ 929: (1974) 4 SCC 754. The first submission of the learned counsel for the appellant has no merit. Accordingly it is held that even in the absence of the charge under section 34 the conviction could be maintained by the courts below."

Q.96. In a case of rape reported by a maid servant, prosecutrix's medical evidence could not prove the offence. Still, the accused was convicted under section 376 read with section 511 IPC, whereas no charge under section 511, IPC was framed against him. Please advise?

Ans. If an accused is charged with a major offence, but after trial he is not found guilty for the said offence, he can still be convicted of a lesser offence though he was not separately charged for the same. Section 222(3) of Cr.P.C provides: "when a person is charged with an offence, he may be convicted of an attempt to commit such an offence although the attempt was not separately charged." Therefore, the accused has been rightly convicted for an attempt to commit rape. The Supreme Court, in *Pandharinath* v. *State of Maharashtra*, (2009) 14 SCC 537: AIR 2010 SC 1453: 2010 AIR SCW 653, held that, "if an accused is charged of a major offence but is not found guilty there-under, he can be convicted of minor offence, if the facts established indicate that such minor offence has been committed. Reference in this regard may be made to the decision of this court in *State of Maharashtra* v. *Rajendra Jawanmal Gandhi*, (1997) 8 SCC 386: 1997 AIR SCW 3923: AIR 1997 SC 3986; and *Tarkeshwar Sahu* v. *State of Bihar*, (2006) 8 SCC 560."

32. Interlocutory Order

Q.97. What is meant by "interlocutory order" in criminal law parlance? Does any revision lie against such order?

Ans. Interlocutory means provisional, interim, temporary and not final. An interlocutory order is one that does not finally determine the cause but decides some intervening matter pertaining to the cause and which requires further steps to be taken in order to enable the court to adjudicate the cause on merits. Though the phrase "interlocutory order" has not been defined in the Code of Criminal Procedure, the Supreme Court and High Courts have interpreted it in several decisions. In the *Amar Nath* case, reported as AIR 1977 SC, the Supreme Court laid down that 'Interlocutory orders, merely denotes orders of a purely interim or temporary nature which do not decide or touch the important rights or the liabilities of the parties. Any order that substantially affects the rights of the accused or decide certain rights of the parties cannot be said to be an interlocutory order. In *Madhu Limaye* v. *State of Maharashtra*, reported as 1978 Cr LJ 165: AIR 1978 SC 47: (1978) 1 SCR 749, the Supreme Court affirmed the views expressed in the *Amar Nath's* case. There is a specific bar of revision under section 397(2) of Cr.P.C. which reads: "The powers of revision conferred by sub-section (1) shall not be exercised in relation to any interlocutory order passed in any appeal, inquiry, trial or other proceeding." Even though revision against an interlocutory order is barred by section 397(2), yet it may be revised by the High Court under its inherent powers under section 482 of Cr.P.C. which reads: "Nothing in this Code shall be deemed to limit or affect the inherent powers of the High Court to make such orders as may be necessary to give effect to any order under this Code, or to prevent abuse of the process of any Court or otherwise to secure the ends of justice."

The powers under section 482, Cr.P.C. can be invoked only where the order clearly creates a situation that is an abuse of the process of the court, or for securing the ends of justice as there is no other provision in the Cr.P.C. to redress grievances of the aggrieved party. [Reference may also be made to *Municipal Corporation of Delhi* v. *Ram Kishan Rohtagi*, AIR 1983 SC 67: (1983) 1 SCC 1: 1983 Cr LJ 159.

33. Appeal against Acquittal

Q.98. A case under sections 325/326/34 IPC was registered against two persons for beating a friend. The court acquitted one of them by giving him benefit of doubt. The State did not file an appeal against acquittal. Can the victim challenge this order in appeal?

Ans. Earlier, there was no provision in section 372 of Cr.P.C for a victim to challenge an order of acquittal. This provision was amended in 2008 providing for victim's right to file an appeal against an order of acquittal or imposing lesser punishment. Section 372 reads: "No appeal shall lie from any judgment or order of a Criminal Court except as provided for by this Code or by any law for the time being in force. Provided that the victim shall have a right to prefer an appeal against any order passed by the court acquitting the accused or convicting for a lesser offence or imposing inadequate compensation, and such appeal shall lie to the court to which an appeal ordinarily lies against the order of conviction of such court."

Thus, now, a victim is entitled to file an appeal against any order of acquittal. The term "victim" means a person who has suffered any loss or injury caused by reason of the act or omission for which the accused person has been charged. The expression 'victim' includes his or her guardian or legal heirs. [*Smt. Ram Kaur* v. *Jagbir Singh*, 2010 (3) RCR (Cri) 391 (P&H)].

Q.99. In a dowry death case, the police charged the husband for offences under sections 304-B/34 but he was acquitted. What is remedy available to deceased's parents?

Ans. The deceased's parents are entitled to challenge the order of acquittal by filing an appeal in view of section 372 of Cr.P.C.

Q.100. In a murder case, two of the accused were convicted and the remaining two were acquitted. The State filed an appeal against acquittal. The complainant filed revision petition in the High Court. The High Court dismissed the appeal as well as revision petition. Can an appeal in the Supreme Court be entertained?

Ans. Article 136 of the Constitution of India is a special jurisdiction which deals with the appellate power vested in the Supreme Court. It is a residuary power which is extraordinary in its amplitude. In express terms, article 136 does not confer a right of appeal on a party as such but it confers a wide discretionary power on the Supreme Court to interfere in suitable cases to meet the ends of justice. In *Suga Ram @ Chuga Ram* v. *State of Rajasthan,* (2006) 8 SCC 641: AIR 2006 SC 3258: 2006 Cr LJ 4643, it was held by the Supreme Court that, "A doubt has been raised in many cases about the competence of a private party as distinguished from the State, to invoke the jurisdiction of this court under Article 136 of the Constitution against a judgment of acquittal by the High Court. We do not see any substance in the doubt. Appellate power vested in this court under article 136 of the Constitution is not to be confused with ordinary appellate power exercised by appellate courts and appellate tribunals under specific statutes. It is a plenary power, 'exercisable outside the purview of ordinary law' to meet the pressing demands of justice (See *Durga Shankar Mehta* v. *Thakur Raghuraj Singh,* AIR 1954 SC 520: 1954 SCJ 728: 1955 SCR 267. Article 136 of the Constitution neither confers on anyone the right to invoke the jurisdiction of this court nor inhibits anyone from invoking the court's jurisdiction. The power is vested in this court but the right to invoke the court's jurisdiction is vested in noone. The exercise of the power of this court is not circumscribed by any limitation as to who may invoke it. Where a judgment of acquittal by the High Court has led to a serious miscarriage of justice, this court cannot refrain from doing its duty and abstain from interfering on the ground that a private party and not the State has invoked the court's jurisdiction. We do not have slightest doubt that we can entertain appeals against judgments of acquittal by the High Court at the instance of interested private parties also."

Q.101. A complaint was lodged under sections 307/34 of IPC. The accused was acquitted by the trial court. What is the period of limitation for filing an appeal?

Ans. In view of the provisions of section 378 of Code of Criminal Procedure, 1973, the complainant may prefer an appeal before the High Court against the acquittal. According to section 378(5), the period of limitation for filing such an appeal is 60 days from the date of order. Section 378(5) of Cr.P.C. reads: "No application under sub-section (4) for the grant of special leave to appeal from an order of acquittal shall be entertained by the High Court after the expiry of six months, where the complainant is a public servant, and sixty days in every other case, computed from the date of that order of acquittal."

34. *Amicus Curie*

Q.102. After dismissal of an appeal after hearing the *amicus curie*, the dismissal being due to the non-appearance of private lawyer, what is the remedy left with the accused?

Ans. The facts of this question are identical with the facts in *Naresh Kumar* v. *Kala Wati*, (2009) 11 SCC 511, in which the Supreme Court set aside the High Court judgment and remitted the matter to the High Court for fresh disposal without expressing any opinion on merits with these observations: "The appellant has indicated the reason for which there was no appearance when the matter was called before Learned Single Judge. That being the position, we set aside the impugned order and remit the matter to the High Court for fresh disposal in accordance with law."

35. Appeal/Revision

Q.103. During trial, an application filed by the accused under section 311 of the Cr.P.C., seeking further cross-examination of an eyewitness, was rejected by the court. What will be the further course of action?

Ans. Section 311 reads:"Power to summon material witness or examine person present.—Any Court may, at any stage of any inquiry, trial or other proceedings under this Code, summon any person as a witness, or examine any person in attendance, though not summoned as a witness, or recall and re-examine any person already examined; and the Court shall summon and examine or recall and re-examine any such person if his evidence appears to it to be essential to the just decision of the case."

In *Jamatraj* v. *State of Maharashtra*, AIR 1968 SC 178: (1967) 3 SCR 415: 1968 Cr LJ 231, the Supreme Court pointed out, "The section is in two parts. The first part gives a discretionary power but the latter part is mandatory. The use of the word 'may' in the first part and of the word 'shall' in the second firmly establishes this difference. Under the first part, which is permissive, the Court may act in one of three ways: (a) summon any person as a witness; (b) examine any person present in Court although not summoned and (c) recall or re-examine a witness already examined. The second part is obligatory and compels the Court to act in these three ways or any one of them, if the just decisions of the case demands it. As the section stands there is no limitation on the power of the Court arising from the stage to which the trial may have reached, provided the Court is bona fide of the opinion that for the just decision of the case, the step must be taken. It is clear that the requirement of just decision of the case does not limit the action to something in the interest of the accused only. The action may equally benefit the prosecution."

In *Mohanlal Shamji Soni* v. *Union of India*, AIR 1991 SC 1346: 1991 Cr LJ 1521: 1991 Supp (1) SCC 271, the Supreme Court held, "It is a cardinal rule in the law of evidence that the best available evidence should be brought before the court to prove a fact or the points in issue. But it is left either for the prosecution or for the defence to establish its respective case by adducing the best available evidence and the court is not empowered under the provisions of the Code to compel either the prosecution or the defence to examine any particular witness or witnesses on their sides. Nonetheless if either of the parties withholds any evidence which could be produced and which, if produced, be unfavourable to the party withholding such evidence, the court can draw a presumption under *illustration* (g) to section 114 of the Evidence Act. In such a situation a question that arises for consideration is whether the presiding officer of a court should simply sit as a mere umpire at a contest between two parties and declare at the end of the combat who has won and who has lost or is there not any legal duty of his own, independent of the parties, to take an active role in the proceedings in finding the truth and administering justice? It is a well accepted and settled principle that a court must discharge its statutory functions - whether discretionary or obligatory - according to law in dispensing justice because it is the duty of a court not only to do justice but also to ensure that justice is being done. In order to enable the court to find out the truth and render a just decision, the salutary provisions of section 540 of the Code (Section 311 of the new Code) are enacted whereunder any court by exercising its discretionary authority at any stage of enquiry, trial or other proceeding can summon any person as a witness or examine any person in attendance though not summoned as a witness or recall or re-examine any person in attendance though not summoned as a witness or recall and re-examine any person already examined who are expected to be able to throw light upon the matter in dispute; because if judgments happen to be rendered on inchoate, inconclusive and speculative presentation of facts, the ends of justice would be defeated."

Q.104. Whether an accused can be compelled by court to provide his specimen signatures or hand-writing for expert opinion to be used against him in evidence?

Ans. There is an amendment in law. Earlier view was that an accused cannot be compelled to supply any material which may incriminate him. The Supreme Court, in *State of Uttar Pradesh* v. *Ram Babu Mishra*, AIR 1980 SC 791: 1980 All LJ 350: (1980) 2 SCC 343, recommended that this law should be amended. Accordingly, by an amendment [Act No. 25 of 2005] inserted on 23-6-2006, section 311A was added in Cr.P.C. which reads: "If a Magistrate of the First Class is satisfied that, for the purposes of any investigation or proceeding under this Code, it is expedient to direct any person, including an accused person, to give specimen signatures or hand-writing, he may make an order to that effect and in that case the person to whom the order relates shall be produced or shall attend at the time and place specified in such order and shall give a specimen signature or hand-writing: Provided that no order shall be made under this section unless the person has at sometime been arrested in connection with such investigation or proceeding."

36. Free Legal Aid

Q.105. What are State 'Legal Services' and who are entitled to get such service free of cost?

Ans. Legal Service has been defined in section 2(c) of Legal Services Authorities Act, 1987 as under:

> "Legal Service includes the rendering of any service in the conduct of any case or other legal proceeding before any court or other authority or Tribunal and the given of advice on any legal matter".

As per section 12 of the said Act the following persons are entitled to get legal services under the Act.

1. Member of Scheduled Caste or Scheduled tribe;
2. A victim of trafficking in human beings or beggar as referred to in Article 23 of the Constitution of India;
3. A woman or a child;
4. A person with disability as defined in clause (1) of section 2 of the Persons with Disabilities Act, 1995;
5. A person under circumstances or undeserved want such as being a victim of a mass disaster, ethnic violence, caste atrocity, blood drought , earthquake or industrial disaster;
6. An industrial workman; or

7. A person in custody including custody in a protective home within the meaning of clause (g) of section 2 of the Immoral Traffic (Prevention) Act, 1956 or in a Juvenile home within the meaning of clause (g) of section 2 of the Juvenile Justice Act or in a psychiatric hospital or psychiatric nursing home within the meaning of clause (g) of section 2 of the Mental Health Act.

Any person in receipt of annual income less then Rs. 9000 per year or such other higher amount as may be prescribed by the State Government if the case is before a court other than Supreme Court and less than 12000 per year or such other higher amount as may be prescribed by the Central Government if the case is before the Supreme Court.

A person who satisfies all or any of the conditions specified in section 12 shall be entitled to receive legal service provided that the concerned Authority is satisfied that such person has a *prima facie* case to prosecute or to defend. An affidavit made by a person as to his income may be sufficient for his entitlement under this Act unless the concerned Authority has reasons to disbelieve such affidavit.

Q.106. Is an Order passed by the Lok Adalat appealable?

Ans. Every Award of the permanent Lok Adalat under the Legal Services Authority Act, 1987 either on merits or in terms of a settlement shall be final and binding on all the parties and shall not be called in question. Every award of the permanent Lok Adalat shall be deemed to be a decree of a civil court. Section 21 (2) of the Act says: "Every award made by a Lok Adalat shall be final and binding on all the parties to the dispute, and no appeal shall lie to any court against the award."

37. Abatement of Appeal

Q.107. An accused was convicted under sections 326/325 IPC. He filed an appeal and his sentence was suspended. During pendency of appeal, he died. What will be the fate of his appeal?

Ans. As per section 394 of Cr.P.C., criminal proceedings abate on death of the accused. The section reads: "(1) Every appeal under section 377 or section 378 shall finally abate on the death of the accused. (2) Every other appeal under this Chapter (except an appeal from a sentence of fine) shall finally abate on the death of the appellant: Provided that where the appeal is against a conviction and sentence of death or of imprisonment, and the appellant dies during the pendency of the appeal, any if his near relatives may, within thirty days of the death of the appellant, apply to the Appellate Court for leave to continue the appeal; and if leave is granted, the appeal shall not abate. *Explanation.* In this section, "near relative" means a parent, spouse, lineal descendant, brother or sister."

However, the sentence of fine will not abate in case the appellate court upheld the conviction of the accused. Recovery of such fine can be made from the estate inherited by the legal representatives of the deceased.

38. Civil and Criminal Liability

Q.108. Whether civil and criminal proceedings with regard to the same matter can run simultaneously?

Ans. The law is well settled that civil and criminal remedies are not mutually exclusive, but clearly co-extensive and can run simultaneously. Even when a civil remedy is available and pending/contemplated, a criminal prosecution is not barred. The object of the criminal law is to punish an offender who commits the offence, but this does not, however, affect the civil remedies for suing the wrongdoer in cases of arson, accidents etc.

The Supreme Court in *Kamaladevi Aggarwal* v. *State of West Bengal,* (2002) 1 SCC 555 has held that criminal proceedings should not be quashed merely because of pendency of civil proceedings between the same parties as the nature and standard of proof required in civil and criminal proceedings are distinct. It was observed: "Criminal prosecution cannot be thwarted at the initial stage merely because civil proceedings are also pending. After referring to judgments in *State of Haryana* v. *Bhajan Lal; Rajesh Bajaj* v. *State NCT of Delhi,* AIR 1992 SC 604: 1992 Cr LJ 527 this court in *Trisuns Chemical Industry* v. *Rajesh Agarwal,* [(1999) 8 SC 686: AIR 1999 SC 3499: 1999 Cr LJ 4325] held: "Time and again this court has been pointing out that quashing of FIR or a complaint in exercise of the inherent, powers of the High Court should be limited to very extreme exceptions (vide *State of Haryana* v. *Bhajan Lal* and *Rajesh Bajaj* v. *State NCT of Delhi,* (1999) 3 SCC 259: AIR 1999 SC 1216: 1999 AIR SCW 881]. In the last referred case this court also pointed out that merely because an act has a civil profile is not sufficient to denude it of its criminal outfit. We quote the following observations:—

> "10. It may be that the facts narrated in the present complaint would as well reveal a commercial transaction or money transaction. But that is hardly a reason for holding that the offence of cheating were committed in the course of commercial and also money transaction. ..... Criminal cases have to be proceeded with in accordance with the procedure as prescribed under the Code of Criminal Procedure and the pendency of a civil action in a different court even though higher in status and authority, cannot be made a basis for quashing of the proceedings."

Q.109. If an employee is acquitted in a criminal trial, can departmental action for the same charge continue against him?

The law is well settled that the two proceedings are independent of each other. A person can suffer criminal prosecution even if he is acquitted in departmental proceedings. In *Commissioner of Police, New Delhi* v. *Narender Singh,* (2006) 4 SCC 265, the Supreme Court held: "It is not in dispute that the standard of proof required in recording a finding of conviction in a criminal case and in a departmental proceeding are distinct and different. Whereas in a criminal case, it is essential to prove a charge beyond all reasonable doubt, in a departmental proceeding preponderance of probability would serve the purpose. [See *Kamaladevi Agarwal* v. *State of W.B.*, (2002) 1 SCC 555: AIR 2001 SC 3846: 2001 AIR SCW 4292]. It is now well-settled by reason of a catena of decisions of this court that if an employee has been acquitted of a criminal charge, the same by itself would not be a ground not to initiate a departmental proceeding against him or to drop the same in the event an order of acquittal is passed."

Q. 110. If a seller of plot refuses to execute the sale-deed but is willing to refund the double amount of the earnest money as per the 'sale agreement', can the purchaser seek his criminal prosecution for offence of 'cheating' in addition to a Civil Suit for specific performance?

Ans. *'Mens rea'* or a 'guilty intention' is the *sine qua non* for the offence of cheating. Cheating is defined in section 415 of the Indian Penal Code which reads: "Whoever, by deceiving any person, fraudulently or dishonestly induces the person so deceived to deliver any property to any person, or to consent that any person shall retain any property, or intentionally induces the person so deceived to do or omit to do anything which he would not do or omit if he were not so deceived, and which act or omission causes or is likely to cause damage or harm to that person in body, mind, reputation or property, is said to cheat". Further it has been provided in the explanation that a dishonest concealment of facts is a deception within the meaning of this section.

In order to secure conviction of a person for the offence of cheating, intention of the accused to deceive the complaint must be established. Violation of an agreement to sell the plot in question discloses only a civil dispute and no offence under section 406/420, IPC is made out. In *S.W. Palanitkar* v. *State of Bihar,* (2002) 1 SCC 241: AIR 2001 SC 2960: 2001 Cr LJ 4765, the Supreme Court quoted with approval the following passage from its earlier judgments in *Haridaya Ranjan Prasad Verma* v. *State of Bihar,* (2000) 4 SCC 168: AIR 2000 SC 2341: 2000 AIR SCW 2077

> "In determining the question it has to be kept in mind that the distinction between mere breach of contract and the offence of cheating is a fine one. It depends upon the intention of the accused at the time to inducement which may be judged by his subsequent conduct but for this subsequent conduct is not the sole test. Mere breach of contract cannot give rise to criminal prosecution for cheating unless fraudulent or dishonest intention is shown right at the beginning of the transaction, that is the time when the offence is said to have been committed. Therefore it is the intention which is the gist of the offence. To hold a person guilty of cheating it is necessary to show that he had fraudulent or dishonest intention at the time of making the promise. From his mere failure to keep up promise subsequently such a

culpable intention right at the beginning, that is, when he made the promise cannot be presumed."

Q. 111. During the pendency of arbitration proceedings between the government and a contractor, can the State also seek criminal prosecution of the contractor under sections 406/409/420 IPC alleging that he used sub-standard material in the construction. Can both the proceedings run simultaneously?

Ans. In this case, the use of sub-standard material by the contractor attracts penal provisions of criminal law, besides civil liability for recovery of loss suffered by the State. Therefore, criminal and arbitration proceedings can continue simultaneously. Arbitration clause in the agreement is thus no bar for criminal prosecution. In *S.W. Palanitkar* v. *State of Bihar*, (2002) 1 SCC 241: AIR 2001 SC 2960: 2001 Cr LJ 4765, the Supreme Court has held that, "... a provision made in the agreement for referring the disputes to arbitration is not an effective substitute for a criminal prosecution when the disputed act constitutes a criminal offence."

Q.112. A person lodged a criminal complaint against his business partner under sections 406/420 of the IPC for misappropriation of business funds. The accused pleaded that a partner cannot commit 'breach of trust' of his own funds. Please advise.

Ans. The plea taken by the accused is not tenable in law because a partner is equally liable for the criminal offences punishable under section 406/420 of the IPC. In *Anil Saran* v. *State of Bihar*, (1995) 6 SCC 142: 1996 Cr LJ 408: AIR 1996 SC 204 it was held by the Supreme Court that, "partnership firm is not a legal entity but a legal mode of doing business by all the partners. Until the firm is dissolved as per law and the account settled, all the partners have domain in common over the property and funds of the firm. Only after the settlement of accounts and allotment of respective share, the partner becomes owner of his share. However, criminal breach of trust under section 406 is not in respect of a property belonging to the partnership firm, but is an offence committed by a person in respect of the property which has been specially entrusted to such a person under a special contract and he holds that property in fiduciary capacity under special contract. If he misappropriates the same, it is an offence."

Q.113. A lawyer filed a criminal complaint against his client under sections 406 and 420 IPC for non-payment of his fee. Please advise.

Ans. A lawyer is entitled to recover his balance fee only in civil proceedings. For non-payment of balance fee, an advocate cannot initiate criminal proceedings against his client. In *Narinder Kumar* v. *N. Balachandra*, 2001 (2) RCR (Cri) 438, the Bombay High Court quashed a lawyer's criminal complaint against his client holding that it was a matter of civil nature and that criminal proceedings were not meant to short-circuit the other remedies.

39. Disposal of Case Property

Q.114 Whether during pendency of criminal trial, a complainant in a theft case can dispose of the ornaments recovered by the police, though he has received the same on superdari?

Ans. The trial Court can permit a complainant to dispose of the recovered ornaments that are already on superdari with him. However, the Court can direct placing of photographs of all ornaments on court file for identification purposes. It can also direct furnishing of indemnity bond equivalent to the value of the recovered ornaments. The Karnataka High Court, in *Prabhakar Vaman Pishe* v. *State of Karnataka*, 2001 (4) RCR (Cri) 204: 2001 Cr LJ 3568: 2001 (4) All Cri LR 342, allowed similar application of the complainant/owner.

Q.115. Whether a complainant can obtain and use a part of the cash recovered in a pending theft case? Please guide.

Ans. The issue in hand is dealt with by section 451 of the Criminal Procedure Code which reads: "When any property is produced before any Criminal Court during an inquiry or trial, the court may make such order as it thinks fit for the proper custody of such property pending the conclusion of the inquiry or trial, and, if the property is subject to speedy and natural decay, or if it is otherwise expedient so to do, the court may, after recording such evidence as it thinks necessary, order it to be sold or otherwise disposed of." It was held by the Supreme Court in *Sunderbhai Ambalal Desai* v. *State of Gujarat*, (2002) 10 SCC 283: AIR 2003 SC 638: 2002 AIR SCW 5301 that if material on record indicates that such articles belong to the complainant at whose house theft, robbery or dacoity has taken place, the seized articles should be handed over to the complainant after—(1) Preparing detailed proper panchnama of such articles; (2) Taking photographs of such articles and a bond that such articles would be produced if required at the time of trial; and (3) After taking proper security. It was further held, "In case, where such articles are not handed over either to the complainant or to the person from whom such articles are seized or to its claimant, then the court may direct that such articles be kept in bank lockers. Similarly, if articles are required to kept in police custody, it would be open to the SHO after preparing proper panchnama to keep such articles in a bank locker. In any case, such articles should be produced before the Magistrate within a week of their seizure. If required, the court may direct that such articles be handed over back to the Investigating Officer for further investigation and identification. However, in no set of circumstances, the Investigating Officer should keep such articles in custody for a longer period for the purpose of investigation and identification. For currency notes, similar procedure can be followed."

Q.116. A person purchased a car on power-of-attorney but did not get it transferred in his name. Later, the vehicle was involved in a criminal case. After conclusion of trial, purchaser's application for release of car was dismissed by the trial court on the ground that the car was not in his name. Please advise.

Ans. After conclusion of trial, the owner is entitled to receive back the case property. Even if the vehicle was not transferred in name of purchaser, he may still be entitled to receive the same on the basis of power-of-attorney. The Trial Court order can be challenged by way of appeal. Alternatively, the car-purchaser may approach the High Court under section 482 of the Cr. P.C. for appropriate directions. In *Pardeep Kumar* v. *State of Haryana*, 2007 (1) RCR (Cri)

284, the Punjab and Haryana High Court held that, ".... On the basis of the alleged General Power-of-Attorney executed by the registered owner, the petitioner is entitled to get the vehicle released, because it is no more required by the police as the accused in the case has already been acquitted...."

Q.117. During the trial of a theft case, one of the accused claimed ownership of a gold chain which was part of the stolen property. After recording of evidence, the Trial Court convicted all the accused for keeping in possession the stolen property under section 411 of the IPC. However, since ownership of the gold chain was disputed, the court advised the parties to get their title established by filing an appropriate civil suit. Please advise.

Ans. The order of the Court is perfectly legal and in accordance with law. Since the chain, which was stolen from the house of owner and later on recovered from one of the accused, has been claimed by both of them, the Trial Court had no option but to direct the parties to establish their ownership in a civil court. In *Thamana Shivalingappa Teli* v. *State of Karnatka,* (2005) 11 SCC 171, the Supreme Court has upheld a similar order of the Trial Court by observing, "...the trial court was quite justified in directing the parties to get their title established by moving the competent civil court.."

Q.118. The police registered a case under sections 457/380 IPC for a theft of cash and ornaments. The trial Court has refused to release the recovered stolen goods observing that these would be required during evidence. What are remedies available to the complainant?

Ans. *Prima facie,* the order of Court is not in consonance with section 451, Cr. P.C. In *Sunderbhai Ambalal Desai* v. *State of Gujarat,* (2002) 10 SCC 283: AIR 2003 SC 638: 2002 AIR SCW 5301, the Supreme Court has laid down guidelines for the Trial Court to meet with such situations: "With regard to valuable articles, such as gold or silver ornaments or articles studded with precious stones, it is submitted that it is of no use to keep such articles in police custody for years till the trial is over. In our view, this submission requires to be accepted. In such cases, Magistrate should pass appropriate orders as contemplated under section 451, Cr. P.C. at the earliest."

40. Damages in a Murder Case

Q.119. During trial of a murder case, can the dependents of the deceased, who was the only bread-winner of family, claim any interim damages from the accused who are financially very strong?

Ans. As of now there is no legal provision for providing immediate financial support to the victims of deceased family in such cases unlike the provisions incorporated in Motor Vechicles Act where the victim is entitled to 'interim compensation' from vehicle owner or insurance company under 'no fault theory'. The court may, under section 357 of Criminal Procedure Code, award compensation to the victims family at the time of conviction and sentence to the accused. Section 357(5) further provides that, "*At the time of awarding compensation in any subsequent civil suit relating to the same matter, the* *court shall take into account any sum paid or recovered as compensation under this section."* In *Lachman Singh* v. *Anita Devi,* 2007 (3) RCR (Cri) 262 (P&H) the Punjab and Haryana High Court has upheld the orders of the civil court awarding damages to the tune of Rs. 4 lakhs for causing death and injuries in similar circumstances.

41. Dismissal of Appeal in Default

Q.120. Appeal of a person convicted of rash and negligent driving under sections 279/304A IPC was dismissed in default for for non-appearance of his lawyer. Please advise.

Ans. There is no provision in Criminal Procedure Code to dismiss an appeal in default. In *Shyam Deo Pandey* v *State of Bihar,* AIR 1971 SC 1606: 1971 Cr LJ 1177: 1973 BLJR 774, the Supreme Court has made it mandatory for the Appellate Court to peruse the records before dismissing the appeal. It has been observed by Allahabad High Court in *Man Singh* v. *State of Uttar Pradesh* 2004 (1) RCR (Cri) (All) that there is no provision in the Cr.P.C. permitting disposal of criminal appeal in default. In case the Appellate Court decides to proceed with the hearing of the appeal and is satisfied that either the appellants themselves or their counsel have not appeared, even though they have notice of the date, it has the right to examine the records and decide the appeal on merits. In *Naresh Kumar* v. *Kala Wati,* (2009) 11 SCC 511, the counsel engaged by the accused could not appear in the High Court but the accused was represented through an *'amicus'* appointed by the court, still the Supreme Court remanded the case to High Court for fresh decision after hearing counsel engaged by the accused.

42. Financier's Right to Seize Vehicle

Q.121. A car, involved in an illegal liquor trade, was seized, confiscated and sold by Excise authorities in public auction under the Excise Act. The vehicle was hypothecated with a financier. Can the financer seek cancellation of auction and re-possess the car?

Ans. Property confiscated by Excise authorities under the Excise Act, vests in the government and the right of the owner/financer in the vehicle ceases with the passing of confiscation order. Therefore, the auction by Excise Authorities is valid. *Ashokan* v. *State of Kerala,* 2004 (4) RCR (Cri) 473 (Ker) is a case on the point.

Q.122. A hirer defaulted in payment of installments under the hire purchase agreement. The financier, a limited company, re-possessed the truck. The hirer lodged an FIR under section 392 of the IPC against Directors of the company. Please advise.

Ans. In cases of hire-purchase agreements, the financer can re-possess the vehicle in case of default of installments if the agreement permits. There is no legal impediment on such possession. In such a situation, no offence under section 392 of the IPC is made out against the finance company or its Directors and/or its employees. The Director may seek quashing of criminal proceedings under section 482 of the Cr.P.C. In *The Managing Director, Orix Auto Finance (India) Ltd.* v. *Shri Jagmander Singh,* 2006 (2) RCR (Cri) 386, the Supreme Court held: "if agreement permits the financier to take possession of the financed vehicle, there is no legal impediment on such possession being taken. Of course, the hirer can avail such statutory remedy as may be available. But mere fact that possession has been taken cannot be a ground to contend that the hirer is prejudiced."

Following this judgment, the Punjab and Haryana High Court quashed an FIR registered against the financier in *Kanwal Aggarwal* v. *State of Haryana,* 2006 (3) RCR (Cri) 920 (P&H).

Q.123. There was a default in payment of two loan installments. The finance company's musclemen forcibly took away the hypothecated car as per the agreement. Whether the hirer can lodge an FIR for theft/robbery?

Ans. The financer can re-possess the financed car as per terms and conditions of the hire-purchase agreement and on account of failure to pay the installments. In the circumstances, no offence of theft or robbery is made out against the financer. In similar circumstances, the Supreme Court in *K.A. Mathai @ Babu* v. *Kora Bibbikutty,* (1996) 7 SCC 212: 1996 SCC (Cri) 281 held that if financier takes possession of the vehicle as per terms and conditions of the hire-purchase agreement, the act does not amount to a criminal offence. Similar view has been taken by the Madhya Pradesh High Court in *Shri Ram City Union Finance Ltd.* v. *State of Madhya Pradesh,* 2006 (1) RCR (Cri) 281.

43. Victim's Right to Engage a Lawyer

Q.124. In a case filed by the police, can an aggrieved person engage his private lawyer?

Ans. Yes, now an aggrieved person is entitled to engage a private lawyer of his choice in view of the Proviso added to section 24(8) of Cr.P.C. w.e.f. 31-12-2009 *vide* Act 5 of 2009. It reads: "Provided that the court may permit the victim to engage an advocate of his choice to assist the prosecution under this sub-section."

44. Manufacturer's Liability

Q.125. An insecticide sample was taken by the Drugs Inspector from a dealer's shop from a sealed container. The sample was found misbranded and a complaint was lodged. The manufacturer of the insecticides had not been summoned by the court, as an accused. Please guide.

Ans. Section 30(3) of the Insecticides Act, 1968 provides that—

> "(3) A person not being an importer or a manufacturer of an insecticide or his agent for the distribution thereof, shall not be liable for a contravention of any provision of this Act, if he proves—
>
> (a) that he acquired the insecticide from an importer or a duly licensed manufacturer, distributor or dealer thereof;
>
> (b) that he did not know and could not, with reasonable diligence, have ascertained that the insecticide in any way contravened any provision of this Act; and
>
> (c) that the insecticide, while in his possession, was properly stored and remained in the same state as when he acquired it."

Since the sample of insecticide was taken from a sealed container, the dealer cannot be held liable for misbranding of the insecticide and only the manufacturer would be liable. The accused may apply to the court for his discharge and for summoning of the manufacturer as an accused. In a similar situation, the Punjab and Haryana High Court, in *Jindal Fertilizers and Chemicals* v. *State of Punjab,* 2010 (4) RCR (Cri) 1461, quashed the criminal proceedings against a dealer. Reliance was placed upon Supreme Court judgment in *M/s Kisan Beej Bhandar, Abohar* v. *Chief Agricultural Officer, Ferozepur,* 1990 SCC (Cri) 623 (SC); followed by the High Court in subsequent cases.

45. Probation after Conviction

Q.126 A lady died in a road accident. After 10 years of trial, the driver was held guilty of an offence under section 304A of Indian Penal Code. Whether the accused can be released on probation?

Ans. The Supreme Court in *Dalbir Singh* v. *State of Haryana,* (2000) 5 SCC 82: 2000 AIR SCW 1653: AIR 2000 SC 1677, held that, "Bearing in mind the galloping trend in road accidents in India and the devastating consequences visiting the victims and their families, criminal courts cannot treat the nature of the offence under section 304A, IPC as attracting the benevolent provisions of section 4 of the Probation of Offenders Act." Again, the Supreme Court followed this judgment in *B. Nagabhushanam* v. *State of Karnataka*, (2008) 5 SCC 730: 2008 AIR SCW 3573: AIR 2008 SC 2557 and declined the benefit of Probation of Offenders Act in cases punishable under section 304A, IPC. Both these judgments were followed by the Punjab and Haryana High Court, in *Mahipal* v. *State of Haryana,* 2010 (4) RCR (Cri) 676. The court refused to grant benefit of probation to the accused.

Q.127. After a milk sample was found adulterated, the Trial Court convicted and sentenced the accused for six months jail and fine of Rs. 1000. The court declined probation on the ground that a minimum punishment has been provided under the Food Adulteration Act. Please guide.

Ans. The Trial Court has rightly declined prayer for probation of the accused. In a case under section 16 of the Food Adulteration Act, the court cannot award below the minimum sentence as provided under the Act even for adequate or special reasons. The Supreme Court in *State Govt. of NCT of Delhi* v. *Amar Singh,* (2005) 10 SCC 279: AIR 2005 SC 3818: 2005 AIR SCW 3983 held that the courts cannot award sentence less than the minimum period prescribed under the statute. In a similar situation, the Punjab and Haryana High Court, in *Pardeep* v. *State of Haryana,* 2010 (1) RCR (Cri) 73, refused to reduce sentence and grant probation.

Q.128. In appeal, an accused was allowed benefit of probation under section 4 of Probation of Offenders Act, but payment of fine was upheld. Whether the court can uphold fine while granting probation? Please guide.

Ans. Once an accused has been granted the benefit of section 4 of Probation of Offenders Act, there is no reason to retain the imposition of fine [*Balbir Singh* v. *State of Punjab*, 2003 (4) RCR 699, following Supreme Court judgment in *Ishar Dass* v. *State of Punjab,* AIR 1973 SC 1293 and a Division Bench judgment of the Punjab and Haryana High Court in *Shri Bhagwan* v. *State of Haryana*, 1985 (1) PLR 649].

Q.129. Whether a convict under section 13(2) of the Prevention of Corruption Act, 1988 is entitled to the benefit of Probation of Offenders Act?

Ans. In *State of Jammu & Kashmir* v. *Vinay Nanda*, 2001 (1) RCR (Cri) 532, the Supreme Court held that, "The mitigating circumstances in a case, if established, would authorise the court to pass such sentence of imprisonment or fine which may be deemed to be reasonable but not less than the minimum prescribed under an enactment." With these observations, the court declined to grant the benefit of probation to the accused and reversed the High Court decision. Again, in *State* v. *A. Parthiban*, 2007 (1) AIR Kar R 45: AIR 2007 SC 51: 2006 AIR SCW 5267, the Supreme Court held that an accused convicted under the Prevention of Corruption Act, is not entitled to the benefit of probation. The court observed, "In the case of *Superintendent Central Excise, Bangalore* v. *Bahubali*, (1979) 2 SCC 279: 1979 Cr LJ 862: AIR 1979 SC 1271, while dealing with rule 126P (2)(ii) of the Defence of India Rules which prescribed a minimum sentence and section 43 of the Defence of India Act, 1962 almost similar to the purport enshrined in section 28 of the Act in the context of a claim for granting relief under the Probation Act, this court observed that in cases where a specific enactment, enacted after the Probation Act prescribes a minimum sentence of imprisonment, the provisions of Probation Act cannot be invoked if the special Act contains any provision to enforce the same without reference to any other Act containing a provision, in derogation of the special enactment, there is no scope for extending the benefit of the Probation Act, to the accused. Unlike the provisions contained in section 5(2) proviso of the Old Act providing for imposition of a sentence lesser than the minimum sentence of one year therein for any "special reasons" to be recorded in writing, the Act did not carry any such power to enable the court concerned to show any leniency below the minimum sentence stipulated. These aspects were highlighted in *State through SP, New Delhi* v. *Ratan Lal Arora*, (2004) 4 SCC 590: 2004 Cr LJ 2105: AIR 2004 SC 2364."

46. Suspension of Sentence

Q.130. Whether an order sentencing an accused for a term of upto rising of the court with a fine of Rs. 1,000 can be challenged in appeal?

Ans. It is settled law that generally the conviction should not be stayed though sentence may be stayed. A sentence of imprisonment till rising of the court is a sentence within the meaning of the Indian Penal Code and the Code of Criminal Procedure and as such, this sentence can be suspended by the appellate court exercising the powers under section 389 of the Code of Criminal Procedure. In *Raju @ Rajiv Sharma* v. *State of Madhya Pradesh*, 2006 (4) RCR (Cri) 578, it was held by the Madhya Pradesh High Court that, "On perusal of section 389, Cr.PC it reveals that the section does not speak about jail sentence but of imprisonment. The dictionary meaning of the word sentence is 'punishment given by a Law Court': a jail/prison/custodial sentence. The meaning of the word "imprisonment" means 'putting an accused in prison' (Oxford Advances Learners Dictionary). A sentence of imprisonment till rising of the court is a sentence, which is in accordance with law. A direction by the court that a person shall be confined in the court premises till the court rises constitute imprisonment within the meaning of the Penal Code and the Code of Criminal Procedure, *Muthu Nadar's* case, AIR 1945 Mad 313: 47 Cr LJ 50. Mulchandani in his esteemed *Law Lexicon Digest*, 1990 Edn., Vol. 1, p. 728, explains the meaning of the words "till the rising of the court" and for "one day" like this: "There is no practical difference because 'day' in this context does not mean 24 hours or does not even include 'night'. 'Day' here means 'Lockup time' which is generally 5 p.m. in the winter and 6 p.m. in the summer. If a convict is ordered to undergo sentence of one day, he must be released before lockup time from the prison". The words imprisonment, confinement and detention have also been explained in the said book. They respectively mean conviction and the last two means without conviction. Therefore, the last two may prove to be unlawful also."

Q.131. In a criminal appeal, if conviction is not suspended though sentence is suspended, what is the remedy in law?

Ans. As per section of 389(1) of Cr.P.C, only sentence can be suspended. However, the High Court under section 432 of the Cr.P.C. may be approached for suspension of conviction on the basis of precedents [*Roop Singh* v. *State of Punjab*, 2005 (2) RCR (Cri) 799 (P&H); *Tarsem Singh* v. *State (Chandigarh Administration)*, 2006 (1) RCR (Cri) 831 (P&H); *Hari Narain* v. *State of Rajasthan*, 2005 (2) RCR (Cri) 507 (Raj HC)].

Q.132. Pending appeal of an accused convicted under sections 307/148/149, IPC, what is the remedy available for suspension of conviction and sentence on the grounds of past good conduct to protect him from losing his government job?

Ans. An order granting stay of conviction is not the rule but is an exception to be resorted to in rare cases depending upon the facts of each case. Appeal is a statutory right but stay of conviction is not. In *K.C. Sareen* v. *CBI Chandigarh,* (2001) 6 SCC 584: AIR 2001 SC 3320: 2001 Cr LJ 4234, the Supreme Court has held that though the power to suspend an order of conviction apart from the order of sentence is not alien to section 389(1) of the Code of Criminal Procedure, its exercise should be limited to very exceptional cases. The Supreme Court has further held that merely because the convicted person has filed an appeal to challenge his conviction, the court should not suspend the operation of the order of conviction. In *Navjot Singh Sidhu* v. *State of Punjab,* (2007) 2 SCC 574: 2007 Cr LJ 1427: AIR 2007 SC 1003 though the Supreme Court exercised its judicial discretion while suspending the conviction of Sidhu, yet it held that such a discretion can be resorted to in rare cases depending upon the special facts of the case. The Punjab & Haryana High Court, in *Ram Singh* v. *State of Haryana,* 2007 (3) RCR (Cri) 201, suspended the sentence as well as conviction of an accused who was a JBT teacher on the ground that he will lose his government job.

47. Transfer of Case

Q.133. An accused, facing trial under section 292 of the IPC for making and selling pornographic videos, is being tried by a lady Magistrate. Can the accused seek trial by a male judge as viewing of pornographic CDs in the presence of male witnesses would embarrass the lady presiding officer and she might become prejudicial?

Ans. A case cannot be transferred to other court presided over by a male judge merely on the ground that viewing of pornographic CDs in the presence of male witnesses would embarrass lady presiding officer because embarrassment is a state of mind which is more individual related than related to the sex of a person. The Supreme Court, in *Fatima Riswana* v. *State,* (2005) 1 SCC 582: 2005 Cr LJ 900: AIR 2005 SC 712, held that, "a judicial officer, be it a female or male, is expected to face this challenge when the call of duty required it. It is expected of a Judicial Officer to get over all prejudices and predilections when situation requires, hence in our considered opinion the High Court was not justified in presuming embarrassment to the Judicial Officer solely on the ground that she is a lady Officer even when the Officer concerned had not expressed any reservation in this regard. If situation requires the Presiding Officer may make such adjustments/arrangements so as to avoid viewing the CDs in the presence of male persons. This is a matter of procedure to be adopted by the Presiding Officer."

48. Statement of Accused under section 313, Cr.P.C.

Q.134. What is the importance of statement of accused under section 313 of Cr.P.C. after the prosecution concludes its entire evidence? Can an accused be convicted on the basis of a circumstance, which he was never asked to explain?

Ans. The object of examination of accused under section 313, Cr.P.C. is to give him an opportunity to explain the circumstances and the prosecution evidence led against him during the trial.

*Section 313 reads: "**Power to examine the accused:***

(1) In every inquiry or trial, for the purpose of enabling the accused personally to explain any circumstances appearing in the evidence against him, the court—

(a) may, at any stage, without previously warning the accused, put such questions to him as the court considers necessary;

(b) shall, after the witnesses for the prosecution have been examined and before he is called on for his defence, question him generally on the case:

Provided that in a summons-case, where the court has dispensed with the personal attendance of the accused, it may also dispense with his examination under clause (b).

(2) No oath shall be administered to the accused when he is examined under sub-section (1).

(3) The accused shall not render himself liable to punishment by refusing to answer such questions, or by giving false answers to them.

(4) The answers given by the accused may be taken into consideration in such inquiry or trial, and put in evidence for, or against him in any other inquiry into, or trial for, any other offence which such answers may tend to show he has committed.

(5) The court may take help of Prosecutor and Defence Counsel in preparing relevant questions which are to be put to the accused and the court may permit filing of written statement by the accused as sufficient compliance of this section.

Such a statement can be taken into consideration in judging his innocence or guilt. But the questions must be put to an accused in such a way as to enable him to understand the prosecution case and the material against him.

The object of this section is to afford the accused a fair and proper opportunity of explaining circumstances which appear against him and as such the questions under section 313, Cr.P.C. should be fair, must be framed in such a form which an ignorant or illiterate person will be able to understand. As such, the accused must be questioned separately about each material substance, which is intended to be used against him. It is settled principle that a conviction based on failure of the accused to explain what he was never asked to explain is not sustainable. But in case an accused offers false answer in his examination against the established facts, it can be considered against him. As held by the Supreme Court, the examination of accused under section 313, Cr.P.C. is not a mere formality since the answers given by the accused to the questions put to him during such examination have practical utility for criminal courts.

In *Vikramjit Singh* v. *State of Punjab*, (2006) 12 SCC 306: 2006 AIR SCW 6197: 2007 Cr LJ 1000, the Supreme Court observed: "It is now a well-settled principle of law that the circumstances which according to the prosecution lead to proof of the guilt against the accused ***must be put to him*** in his examination under section 313 of the Code of Criminal Procedure."

Q.135. What is the value of accused's statement under section 313 where his version appears to be equally probable *vis-à-vis* the prosecution story?

Ans. It is now beyond any cavil that where two views of a story appear to be probable, the one that was contended by the accused should be accepted. [See *K. Gopal Reddy* v. *State of Andhra Pradesh*, (1979) 1 SCC 355: AIR 1979 SC 387: (1979) 2 SCR 363; *Sharad Birdhichand Sarda* v. *State of Maharashtra*, (1984) 4 SCC 116: AIR 1984 SC 1622: 1984 Cr LJ 1738; *Tota Singh* v. *State of Punjab*, AIR 1987 SC 1083: 1987 Cr LJ 974: 1987 (2) SCJ 193; *Divakar Neelkantha Hegde* v. *The State of Karnataka*, JT 1996 (7) SC 63; *State of Orissa* v. *Babaji Charan Mohanty*, (2003) 10 SCC 57: AIR 2003 SC 3926: 2003 Cr LJ 3744 and *Hem Raj* v. *State of Haryana*, (2005) 10 SCC 614: AIR 2005 SC 2110: 2005 Cr LJ 2152].

49. Statement of a witness before Magistrate [under section 164]

Q.136. After getting her statement recorded before a Magistrate under section 164, Cr.P.C., a rape victim died before she could depose in court. The doctor who medically examined the victim also could not depose during the trial. Whether the accused can still be held guilty?

Ans. In a rape case, the victim is the material witness to un-fold the entire story and similarly the doctor who medically examined her is a very important witness. Non-examination of both these witnesses is fatal to the prosecution. Moreover, the statement of the prosecutrix recorded under section 164, Cr.P.C. before a Magistrate is not substantive evidence. In these circumstances the accused may get benefit of doubt. [Reference: *Uppari Siddi Ramula* v. *State of Andhra Pradesh*, 2005 (3) RCR (Cri) 513. Allahabad High Court]

Q.137. The statement of a kidnapped minor girl was recorded before a Magistrate under section of 164, Cr.P.C. who did not appear in court for giving her evidence. On the basis of her statement under section 164, Cr.P.C.,

the trial court convicted the accused under section 363/366 IPC. Is the conviction sustainable?

Ans. The order of the trial Court is not sustainable in law. It has been held by the Supreme Court that a statement under section 164, Cr.P.C. is not a substantive evidence and it can be utilized only to corroborate or contradict a witness. [Reference: *Ram Kishan Singh* v. *Harmit Kaur*, (1972) 3 SCC 280: AIR 1972 SC 468: 1972 Cr LJ 267; *Brij Nath Sah* v. *State of Bihar*, (2010) 6 SCC 736].

50. Withdrawal from Prosecution

Q.138. A false case under section 409, IPC was registered against a government employee for embezzlement of funds. The employee deposited the money and the government directed the Public Prosecutor to file an application under section 321 of Code of Criminal Procedure for withdrawal of the case. The Trial Court dismissed this application. Whether order of the Magistrate is sustainable in law?

Ans. No doubt section 321 of Cr.P.C empowers the Public Prosecutor to withdraw prosecution of any case with the consent of the court. However, the Magistrate may refuse such request if he is satisfied that such a withdrawal is not in public interest. The court has thus rightly refused withdrawal of prosecution. In *Yereni Raja Ram Chander* v. *State of Andhra Pradesh*, [2009] 15 SCC 604, the Supreme Court upheld a similar order by observing, "The action on the part of State in our opinion suffers from malice on facts. The State is the protector of law. When it deals with a public fund, it must act as per procedure established by law. In respect of public funds the doctrine of public trust would be applicable. So far as the State and its officers are concerned, the State was not acting in public interest but in private interest."

51. Video Conferencing

Q.139. In which cases may evidence be recorded by video conferencing? Is presentation of evidence or witness testimony *via* video conferencing admissible in our country?

Ans. Where the attendance of a witness cannot be procured without inordinate delay, expense or inconvenience, the court can consider issuing a commission to record the evidence by way of video conferencing. Evidence of such witness can be recorded by video conferencing if the accused and/or his pleader are present when evidence is recorded in the presence of accused and as a matter of prudence evidence by video conferencing in open court should be permitted only if the witness is in a country which has an extradition treaty with India and under whose laws contempt of court and perjury are punishable. Refer to a Supreme Court judgment, *State of Maharashtra* v. *Dr. Praful B. Desai,* 2003 (3) CCC 320 (SC).

52. Set-off and Parole

Q.140. An accused facing criminal trial in two cases under the NDPS Act was convicted in both the cases after he had spent six months in jail. The court gave the benefit of set-off only in one case. Please guide.

Ans. In view of the latest judgment of the Supreme Court in *State of Maharashtra* v. *Najakat Alias Mubarak Ali,* (2001) 6 SCC 311: 2001 AIR SCW 2059: AIR 2001 SC 2255, the accused is entitled to the benefit of set-off in both the cases under section 428 of the Cr.P.C. which reads:

> "Where an accused person has, on conviction, been sentenced to imprisonment for a term not being imprisonment in default of payment of

fine, the period of detention, if any, undergone by him during the investigation, inquiry or trial of the same case and before the date of such conviction, shall be set off against the term of imprisonment imposed on him on such conviction, and the liability of such person to undergo imprisonment on such conviction shall be restricted to the remainder, if any, of the term of imprisonment imposed on him:

Provided that in cases referred to in section 433A, such period of detention shall be set off against the period of fourteen years referred to in that section."

Q.141. An accused facing a trial under section 307 of the IPC, while on bail, committed another offence punishable under section 326 of the IPC and was sent to jail. Finally, he was convicted in both the cases, but was denied the benefit of set-off as provided under section 428, Cr. P.C. for the jail period in the first case. Is the order of the Trial Court legally sustainable?

Ans. The order of the Trial Court is legally sustainable since benefit of a set-off cannot be extended for the period spent by him in the subsequent case under section 326 of the IPC. The Punjab and Haryana High Court had taken a similar view in *Raj Kumar @ Raju* v. *State of Haryana* 2005 (2) RCR (Cri) 960 while relying upon a Supreme Court ruling in *State of Maharashtra* v. *Najakat Alias Mubarak Ali*, 2001 (2) RCR 778: (2001) 6 SCC 311: 2001 AIR SCW 2059. The High Court Court ruled: "The view taken in *Raghbir Singh's* case, AIR 1984 SC 1796: 1984 2 Crimes 569: (1984) 4 SCC 348 (*supra*), however, was dissented by their Lordships of the Supreme Court in the case of *State of Maharashtra* v. *Najakat alias Mubarak Ali*, 2001 Cr LJ 2588: 2001 AIR SCW 2059: AIR 2001 SC 2255 (*supra*) holding as follows:—

"18. Reading section 428 of the Code in the above perspective, the words "of the same case" are not to be understood as suggesting that the set off is allowable only if the earlier jail life was undergone by him exclusively for the case in which the sentence is imposed. The period during which the accused was in prison subsequent to the inception of a particular case, should be credited towards the period of imprisonment awarded as sentence in that particular case. It is immaterial that the prisoner was undergoing sentence of imprisonment in another case also during the said period. The words "of the same case" were used to refer to the pre-sentence period of detention undergone by him. Nothing more can be made out of the collocation of those words."

53. Tutoring of Witnesses

Q.142. A ten-year-old rape victim, during her cross-examination, admitted that she was briefed by her mother outside the court. Will such an admission have an adverse effect on the prosecution case?

Ans. In the case of a child witness, the court has to carefully consider whether the child is under the influence of any tutoring, and in case it is found that she was under the influence of tutoring and was asked to make a particular statement, it is highly unsafe to place reliance on such a statement. In a similar case, the Punjab and Haryana High Court gave the benefit of doubt to the accused in *Rajbir Fauji* v. *State of Haryana*, 2004 (4) RCR (Cri) 436, relying upon observations of the Supreme Court in *Chhagan Dame* v. *State of Gujarat*, AIR 1994 SC 454: 1994 Cr LJ 56: 1993 AIR SCW 3865, "In the case of a child witness, the Court has to carefully consider whether the child was under the influence of any tutoring. In the case, her answers to the questions in the cross-examination clearly indicate that she was tutored and she was made to give evidence in accordance with the earlier statement recorded under section 162. Therefore, we find it highly unsafe to place reliance on her evidence."

54. Compounding/Quashing of FIR on the Basis of Compromise

Q.143. Two groups involved in cross cases under sections 307/34, IPC and 326/34, IPC respectively, reached a compromise. Whether the criminal cases against them can be dropped?

Ans. Since the cases are of serious nature and non-compoundable, the compromise reached by the parties cannot bring the criminal cases to an end. However, a Full Bench of Punjab & Haryana High Court, in *Kulwinder Singh* v. *State of Punjab*, 2007 (3) RCR (Cri) 1052: (2007) 10 SCC 455: AIR 2007 SC 2868, has held that the High Court can allow compounding of non-compoundable offences and quash the proceedings where it is felt necessary to prevent the abuse of process of the court or to secure the ends of justice. Therefore, after reaching a compromise, the parties may approach the High Court for quashing of criminal cases. [Also refer: *Balraj Singh* v. *State of Punjab*, 2010 (4) RCR (Cri) 406].

Q.144. A person was arrested in a case under section 420, IPC for not effecting sale of his plot despite having received advance money. After the owner was arrested and bailed, the parties compromised. The seller refunded the advance amount to the buyer. Whether the criminal proceedings can be quashed on the basis of this compromise?

Ans. Since the matter has been settled and the grievance of the complainant has been redressed, the High Court may quash the criminal proceedings on the basis of compromise. [Reference: *Kulwinder Singh* v. *State of Punjab*, 2007 (3) RCR (Cri) 1052 (P&H)].

In similar circumstances the High Court of Punjab & Haryana quashed the FIR under section 420 IPC in *B.C. Jain* v. *State of U.T. Chandigarh*, 2010 (1) RCR (Cri) 662.

55. Powers of Magistrate to Direct Police to Add or Delete Offences

Q.145. In a case under sections 326/325/324/34 IPC (for causing injuries), on victim's application, the Magistrate directed the investigating officer to file challan by adding section 307 IPC. Is this order legal?

Ans. The functions of the judiciary and the police are complementary and not overlapping. There is a statutory right on the part of the police to investigate without requiring any authority or direction from the judicial authorities. The Supreme Court in *State of Bihar* v. *J.A.C. Saldanha*, (1980) 1 SCC 544: AIR 1981 SC 431: 1980 Cr LJ 1487 has held that there is clear-cut and well demarcated sphere of activity in the field of crime detection and crime punishment. The Court held, "Investigation of an offence is the field exclusively reserved by the executive through the police department, the superintendence over which vests in the State Government. It is the bounden duty of the executive to investigate, if an offence is alleged, and bring the offender to book. Once it investigates and finds an offence having been committed, it is its duty to collect evidence for the purpose of proving the offence. Once that is completed and the investigating officer submits report to the Court requesting the Court to take cognizance of the offence under section 190 of the Code of Criminal Procedure, its duty comes to an end. On a cognizance of the offence being taken by the Court, the police function of investigation comes to an end subject to the provision contained in section 173(8), then commences the adjudicatory function of the judiciary to determine whether an offence has been committed and if so, whether by the person or persons charged with the crime."

The observations in Saldanha were cited with approval by the Supreme Court in *Shariff Ahmed* v. *State (NCT of Delhi)*, (2009) 14 SCC 184: AIR 2009 SC

2691: 2009 AIR SCW 4131 holding: "It is the statutory duty of the investigating agency to fully investigate the matter and then submit a report to the concerned Magistrate. The Magistrate will thereafter proceed to pass appropriate order in accordance with law. It was not appropriate for the High Court in these circumstances to issue a direction that the case should not only be investigated, but a charge-sheet must be submitted. In our view the High Court exceeded its jurisdiction in making this direction which deserves to be set aside. While it is open to the High Court in appropriate cases to give directions for prompt investigation etc., the High Court cannot direct the investigating agency to submit a report that is in accord with its views as that would amount to unwarranted interference with the investigation of the case by inhibiting the exercise of statutory power by the investigating agency."

Thus the order of Magistrate is not sustainable in law.

SECTION II

SECTION II

- Indian Evidence Act
- Narcotic Drugs and Psychotropic Substances Act
- Negotiable Instruments Act
- Juvenile Justice Act
- Protection of Women from Domestic Violence Act
- Prevention of Corruption Act
- Gambling Act, 1867
- Motor Vehicles Act
- Insurance Act
- Oaths Act

56. Hostile Witnesses

Q.146. Can an eye-witness be declared hostile by the Public Prosecutor only during the cross-examination or even after the Cross?

Ans. It is settled proposition that a prosecution witness, who introduces a new story in his cross-examination in subtle way contradicting his own statement made under section 161 of the Cr.P.C., can be declared hostile with the permission of the court even after cross-examination of such a witness is complete. The prosecution is entitled to cross-examine him on the point which is destructive to its case. In *Daya Bhai* v. *State of Gujarat*, AIR 1964 SC 1563: (1964) 2 Cr LJ 472: (1964) 1 SCWR 831, the Supreme Court observed: "Section 137 of the Evidence Act gives only the three stages in the examination of a witness, namely, examination-in-chief, cross- examination and re-examination. This is a routine sequence in the examination of a witness. This has no relevance to the question when a party calling a witness can be permitted to put to him questions under section 154 of the Evidence Act: that is governed by the provisions of section 154 of the said Act, which confers a discretionary power on the court to permit a person who calls a witness to put any questions to him which might be put in cross-examination by the adverse party. Section 154 does not in terms, or by necessary implication confine the exercise of the power by the court before the examination-in-chief is concluded or to any particular stage of the examination of the witness. It is wide in scope and the discretion is entirely left to the court to exercise the power when the circumstances demand. To confine this power to the stage of examination-in-chief is to make it ineffective in practice. A clever witness in his examination in-chief faithfully conforms to what he stated earlier to the police or in the committing court, but in the cross-examination introduces statements in a subtle way contradicting in effect what he stated in the examination-in-chief. If his design is obvious, we do not see why the court cannot, during the course of his cross- examination, permit the person calling him as a witness to put questions to him which might be put in cross-examination by the adverse party. To confine the operation of section 154 of the Evidence Act to a particular stage in the examination of a witness is to read words in the section which are not there."

In *G.S. Bakshi* v. *State (Delhi Administration)*, AIR 1978 SC 569: 1979 Cr LJ 476: (1978) 4 SCC 482, the Supreme Court ruled, "When a prosecution witness turns hostile by stating something which is destructive of the prosecution case the prosecution is entitled to pray that the witness be treated as hostile."

Q.147. How can a working woman prevent sexual harassment by her male colleagues?

Ans. The Supreme Court of India in a landmark judgment on this subject reported as *Vishaka* v. *State of Rajasthan*, (1997) 6 SCC 241: 1997 AIR SCW 3043: AIR 1997 SC 3011, while discussing the rights of working women, has held that they have rights to gender equality, to work with dignity and to a working environment which is safe and where they are protected from sexual harassment or abuse. The Supreme Court has prescribed guidelines and norms in this judgment to prevent sexual harassment of women at work places. The Haryana Government has issued instructions to constitute complaint committees in every department in this regard. A working woman may thus file a complaint against her male colleagues before the Head of her Department who is then bound to take appropriate action to redress her grievances.

57. Dying Declaration

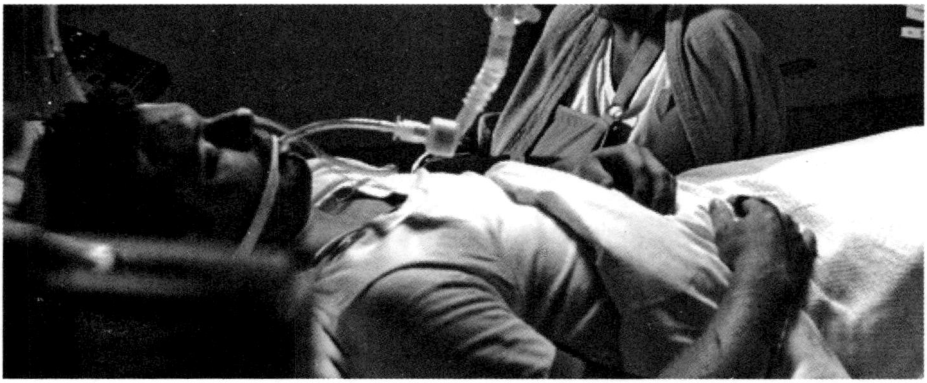

Q.148. Can an accused be convicted solely on the basis of a dying declaration made by the victim who died one month after the burns even though the major prosecution witnesses resiled?

Ans. Law is settled that conviction can be based even on the sole and uncorroborated testimony of the dying declaration. Dying declaration is preferred and believed on the basis of philosophy that no one at the point of death will make any untrue statement and that a man will not meet his maker with a lie in his mouth as the shadow of impending death by itself is the guarantee of the truth. It is also settled that a dying declaration does not cease to be dying declaration even if the victim dies after one month of making such a statement. Though all the material prosecution witnesses had resiled in this case, the court can convict the accused on the basis of declaration alone. The court ought to be satisfied that it was made voluntarily by the deceased while she was fit to make such a statement.

In *Laxman* v. *State of Maharashtra,* (2002) 6 SCC 710: AIR 2002 SC 2973: 2002 Cr LJ 4095, a Constitution Bench of the Supreme Court while settling down the contrary opinions expressed by two different benches of the said Court in *Paparambaka Rosamma* v. *State of Andhra Pradesh,* AIR 1999 SC 3455: (1999) 7 SCC 695: 1999 Cr LJ 4321 and *Koli Chunilal Savji* v. *State of Gujarat,* AIR 1999 SC 3695: (1999) 9 SCC 562 laid down, the principle of admissibility of dying declaration in evidence against the accused in following terms:

> "The justice theory regarding acceptability of a dying declaration is that such declaration is made in extremity, when the party is at the point of death and when every hope of this world is gone, when every motive to falsehood is silenced, and the man is induced by the most powerful consideration to speak only the truth. Notwithstanding the same, great caution must be exercised in considering the weight to be given to this species of evidence on account of the existence of many circumstances which may affect their truth. The situation in which a man is on death bed is so solemn and serene, is the reason in law to accept the veracity of his statement. It is for this reason the requirements of oath and cross-examination are dispensed with. Since the accused has no power of cross-examination, the court insist that the dying declaration should be of such a nature as to inspire full confidence of the court in its truthfulness and correctness. The court, however has to always be on guard to see that the statement of the deceased was not as a result of either tutoring or promoting or a product of imagination. The court also must further decide that the deceased was in a fit state of mind and had the opportunity to observe and identify the assailant. Normally, therefore, the court in order to satisfy whether the deceased was in a fit mental condition to make the dying declaration look up to the medical opinion. But where the eyewitnesses state that the deceased was in a fit and conscious state to make the declaration, the medical opinion will not prevail, nor can it be said that since there is no certification of the doctor as to the fitness of the mind of the declarant, the dying declaration is not acceptable. A dying declaration can be oral or in writing and in any adequate method of communication whether by words or by signs or otherwise will suffice provided the indication is positive and definite. In most cases, however, such statements are made orally before death ensues and is reduced to writing by someone like a magistrate or a doctor or a police officer. When it is recorded, no oath is necessary nor is the presence of a magistrate

absolutely necessary, although to assure authenticity it is usual to call a magistrate, if available for recording the statement of a man about to die. There is no requirement of law that a dying declaration must necessarily be made to a magistrate and when such statement is recorded by a magistrate there is no specified statutory form for such recording. Consequently, what evidential value or weight has to be attached to such statement necessarily depends on the facts and circumstances of each particular case. What is essentially required is that the person who records a dying declaration must be satisfied that the deceased was in a fit state of mind. Where it is proved by the testimony of the magistrate that the declarant was fit to make the statement even without examination by the doctor the declaration can be acted upon provided the court ultimately holds the same to be voluntary and truthful. A certification by the doctor is essentially a rule of caution and therefore the voluntary and truthful nature of the declaration can be established otherwise."

However, the Supreme Court, in *Chacko* v. *State of Kerala*, AIR 2003 SC 265: 2002 AIR SCW 4726: 2003 Cr LJ 441, observed: "Further in the absence of any certificate by a competent doctor as to the mental and physical condition of the deceased to make such a dying declaration, we think it is not safe to rely on the same. We are aware of the judicial pronouncements of this Court that it is not always necessary that a dying declaration should be certified by a doctor before reliance could be placed on the same. But then in the absence of any such certificate, the courts should be satisfied that from the material on record it is safe to place reliance on such uncertified declaration. [See: *Ram Bai* v. *State of Chhattisgarh*, (2002) 8 SCC 83: AIR 2002 SC 3492: 2002 AIR SCW 4085]."

Q.149. Whether a dying declaration should be recorded by a Judicial Magistrate or an Executive Magistrate?

Ans. Although the High Court Rules and Punjab Police Rules require that dying-declaration should be recorded by a Judicial Magistrate, yet these provisions are not mandatory in nature and are in the shape of guidelines. As such, a dying-declaration recorded by an Executive Magistrate by taking all precautions cannot be excluded merely because it was not recorded by a Judicial Magistrate. In *Raj Kumar* v. *State of Punjab*, 2000 (2) RCR (Cri) 595, since the dying-declaration was recorded by a Executive Magistrate after taking all the necessary precautions, the Punjab & Haryana High Court upheld the conviction.

Q.150. Can a dying declaration made solely by nods and gestures before a Magistrate and the consciousness of the maker duly certified by a doctor, be made the basis of conviction?

Ans. The Supreme Court in *Meesala Rama Krishan* v. *State of Andhra Pradesh*, 1994 SCC (Cri) 838 has held that dying declaration recorded on the basis of nods and gestures is admissible. In the said case the recorder of such dying declaration was a Magistrate and the mental consciousness of the victim was duly certified by a doctor. The Court ruled, "...we hold that dying declaration recorded on the basis of nods and gestures is not only admissible but possesses evidentiary value, the extent of which shall depend upon who recorded the statement, what is his educational attainment, what gestures and nods were made, what were the questions asked whether they were simple or complicated and how effective or understandable the nods and gestures were."

Q.151. In a burn case, a statement was made by the lady to the Inspector describing the incident as an accident in the presence of the doctor. Two days later, before her death, she made a declaration before a Magistrate implicating her husband. Is the conviction of the husband sustainable?

Ans. In her first dying declaration which was recorded soon after the incident she did not implicate the accused in any manner although it was recorded by the police inspector in the presence of the doctor who declared her mentally fit to make statement. It is not necessary that a dying declaration must always be recorded by a Magistrate. In this case the implication appears to be an after-thought and chances of her being tutored cannot be ruled out as she changed her version. In *Sharda* v. *State of Rajasthan,* (2010) 2 SCC 85: AIR 2010 SC 408: 2010 AIR SCW 1 the Supreme Court upheld acquittal of the accused by disbelieving the subsequent dying declaration recorded by the executive Magistrate.

However, in *Sayarabano@Sultanabegum* v. *State of Maharashtra,* (2007) 12 SCC 562: AIR 2007 SC (Supp) 398, the Court accepted the second dying declaration as correct. In this case two Dying Declarations had been recorded. As per the first declaration, the deceased had met with an accident. She was hit by the kerosene lamp which fell on her body and caught fire. While recording the second declaration, the Judicial Magistrate asked her why she was changing her statement. The deceased replied that her Mother-in-Law had told her not to give any statement against the family members of her in-laws and that was the reason, why she had not involved any person in the earlier statement. But, in fact, it was her Mother-in-Law who threw the kerosene lamp on her and thus, she was burnt. She also stated that her Mother-in-Law was harassing her. In such a situation, the Supreme Court held that the second dying declaration was true and inspired confidence since ill-treatment of the decreased was clearly established and completely proved on the basis of the evidence of other witnesses.

In *Lakhan* v. *State of Madhya Pradesh,* (2010) 8 SCC 514, the Supreme Court ruled: "The law is that if the court is satisfied that the dying declaration is true and made voluntarily by the deceased, conviction can be based solely on it, without any further corroboration. It is neither a rule of law nor of prudence that a dying declaration cannot be relied upon without corroboration. When a dying declaration is suspicious, it should not be relied upon without having corroborative evidence. The court has to scrutinize the dying declaration carefully and must ensure that the declaration is not the result of tutoring, prompting or imagination. The deceased must be in a fit state of mind to make the declaration and must identify the assailants. Merely because a dying declaration does not contain the details of the occurrence, it cannot be rejected and in case there is merely a brief statement, it is more reliable for the reason that the shortness of the statement is itself a guarantee of its veracity. If the dying declaration suffers from some infirmity, it cannot alone form the basis of conviction. Where the prosecution's version differs from the version given in the dying declaration, the said declaration cannot be acted upon. (vide: *Kushal Rao* v. *State of Bombay*, AIR 1958 SC 22: 1958 Cr LJ 106: 1958 SCR 552; *Rasheed Beg* v. *State of Madhya Pradesh*, AIR 1974 SC 332: 1974 Cr LJ 361: (1974) 4 SCC 264; *K.R. Reddy* v. *The Public Prosecutor*, AIR 1976 SC 1994: 1976 Cr LJ 1548: (1976) 3 SCC 618; *State of Maharashtra* v. *Krishnamurti Laxmipati Naidu*, AIR 1981 SC 617: 1981 Cr LJ 9; *Uka Ram* v. *State of Rajasthan*, (2001) 5 SCC 254: AIR 2001 SC 1814: 2001 Cr LJ 1821; *Babulal* v. *State of Madhya Pradesh*, (2003) 12 SCC 490: AIR 2004 SC 846: 2003 AIR SCW 7074; *Muthu Kutty* v. *State*, (2005) 9 SCC 113: AIR 2005 SC 1473: 2004 AIR SCW 7396; *State of Rajasthan* v. *Wakteng*, AIR 2007 SC 2020: 2007 AIR SCW 3802: (2007) 14 SCC 550; and *Sharda* v. *State of Rajasthan*, (2010) 2 SCC 85: AIR 2010 SC 408: 2010 AIR SCW 1]."

It was further ruled in this very case: "...the law on the issue of dying declaration can be summarized to the effect that in case, the Court comes to the conclusion that the dying declaration is true and reliable, has been recorded by a person at a time when the deceased was fit physically and mentally to make the declaration and it has not been made under any tutoring/duress/prompting; it can be the sole basis for recording conviction. In such an eventuality no corroboration is required. In case, there are multiple dying declarations and there are inconsistencies between them, generally, the dying declaration recorded by the higher officer like a Magistrate can be relied upon, provided that there is no circumstance giving rise to any suspicion about its truthfulness. In case, there are circumstances wherein the declaration had been made, not voluntarily and even otherwise, it is not supported by the other evidence, the Court has to scrutinize the facts of an individual case very carefully and take a decision as to which of the declarations is worth reliance."

58. False Evidence

False

Evidence

Appearing

Real

Q.152. In a rent proceeding, the tenant filed an affidavit which was proved to be false. Is the Court competent to take action? Please advise.

Ans. Filing of a false affidavit in a court of law is a serious matter which must be handled with strict action in order to eradicate the evil of perjury. However, the said court cannot take any action itself. In such circumstances, one should request the court concerned to get a criminal complaint registered against the said person and set the criminal law in motion. [Reference: *Mohan Singh* v. *Late Amar Singh through LRs.*, (1996) 6 SCC 686: AIR 1999 SC 482: 1998 AIR SCW 3648; *Ircon International Ltd.* v. *Union of India*, 2004 (3) RCR (Cri) 759 (Del)]

Q.153. After framing of charges, can the police declare the accused as innocent and recommend prosecution of the complainant on the basis of further investigation u/s 173 (8)?

Ans. After the Trial Court has framed charges against the accused, the complainant cannot be prosecuted under section 182/211 of the IPC merely on the basis of 173(8) report. The complainant may file a protest petition opposing 173(8) report. The complainant can be prosecuted only after the trial court records a finding of acquittal in favour of the accused and reaches a conclusion that the complaint was false. [Reference: *Pawan Kumar* v. *State of Punjab*, 2002 (4) RCR (Cr) 716].

Q.154. After acquittal in a corruption case, can the police submit a calendra under section 182 IPC for furnishing a false complaint? Is the summoning order by the Magistrate legal?

Ans. It is well-settled that after a full-fledged trial, the complainant cannot be bounded under section 182 of the IPC for giving false information to the police. In these circumstances, only the court, which conducted the trial, can initiate action under section 193 or 194, IPC after recording a finding of guilt against the complainant. But after the accused was acquitted, the police have no power to book a case under section 182, IPC. Therefore, the summoning order of the Magistrate in the said calendra is not sustainable. In *Balraj Singh* v. *State of Punjab*, 2006 (4) RCR (Cri) 8 (P&H), the Punjab and Haryana High Court quashed proceedings in a similar situation.

Q.155. In a trap case, two significant witnesses were declared hostile. After acquittal, the police filed a Complaint under section 182 IPC against them for giving false evidence. Please advise.

Ans. A person can be booked under section 182 of the IPC only if the prosecution agency, instead of filing the challan against the aforesaid public servant, had come to the conclusion that he had given false information knowing it to be false. But after the trial of the case, he cannot be booked. At the most perjury proceedings can be taken against him by the court under sections 193 and 194 of the IPC after recording a finding that the complainant had deposed falsely during trial.

Q.156. A complaint was made to the Superintendent of Police (SP) for registration of a case. The official marked the complaint to Station House Officer (SHO). After investigation, the SHO filed a calendra under section 182 IPC. Is the calendar maintainable?

Ans. Since the complaint was lodged with the Superintendent of Police, so prosecution under section 182, IPC can be launched by SP himself or his controlling officer and not by a person who is subordinate to him. In this case, the complaint under section 182 of the IPC launched by SHO is not maintainable in view of the provisions contained in section 195 of Code of Criminal Procedure and as such these proceedings under section 182 of the IPC can be got quashed by filing a petition under section 482 Cr.P.C. in the High Court [Reference: (1) *Devinder Singh Kapoor* v. *State of Punjab*, 1991 (1) RCR (Cri) 149 (P&H), (2) *Randhir* v. *State of Haryana*, 2003 (4) RCR (Cri) 651.]

Q.157. In an FIR under sections 307/34 IPC, the police filed cancellation report. Thereafter, a private complaint was filed in the court on the same allegations. The accused were summoned. Can the police file a calendra under section 182 IPC for lodging a false FIR?

Ans. In the instant case, the prosecution under section 182 of the IPC cannot be launched because the complaint, based on the same facts as mentioned in the FIR, is pending in the court. One may approach the High Court under section 482 of the Cr.P.C. for the quashing of proceedings under section 182 of the IPC.

[Reference: (1) *State of Punjab* v. *Brij Lal Palta*, AIR 1969 SC 355: (1969) 1 SCR 853 (SC); (2) *Banta Singh* v. *State of Haryana*, 1995 (3) RCR (Cri) 133 (P&H); (3) *Kulwant Kaur* v. *State of Punjab*, 1997 (2) RCR (Cri) 780 (P&H)].

Q.158. A witness in a murder case, having fully supported the prosecution in evidence later filed an affidavit that his testimony was under duress. The Judge rejected the affidavit. Please advise.

Ans. In the given circumstance, order of the Judge is sustainable because once the witness is examined as a prosecution witness, he cannot be allowed to perjure himself by resiling from his testimony given in the court on oath. In *Yakub Ismailbhai Patal* v. *State of Gujarat*, (2004) 12 SCC 229: 2004 Cr LJ 4205: AIR 2004 SC 4209 Supreme Court ruled: "Once the witness is examined as a prosecution witness, he cannot be allowed to perjure himself by resiling from the testimony given in Court on oath."

Q.159. After cancellation of F.I.R., the police launched prosecution against complainant under section 182, I.P.C. Legal advice was given to file a complaint in Criminal Court on same facts as recorded in F.I.R. Please advise.

Ans. The complainant is entitled to file a complaint in the court because prosecution under section 182, IPC cannot be launched when the complaint case is pending in the court. In these circumstances, the High Court has quashed the proceedings under section 182, IPC in *Kulwant Kaur* v. *State of Punjab*, 1997 (2) RCR (Cri) 780.

Q.160. What is the evidentiary value of affidavits of eye-witnesses to the occurrence denying knowledge about the incident in a murder trial?

Ans. It has been held by the Supreme Court in *Asha* v. *State of Rajasthan*, 1997 (2) SCC (Cri) 712: AIR 1997 SC 2828: 1997 AIR SCW 2831 that the affidavits of eye-witnesses denying knowledge about the incident shows only an attempt on the part of the accused/defence to win over the prosecution witnesses. In *Rachapalli Abbulu* v. *State of Andhra Pradesh,* 2002 SCC (Cri) 748: AIR 2002 SC 1805: 2002 AIR SCW 1774 the Supreme Court ruled: "The practice adopted by the defence side in getting the affidavits of these witnesses in advance is to be deprecated. That, in a way, amounts to an attempt aimed at dissuading the witnesses from speaking truth before the court. The trial Judge as well as the High Court rightly rejected the defence contention. These witnesses appear to be illiterate persons. Their so-called affidavits must have been either cooked-up or obtained by playing a fraud on them. This type of interference in the criminal justice shall not be encouraged and is to be viewed seriously."

Q.161. A complaint was lodged against a dealer for manhandling and obstructing performance of duty by the Deputy Excise and Taxation Commissioner. The complaint was found false. Later, F.I.R. was lodged by the police under section 182 IPC. Please advise.

Ans. In this case the provisions of section 195(1), Cr.P.C. have not been complied with because the complaint under section 182, IPC has been filed by the police and has not been made by the Deputy Excise and Taxation Commissioner to whom the initial complaint was made. In these circumstances the court cannot take cognizance. In *Daulat Ram* v. *State of Punjab,* AIR 1962 SC 1206: (1962) 2 Cr LJ 286: AIR 1962 SC 1206, the Supreme Court observed that "Section 182 does not require that action must always be taken if the person who moves the public servant knows or believes that action would be taken. In making his report to the Tehsildar, therefore, if the appellant believed that some action would be taken (and he had no reason to doubt that it would not) the offence under that section was complete. It was therefore incumbent, if the prosecution was to be launched, that the complaint in writing should be made by the Tehsildar as the public servant concerned in this case. ... ... What the section comtemplates is that the complaint must be in writing by the public servant concerned..." This view was followed by the Punjab and Haryana High Court in *Kulwinder Singh* v. *State of Punjab,* 2008 (4) RCR (Cri) 418 (P&H); and again in *Vipin Kumar* v. *Manjit Kaur,* 2010 (1) RCR (Cri) 515 (P&H)].

59. Medical and Oral Evidence

Q.162 In a murder case there was a discrepancy in the Post-Mortem Report and the Medico-legal report (MLR) regarding presence of injuries caused by blunt and sharp weapon. Please advise on the possible effect.

Ans. It has been repeatedly held by the Supreme Court that in case of any discrepancy between ocular and medical evidence, the ocular evidence has to get primacy as medical evidence is only an opinion. In *Maju* v. *State of Madhya Pradesh,* 2002 SCC (Cri) 597, it was held by the Supreme Court that the doctor who firstly examined the deceased and described the nature of injuries (sharp/ incised) fully in conformity with the oral evidence given by the eye witnesses should be preferred to the opinion of the doctor who conducted post mortem.

In *Shyam* v. *State of Madhya Pradesh,* 2007 (2) RCR (Cri) 61 (SC), the Supreme Court ruled: "It has now become axiomatic that medical evidence can be used to repel the testimony of eyewitness only if it is so conclusive as to rule out even the possibility of the eyewitness's version to be true. A doctor usually confronted with such questions regarding different possibilities or probabilities of causing those injuries or post- mortem features which he noticed in the medical report may express his views one way or the other depending upon the manner the question was asked. But the answers given by the witness to such questions need not become the last word on such possibilities. After all he gives only his opinion regarding such questions. But to discard the testimony of an eyewitness simply on the strength of such opinion expressed by the medical witness is not conducive to the administration of criminal justice. (See, *State of Uttar Pradesh* v. *Krishna Gopal*, AIR 1988 SC 2154: 1989 Cr LJ 288: (1988) 4 SCC 302 and *Ramanand Yadav* v. *Prabhu Nath Jha*, (2003) 12 SCC 606: AIR 2004 SC 1053: 2004 Cr LJ 640." [Also: *Jasbir Singh* v. *State of Punjab*, 2010 (3) RCR (Cri) 351 (P&H)].

Q.163. A lady died during delivery. Her husband alleged negligence and claimed compensation which was rejected by the Consumer Forum for lack of expert medical evidence. Please advise.

Ans. It is settled law that in cases where medical negligence is alleged and medical expert opinion is required, compensation should not be awarded without cogent expert medical evidence. The Supreme Court laid down following principles in *Kusum Sharma* v. *Batra Hospitaland Medical Research Centre*, (2010) 3 SCC 480: AIR 2010 SC 1050: 2010 AIR SCW 1315

> "On scrutiny of the leading cases of medical negligence both in our country and other countries specially United Kingdom, some basic principles emerge in dealing with the cases of medical negligence. While deciding whether the medical professional is guilty of medical negligence following well known principles must be kept in view:—
>
> I. Negligence is the breach of a duty exercised by omission to do something which a reasonable man, guided by those considerations which ordinarily regulate the conduct of human affairs, would do, or doing something which a prudent and reasonable man would not do.
>
> II. Negligence is an essential ingredient of the offence. The negligence to be established by the prosecution must be culpable or gross and not the negligence merely based upon an error of judgment.
>
> III. The medical professional is expected to bring a reasonable degree of skill and knowledge and must exercise a reasonable degree of care. Neither the very highest nor a very low degree of care and competence judged in the light of the particular circumstances of each case is what the law requires.
>
> IV. A medical practitioner would be liable only where his conduct fell below that of the standards of a reasonably competent practitioner in his field.
>
> V. In the realm of diagnosis and treatment there is scope for genuine difference of opinion and one professional doctor is clearly not negligent merely because his conclusion differs from that of other professional doctor.
>
> VI. The medical professional is often called upon to adopt a procedure which involves higher element of risk, but which he honestly believes as providing greater chances of success for the patient rather than a procedure involving lesser risk but higher chances of failure. Just because a professional looking to the gravity of illness has taken higher element of risk to redeem the patient out of his/her suffering which did not yield the desired result may not amount to negligence.
>
> VII. Negligence cannot be attributed to a doctor so long as he performs his duties with reasonable skill and competence. Merely because the doctor

chooses one course of action in preference to the other one available, he would not be liable if the course of action chosen by him was acceptable to the medical profession.

VIII. It would not be conducive to the efficiency of the medical profession if no Doctor could administer medicine without a halter round his neck.

IX. It is our bounden duty and obligation of the civil society to ensure that the medical professionals are not unnecessary harassed or humiliated so that they can perform their professional duties without fear and apprehension.

X. The medical practitioners at times also have to be saved from such a class of complainants who use criminal process as a tool for pressurizing the medical professionals/hospitals particularly private hospitals or clinics for extracting uncalled for compensation. Such malicious proceedings deserve to be discarded against the medical practitioners.

XI. The medical professionals are entitled to get protection so long as they perform their duties with reasonable skill and competence and in the interest of the patients. The interest and welfare of the patients have to be paramount for the medical professionals.

"In our considered view, the aforementioned principles must be kept in view while deciding the cases of medical negligence. We should not be understood to have held that doctors can never be prosecuted for medical negligence. As long as the doctors have performed their duties and exercised an ordinary degree of professional skill and competence, they cannot be held guilty of medical negligence. It is imperative that the doctors must be able to perform their professional duties with free mind."

60. Defence Witness

India
Against
Corruption

Q.164. During trial of an offence under section 13 of the Prevention of Corruption Act 1988, the shadow witness was given up by the prosecution. The witness was produced in defence. The public prosecutor confronted the witness with his statement recorded by the police under section 161 of the Cr.P.C. Please advise.

Ans. It is well-settled that a witness can be confronted with his earlier statement recorded by the police under section 161 of the CrPC only when he is called as a prosecution witness and the prosecution cannot confront him in case he is given up by the prosecution and he chose to turn up as defence witness.

In *State of Kerala* v. *Ram Chanderan,* 2002 (4) RCR (Cri) 673, the Kerala High Court interpreted provisions of sections 161 and 162 of the Criminal Procedure Code as follows:—

> "Section 162 of the Cr.P.C. reads as follows: "Section 162: Statements to police not to be signed: Use of statements in evidence:—(1) No statement made by any person to a police officer in the course of an investigation under this Chapter shall, if reduced to writing, be signed by the person making it, nor shall any such statement or any record thereof, whether in a police diary or otherwise, or any part of such statement or record, be used for any purpose, save as hereinafter provided, at any inquiry or trial in respect of any offence under investigation at the time when such statement was made:
>
> Provided that when any witness is called for the prosecution in such inquiry or trial whose statement has been reduced into writing as aforesaid, any part of his statement, if duly proved, may be used by the accused, and with the permission of the Court, by the prosecution, to contradict such witness in the manner provided by section 145 of the Indian Evidence Act, 1872 (1 of 1872); and when any part of such statement is so used, any part thereof may also be used in the re-examination of such witness, but for the purpose only of explaining any matter referred to in his cross examination". [Sub-section (2) and explanation omitted]

"What is obvious from the proviso is that the statement recorded under section 161 can be confronted only to a witness called for the prosecution. There is no mention in the proviso of any such confrontation being possible to a defence witness. Actually it enables the accused to rely upon it for a limited purpose of contradicting a witness in the manner provided under section 145 of the Evidence Act by drawing his attention to parts of the statements intended for contradiction. It cannot certainly be used for corroboration of a prosecution or a defence witness or even in the matter of court witness. It cannot be used for contradicting a defence or a court witness. The bar contemplated in section 162(1) is of general application and the limited exception is the confrontation to the witness for the prosecution in the interest of the accused. The statement of the witness under section 161 cannot also be used as substantive evidence and can only be used to contradict the witness within the limitation specified in the proviso. The veracity of the defence witness, therefore, has to be assessed independent of any such statement and based on his performance in the box as also corroboration, if any, forthcoming thereto. It is clear that neither the prosecution nor the defence can contradict or corroborate the version of a defence witness with the aid of a statement recorded under section 161 of the Cr.P.C."

61. Relationship with Witness

Q.165. In a murder case, deceased's 10 year old son was the only eye-witness. The police recorded child's statement. Whether conviction based on sole testimony of the child is sustainable?

Ans. The Evidence Act, does not prescribe any particular age as a demarcating line for treating a witness competent to testify. The intellectual capacity of the child to understand the question and to give rational answers is the sole test of testimonial competency. Generally, witness aged 10/12 years is believed to possess minimal required understanding. In *Dalbir Singh* v. *State of Haryana*, 2003 (1) RCR (Cri) 727 (P&H) and in *State of Punjab* v. *Jagjit Singh*, 2004 (1) RCR (Cri) 799 (P&H); two Division Benches of Punjab and Haryana High Court have upheld the conviction of accused on the basis of evidence of child witnesses.

Q.166. On a secret information, the officials of Central Excise and Customs Department seized 100 gold biscuits from a smuggler. As per government rules, the informer is entitled to 20 percent of the value of seized goods but the Department paid him only 10 per cent. Can the informer claim the entire award money?

Ans. As per paragraph 3.1.1 of the government instructions dated 30-3-1985, the informer is entitled to a reward of up to 20 per cent of the market value of goods seized and as per paragraph 4.1 of said instructions a lesser amount can be given if the competent authority gives a cogent reason. The grant of award is not a statutory right and cannot be claimed through a court of law, if the authorities decide to award a lesser or no amount to the informant. Reversing the view expressed by a Single Bench in *Krishan Gopal Dhawan* v. *Union of India*, 2005 (4) PLR 721, a Division Bench of the High Court in appeal [L.P.A. No. 164 of 2005 decided on 5 February, 2009 *Union of India* v. *Krishan Gopal Dhawan*] ruled, "If the grant of reward cannot be claimed as a matter of right it is not understandable as to how a writ of mandamus can be issued commanding the Government to give a particular amount by way of reward. .... Hon'ble the Supreme Court further held that a writ of mandamus can only be granted in a case where there is a statutory duty imposed upon the officer concerned and failure on the part of that officer to discharge the statutory obligation. Therefore, it is required to be shown that a statute imposes a legal duty and the aggrieved party has a legal right under the statute to enforce its performance. The Supreme Court relied upon its earlier judgments rendered in *Bihar Eastern Gangetic Fishermen Co-operative Society Ltd.* v. *Sipahi Singh*, AIR 1977 SC 2149: 1978 BLJ 60: (1978) 1 SCR 375; *Lekhraj Sathram Dass Lalvanai* v. *Deputy Custodian-cum-Managing Officer*, AIR 1966 SC 334: 1966 (1) SCJ 24: (1966) 1 SCR 120 and *Dr. Umakant Saran* v. *State of Bihar*, AIR 1973 SC 964: (1973) 1 SCC 485: (1973) 1 SCWR 313. The principles laid down by the Hon'ble Supreme Court in *C. Krishna Reddy's* case when applied to the facts of the present case would show that no direction could be issued to the appellant for rewarding the full amount ."

62. Tape Recorded Evidence

Q.167. Can the court order tape-recording of a person's voice for comparison against his wishes?

Ans. The Court is competent to grant such permission during investigation The Bombay High Court, in *CBI* v. *Abdul Karim Ladsab Telgi,* 2005 (4) RCR (Cri) 259, while permitting the investigating agency to tape-record the voice of the accused for comparison, held that it does not infringe accused's rights under Article 20(3) of the Constitution of India. It was further held that under section 114(g) of the Indian Evidence Act, 1872 the court may draw adverse inference against the accused if he refuses to allow his voice to be tape-recorded for comparison. In *R.M. Malkani* v. *State of Maharashtra,* (1973) 1 SCC 471: 1973 Cr LJ 238: AIR 1973 SC 157 the Supreme Court held as under:

> "Tape recorded conversation is admissible provided first the conversation is relevant to the matters in issue; secondly, there is identification of the voice; and thirdly, the accuracy of the tape recorded conversation is proved by eliminating the possibility of erasing the tape record. A contemporaneous tape record of a relevant conversation is a relevant fact and is admissible under section 8 of the Evidence Act. It is *res gestae.* It is also comparable to a photograph of a relevant incident. The tape recorded conversation is therefore a relevant fact and is admissible under section 7 of the Evidence Act. The conversation between Dr. Motwani and the appellant in the present case is relevant to the matter in issue. There is no dispute about the identification of the voices. There is no controversy about any portion of the conversation being erased or mutilated. The appellant was given full opportunity to test the genuineness of the tape recorded Conversation. The tape recorded conversation is admissible in evidence."

Q.168. Can the court order an accused to be measured or photographed against his wishes for comparison purposes?

Ans. Section 5 of the Identification of Prisoners Act, 1920 which deals with Power of Magistrate to order a person to be measured or photographed which reads as under:

> "If a Magistrate is satisfied that, for the purposes of any investigation or proceeding under the Code of Criminal Procedure, 1898 (5 of 1898), it is expedient to direct any person to allow his measurements or photograph to be taken, he may make an order to that effect, and in that case the person to whom the order relates shall be produced or shall attend at the time and place specified in the order and shall allow his measurements or photograph to be taken, as the case may be, by a police officer:
>
> Provided that no order shall be made directing any person to be photographed except by a Magistrate of the first class:
>
> Provided further, that no order shall be made under this section unless the person has at some time been arrested in connection with such investigation or proceeding."

In view of the said provision, the court is empowered to permit the investigating agency to take accused's measurements or photograph for the purpose of comparison.

Q.169. Whether the court can order an accused to give impressions of his thumb, foot and other body parts during investigation?

Ans. The court can order an accused to give his thumb, foot and other body part impressions for comparison by investigating agency. Such an order will not be hit by article 20(3) of the Constitution of India. In *State of Bombay* v. *Kathi Kalu Oghad*, AIR 1961 SC 1808: (1961) 2 Cr LJ 856: (1962) 3 SCR 10 a Constitution Bench of 11 Judges of the Supreme Court held as under:

> "(3) 'To be a witness' is not equivalent to garnishing evidence in its widest significance; that is to say, as including not merely making of oral or written statements but also production of documents or giving materials which may be relevant at a trial to determine the guilt or innocence of the accused.
>
> (4) Giving thumb impressions or impressions of foot or palm or fingers or specimen writings or showing parts of the body by way of identification were not included in the expression 'to be a witness'.
>
> (5) 'To be a witness' means imparting knowledge in respect of relevant facts by an oral statement or a statement in writing, made or given in court or otherwise.
>
> (6) 'To be a witness' in its ordinary grammatical sense means giving oral testimony in court. Case law has gone beyond this strict literal interpretation of the expression which may now bear a wider meaning, namely, bearing testimony in court or out of court by a person accused of an offence, orally or in writing."

63. Chance Witness

Q.170. Who is a chance witness? Can conviction be based on the testimony of such a witness?

Ans. If by coincidence or chance, a person happens to be present at the place of event at the time of its occurrence, he is called a chance witness. When an incident takes place in broad daylight, different persons are found to follow their own avocations of life and while doing so they are likely to come across incidents, which in the ordinary course they never contemplated to witness. The Supreme Court in *Sachchey Lal Tewari* v. *State of Uttar Pradesh*, (2004) 11 SCC 410: AIR 2004 SC 5039: 2004 AIR SCW 5672, held that, "the expression 'chance witness' is borrowed from countries where every man's home is considered his castle and everyone must have an explanation for his presence elsewhere or in another man's castle. It is quite unsuitable an expression in a country where people are less formal and more casual, at any rate in the matter of explaining their presence."

Similarly, in *Chanakya Dhibar* v. *State of West Bengal*, (2004) 12 SCC 398: (2003) 8 Supreme 884 the Supreme Court has observed: "Murders are not committed with previous notice to witnesses soliciting their presence. If murder is committed in a dwelling house, the inmates of the house are natural witnesses. If murder is committed in a street, only passerby will be witness. Their evidence cannot be brushed aside or viewed with suspicion on the ground that they are mere chance witnesses."

In case the presence of such a witness at the time of occurrence is proved satisfactorily, his evidence cannot be discarded simply because he is a chance witness.

64. Child Witness

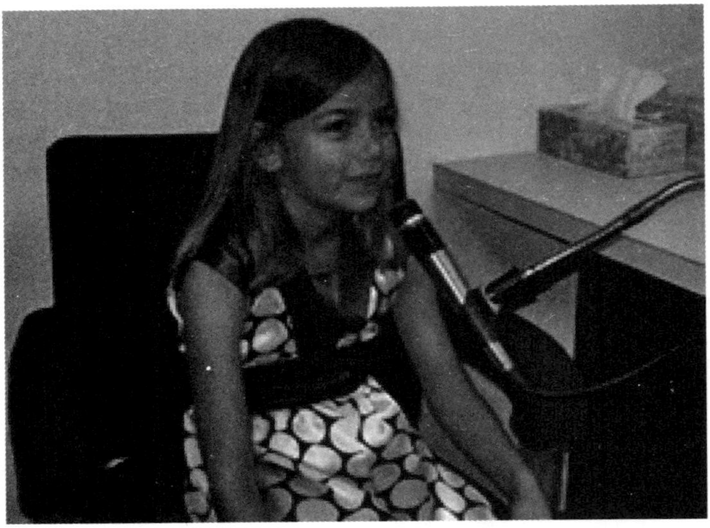

Q.171. A person has been convicted of 'murder' solely on the basis of statement of deceased's son aged about 8-9 years. Whether the conviction is maintainable?

Ans. The Evidence Act, does not prescribe any particular age as a demarcating line for treating a witness incompetent to testify by reason of his tender age. However, the trial court should always record their opinion that the child understands the duty of speaking the truth. In *Ratan Singh* v. *State of Gujarat*, 2003 (4) RCR Criminal 970 the Supreme Court has held that a child of tender age can be allowed to testify if he has intellectual capacity to understand questions and give rational answerer thereto. In a number of cases, the Supreme Court has relied upon the testimony of child witness while convicting the accused. In *Surya Narayana* v. *State of Karnataka*, 2002 SCC (Cri) 413: 2001 (1) Supreme 1, it was held, "The evidence of the child witness cannot be rejected *per se*, but the court, as a rule of prudence, is required to consider such evidence with close scrutiny and only on being convinced about the quality of the statements and its reliability, base conviction by accepting the statement of the child witness."

In *State of Uttar Pradesh* v. *Krishna Master*, AIR 2010 SC 3071: 2010 Cr LJ 3889: 2010 AIR SCW 4733, the Supreme Court held, "There is no principle of law known to this court that it is inconceivable that a child of tender age would not be able to recapitulate facts in his memory witnessed by him long ago."

65. Age Proof

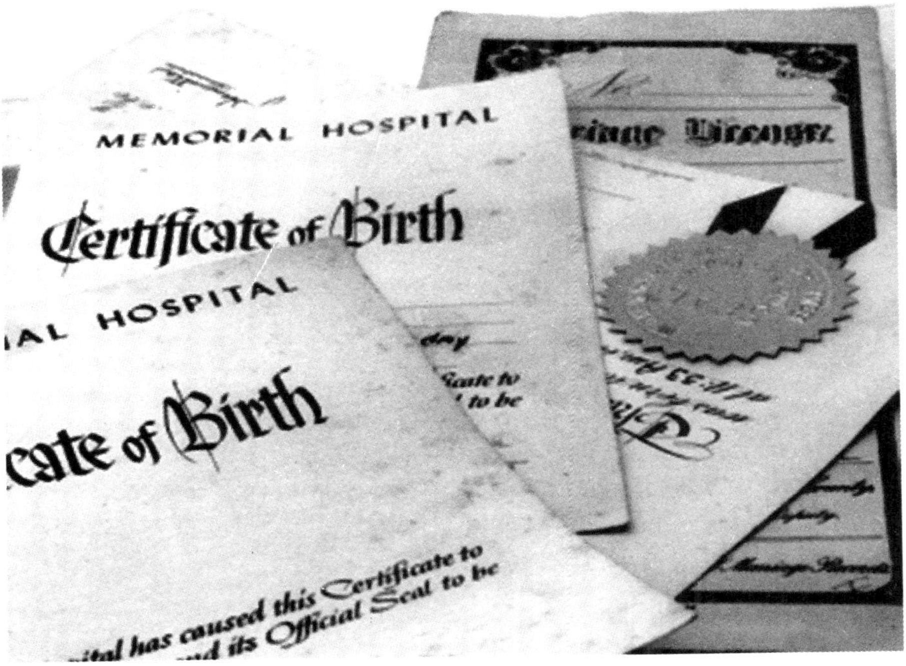

Q.172. In a rape case of a girl below 16 years, there was a discrepancy in the ossification test report and the statement of girl's parents before the police. The statement was supported by birth record of hospital. How age of the victim is to be determined in such situations?

Ans. It is well-settled that expert medical evidence is of advisory character and not binding on the witness. Very often parents furnish incorrect date of birth to the school authorities to make the age in order to secure admission for their children. The Supreme Court ruled in *Vishnu @ Undrya* v. *State of Maharashtra,* (2006) 1 SCC 283: AIR 2006 SC 508: 2005 AIR SCW 6149, "..... the expert medical evidence is not binding on the ocular evidence. The opinion of the medical officer is to assist the court as he is not a witness of fact and the evidence given by the medical officer is really of an advisory character and not binding on the witness of fact. In the case of *Madan Gopal Kakkad* v. *Naval Dubey,* (1992) 3 SCC 204: 1992 AIR SCW 1480 this Court has considered a similar question and pointed out in paragraph 34 at page SCC 221 as under:

> "A medical witness called in as an expert to assist the Court is not a witness of fact and the evidence given by the medical officer is really of an advisory character given on the basis of symptoms found on examination. The expert witness is expected to put before the Court all materials inclusive of the data which induced him to come to the conclusion and enlighten the

Court on the technical aspect of the case by explaining the terms of science so that the Court although, not an expert may form its own judgment on those materials after giving due regard to the expert's opinion because once the expert's opinion is accepted, it is not the opinion of the medical officer but of the Court."

Q.173. Can a person aged 15 years get benefit of the Juvenile Justice Act, 2000 on the basis of horoscope (janam patri) as a proof?

Ans. One cannot get any benefit of a horoscope entry, as it is not a reliable piece of evidence. This was so held by the Supreme Court in *Hawaldar Singh* v. *State of Uttar Pradesh,* (1984) 3 SCC 617: AIR 1985 SC 955: 1984 All LJ 6 by observing, "Such documents could always be brought into existence at any time. We cannot rely upon the two horoscopes produced before us."

66. Plea of *Alibi*

Q.174. What is *alibi* and its evidentiary value?

Ans. The word *alibi* means 'elsewhere'. It is a defence based on the physical impossibility and participation in the crime by an accused person by placing a letter in a location other than the scene of crime at the relevant time. Plea of *alibi* can succeed only if it is shown that the accused was so far away at the relevant time that he could not be present at the place where the crime was committed.

In *State of Maharashtra* v. *Narsingrao Gangaram Pimple,* AIR 1984 SC 63: 1984 Cr LJ 4: (1984) 1 SCC 446 (SC), it was held by the Supreme Court that "It is well settled that a plea of alibi must be proved with absolute certainty so as to completely exclude the possibility of the presence of the person concerned at the place of occurrence."

Thus 'burden of proof' lies upon the accused to prove *alibi*. In *Jasbir Singh @ Beeraand* v. *State of Punjab*, 2010 (3) RCR (Criminal) 351, the High Court has rejected such plea of the accused as the same was found unreliable.

67. Circumstantial Evidence

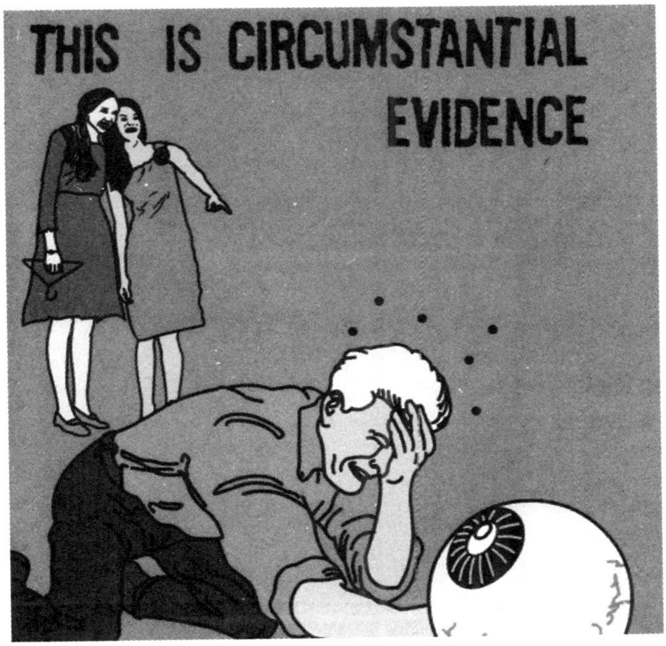

Q.175. In case of a blind murder, two persons were tried on the basis of circumstantial evidence of 'last seen together' and extra-judicial confessional statement allegedly made by them. The Trial Court convicted one accused and acquitted the other by giving him benefit of doubt. Is the conviction sustainable?

Ans. An extra judicial confession, in the very nature of things, is a weak piece of evidence. The extra-judicial confession made jointly by the two accused is no confession in the eyes of law being joint in nature. Moreover, if co-accused is to given the benefit of doubt, the other accused should also be entitled to the same benefit as evidence against both the accused is same. In *Charan Singh* v. *State of Punjab*, 2007 (3) RCR (Cri) 781 (P&H), the Punjab and Haryana High Court held that joint extra-judicial confession made by two accused was not reliable.

Local and Special Laws

68. Narcotic Drugs and Psychotropic Substances Act

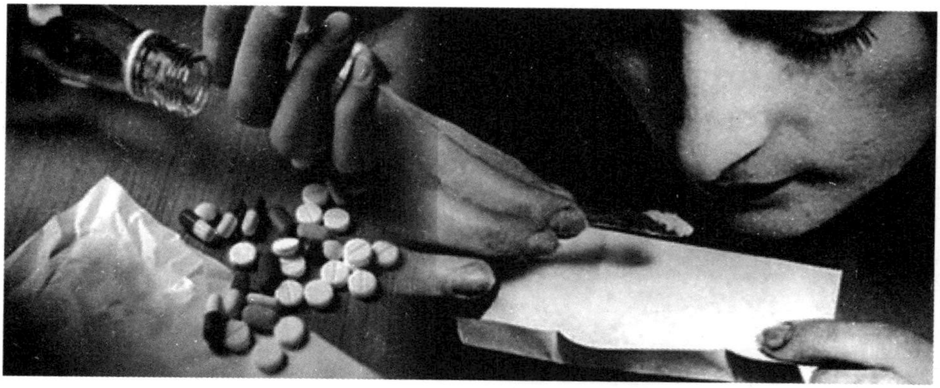

Q.176. An accused has challenged his conviction of 10 years term under section 15 of NDPS Act. He had remained in jail for three years during trial and one year after conviction. Can he be released on bail, pending appeal in High Court?

Ans. In *Daler Singh* v. *State of Punjab*, 2007 (1) RCR (Cri) 316 (P&H), a Division Bench of the Punjab and Haryana High Court has laid down certain guidelines for suspension of sentence under section 389 of the Cr. P.C. in the cases related to NDPS Act. According to these guidelines, where the convict is sentenced for 10 years for having in his possession commercial quantity of the contraband, he shall be entitled to bail if he has already undergone a total sentence of four years, which must include at least 15 months' jail period after conviction. Since in this case, the accused has undergone only 12 months' period in jail after his conviction, he is presently not entitled for bail. He should wait for another three months to avail the benefit.

Q.177. In a case of heroine recovery under the NDPS Act, can a second sample of the recovered substance be got tested from another Laboratory?

Ans. Though there is no provision in the NDPS Act to send the second sample for re-analysis, the court can allow re-testing in the interest of justice. The Kerala High Court in *State of Kerala* v. *Deepak*, 2001 (3) RCR (Cri) 216 has held that even in the absence of any specific provision, a request for sending second sample for analysis can be allowed. The Delhi High Court has also taken a similar view in *Nihal Khan* v. *State (Govt. of NCT Delhi)*, 2007 (3) RCR (Cri) 860 holding that the court can allow such a request in the interest of justice.

Q.178. The police recovered five bags of poppy husk from the car driven by a driver but the owner was not travelling at the time of the alleged recovery. The owner has also been booked under section 29 of the Narcotic

Drugs and Psychotropic Substances Act, for abetment. Can the owner be granted anticipatory bail?

Ans. In the instant case, there is no legal evidence to connect the owner with the offence of abetment or criminal conspiracy punishable under section 29 of the NDPS Act, because firstly, the secret information is not admissible unless and until the provider of such an information is examined in the court and secondly, statement of the co-accused recorded by the police implicating him is not admissible under section 30 of the Indian Evidence Act, unless he implicates himself also in the said offence. Thus, it is a good case for anticipatory bail. This view finds support from a Delhi High Court Judgement in *Karan Singh* v. *State (NCT of Delhi)*, 2006 (3) RCR 707 (Del), relying upon a Supreme Court judgement in *Amar Singh Ramjibhai Barot* v. *State of Gujarat*, (2005) 7 SCC 550: AIR 2005 SC 4248: 2005 AIR SCW 5075.

Q.179. The court rejected owners application for release of his car on superdari. The vehicle was allegedly involved in smuggling of poppy husk with a recovery of 20 kg. Please advise.

Ans. There is no bar under the Narcotic Drugs and Psychotropic Substances Act to release the vehicle involved in the crime on superdari to its registered owner as no useful purpose is served in keeping the vehicle at the police station. The vehicle can be confiscated under section 60 of the Narcotic Drugs and Psychotropic Substances Act only after the offence is proved.

In *Sant Lal* v. *State of Rajasthan*, 2006 (2) RCR (Cri) 803, it was ruled by the Rajasthan High Court that, : "In catena of cases, this Court has held that no fruitful purpose is served in keeping the vehicle at police station. Therefore, this Court has repeatedly directed that the vehicle be handed over back to the registered owner. This view has been expressed in the case of *Raj Kumar* v. *Union of India*, 2001 (2) RCC 1370, wherein this High Court handed the possession of the jeep to the registered owner and had held that under section 60 of the NDPS Act, the jeep can be confiscated only after the offence is proved."

The Punjab and Haryana High Court has also taken a similar view in *Gurdev Singh* v. *State of Punjab*, 2002 (4) RCR (Cri) 440 (P&H).

Q.180. 100 grams of *charas* was recovered for which a person was convicted under the Narcotic Drugs and Psychotropic Substances Act. Pending appeal, the law has been amended providing reduced sentence for small quantities of Narcotics. Can the benefit accrue to the accused/appellant in a pending appeal?

Ans. It is a settled principle of law that an appeal being a rehearing of the entire case and pending before the court, the accused would be entitled to the benefit of amendment. The appellant is entitled to the benefit of amended provision.

In *Pappoo* alias *Moochh* alias *Aneas* v. *State of Madhya Pradesh*, 2004 (1) RCR (Cri) 421 (MP), it was held by the Madhya Pradesh High Court: The Act has been amended in 2001 with effect from 2-10-2001. The amended provisions have been considered by this Court in *Mahesh Chandra* v. *State of Madhya Pradesh,* 2002 (4) MPHT 174: 2003 (2) MPLJ 109. There is rationalisation of quantum of sentence. There are three categories of cases for determining the question of punishment depending upon the quantity of the narcotic drug or psychotropic substance which is involved. The severity of punishment would depend upon that quantity. The benefit of rationalisation of sentence structure has been extended to those cases which were "pending before the Courts" on the date of amendment. There was a proviso to section 41 of Amending Act. It reads "Provided that nothing in this section shall apply to cases pending in appeal". The Constitutional validity of this proviso has been examined by a Division Bench of this Court in *Ramesh* v. *State of Madhya Pradesh,* 2003 (4) MPHT 78, and it has been held that "appeal being rehearing of the entire case and if pending before the Court would be entitled to the benefit of Amending Act No. 9 of 2001. As mentioned above the exclusion of benefit of liberalised provisions of the Act as substituted by Act No. 9 of 2001 to cases pending in appeal is without any intelligible differentia and without having any reasonable nexus with the object to be achieved, therefore, we hereby strike down the proviso and issue a writ in the nature of mandamus directing that the proviso to sub-section (1) of section 41 of Act No. 9 of 2001 "provided that nothing in the section shall apply to the cases pending in appeal" shall not be given effect to being violative of article 14 of the Constitution of India being a classification without any reasonable nexus with the object to be achieved. Consequently, it is held that Act No. 9 of 2001 shall be applicable to all cases pending before the Courts or under investigation at the commencement of the said Act and shall be disposed of in accordance with the provisions of the Principal Act as amended by Act No. 9 of 2001 irrespective of the fact whether such cases are pending in appeal or before the trial Court. Applying the science of interpretation and taking recourse to the art of acceptation, we are inclined to interpret that the main provision shall apply to the appeals because the language employed in the provision is 'all cases pending before the Court'. When the word Court has been used there is no reason or justification to exclude the Appellate Court. We may reiterate that once the proviso has been struck down being unconstitutional, the main provision, *propio vigore,* would apply to appeals".

Q.181. A person was convicted under Narcotic Drugs and Psychotropic Substances Act. He had taken lift in a car in which one kg opium was found by the police. Please advise.

Ans. In such circumstances sections 35 and 54 of the Narcotic Drugs and Psychotropic Substances Act raise a presumption of culpable mental state and the burden lies on the accused to prove the fact that he had no such mental state with respect to the act charged as an offence. In such case, the prosecution is only required to prove that the accused was found in possession of the contraband and thereafter, the onus lies on the accused to prove that he was not in conscious possession of the contraband. In *Madan Lal* v. *State of Himachal Pradesh,* (2003) 7 SCC 465: AIR 2003 SC 3642: 2003 AIR SCW 3969, the Supreme Court upheld conviction of the accused who was found travelling in a car alongwith other co-accused from which charas was recovered from a steel container (dollu) concealed in a bag, when the said car was subjected to search by the police.

69. Negotiable Instruments Act

Q.182. A person could not repay the loan amount of Rs. 1 lakh. However, after three years, he issued a cheque for Rs. 50,000 to the lender. The cheque was dishonored for want of insufficient funds. The lender has filed a complaint under section 138 of the Negotiable Instruments Act. Please guide?

Ans. In *S.A. Mamman, Sakthimangalam* v. *C.P. Gopalan Achari, Thekke* CRL. A. No. 225 of 2002, decided on 29 June, 2010 – A Division Bench of Kerala High Court ruled, "section 138 of Negotiable Instruments Act provides that if the dishonoured cheque was issued in discharge of whole or any part of the debt or other liability, it would attract the offence under section 138 of Negotiable Instruments Act, provided, other requirements are complied. The question is whether the debt so provided would include a time barred debt also.. ...The question was settled by a Division Bench in *Ramakrishnan* v. *Parthasaradhy,* 2003 (2) KLT 613, followed by the decisions of the learned single Judge in *Gopinathan* v. *Sivadasan,* 2006 (4) KLT 779 "and *Ramakrishnan* v. *Gangadharan Nair,* ILR 2006 (3) Ker 657. The Division Bench held that under section 25(3) of Contract Act, a promise can be made even in a case where limitation for recovery of the amount has already expired and that promise is in writing and such writing can also be in the form of a cheque and when a cheque is delivered to the payee, the person is entitled to present the cheque to the Bank and seek payment and in the event of dishonour, an offence under section 138 of Negotiable Instruments Act is attracted. In view of the legal position, the finding of the learned Magistrate that as the amount covered by Exhibit P1 cheque is a time barred debt, an offence under section 138 of Negotiable Instruments Act is not attracted is unsustainable."

Q.183. If a cheque issued for discharge of liability arising out of a wagering contract is dishonoured, can the payee institute proceedings under section 138 of the Negotiable Instruments Act?

Ans. In *A.V. Murthy* v. *B.S. Nagabasavanna,* (2002) 2 SCC 642: AIR 2002 SC 985: 2002 Cr LJ 1479, it was held by the Supreme Court that the cheque in question must represent a legally enforceable debt. The Court ruled, "If for example, the cheque was drawn in respect of a debt or liability payable under a wagering contract, it could have been said that that debt or liability is not legally enforceable as it is a claim, which is prohibited under law."

Q.184. 'X' had filed a criminal complaint within limitation under the Negotiable Instruments Act but the Trial Court took cognizance after expiry of limitation as prescribed under section 468 of Code of Criminal Procedure. The court discharged him on this ground. What is the remedy of cheque holder?

Ans. As the complaint was filed within the period of limitation, it cannot be made infructuous by an act of the court. Therefore, the court order discharging the accused is not legally sustainable. The complainant cannot be held responsible for any delay on the part of the court in issuing process or taking cognizance of an offence.

It has been held by the Supreme Court in *Japani Sahoo* v. *Chander Sekhar Mahanty,* (2007) 7 SCC 394: AIR 2007 SC 2762: 2007 Cr LJ 4068 that the relevant date for computing period of limitation must be considered the date of filing of complaint and not the date of taking cognizance by a Magistrate or issuance of process by a court.

The court observed, "The general rule of criminal justice is that "a crime never dies". The principle is reflected in the well-known maxim *nullum tempus aut locus occurrit regi* (lapse of time is no bar to Crown in proceeding against offenders). The Limitation Act, 1963 does not apply to criminal proceedings unless there are express and specific provisions to that effect, for instance, articles 114, 115, 131 and 132 of the Act. It is settled law that a criminal offence is considered as a wrong against the State and the Society even though it has been committed against an individual. Normally, in serious offences, prosecution is launched by the State and a Court of Law has no power to throw away prosecution solely on the ground of delay. Mere delay in approaching a Court of Law would not by itself afford a ground for dismissing the case though it may be a relevant circumstance in reaching a final verdict."

It was further observed, "At the same time, however, ground reality also cannot be ignored. Mere delay may not bar the right of the 'Crown' in prosecuting 'criminals'. But it also cannot be overlooked that no person can be kept under continuous apprehension that he can be prosecuted at 'any time' for 'any crime' irrespective of the nature or seriousness of the offence. "People will have no peace of mind if there is no period of limitation even for petty offences".

After detailed examination of the law on the point, the Supreme Court concluded in the said judgment, "The Code imposes an obligation on the aggrieved party to take recourse to appropriate forum within the period provided by law and once he takes such action, it would be wholly unreasonable and inequitable if he is told that his grievance would not be ventilated as the court had not taken an action within the period of limitation. Such interpretation of law, instead of promoting justice would lead to perpetuate injustice and defeat the primary object of procedural law..... . In view of the above, we hold that for the purpose of computing the period of limitation, the relevant date must be considered as the date of filing of complaint or initiating criminal proceedings and not the date of taking cognizance by a Magistrate or issuance of process by a court. We, therefore, overrule all decisions in which it has been held that the crucial date for computing the period of limitation is taking of cognizance by the Magistrate/ Court and not of filing of complaint or initiation of criminal proceedings."

Q.185. In a complaint under section 138 of the Negotiable Instruments Act, the trial Court convicted the (accused) to undergo rigorous imprisonment for a period of three months and also to pay a fine of Rs. 10,000 and in default, to further undergo rigorous imprisonment for one month. The Appellate Court reduced the sentence of imprisonment from three months to till rising of court but at the same time awarded a sum of Rs. 50,000 as compensation to the complainant. The accused is unable to pay. Please advise.

Ans. The Appellate Court could not award any compensation to the complainant because the court had imposed a sentence which also included fine. The order of the Appellate Court to pay compensation of Rs. 50,000 is not legally sustainable in view of section 357(3) of the Code of Criminal Procedure. In *Sivasuriyan* v. *Thangavelu,* (2004) 13 SCC 795 the Supreme Court ruled, " ... the only question that arises for consideration is whether the Court can direct payment of compensation in exercise of power under sub-section (3) of section 357 in a case where fine already forms a part of the sentence. Apart from sub-section (3) of section 357 there is no other provision under the Code whereunder the Court can exercise such power.

> "Sub-section (3) of section 357: when a Court imposes a sentence, of which fine does not form a part, the Court may, when passing judgment, order the accused person to pay, by way of compensation, such amount as may be specified in the order to the person who has suffered any loss or injury by reason of the act for which the accused person has been so sentenced."
>
> "On a plain reading of the aforesaid provision, it is crystal clear that the power can be exercised only when the court imposes sentence by which fine does not form a part. In the case in hand, a Court having sentenced to imprisonment, as also fine, the power under sub-section (3) of section 357 could not have been exercised. In that view of the matter, the impugned direction of the High Court directing payment of compensation to the tune of Rs. one Lakh by the appellant is set aside."

Q.186. A case of theft was registered on April 16, 2002. The police, after investigation, filed a challan in the court on July 21, 2004. The court framed charge under section 380, IPC on May 20, 2005. Are the proceedings barred by limitation?

Ans. As per section 468 of the Code of Criminal Procedure, the limitation for taking cognizance of offence punishable under section 380, IPC is up to three years as the maximum punishment provided for the offence under this section is only three years. In *Baljit Singh* v. *State of Punjab*, 2006 (3) RCR (Cri) 39; relying upon an earlier judgment of the Supreme Court in *Nar Singh Dass Tapadra* v. *Goverdhan Dass Partani*, (2000) 7 SCC 183: AIR 2000 SC 2946: 2000 (3) KLT 605, the High Court *quashed the proceedings being time barred holding* that mere filing of a challan or presentation of complaint in the court cannot be held to mean that the Magistrate has taken cognizance and that taking cognizance of an offence by the Magistrate would only be on the date when he applied his mind to the facts of the case. However, there is a change in legal position. The Supreme Court, in *Japani Sahoo* v. *Chander Sekhar Mahanty*, (2007) 7 SCC 394: AIR 2007 SC 2762: 2007 Cr LJ 4068, has held that for the purpose of computing the period of limitation, the relevant date must be considered as the date of filing of complaint or initiating criminal proceedings and not the date of taking cognizance by a Magistrate or issuance of process by a court. Further, in *Japani Sahoo*, the Supreme Court declared, "We, therefore, overrule all decisions in which it has been held that the crucial date for computing the period of limitation is taking of cognizance by the Magistrate/Court and not of filing of complaint or initiation of criminal proceedings."

In view of this change in law, the proceedings are not barred by limitation.

Q.187. During the pendency of a criminal complaint under section 138 of the Negotiable Instruments Act (dishonour of cheque), the complainant died. Can the legal representatives of deceased complainant continue proceedings?

Ans. A criminal complaint does not necessarily abate on the death of the complainant. As such, the legal representative of the deceased complainant can be permitted to continue the proceedings. In *Ashwin Nanubhai Vyas* v. *State of Maharashtra*, AIR 1967 SC 983: 1967 Cr LJ 943: AIR 1967 SC 983, it was held by the Supreme Court that, "the power of the court to substitute another prosecution agency (subject to such restrictions as may be found) under section 495 of the Code of Criminal Procedure is always available." In this case the court had allowed the mother to carry on the prosecution after the death of the complainant. It was further held that the Magistrate was right in proceeding with the inquiry by allowing the mother to carry on the prosecution, observing that under section 495, CrPC (old), the mother may continue the prosecution herself or through a pleader. It was further held,

> "We see no reason why we should be astute to find a lacuna in the procedural law by which the trial of such important cases would be stultified by the death of a complainant when all that the section 198 requires is the removal of the bar."

Section 495, Cr.P.C. (old) has been substituted by section 256 of the Cr.P.C., 1973, which reads as under:

"256. *Non-appearance or death of complainant.*—(1) If the summons has been issued on complainant, and on the day appointed for the appearance of the accused, or any day subsequent thereto to which the hearing may be adjourned, the complainant does not appear, the Magistrate shall, notwithstanding anything hereinbefore contained, acquit the accused, unless for some reason he thinks it proper to adjourn the hearing of the case to some other day; provided that where the complainant is represented by a pleader or by the officer conducting the prosecution or where the Magistrate is of the opinion that the personal attendance of the complainant is not necessary, the Magistrate may dispense with his attendance and proceed with the case.

(2) The provisions of sub-section (1) shall so far as may be, apply also to cases where the non-appearance of the complainant is due to his death."

Relying upon the aforesaid Supreme Court judgment, the Punjab and Haryana High Court, in *Bhag Singh* v. *State of Punjab*, 2001 Cr LJ 2997: 2001 (4) All Cri LR 521: 2001 (2) Chand Cri C 347, held that, " .. ... it would be clear that under sub-section (1), where the complainant is absent from the court, the Magistrate is competent to adjourn the hearing of a case to some other day and where the complainant is represented by a counsel and where the Magistrate is of the opinion that the personal presence of the complainant is not necessary, the Magistrate is empowered to dispense with the attendance of the complainant and to proceed with the case. Under sub-section (2), it is provided that the provisions of sub-section (1) shall also apply to the cases where the non-appearance of the complainant is due to his death. Under these circumstances, it would be clear that the Magistrate is competent to proceed with the criminal complaint, even where the complainant is absent due to his death."

In *S. Reddappa* v. *M. Vijaya*, 1997 (1) CCC 248 (Karn), the complainant had filed a criminal complaint before the Magistrate under section 138 of the Negotiable Instruments Act. After recording preliminary evidence of the complainant, the Magistrate ordered summoning of the accused. Thereafter, the charge was framed and the case was fixed for evidence. Meanwhile, the complainant died and subsequently his son filed an application praying the court to substitute him in place of the complainant and to permit him to continue the proceedings. The said application was opposed by the accused. After hearing both the sides, the learned Magistrate dismissed the application filed by the son of the complainant and acquitted the accused. Aggrieved against the same, a revision petition was filed before the Karnataka High Court. After hearing both the sides, the Karnataka High Court allowed the revision petition, set aside the order passed by the trial Magistrate and remitted the case to the trial Magistrate, with a direction to take up the case at its original number and to grant permission to the petitioner to continue the proceedings from the stage at which these were interrupted and to dispose of the same in accordance with law. While allowing the said revision petition, it was held by the Karnataka High Court that on reading whole of the sections 256 and 302, Cr. P.C. 1973, and keeping in mind that a criminal case does not abate on the death of the complainant, section 256, Cr. P.C., empowers the Magistrate in a given case to permit a fit and proper person to continue the prosecution on the death of the complainant.

In *Associated Cement Companies* v. *Keshvanand,* (1998) 1 SCC 687: AIR 1998 SC 596: 1998 Cr LJ 856, the Supreme Court ruled, "The above scheme of the new Code makes it clear that complainant must be a corporeal person who is capable of making physical presence in the court. Its corollary is that even if a complaint is made in the name of an incorporeal person (like a company or corporation) it is necessary that a natural person represents such juristic person in the court and it is that natural person who is looked upon, for all practical purposes to be the complainant in the case. In other words, when the component to a body corporate it is the *de jure* complainant, and it must necessarily associate a human being as *de facto* complainant to represent the former in court proceedings.

Q.188. Can a case under Negotiable Instruments Act be filed through a power of attorney when it relates to a cheque not filled in with the own hand-writing of the complainant?

Ans. The Supreme Court in *Shankar Finance and Investments* v. *State of Andhra Pradesh,* (2008) 8 SCC 536 followed in *Praveen* v. *Mohd. Tajuddin,* (2009) 12 SCC 706 has held that a compliant under section 138 of the Negotiable Instruments Act, can be filed by the payee through his power of attorney holder.

It was held, "Where the proprietor of the proprietary concern has personal knowledge of the transaction and the proprietor has signed the complaint, he has to be examined under section 200 of the Code. A power of attorney holder of the complainant who does not have personal knowledge, cannot be examined. But where the attorney holder of the complainant is in charge of the business of the payee-complainant and the Attorney holder alone is personally aware of the transactions, and the complaint is signed by the attorney holder on behalf of the payee-complainant, there is no reason why the attorney holder cannot be examined as the complainant. We may, in this connection, refer to the decision of this court in *Janki Vashdeo Bhojwani* v. *Indusind Bank Ltd.,* (2005) 2 SCC 217: AIR 2005 SC 439: 2004 AIR SCW 7064, where the scope of an attorney holder acting on behalf of the principal in a civil suit governed by Code of Civil Procedure was examined. This court observed:

> "Order 3, rules 1 and 2, CPC empower the holder of power of attorney to "act" on behalf of the principal. In our view the word "acts" employed in Order 3, rules 1 and 2, CPC confines only to in respect of "acts" done by them, power-of-attorney holder, in exercise of power granted by the instrument. The term "acts" would not include deposing in place and instead of the principal. In other words, if the power-of-attorney holder has rendered some "acts" in pursuance of power of attorney, he may depose for the principal in respect of such acts, but he cannot depose for the principal for the acts done by the principal and not by him. Similarly, he cannot depose for the principal in respect of the matter of which only the principal can have a personal knowledge and in respect of which the principal is entitled to be cross-examined."

"The principle underlying the said observations will apply to cases under section 138 of the Act. In regard to business transactions of companies, partnerships or proprietary concerns, many a time the authorized agent or attorney holder may be the only person having personal knowledge of the particular transaction; and if the authorized agent or attorney-holder has signed the complaint, it will be absurd to say that he should not be examined under section 200 of the Code, and only the Secretary of the company or the partner of the firm or the proprietor of a concern, who did not have personal knowledge of the transaction, should be examined."

It is not necessary that body of the cheque must necessarily be written by the person who has signed the cheque. It can be in the handwriting of anybody else or typed on a type machine or by computer printing so long as the person signing the cheque does not dispute the genuineness of his signatures on the cheque in question. What is material is signatures of the drawer or maker and not the body-writing. The same view was reiterated by the High Court of A.P. in *D. Atchyutha Reddy* v. *State of Andhra Pradesh,* 2010 (2) RCR (Cri) 860.

Q.189. A person convicted under section 138 Negotiable Instruments Act, compromised with the complainant during pendency of the appeal by paying the disputed amount. Can any mileage be gained by the convict during appeal?

Ans. Section 138 of Negotiable Instrument Act, 1881 is compoundable. The conviction and sentence can be set aside on the basis of compromise.

After taking note of the fact that the complainant keeps on delaying the proceedings and then enter into compromise, and in order to mitigate the sufferings of check-holders, the Supreme Court held as under in *Damodar S. Prabhu* v. *Sayeed Babalal,* (2010) 5 SCC 663

"With regard to the progression of litigation in cheque bouncing cases, the learned Attorney General has urged this court to frame guidelines for a graded scheme of imposing costs on parties who unduly delay compounding of the offence. It was submitted that the requirement of deposit of the costs will act as a deterrent for delayed composition, since at present, free and easy compounding of offences at any stage, however belated, gives an incentive to the drawer of the cheque to delay settling the cases for years. An application for compounding made after several years not only results in the system being burdened but the complainant is also deprived of effective justice. In view of this submission, we direct that the following guidelines be followed:—

(a) That directions can be given that the Writ of Summons be suitably modified making it clear to the accused that he could make an application for compounding of the offences at the first or second hearing of the case and that if such an application is made, compounding may be allowed by the court without imposing any costs on the accused.

(b) If the accused does not make an application for compounding as aforesaid, then if an application for compounding is made before the

Magistrate at a subsequent stage, compounding can be allowed subject to the condition that the accused will be required to pay 10% of the cheque amount to be deposited as a condition for compounding with the Legal Services Authority, or such authority as the court deems fit.

(c) Similarly, if the application for compounding is made before the Sessions Court or a High Court in revision or appeal, such compounding may be allowed on the condition that the accused pays 15% of the cheque amount by way of costs.

(d) Finally, if the application for compounding is made before the Supreme Court, the figure would increase to 20% of the cheque amount."

Q.190. A person was convicted under the Negotiable Instruments Act, on the basis of notice received by his wife during his absence. Is the conviction maintainable?

Ans. In *M.D. Thomas* v. *P.S Jaleeland*, (2009) 14 SCC 398, the Supreme Court held that, "Proviso to section 138 specifies the conditions which are required to be satisfied before a person can be convicted for an offence enumerated in the substantive part of the section. clause (b) of the proviso to section 138 cast on the payee or the holder in due course of the cheque, as the case may be, a duty to make a demand for payment of the said amount of money by giving a notice in writing, to the drawer of the cheque, within thirty days of the receipt of information by him from the bank regarding the return of the cheque as unpaid. In the present case, the notice of demand was served upon the wife of the appellant and not the appellant. Therefore, there is no escape from the conclusion that complainant-respondent had not complied with the requirement of giving notice in terms of clause (b) of proviso to section 138 of the Act."

Q.191. Whether a notice of demand under section 138 of Negotiable Instruments Act, sent to the accused by e-mail, constitute a valid service under the Act?

Ans. A notice demanding payment of amount represented by a dishonored cheque can be sent by E-mail also. No format is prescribed under the Act in respect of such demand notice. The Bombay High Court in *M/s Paul Dias and Sons* v. *M/s SDS Shipping Pvt. Ltd.*, 2010 (2) RCR (Cri) 207 held that an e-mail sent to the accused was a valid notice under section 138 of Negotiable Instruments Act.

70. Scheduled Castes and Scheduled Tribes Act, 1989

Q.192. A person belonging to the Scheduled Caste, invited in a party, was insulted on the basis of his caste. On his complaint under section 3 of Scheduled Caste and Scheduled Tribe Act, 1989, the court discharged the accused on the ground that the incident did not take place in a public place. Please advise.

Ans. The order of the Trial Court discharging the accused is not legally sustainable. A bare reading of the said section 3(1)(x) of Scheduled Caste and Scheduled Tribe Act, 1989 would reveal that such an Act should have been done by the accused at any place within the public view and it is not necessary that it should be a public place. The Legislature, in its wisdom, has used the word "in any place within the public view" in section 3(1)(x) of the Act instead of using the word public place. Section 3(1)(x) of the Scheduled Caste & Scheduled Tribe Act lays down that: "Whoever, not being a member of a Scheduled Caste or a Scheduled Tribe, intentionally insults or intimidates with intent to humiliate a member of a Scheduled Caste or a Scheduled Tribe in any place within public view shall be punishable with imprisonment for a term which shall not be less than six months but which may extend to five years and with fine."

Although somebody's residence is not a public place, yet if he invites members of public to a wedding or some social function to his house, it becomes a place within the public view. In *E. Tirupem Reddy* v. *Dy Supdt. of Police Nandy*, 2006 (3) RCR (Cri) 435, a Division Bench of the Andhra Pradesh High Court has held:

> "Again a mistake was committed in taking the term "in a place within the public view" as a "public place". A public place is a place where the public generally are permitted to assemble, but somebody's office, chamber or residence can never be a public place. The learned single Judge in this judgment has correctly come to the conclusion, while taking the definition of "public" from section 12 of the Indian Penal Code, that public place is a place where ordinarily the public visit for some purpose or other than with uninterrupted regularity though not continuously, but a mistake was committed when the term "within the public view" was taken as synonymous to "place within public view". For instance, somebody's residential house is not a public place, but if somebody invites members of public to a wedding in his house, it becomes, on that count, a place within the public view, though it does not become a public place. The distinction is unambiguous between the terms "public place" and "within the public view". Private places, as opposed to public places, can become places within the public view. The learned single Judge in this judgment also mentioned the definition of "place within the public view" as contained in Words and Phrases (Vol. 35A Permanent Edition West Publishing Company, 2002 Cumulative Supplementary Pamphlet, P51) that the term "in view of the public" has been defined as under, "When accused exposed himself to a babysitter in his bedroom, he exposed himself to "public view" as required for offense of indecent exposure, since term does not mean a "public place" but "in view of the pubic".

71. Oaths Act

Q.193. What is the evidentiary value of a statement made by a person under oath administered to him under the Oaths Act, 1969?

Ans. An oath administered to a person is binding on the parties and constitutes 'admission' under section 20 of the Evidence Act which reads as under:

> "20 *Admissions by persons expressly referred to by party to suit.*—Statements made by persons to whom a party to the suit has expressly referred for information in reference to a matter in dispute are admissions.

Illustration

The question is, whether a horse sold by A to B is sound.

A says to *B* "Go and ask *C*, *C* knows all about it. *C's* statement is an admission."

In *Hirachand Kothari (dead) by Lrs* v. *State of Rajasthan*, (1985) (Supp) SCC 17, the Supreme Court held thus "section 20 is the second exception to the general rule laid down in section 18. It deals with one class of vicarious admissions. Where a party refers to a third person for some information or an opinion on matter in dispute, the statements made by the third person are receivable as admission against the person referring. The word `informa- tion' occurring in section 20 is not to be understood in the sense that the parties desired to know something which none of them had any knowledge of. Where there is a dispute as regards a certain question and the Court is in need of information regarding the truth on that point any statement which the referee may make is nevertheless information within the purview of section 20 and is admissible. The reason behind admissibility of the statement is that when a party refers to another person for a statement of his views the party approves of the utterance in anticipation and adopts that as his own. The principle is the same as that of reference to arbitration.

The reference under section 20 may be by express words or by conduct but in any case there must be a clear admission to refer and such admission are generally conclusive. Admissions may operate as estoppel and they do so where parties had agreed to abide by them "

The said judgement was cited with approval by the Supreme Court in *K.M. Singh* v. *Secretary, Association of Indian Universities*, (1992) 3 SCC 129: AIR 1992 SC 1356: 1992 AIR SCW 1346 by holding, "the compromise arrived at between the counsel for the plaintiff on behalf of his client and the defendant appellant would be covered by section 20 the Evidence Act and the plaintiff would be bound by the statement made by the defendant if the same is found to have been made strictly in accordance with the terms offered by him"

72. Punjab Excise Act

Q.194. The police recovered three boxes (36 bottles) of liquor from the accused in an Excise case but the investigating officer preferred to take only three representative samples of liquor (sample from one bottle out of each of the three boxes). He did not take sample from each of the recovered bottles. The chemical examination report had been received in respect of only three

samples taken from the three bottles. One is allowed to possess up to six bottles of liquor. Whether the accused can get any benefit?

Ans. The possession by the accused of only three bottles is proved but there is no proof that the remaining 33 bottles also contained liquor. This is below the prescribed limit of six bottles. The accused can get benefit for the lapse of the Investigating Officer. In *Mahajan* v. *State of Himachal Pradesh,* 2003 (2) RCR (Cri) 654: 2003 Cr LJ 1346: 2003 (3) Cur Cri R 490 it was held that the prosecution has to prove that the accused was in conscious possession of IMFL in excess of the prescribed limit of the bottles.

73. Electricity Act

Q.195. A tenant was booked for Electricity theft. The department imposed upon him a penalty of Rs. 50,000. Subsequently, the police also implicated the landlord on charges of criminal conspiracy under section 120B, IPC. Please advise.

Ans. Though the landlord is not liable for the criminal liability, yet he cannot be absolved from the civil liability to pay the penalty imposed by the Electricity department being a registered consumer as the tenant used the electricity with his consent. It is a case of quashing of criminal proceedings in view of law laid down by the Punjab and Haryana High Court in *UHBVNL* v. *Mehtab Singh,* 2006 (4) RCR (Civil) 844.

Q.196. On the allegations by Electricity department that the seal of electric meter was tampered with, the police registered a case under section 379 of

IPC read with section 39 of the Indian Electricity Act. Subsequently, the Electricity Board imposed a penalty of Rs. One lakh. The owner deposited the amount on Board's assurance of compounding the offence. But the police presented challan in the court. Whether accused can be tried for the theft despite payment of penalty amount?

Ans. Since the accused had already deposited the entire penalty amount with the Board, the continuance of criminal proceedings is an abuse of process of law. In similar circumstances the Punjab and Haryana High Court had quashed the criminal proceeding. The following judgments are applicable in the instant case:

1. *Harish Kumar* v. *State of Haryana*, 2003 (3) RCC 784.
2. *Pawan Kumar* v. *State of Haryana*, 2003 (1) RCR (Cri) 104: (2003) 11 SCC 241: 2003 AIR SCW 3671.
3. *Chaman Lal* v. *State of Haryana*, 2000 (1) RCC 143.
4. *Rajnish* v. *State of Haryana*, 2004 (1) RCR (Cri) 739.
5. *Malkiat Singh* v. *State of Punjab*, 2010 (1) RCR (Cri) 876.

74. Gambling Act, 1867

Q.197. A group of friends were playing rummy in a house. The neighbour called the police acussing them of gambling. Police raided the house, seized cash of Rs. 1 lakh, and charged them under the Gambling Act. Please advise.

Ans. The Supreme Court has ruled that rummy is a game of skill and not of chance; it is not an offence under the Gambling Act. In *State of Andhra Pradesh* v. *Satya Narain*, AIR 1968 SC 825: (1968) 2 SCR 387 it was held that, "The game of Rummy is not a game entirely of chance like the 'three-card' game mentioned in the Madras case to which we were referred. The 'three card' game which goes under different names such as 'flash', 'brag' etc. is a game of pure chance. Rummy, on the other hand, requires certain amount of skill because the fall of the cards has to be memorised and the building up of Rummy requires considerable skill in holding and discarding cards. We cannot, therefore, say that the game of Rummy is a game of entire chance. It is mainly and preponderantly a game of skill. The chance in Rummy is of the same character as the chance in a deal at a game of bridge. Infact in all games in which cards are shuffled and dealt out, there is an element of chance, because the distribution of the cards is not according to any set pattern but is dependent upon how the cards find their place in the shuffled pack. From this alone it cannot be said that Rummy is a game of chance and there is no skill involved in it. Of course, if there is evidence of gambling in some other way or that the owner of the house or the club is making a profit or gain from the game of Rummy or any other game played for stakes, the offence may be brought home."

Q.198. In a club members used to play rummy with stakes. The police warned its members against indulging in gambling. Please advise?

Ans. In order to prove gambling it must be established that:

(i) the game being played was a game of chance.

(ii) It was being played with stakes.

Since rummy is mainly a game of skill and not of chance, as held by the Supreme Court in *State of Bombay* v. *RMD Chamarbaugwala,* AIR 1957 SC 699: 1957 SCJ 607: 1957 SCA 867 and in *K.R. Lakshaman* v. *State of Tamil Nadu,* (1996) 2 SCC 226, no offence under the Gambling Act is made out against the club members.

In *D. Krishna Kumar* v. *State of Andhra Pradesh,* 2003 (1) RCR (Cri) 761: 2003 Cr LJ 143 the Andhra Pradesh held that, "In view of section 15 of the Act, the provisions of the Act do not apply to game of rummy, which is to be treated as a game of skill only. Therefore, the question whether the management of the club or the club is making profits, and what is the rate of profit that is being made from out of the game of rummy with 13 cards/syndicate may not be of any relevance. Therefore, even if the petitioners, who are running the club that was raided by the police, were making profits by allowing persons to use the premises for playing the game of rummy with 13 cards/syndicate, they cannot be said to be running a 'common gaining house' as defined in section 3 of the Act, because section 3 of the Act, in view of section 15 of the Act, does not apply to a place where Rummy is being played."

However, in case one plays the game of 'flash' with stakes, which is definitely a game of chance, one can be booked under section 13 of the Act.

75. Dowry Prohibition Act, 1961

Q.199. A girl's in-laws demanded Rs. 10,000 and a gold ring at the time of child birth on the pretext of their family customs. Whether the girl or her parents can take any legal action for this demand?

Ans. Any payment made after the marriage and which is a customary payment *i.e.*, given at the time of birth of a child or other ceremonies as are prevalent in different societies are not covered by the expression 'dowry'. However, if the demand is coupled with harassment of the girl in any manner, it will constitute 'cruelty' within the meaning of section 498A, IPC. Thus, if the girl has suffered any kind of cruelty, she or her parents may lodge a report with the local police for appropriate action.

It has been held by the Supreme Court in *Kamlesh Panjiyar* v. *State of Bihar*, (2005) 2 SCC 388: AIR 2005 SC 785: 2005 Cr LJ 1418 that, "There are three occasions related to dowry. One is before the marriage, second is at the time of marriage and the third "at any time" after the marriage. The third occasion may appear to be unending period. But the crucial words are "in connection with the marriage of the said parties". Other payments which are customary payments *e.g.*, given at the time of birth of a child or other ceremonies as are prevalent in different societies are not covered by the expression "dowry".

There is thus, in law, a clear demarcation between 'demand' and 'customary payments'. Whereas 'customary payments' by girl's family will not constitute 'dowry', any demand from the girl or her parents will be covered within the mischief of dowry more particularly if the demand is persisted and followed by harassment of the girl.

Q.200. After five years of marriage, a girl married at Delhi shifted to Ambala at her parent's residence on account of harassment for dowry by her in-laws. Can she lodge FIR under sections 406, 498A of I.P.C at Ambala? Whether the demand for return of her 'istridhan' is time barred?

Ans. Section 181(4) of the Code of Criminal Procedure lays down that any offence of criminal misappropriation or of criminal breach of trust may be inquired into or tried by a court within whose local jurisdiction the offence was committed or any part of the property which is the subject to the offence was received or retained, or was required or accounted for by the accused person. The courts at the bride's residence has the territorial jurisdiction to try the offence punishable under sections 406 and 498A of the IPC as the effect of the physical cruelty in the shape of mental cruelty travels to said place. Section 181(4) of the Cr.P.C. permits the lodging of FIR at Ambala in these circumstances. Secondly, an offence under section 406, IPC, which entitles a girl to demand return of her 'istridhan' is a continuing offence and therefore, the demand is not time-barred.

The law on the point has been fully explained by the Punjab and Haryana High Court in *Dayal Arora* v. *Renu Arora,* 2007 (3) RCR (Cri) 10 (P&H) holding that ".. the matrimonial courts at the bride's residence have the jurisdiction to try the offences both under sections 406 and 498A, Indian Penal Code. ... We find an element of continuance in the offence of criminal misappropriation in view of the extended definition of 'stolen property'. The offence continues until the property which has been criminally misappropriated is restored to the true owner. ... the offence under section 406 of the Indian Penal Code is a continuing offence."

76. Prevention of Corruption Act

Q.201. On the basis of an anonymous complaint, the police registered a case of assets disproportionate to known sources of income under section 13(1)(e) of Prevention of Corruption Act, 1988. During investigation, the police found that assets acquired were held in the name of the wife. Now the police have challaned her also for abetment under section 109, IPC read with section 13(1)(e) of the Prevention of Corruption Act, 1988. Please advise.

Ans. The Supreme Court in *P. Nallammal* v. *State,* (1999) 6 SCC 559: 1999 AIR SCW 2725: 1999 Cr LJ 3967 has held that if an offence under section 13(1)(e) is abetted by a private person, he can also be prosecuted with the public servant. The court observed, "If a non-public servant is also a member of the criminal conspiracy for a public servant to commit any offence under the P.C. Act, or if such non-public servant has abetted any of the offences which the public servant commits, such non-public servant is also liable to be tried alongwith the public servant..."

In similar circumstances, the Andhra Pradesh High Court in *State represented by CBI* v. *D.J. Prabhakar Anand,* 2006 (1) RCR (Cri) 516 has allowed the application of CBI holding that the wife cannot be discharged from the charge of being an abettor of the crime and cognizance has to be taken against her.

Q.202. A case under section 5(2) of Prevention of Corruption Act, was registered in 1987. The charges were framed under the old Act. Later in 1988, the new Act (Prevention of Corruption Act, 1988) came into force on 9-9-1988. Can the accused be tried and convicted under the provisions of old Act of 1947 which stands repealed with the coming into force of the new Act?

Ans. In view of the saving clause of section 30(2) of the new Act, 1988 read with Article 20(1) of the Constitution of India, the prosecution of the accused under the old Act of 1947 is legally permissible even subsequent to its repeal.

Q.203. A case was being investigated by an inspector duly authorized by the State Government under the old Prevention of Corruption Act, 1947. In 1988 the new Prevention of Corruption Act, came into force repealing the old Act of 1947. No fresh Notification was issued by the Government under the

new Act of 1988. Can the investigation be continued by Inspector authorized under old Act?

Ans. The notification issued by the State Government under the old Act *i.e.*, of 1947 is saved by section 30(2) of the new Act of 1988 read with sections 6(b) and 24 of the General Clauses Act, 1897. As there is no inconsistency between section 5A of the old Act under which the said notification was issued and section 17 of the new Act of 1988, the earlier notification would remain in force and would be deemed to have been issued under the new Act till the same is superseded or specifically withdrawn. The Supreme Court held in *State of Punjab* v. *Harnek Singh*, (2002) 3 SCC 481: AIR 2002 SC 1074: 2002 Cr LJ 1494 "....the notifications issued by the Government of Punjab, in exercise of the powers conferred under section 5A of the 1947 Act, empowering and authorising the Inspectors of Police posted in Special Inquiry Agency of the Vigilance Department, Govt. of Punjab to investigate the cases registered under the said Act were saved under the saving provision of the re-enacted 1988 Act. Such notifications are not inconsistent with the provisions of re-enacted Act and are deemed to continue in force as having been issued under the re-enacted 1988 Act till the aforesaid notifications are specifically superseded or withdrawn or modified under the 1988 Act. The investigation conducted by the Inspectors of Police authorised in that behalf under the 1947 Act are held to be proper, legal and valid investigation under the re-enacted Act and do not suffer from any vice of illegality or jurisdiction."

Q.204. A person was falsely implicated in a corruption case at the instance of his colleague. In his absence, some currency notes were placed in his office drawer. Can he be convicted?

Ans. Merely finding money in a drawer is no proof of acceptance of illegal gratification especially when the accused pleads that the notes were put in the drawer without his knowledge. However, in case it is found and proved that the currency notes were handled by the accused and were placed in the drawer, he can be convicted. For this purpose, the police generally applies phenolphthalein powder test. In case this test is found positive, then the accused can be held guilty with the help of other corroborative evidence. In the absence of any such evidence, he may get benefit of doubt.

In *M.K. Harshan* v. *State of Kerala*, (1996) 11 SCC 720: AIR 1995 SC 2178: 1995 AIR SCW 3385, the Supreme Court ruled: "In all this type of cases of bribery, two aspects are important. Firstly, there must be a demand and secondly there must be acceptance in the sense that the accused has obtained the illegal gratification. Mere demand by itself is not sufficient to establish the offence. Therefore, the other aspect, namely, acceptance is very important and when the accused has come forward with a plea that the currency notes were put in the drawer without his knowledge, then there must be clinching evidence to show that it was with the tacit approval of the accused the money had been put in the drawer as an illegal gratification. .... By preponderance of probabilities, the accused has sufficiently shown that the plea put forward by him, namely, that in his absence somebody else might have put the tainted money in his drawer, is plausible."

77. Post Office Act

Q.205. Indira Vikas Patras worth Rs. 10,000 were eaten-up by moths. However, their record along with serial numbers remained intact. The Post Office refused to issue duplicate Patras. Please advise.

Ans. The refusal on the part of the Postal Authorities is in accordance with the rule 7(2) of Indira Vikas Patra Rules, 1986 which reads: "A certificate lost, stolen, mutilated defaced or destroyed beyond recognition will not be replaced by any Post Office."

In *Central Government of India* v. *Krishnaji Parvetesh Kulkarni*, (2006) 4 SCC 275: AIR 2006 SC 1744: 2006 AIR SCW 1946 the Supreme Court had held that, "An IVP is akin to an ordinary currency note. It bears no name of the holder. Just as a lost currency note cannot be replaced, similarly the question of replacing a lost IVP does not arise."

78. Juvenile Justice Act

Q.206. Five accused were facing trial. One of them claimed to be a "juvenile', as on the date of alleged occurrence he was 17 years and 11 months as per his school certificate, whereas in the voter list his age has been shown as 19 years. The court rejected application of the "juvenile" seeking trial under Juvenile Justice Act. Please guide.

Ans. The entry made in the High school register is presumed to be correct and the burden lies on the person who disputes its correctness to prove it otherwise. It has been held by various High Courts that the entry of age in the voters list is not a conclusive piece of evidence because it is a matter of common knowledge that the age of voters in the voter list/electoral list is entered on the basis of enquiries made by the government employees who are put on such duty temporarily. It is also a common knowledge that there is general tendency to somewhat exaggerate the age of minors when the electoral rolls are prepared and elections are round the corner, with an intention to include their minor children also in the voters list. The High Court of Allahabad has expressed similar views in *Mayank Rajput* v. *State of Uttar Pradesh,* 1998 (3) RCR (Cri) 227. In *Surendra Kumar* v. *State of Rajasthan,* 2009 (1) RCR (Cri) 112, Rajasthan High Court held that age recorded in voters list cannot be relied has also taken similar view.

79. Protection of Women from Domestic Violence Act

Q.207. The victim was maltreated and was driven out of the matrimonial home after about one year of marriage in 2005. A Petition was filed under section 12 of the Protection of Woman from Domestic Violence Act, 2005. The husband took the objection that complaint was not maintainable because the alleged acts of domestic violence took place prior to enactment of the said Act which was enforced on 26-10-2006. The court dismissed the complaint. Whether the order is legally sustainable?

Ans. A petition under the Protection of Women from Domestic Violence Act, 2005 is maintainable even if the acts of domestic violence were committed prior to the coming into force of the said Act. It has retrospective effect. In *Savita Bhanot* v. *Lt. Col. V.D. Bhanot*, 2010 (2) RCR (Cri) 872 (Del), it was held by the Delhi High Court that, "...a petition under the provisions of the Protection of Women from Domestic Violence Act, 2005 is maintainable even if the acts of domestic violence have been committed prior to coming into force of the Act or despite her having in the past lived together with the respondent and shared household, woman is no more living with him at the time of coming into force of the Act. It is be open for the Magistrate to pass appropriate order under the provisions of sections 12, 18, 19, 20, 21, 22 or 23 of the Act on a petition filed by such a woman and the person who commits breach of the protection order or interim protection order passed on an application filed by such a woman will be liable to punishment under section 31 of the Act." Similar view was taken by the Andhra Pradesh High Court in *Mohit Yadam* v. *State of Andhra Pradesh,* 2010 (2) RCR (Cri) 780 (AP).

Q.208. A married woman made a complaint against her in-laws under section 12 of the Protection of Woman from Domestic Violence Act, 2005 on the allegations of domestic violence. Can the complaint be quashed by the High Court?

Ans. Relatives of a husband, including female relatives, can be booked under the Domestic Violence Act on a complaint lodged by the wife. In *Sandhya Manoj Wankhade* v. *Manoj Bhimrao Wankhade,* (2011) 3 SCC 650, the Supreme Court set aside the concurrent orders of a Sessions Court and the Bombay High Court to the effect that female relatives of the husband cannot be booked under the Act as the legislation was meant only against the husband or any other male member. The court observed,

> "No restrictive meaning has been given to the expression 'relative' nor has the said expression been specifically defined in the Domestic Violence Act, 2005, to make it specific to males only............
>
> In such circumstances, it is clear that the legislature never intended to exclude female relatives of the husband or male partner from the ambit of a complaint that can be made under the provisions of the Domestic Violence Act, 2005."

Q. 209. Despite receiving a handsome amount of dowry, a husband did not provide sufficient money to the wife for meeting her personal expenses. Can the wife make a complaint of "domestic violence"?

Ans. Section 3 of the Protection of Women From Domestic Violence Act, 2005 defines "domestic violence" as follows:

"For the purposes of this Act, any act, omission or commission or conduct of the respondent shall constitute domestic violence in case it—

(a) harms or injures or endangers the health, safety, life, limb or well-being, whether mental or physical, of the aggrieved person or tends to do so and includes causing physical abuse, sexual abuse, verbal and emotional abuse and economic abuse; or

(b) harasses, harms, injures or endangers the aggrieved person with a view to coerce her or any other person related to her to meet any unlawful demand for any dowry or other property or valuable security; or

(c) has the effect of threatening the aggrieved person or any person related to her by any conduct mentioned in clause (a) or clause (b); or

(d) otherwise injures or causes harm, whether physical or mental, to the aggrieved person.

Explanation I.—For the purposes of this section,—

(i) "physical abuse" means any act or conduct which is of such a nature as to cause bodily pain, harm, or danger to life, limb, or health or impair the health or development of the aggrieved person and includes assault, criminal intimidation and criminal force;

(ii) "sexual abuse" includes any conduct of a sexual nature that abuses, humiliates, degrades or otherwise violates the dignity of woman;

(iii) "verbal and emotional abuse" includes—

(a) insults, ridicule, humiliation, name calling and insults or ridicule specially with regard to not having a child or a male child; and

(b) repeated threats to cause physical pain to any person in whom the aggrieved person is interested.

(iv) "economic abuse" includes—

(a) deprivation of all or any economic or financial resources to which the aggrieved person is entitled under any law or custom whether payable under an order of a court or otherwise or which the aggrieved person requires out of necessity including, but not limited to, household necessities for the aggrieved person and her children, if any, stridhan, property, jointly or separately owned by the aggrieved person, payment of rental related to the shared household and maintenance;

(b) disposal of household effects, any alienation of assets whether movable or immovable, valuables, shares, securities, bonds and the like or other property in which the aggrieved person has an interest or is entitled to use by virtue of the domestic relationship or which may be reasonably required by the aggrieved person or her children or her stridhan or any other property jointly or separately held by the aggrieved person; and

(c) prohibition or restriction to continued access to resources or facilities which the aggrieved person is entitled to use or enjoy by virtue of the domestic relationship including access to the shared household.

Explanation II.—For the purpose of determining whether any act, omission, commission or conduct of the respondent constitutes "domestic violence" under this section, the overall facts and circumstances of the case shall be taken into consideration."

Thus a complaint against the husband can be made.

80. Live-in Relationship

Q.210. What is a 'live-in relationship'? Can a woman living with a man in 'live-in relationship' claim maintenance from her male partner?

Ans. A relationship between a man and a woman living as husband and wife, without performance of matrimonial rites, is called as 'live-in relationship'.

In *D. Velasamy* v. *D. Patchaiammel,* (2010) 10 SCC 469, the Supreme Court held that 'relationship in the nature of marriage' is akin to a common law marriage which require that although not being formally married—

(a) The couple must hold themselves out to society as being akin to spouses.

(b) They must be of legal age to marry.

(c) They must be otherwise qualified to enter into a legal marriage, including being unmarried.

(d) They must have voluntarily cohabited and held themselves out to the world as being akin to spouses for a significant period of time.

In *Savitaben Somabhat Bhatiya* v. *State of Gujarat*, AIR 2005 SC 1809: 2005 AIR SCW 1601: 2005 Cr LJ 2141, the Supreme Court held that however desirable it may be to take note of the plight of an unfortunate woman, who unwittingly enters into wedlock with a married man, there is no scope to include a woman not lawfully married within the expression of 'wife'. The Bench held that this inadequacy in law can be amended only by the Legislature.

Subsequent to this judgment, the 'live-in' relationship was given legal recognition by the Parliament in Protection of Domestic Violence Act, 2005. Section 20(3) of this Act provides that if a woman had been living with the man like a wife, she would be entitled to claim maintenance. The Supreme Court has held that a 'maid' living with his employer in 'live-in relationship' having given birth to his child, is entitled to maintenance.

81. Motor Vehicles Act

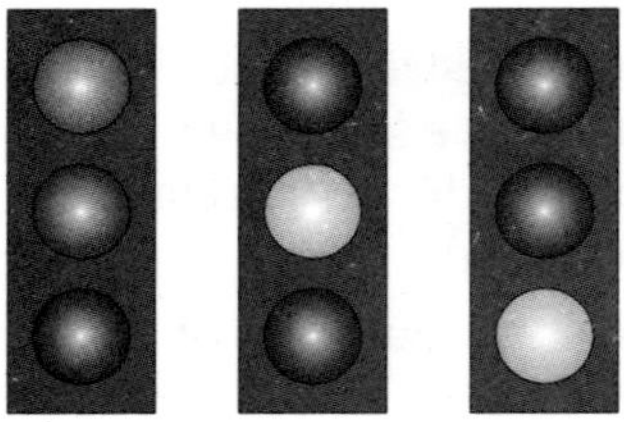

Q.211. A servant lost his life while riding a tractor, which overturned due to rash and negligent driving of the owner. The insurance company rejected the claim for compensation stating that it was not liable since the deceased was travelling in a goods carriage. The legal representative of the deceased have filed a claim petition in the Motor Accident Claims Tribunal claiming compensation from the owner as well as the insurance company. Is the company liable?

Ans. A tractor falls within the category of "goods vehicle". The Supreme Court in *New India Assurance Co. Ltd.* v. *Vedwati,* (2007) 9 SCC 486: (2007) 3 SCALE 397: AIR 2007 SC 1334, held that insurance company is not liable to pay any compensation for death of a traveler riding a tractor. The court held, "The difference in the language of "goods vehicle" as appear in the old Act and "goods carriage" in the Act is of significance. A bare reading of the provisions makes it clear that the legislative intent was to prohibit goods vehicle from carrying any passenger. This is clear from the expression "in addition to passengers" as contained in definition of "good vehicle" in the old Act. The position becomes further clear because the expression used is "good carriage" is solely for the carriage of goods. Carrying of passengers in a goods carriage is not contemplated in the Act. There is no provision similar to clause (ii) of the proviso appended to section 95 of the old Act prescribing requirement of insurance policy. Even section 147 of the Act mandates compulsory coverage against death of or bodily injury to any passenger of "public service vehicle". The proviso makes it further clear that compulsory coverage in respect of drivers and conductors of public service vehicle and employees carried in goods vehicle would be limited to liability under the Workmen's Compensation Act, 1923 (in short 'WC Act"). There is no reference to any passenger in "goods carriage". ... The inevitable conclusion, therefore, is that provisions of the Act do not enjoin any statutory liability on the owner of a vehicle to get his vehicle insured for any passenger travelling in a goods carriage and the insurer would have no liability therefor."

Thus the insurance company cannot be saddled with any liability.

Q.212. Can a claim petition be filed under the Motor Vehicles Act, when the police did not register an FIR against the driver of the car.

Ans. The provisions regarding claim under the Motor Vehicles Act, have been enacted by keeping in view the social welfare justice. Whenever an accident takes place causing injuries to any person, the victim is entitled to get compensation, irrespective of the fact whether the police registered an FIR or not. No claim case can be left over to the mercy of the police. The following cases supports this view: (1) *Brestu Ram* v. *Anant Ram,* 1999 ACJ 333; (2) *Yashwant Singh Baghel* v. *Shiv Parshad,* 2006 (1) RCR (Civil) 373 (MP).

Q.213. The claim tribunal in an accident case awarded compensation to the tune of Rs. 2.5 lakhs under the head of permanent disability, but it rejected the claim under the head of loss of earning capacity. Is the order legally sustainable?

Ans. As loss of earning power is one of the consequences that follows permanent disability, order of the Tribunal denying compensation under the head of loss of earning capacity while allowing compensation for permanent disability is legally sustainable. A similar view was taken by a Full Bench of the Kerala High Court in *Oriental Insurance Company Ltd.* v. *Hari Parshad,* 2006 (1) RCR (Civil) 419 (Ker). Thus, "we find that, (1) Loss of earning power is one of the consequences that follows from a permanent disability; (2) Permanent disability is a physical impairment which results in distinct personal, social and financial consequences to be classified as one head requiring compensation to be worked out as one entitling for non-pecuniary damages; (3) An injured, who sustained a disability is entitled to claim compensation under the head "permanent disability". If the resultant deprivation is categorized and claim is made under separate heads and compensation is awarded under the above heads, over and above the same, for the deprivation suffered compensation is not to be granted under the general head "permanent disability"; (4) all the eventualities that may surface on account of a disability, which deserve to be compensated may not be possible to be catalogued and essentially the Tribunal has to determine the claim bearing in mind the statutory mandate that what is payable is a just compensation; and (5) While awarding compensation under the head "permanent disability", the Tribunal should take notice of the loss of earning power, in each individual case, in case a claim, is made as one of the contributory to the total packet of compensation and shall not take into consideration the loss of earning power as a separate head after fixation of compensation for permanent disability."

Q.214. A person travelling in a "Toka/Jugar" (fitter rehra), met with an accident. He filed a claim petition before the Motor Accident Claims Tribunal. The defence pleaded that the claim was not maintainable because 'Jugar' (fitter rehra) was not a 'motor vehicle'. Please guide.

Ans. Section 2(28) of Motor Vehicles Act, 1988, which defines a motor vehicle, reads as under:

> "motor vehicle" or "vehicle" means any mechanically propelled vehicle adapted for use upon roads whether the power of propulsion is transmitted thereto from an external or internal source and includes a chassis to which a body has not been attached and a trailer; but does not include a vehicle running upon fixed rails or a vehicle of a special type adapted for use only or a vehicle having less than four wheels fitted with engine capacity of not exceeding twenty-five cubic centimeters."

A mechanically propelled "Toka/Jugar" also falls within the definition and as such a person who sustains injury in an accident caused by a 'Jugar' is entitled to get compensation. The objection in this case is not tenable. In *Dharamvir* v. *Inderjit*, 2006 (4) RCR (Civil) 65 the Punjab and Haryana High Court held, "A reading of the said section makes it clear that any mechanically propelled vehicle adapted for use on road whether the power of propulsion is transmitted thereto from any external or internal source, would be covered. The word "chassis" has been added to include those vehicles also where the body is yet to be put. The Jugar fits in the definition and, therefore, it cannot be held that the claim petition was not maintainable under the Motor Vehicles Act."

82. Insurance Act

Q.215. The insurance company objected to maintainability of a claim petition on the ground that the company was not informed of sale and transfer of the vehicle by the original owner in favour of the purchaser. Whether this objection of insurance company is legally tenable?

Ans. It is not the transfer of vehicle but the accident which furnished the cause of action and as such, the liability of the insurance company does not cease even if the owner or purchaser fails to give intimation of such transfer to the insurance company. The claimant is entitled to get compensation. The said objection raised by the insurance company is liable to be rejected. In *United India Insurance Co. Ltd.* v. *Tilak Singh*, (2006) 4 SCC 404: AIR 2006 SC 1576: 2006 AIR SCW 1822, the Supreme Court, following a previous 3-Judges Bench judgment in *Rikhi Ram* v. *Sukhrania (Smt.)*, [2003] 3 SCC 97: AIR 2003 SC 1446: 2003 AIR SCW 780, held, "the liability of an insurer does not cease even if the owner or purchaser fails to give intimation of transfer to the insurance company, as the purpose of the legislation was to protect the rights and interests of the third party."

83. Army Act

Q.216. An army personnel, while on leave, entered into a scuffle resulting in the death of a person. The police registered a case of murder against him and after investigation, filed the challan before the Illaqa Magistrate. He wants to be tried by the Army authorities instead of by the Sessions Judge. What is the legal position?

Ans. It is not in dispute that the personnel was on leave when the incident occurred which meant that he was not on active service within the meaning of section 70 of the Army Act. Moreover, the person who is stated to have been murdered was not subject to military law. As such, provisions of section 475 Cr.P.C. will not be attracted in the case. Refer to the Supreme Court judgment in *Madan Lal* v. *Union of India*, (2002) 10 SCC 185 and judgment of Bombay High Court in *Sandeep @ Sanjay Vithal Shinde* v. *State of Maharashtra*, 2004 (4) RCR (Cri) 863 (Bom).

Q.217. A contractor allotted construction work to another contractor. On the work-site, a worker fell and died on the spot. An FIR under section 304A was lodged against the original contractor. Can the FIR be quashed?

Ans. Section 304A reads: "Whoever causes the death of any person by doing any rash or negligent act not amounting to culpable homicide shall be punished with imprisonment of either description for a term which may extend to two years, or with fine, or with both."

In *Kurban Hussein Mohamedalli* v. *State of Maharashtra*, AIR 1965 SC 1616: 1965 1 SCWR 718: (1965) 2 SCR 622, the Supreme Court ruled, "What section 304A requires is causing of death by doing any rash or negligent act and this means that death must be the direct or proximate result of the rash or negligent act." Similarly, the Punjab and Haryana High Court held in *State of Punjab* v. *Amrit Lal Jain*, 2006 (1) RCR (Cri) 339, dealing with an identical situation held that the owner was not guilty. The Delhi High Court, in *Gulijeet Singh* v. *State*, 2006 (1) RCR (Cri) 618, held that in such circumstances no rash and negligent act could be attributed to the owners who gave a contract to a contractor for construction of a building.

Q.218. A vehicle carrying tourists from India met with an accident in Nepal. Can a claim petition be filed in India?

Ans. Section 1 of the Motor Vehicles Act, 1988 provides that the provisions of the Act would extend to whole of India. Since the accident took place outside the territory of India, the provisions would not be attracted in the present case and as such no Court/Tribunal would entertain any claim petition in India due to lack of jurisdiction. Therefore, the victims may seek his remedy in the competent court of jurisdiction in Nepal. However, it is pertinent to mention that in case Nepalese courts award any compensation, the then insurance company of the bus would be liable to pay.

Q.219. After a love affair lasting three years, the girl refused to marry under family pressure. The boy committed suicide. Can the girl and her parents be tried for abetment to commit suicide?

Ans. It cannot be said that the girl and/or her parents instigated the victim to take the extreme step of committing suicide. Merely, because the family did not agree for marriage with the deceased, it will not amount to abetment to suicide as the victim had taken his life out of frustration. In *Jaikab Pal* v. *State of Punjab,* 2006 (3) RCR (Criminal) 84 in similar circumstances, the Punjab and Haryana High Court quashed the charges against the accused and discharged them under section 306/34 of the IPC.

Q.220. A lady committed suicide within five years of her marriage. She and her husband had been residing separately in a different town. Her father also implicated the in-laws for dowry death under section 304B IPC. Please advise.

Ans. The Courts have noticed that a general tendency has developed for roping in all the members of husband's family in dowry cases and provisions of sections 498A and 304B/306 IPC are being misused. The Courts have deprecated the practice of wholesale implication of husband's relatives in such cases. In *Mrs. Poonam* v. *State of Punjab,* 2007 (2) RCR (Cri) 712, the Punjab and Haryana High Court quashed criminal proceedings under section 498A/406 of IPC against married sister of husband of the deceased.

Earlier, in *Kans Raj* v. *State of Punjab,* (2000) 5 SCC 207: AIR 2000 SC 2324: 2000 AIR SCW 2093, the Supreme Court had ruled: "For the fault of the husband, the in-laws or the other relations cannot, in all cases, be held to be involved in the demand of dowry. In cases where such accusations are made, the overt acts attributed to persons other than husband are required to be proved beyond reasonable doubt. By mere conjectures and implications such relations cannot be held guilty for the offence relating to dowry deaths. A tendency has, however, developed for roping in all relations of the in-laws of the deceased wives in the matters of dowry deaths which, if not discouraged, is likely to affect the case of the prosecution even against the real culprits. In their over enthusiasm and anxiety to seek conviction for maximum people, the parents of the deceased have been found to be making efforts for involving other relations which ultimately weaken the case of the prosecution even against the real accused...."

Q.221. A case originally registered under section 324/34 IPC was later converted to 307 IPC on receipt of x-ray report, and on the doctor declaring the injuries as dangerous to life. During trial, the doctor who conducted the X-ray was not produced. Please advise.

Ans. The accused cannot be convicted under section 307 of the IPC since the X-ray report has not been proved due to non-examination of the radiologist. If the X-ray report is excluded due to non-examination of the radiologist, the opinion of doctor declaring the injury as dangerous to life is not valid. At the most he can be convicted on charges of voluntarily causing hurt by dangerous weapons or means under section 324 of the IPC. [Reference: *State of Haryana* v. *Prem Singh,* 2007 (2) RCR (Cri) 537 (P&H) (DB)]

Q.222. A Bank registered a case under sections 420/468/471 IPC against its employees who were involved in fraud. The accused had deposited the embezzled amount of Rs. 2 lakhs with another bank. Can the police seize the amount from the other bank with whom the amount is deposited and freeze that account?

Ans. The police are competent to seize the said amount or freeze that bank account under sections 102 and 452 of the Cr. P.C. The Supreme Court has held in *State of Maharashtra* v. *Tapas D. Neogy,* (1999) 7 SCC 685 that a police officer has the powers to seize any property which may be found under suspicious circumstances regarding commission of any offence.

Bail of a Juvenile

Q.223. A 15-year-old boy, charged for attempt to murder under section 307 IPC, applied for bail under the Juvenile Justice Act. The Trial Court refused bail on the ground that he has committed a serious offence. During inquiry it was established that accused was a juvenile on the day of alleged offence. He is a first time offender. Please advise.

Ans. Since the accused is a first offender with no criminal background and is a juvenile, he is entitled to bail in view of section 12 of the Juvenile Justice Act, 2000 which reads as under:

> "*12. Bail of juvenile.*—(1) When any person accused of a bailable or non bailable offence, and apparently a juvenile, is arrested or detained or appears or is brought before a Board, such person shall, notwithstanding anything contained in the Code of Criminal Procedure, 1973 (2 of 1974) or

in any other law for the time being in force, be released on bail with or without surety but he shall not be so released if there appear reasonable grounds for believing that the release is likely to bring him into association with any known criminal or expose him to moral, physical or psychological danger or that his release would defeat the ends of justice.

(2) When such person having been arrested is not released on bail under sub-section (1) by the officer incharge of the police station, such officer shall cause him to be kept only in an observation home in the prescribed manner until he can be brought before a Board.

(3) When such person is not released on bail under sub-section (1) by the Board it shall, instead of committing him to prison, make an order sending him to an observation home or a place of safety for such period during the pendency of the enquiry regarding him as may be specified in the order."

Sub-section (1) of section 12 provides that any juvenile accused of a bailable or non-bailable offence if arrested or detained or appeared or brought before the Board, he/she shall be released on bail notwithstanding anything contained in the Code of Criminal Procedure or any other law for the time being in force. The words used by the Legislature like "notwithstanding anything contained in the Code of Criminal Procedure, 1973" or "in any other law for the time being in force", indicate that the considerations which are germane for granting or refusing bail to the persons who are not juvenile delinquents shall not come into play for granting or refusing bail to them". [2001 (1) MPLJ 172, *Rahul Rajendra Mishra* v. *State of Madhya Pradesh*]. The bail can only be denied if it appears that his release is likely to bring him in association with any known criminal or expose him to moral, physical or psychological danger or his release would defeat the ends of justice. It is well-settled that the nature of offence alleged to have been committed by the juvenile is not to be seen while granting bail.

In *Bharat* v. *State of Chhattisgarh,* 2005 (4) MPHT 33 CG, the Chattisgarh High Court held that, "....ordinarily the Board is under obligation to release the juvenile on bail with or without surety, but the juveniles shall not be so released in certain circumstances as the latter part of the section also uses the word "shall" imposing certain mandatory conditions prohibiting the release of the juvenile by the Board. These conditions are as follows:—

(i) if there appears reasonable grounds for believing that the release is likely to bring him into association with any known criminal; or

(ii) expose him to moral, physical or psychological danger; or

(iii) that his release would defeat the ends of justice.

"Therefore, it is clear that when an application is filed by the juvenile for releasing him on bail under section 12 of the Act, ordinarily it would be obligatory on the part of the Board to release him on bail, but he shall not be released on bail if it appears to the Board that either of the 3 conditions, referred to above, is coming in the way of so releasing the applicant or the juvenile on bail. The provisions of section 12 of the Act are balancing from both the sides. On one hand, it creates an obligation on the Board for releasing the juveniles on bail and on the other hand it prohibits the Board from so releasing the juveniles in the particular circumstances enumerated therein. If we divide sub-section (1) of section 12 into two parts— one with relation to obligation to release on bail and the other with relation to prohibitions against the said obligation, we find that the word "shall" used by the Legislature in both the parts is a common factor. The intention of the Legislature in commanding the release of a juvenile on bail is referable to the object of the Legislation, which in fact provides for proper care, protection and treatment by catering to their developmental needs, and by adopting a child friendly approach in the adjudication and disposition of matters in the best interest of the children and for their ultimate rehabilitation through various institutions established under this enactment. Since the enactment is a beneficial legislation, it is for this reason various prohibitions in mandatory forms have been provided in the latter part of section 1(1) of the Act.

"Therefore, it is clear that ordinarily the bail is to be granted to the juvenile under section 12 of the Act, but it shall not be granted to them if it appears to the Board that either of the 3 conditions mentioned above is existing in the matter on the reasonable grounds placed before it."

Q.224. A government employee was charged under the Prevention of Corruption Act but was exonerated in the departmental enquiry. After retirement, the police submitted a challan under section 173 Cr.P.C. Please advise.

Ans. The report of inquiry officer holding the accused innocent in the departmental probe is no ground to drop the criminal proceedings since the scope of departmental inquiry was different. Moreover, the standard of proof required in a departmental inquiry and in a criminal prosecution also differs. Besides, after retirement of a public servant no sanction for prosecution as envisaged by section 19 of the Prevention of Corruption Act, 1988 is required. [Ref: *Sat Pal Joshi* v. *State of Punjab,* 2007 (3) RCR (Cri) 193 P&H HC].

Q.225. A 17 year old was charged with dowry allegations in 2000. After enforcement of Juvenile Justice Act, 2000 he is covered within the definition of a 'juvenile'. Please guide further course of action under the new legislation.

Ans. The Juvenile Justice Act, 2000 came into force w.e.f. April 1, 2001. According to this, a juvenile means a person who has not completed 18 years of age. Earlier, in the old legislation of 1986, the age was 16 years. The age of the offender should be reckoned from the date when the alleged offence was committed. Moreover, the new legislation would be applicable on pending proceedings in any court or authority initiated under the 1986 Act. Since the accused has not completed 18 years on the date of alleged offence and his case is pending when the new Act came into force, he is covered by the provisions of the Juvenile Justice Act, 2000.

Q.226. A lady suffering from depression committed suicide within two years of marriage. Though the husband was charged under section 302, IPC

for murder, he was finally convicted for the dowry death under section 304B IPC. No charge under section 304B was framed earlier. Please advice.

Ans. The offence punishable under section 304B, IPC (*i.e.*, Dowry death) cannot be considered to be minor to section 302, IPC (*i.e.*, murder) and in the absence of specific charge for a distinct offence under section 304B, IPC, the accused cannot be convicted on that account, because the accused does not get any opportunity to place his defence to that charge and that there is a presumption as to dowry death under section 113B of the Indian Evidence Act. In a three-judge Bench judgment, the Supreme Court in *Shamnsaheb M. Multani* v. *State of Karnataka*, (2001) 2 SCC 577: AIR 2001 SC 921: 2001 Cr LJ 1075 held that,".... if the trial court finds that the prosecution has failed to make out the case under section 302 IPC, but the offence under section 304B, IPC has been made out, the court has to call upon the accused to enter on his defence in respect of the said offence. Without affording such an opportunity to the accused, a conviction under section 304B, IPC would lead to real and serious miscarriage of justice. Even if no such count was included in the charge, when the court affords him an opportunity to discharge his burden by putting him to notice regarding the prima facie view of the court that he is liable to be convicted under section 304B, IPC, unless he succeeds in disproving the presumption, it is possible for the court to enter upon a conviction of the said offence in the event of his failure to disprove the presumption."

Q.227. Can a person, sentenced to one month simple imprisonment and fine of Rs. 10,000, under section 138 of the Negotiable Instruments Act, file an appeal without depositing fine?

Ans. An appeal is maintainable without deposit of fine. In *Vijay D. Salvi* v. *State of Maharashtra*, (2007) 5 SCC 741 the Supreme Court held that in the event of non-deposit of fine, the appeal should be decided on merits.

Q.228. An NRI (Non Resident Indian) visiting India had a fight. An FIR was lodged against him and his passport was impounded. Please advise.

Ans. As per sections 10 and 10A of the Passport Act, the police have no powers to impound the passport. Such power vests only in the passport authority and the police have to approach them for impounding the passport in accordance with law. In view of law laid down by the Supreme Court in *Suresh Nanda* v. *CBI,* (2008) 3 SCC 674: AIR 2008 SC 1414: 2008 Cr LJ 1599, an application before the Illaqa Magistrate may be made for return of passport.

Q.229. An accused was convicted and sentenced to undergo rigorous imprisonment for a period of seven years under section 307, IPC. During sentence, he remained on parole for six months. At the time of release after serving six-and-a-half years in jail, the authorities did not count parole period towards the actual sentence. Is the action of authorities legally sustainable?

Ans. The challenge to legality of section 3(3) of the Haryana Good Conduct Prisoners (Temporary Release) Act, 1988, was upheld by the Supreme Court in *Avtar Singh* v. *State of Haryana,* (2002) 3 SCC 18: AIR 2002 SC 1109: 2002 AIR SCW 858. Therefore, action of the authorities in denying the benefit of parole period to the convict is justified as the period of parole cannot be counted towards the actual sentence.

Q.230. Two accused were facing a criminal trial for embezzlement of funds under section 409, IPC. During trial, the co-accused made a confessional statement implicating him in another offence. Can such a statement of the co-accused be read against the accused?

Ans. Under section 30 of the Indian Evidence Act, a confession of an accused is admissible against his co-accused in case the following three conditions are fulfilled:—

- There should be joint trial of the same offence of the maker of the confession and the co-accused.
- There should be a confession of the maker of inculpatory nature (implicating him also in the crime).
- The confession made by one accused should affect him as well the co-accused, meaning that, the person making the confessional statement cannot absolve himself from the said offence and involve his co-accused in it.

Since in the instant case, all the above three conditions appear to be satisfied, thus the confessional statement can be read against others also.

However, such a statement of a co-accused cannot be treated as substantive evidence but only as a corroborative piece of evidence. It was held by the Supreme Court in *Sidharath* v. *State of Bihar,* (2005) 12 SCC 545: AIR 2005 SC 4352: (2005) Cr LJ 4499 that:

> "It is true that the confession made by a co-accused shall not be the sole basis for a conviction. This Court in *Kashmira Singh* v. *The State of Madhya Pradesh,* AIR 1952 SC 159: 1952 Cr LJ 839: 1952 SCR 526 held that the confession of an accused person is not evidence in the ordinary sense of the term as defined in section 3. It cannot be made the foundation of a conviction and can only be used in support of other evidence. The proper way is, first, to marshall the evidence against the accused excluding the confession altogether from consideration and see whether, if it is believed, a conviction

could safely be based on it. If it is capable of belief independently of the confession, then of course it is not necessary to call the confession in aid. But cases may arise where the Judge is not prepared to act on the other evidence as it stands, even though, if believed, it would be sufficient to sustain a conviction. In such an event the Judge may call in aid the confession and use it to lend assurance to the other evidence and thus fortify himself in believing what without the aid of the confession he would not be prepared to accept.

"This view was later followed in *Haricharan Kurmi* v. *State of Bihar,* AIR 1964 SC 1184: (1964) 1 SCWR 446: (1964) 6 SCR 623. The Constitution Bench held that the confession of a co-accused person cannot be treated as substantive evidence and can be pressed into service only when the Court is inclined to accept other evidence and feels the necessity of seeking for an assurance in support of its conclusion deducible from the said evidence.".

Q.231. During the pendency of appeal on conviction in a murder case, the appellant sought parole on the ground of his wife's serious ailment. The authorities refused parole application being not maintainable. Please advise.

Ans. Parole is a form of temporary release of a convict from custody and it is granted in cases of emergency like death, illness of close relative or in the cases of natural calamity such as house collapse, fire or flood. A Constitution Bench of the Supreme Court in *Sunil Fulchand Shah* v. *Union of India,* (2000) 3 SCC 409: AIR 2000 SC 1023: 2000 AIR SCW 582 has categorically observed that parole is a form of temporary release from custody, which does not suspend the sentence or period of detention and as such it would not be covered by section 432 of the Code of Criminal Procedure. A full Bench of the Bombay High Court has also taken a similar view in the case of *S. Sant Singh* v. *Secretary, Home Department, Maharashtra Government,* 2006 (2) RCR (Cri) 677 (Bom). In view of these judgments, the appellant is entitled to parole.

Q.232. In a loan case, the borrower died during the pendency of a notice under section 138, Negotiable Instruments Act. Whether a criminal complaint under section 138, Negotiable Instruments Act can be filed against legal representative of the deceased?

Ans. It is well-settled that criminal liability cannot be fastened to the heirs and the legal representatives of a person, who is said to have been guilty of a criminal offence. Section 118 of the Negotiable Instruments Act, provides that proceedings under section 138 of the said Act cannot be filed against legal representatives of the person who had issued the cheque. The complaint filed by the financer is nothing but abuse of the process of court. The legal representatives may seek quashing of the said complaint by filing a petition under section 482 of the Code of Criminal Procedure. [Reference: *Savita H. Sarode* v. *Rajesh Damidar Sarode,* 2006 (3) RCR (Cri) 216 (Bom)].

Q.233. In a theft case, though the State has not filed any appeal for enhancement of sentence, yet the Appellate Court, while maintaining the conviction order, enhanced the amount of fine to Rs. 6,000, which is beyond the maximum permissible statutory limit of Rs. 5,000 as per section 29(2) of Cr.P.C. Please guide.

Ans. It is a well-settled principle of criminal jurisprudence that the Appellate Court cannot pass sentence beyond the statutory embargo. The jurisdiction in appeal is only limited and the power of the Appellate Court to pass a sentence is measured by the power of the original court from where the judgment in appeal has been preferred. Since the offence of theft under section 379 of the IPC is punishable to a maximum term of three years RI and fine of Rs. 5000 only, the Appellate Court is not competent to enhance the imprisonment beyond three years and the amount of fine beyond Rs. 5000. Reference: (1) *Jagat Bahadur* v. *State of Madhya Pradesh,* AIR 1966 SC 945: 1966 Cr LJ 709: (1966) 2 SCR 822; (2) *Raghu Raj Singh* v. *State of Madhya Pradesh,* 2006 (3) RCR 452 (MP HC).

Q.234. In a trial for house trespass under section 452 I.P.C. (punishable by 7 years), after recording evidence of the injured and statements of the eye-witness, the Magistrate found that an offence under section 458, IPC (punishable by 14 years), triable by Sessions Court, was made out. Before he could be examined in Sessions Court, the injured died in an accident. Is the injured person's statement recorded by the Magistrate admissible in evidence?

Ans. As the judicial proceedings before the trial Magistrate were in respect of the same FIR and the occurrence and complete cross-examination had been conducted on behalf of the accused in that court, so the statement of such victim/injured is relevant and admissible in view of section 33 of the Evidence Act. In *Gurdev Singh* v. *State of Punjab,* 2006 (2) RCR (Cri) 181, the Punjab and Haryana High Court held that statement of a witness made before committing Magistrate is admissible under section 33 of the Evidence Act.

Q.235. Having lost a government job, a person requested his influential father-in-law to procure him a job. His wife committed suicide within seven years of marriage. The girl's father lodged an F.I.R under section 304B alleging torture of his daughter by her husband on the account of non-procurement of the job. Please guide.

Ans. As service is a property it comes within the definition of dowry so *prima facie* an offence under section 304B, IPC is made out. All the three ingredients to constitute the offence of dowry death are present, *viz.,* unnatural death within seven years of marriage, demand for dowry, and harassment of bride due to non-fulfillment of demand for dowry (service). The Jharkhand High Court in *Kamdeo Mehta* v. *State of Bihar,* 2006 (1) RCR (Cri) 495 (now Jharkhand) had taken a similar view where the court has said that yes, demand of service amounts to demand of dowry.

Q.236. One of the prosecution witnesses in a case under sections 406/467/471 of IPC made certain statements before the investigating officer in another case concerning the matter at issue, but the prosecution has not furnished copies of those documents to the accused. Can the defence summon the said statement?

Ans. Court has ample powers under section 91 of Cr.P.C. to summon statements made before the police in another case, if the court considers that

documents in Punjabi. Can the accused ask for the document in Hindi or English so that he can know exact nature of charges leveled against him?

Ans. Code of Criminal Procedure has no provision to supply documents in language known to the accused, so the court cannot accept a request to supply documents in Hindi or English. Police has to supply documents in the language of the court only. One may get documents translated as provided in section 279 (Code of Criminal Procedure). [Refer *Sajal Suresh Kumar Jain* v. *State of Gujarat,* 2005 (4) RCR (Cri) 52].

Q.240. What is a *zimni*? What is its evidentiary value? Can an accused see the *zimni*?

Ans. The case diary, commonly known as *zimni* is recorded by the police so the investigating officer in every case can know what the police officer did, places he visited, whose statements he recorded and what steps he took while conducting investigation. *Zimni* entries are neither substantive nor corroborating evidence and they cannot be used by or against any witness other than the police officer.

The right of the accused to see the *zimni* entries is limited and even that limited scope arises only when the court uses the entries to contradict the police officer or when the police officer uses it for refreshing his memory and then again it is subject to limitations of sections 145 and 161 of the Evidence Act and for that limited purpose only. At the court's discretion, the accused may be permitted to peruse a particular entry. If the court does not use such entries for the purpose of contradicting the police officer or if the police officer does not use the same for refreshing his memory, then the question of an accused getting any right to use the entries even to that limited extent does not arise. Sub-section (3) of section 172, Cr P.C. lays down that neither the accused nor his agents shall be entitled to call for such diaries nor he or they may be entitled to see them merely because they are referred to by the courts. Only if the police officer uses the *zimni* to refresh his memory or if the court uses them for the purpose of contradicting the officer, then in that eventually the accused may be permitted to peruse the case diaries.

Q.241. A trial judge refused to consider certain documents at the time of framing of charge on the ground that the documents may be produced later as defence evidence. Is the order sustainable?

Ans. There is no provision in the Code of Criminal Procedure, which gives a right to the accused to file any material or document at the stage of framing of charge. This right is only granted at the trial stage. The order is legally sustainable. [*State of Orissa* v. *Debendra Nath Padhi,* (2005) 1 SCC 568: AIR 2005 SC 359: 2004 AIR SCW 6813].

Q.242. The police, after investigation, filed a cancellation report which was accepted by the Magistrate. However, after some time, the police submitted an application in the court seeking permission to further investigate the matter. Is such an application maintainable at this stage especially when the Magistrate has already accepted the final police report?

Ans. Even after filing of final report, further investigation can be conducted by the same investigating agency with the permission of the court. It is not necessary to hear the accused before granting such permission. In the case of *Yeshodharan* v. *State of Kerala,* 2004 (3) RCR (Cri) 557 the Kerala High Court held that further investigation can be conducted by the same investigating agency with the permission of the court.

Q.243. During trial, a question arose regarding intricacies of a gun fire and its range. The accused sought the judge to inspect the site in order to arrive at a correct conclusion. Please advise.

Ans. An application under section 310 of Code of Criminal Procedure can be made for the local/spot inspection by the court. Local inspection under section 310 of Cr.P.C. is for properly appreciating the evidence already recorded during the trial. A spot inspection can be carried by the judge in the presence of the accused, his counsel and the public prosecutor. To arrive at a correct conclusion, the trial Court may also conduct a test by firing the same type of gun from the place where the accused had allegedly fired at the victim. [*State of Himachal Pradesh* v. *Mast Ram,* (2004) 8 SCC 660: 2004 Cr LJ 4973: AIR 2004 SC 5056].

84. Enabling Speech – Impaired To Testify

Q.244. A person sustained injuries that left him incapable of speaking. A case of attempt to murder (section 307 of IPC) was registered against the assailant. During trial the victim was unable to depose before the court. How can his evidence be recorded in these circumstances?

Ans. Section 119 of Evidence Act reads: "*Dumb witnesses.*—A witness who is unable to speak may give his evidence in any other manner in which he can make it intelligible, as by writing or by signs; but such writing must be written and the signs made in open court. Evidence so given shall be deemed to be oral evidence."

Thus the victim may be examined in the trial Court with the help of an expert or a person familiar with the modes of conversing with him. But a person who has already been cited as prosecution witness in the said case should not be chosen as interpreter. Moreover, during examination, with the help of such an expert/interpreter, the Trial Court may be requested to record the signs made by the victim and their interpretations in answer to the questions put by the defence counsel.

Hans Raj v. *State of Punjab,* 1980 (2) FAC 396: 1980 Chandigarh Criminal Cases 27 (P&H);

K. Alavi v. *State of Kerala,* 1982 Ker LT 287: 1982 Cr LJ 94 (Ker HC).

Q.245. A father and son are facing trial under Dowry Prohibition Act read with section 498A of IPC. After the prosecution evidence was closed, the son shifted to USA. Now the case is at the stage of examination of accused under section 313, Cr.P.C. Can the Trial Court exempt the son from appearance in court?

Ans. Yes, the court can exempt the accused from personal appearance at this stage of examination under section 313, Cr. P.C. and his counsel can represent the accused and answer questions on his behalf. However, the accused has to file an affidavit in the trial Court factually explaining to the court as to why he is unable to be physically present in court and further assuring the court that no prejudice would be caused to him in any manner by dispensing with his personal presence during such questioning. He must give a further undertaking that he would not have any grievance on this score at any stage of the case. The Supreme Court in case of *Basavaraj R. Patil* v. *State of Karnataka,* (2000) 8 SCC 740: AIR 2000 SC 3214: 2000 AIR SCW 3692 held that though court has to question the accused "personally" but in exigent conditions, court can allow the counsel for the accused to answer the questions on his behalf.

Q.246. During trial in a hurt case, the Public Prosecutor gave up one of the eye witnesses as 'won over'. Later on, an application of the Public Prosecutor, whether the Trial Court can permit recalling of that witness?

Ans. The court is competent to summon/recall the witness for his examination under section 311 of Cr. P.C., if it comes to the conclusion that examination of the witness is essential for the just decision of the case. In *Kale and Kamall Singh* v. *State of Haryana,* 1998 (1) Cri CJ 529, the Punjab and Haryana High Court has allowed the prosecution request to recall such a witness.

Q.247. A person was granted bail in a case of dowry death registered on a complaint of victim's father. Can the complainant seek cancellation of bail?

Ans. The father of victim can move for cancellation of bail even if State has not moved for cancellation. In *Puran* v. *Ram Bilas,* (2001) 6 SCC 338: AIR 2001 SC 2023: 2001 Cr LJ 2566 the Supreme Court held, "When section 439(2) grants to the High Court the power to cancel bail, it necessarily follows that such powers can be exercised also in respect of Orders passed by the court of Sessions. Of course cancellation of bail has to be on principles set out hereinabove and only in appropriate cases. Further, even if it is an interlocutory order, the High Court's inherent jurisdiction under section 482 is not affected by the provisions of section 397(3) of the Code of Criminal Procedure. That the High Court may refuse to exercise its jurisdiction under section 482 on the basis of self-imposed restriction is a different aspect. It cannot be denied that for securing the ends of justice, the High Court can interfere with the order which causes miscarriage of justice or is palpably illegal or is unjustified."

Q.248. After the trial court had framed charges against the accused, on further investigation, the police found the accused innocent and submitted a report under section 173 (8), Cr.P.C. seeking prosecution of the complainant under section 182/211, IPC for making a false complaint. Please advise.

Ans. When the Trial Court has framed charges against the accused persons on the basis of a challan submitted by the police, the complainant cannot be prosecuted under section 182/211 of the IPC, unless there is a positive finding by the Trial Court that the complaint was false. Reliance may be placed upon the judgment of the Punjab and Haryana High Court reported as *Pawan Kumar* v. *State of Punjab*, 2002 (4) RCR (Cri) 716.

Q.249. The trial Court convicted an accused under sections 307/34 of IPC along with three other co-accused. Thereafter, the three co-accused filed an appeal before the Appellate Court against their conviction but the main accused did not prefer any appeal. The appeal filed by the three accused was allowed. What would be fate of other co-accused, although he had not filed any separate appeal?

Ans. The Supreme Court in *Suresh Chaudhary* v. *State of Bihar,* (2003) 4 SCC 128: AIR 2003 SC 1981: 2003 AIR SCW 1483 has held that benefit of acquittal in appeal is also available to the accused who has not filed any appeal against his conviction. Similar view was taken by the Supreme Court in *Gurcharan Kumar* v. *State of Rajasthan,* (2003) 2 SCC 698: AIR 2003 SC 992: 2003 AIR SCW 490. Thus, the accused who did not file appeal is also entitled to be acquitted even though he did not file any appeal.

Q.250. In a civil proceeding pending in court, the opposite party filed a false affidavit. Can the court take action against the maker of this affidavit?

Ans. Yes, the court can direct its official to file a criminal complaint against those who had filed the false affidavit and set the law in motion against the deponent/maker in view of law laid down by the Supreme Court in *Mohan Singh* v. *Late Amar Singh through LRs.,* (1998) 6 SCC 686: 1998 AIR SCW 3648: AIR 1999 SC 482 and in *M.S. Ahlawat, IPS* v. *State of Haryana,* (2000) 1 SCC 278: AIR 2000 SC 168: 1999 AIR SCW 4255.

Q.251. During trial in a rape case, the police requested the Magistrate for taking samples of accused's blood and hair for comparison. The Magistrate allowed the application despite protest by the accused. Is such an order sustainable?

Ans. Taking the accused's blood sample for testing and verifying the fact to see if he could have committed the crime alleged against him will not amount to compelling the accused to be a witness against himself within the meaning of Article 20(3) of the Constitution of India. The Bombay High Court took a similar view in *State of Maharasthra* v. *Ranjit*, 2004 (1) RCR (Cri) 616. Similarly Rajasthan High Court in *Miss Swati Lodha* v. *State of Rajasthan*, 1991 Cr LJ 939: 1991 APLJ (Cri) 228: 1991 (2) All Cri LR 168 has also expressed the view that taking blood from the veins of accused is not violative of Article 20(3) of the Constitution of India. The Delhi High Court in the case of *Sandeep Kalson* v. *State*, 1994 (1) RCR 596 has also taken a similar view.

Q.252. A public servant, while performing his official duties, had taken legal action against a private person, who in turn, filed a false criminal complaint against him. Can the employees' case be defended by the Government Advocate (APP) at government expense?

Ans. The Government Advocate (APP) cannot defend his case in view of the judgment of the Supreme Court in *Sunil Kumar* v. *Phota Sheikh*, (1984) 4 SCC 533: AIR 1984 SC 1591: 1984 Cri LR (SC) 374. Under the circumstances, he will have to engage a private counsel but can request the government to reimburse his expense.

Q.253. A complaint was made to the SSP who further forwarded it to the SHO. On investigation it was found false. To whom should the accused approach for redress under section 182 IPC – the SSP or the SHO?

Ans. Since the complaint was filed before the Superintendent of Police who forwarded it for investigation to the SHO, only the Superintendent of Police is competent to file calendra under section 182, IPC. The SHO is not competent to do this. This has been so held in various judgments of the Punjab and Haryana High Court in the case of *Randhir* v. *State of Haryana*, 2003 (4) RCR (Cri) 651 and *Malkiat Singh* v. *State of Haryana*, (1999) 1 Cri CJ 702: 1999 (2) RCR (Cri) 10 (P&H).

Q.254. During trial of a theft case, the magistrate refused the police application for seeking remand of the accused to recover the stolen articles. Does the complainant have a remedy?

Ans. The complainant may file a revision under section 497 of the Code of Criminal Procedure against the Magistrate's order in view of the law laid down by the Punjab and Haryana High Court in *Kashmir Singh* v. *State of Punjab,* 1984 (1) CLR 70: 1984 Cr LJ 51 (P&H): 1984 Chand Cri C 128. But it is pertinent to point out that if the accused is in judicial custody in a case for more than 15 days from the date of his arrest, he cannot be remanded to police custody in the same case after the expiry of 15 days as per section 167 of Code of Criminal Procedure. In *CBI* v. *Anupum Kulkarni,* (1992) 3 SCC 141: AIR 1992 SC 1768: 1992 Cr LJ 2768 the Supreme Court ruled that police remand can be granted within 15 days of the date of arrest.

Q.255. Can a person apprehending his arrest in a non-bailable offence, directly approach the High Court for anticipatory ball under section 438 Cr.P.C.?

Ans. Section 438(1), Cr.P.C. provides: "*Direction for grant of bail to person apprehending arrest.*—Where any person has reason to believe that he may be arrested on an accusation of having committed a non-bailable offence, he may apply to the High Court or the court of Session for a direction under this section that in the event of such arrest, he shall be released on bail."

The right to choose the forum is with the person who is apprehending his arrest. A citizen has a right to move application for anticipatory bail even directly to High Court without approaching the Sessions Court. [Ref *Mohan Lal* v. *Prem Chand,* ILR (1980) HP 117: 1980 Sim LC 241: AIR 1980 HP 36 FB; *Onkar Nath* v. *State of Himachal Pradesh,* 1976 Cr LJ 1142 All (FB): 1976 All WC 81: 1976 All LJ 223]. However, it may be better to first make such application to the Sessions Court.

Q.256. In a trial, the court passed adverse remarks against a government servant cited as prosecution witness without affording any opportunity. Is there any remedy?

Ans. The procedure adopted by the court is not legal as no opportunity was afforded to the person before passing adverse remarks. The order is contrary to law laid down by the Supreme Court in *Manish Dixit* v. *State of Rajasthan,* (2001) 1 SCC 596: AIR 2001 SC 93: 2001 Cr LJ 133: and *Ram Sarup Rohilla J.E (HSEB)* v. *State of Haryana,* 2003 (1) RCR (Cri) 640 (P&H).

Q.257. In a murder case the police failed to recover the victim's corpse. Without the body, can the police implicate anyone of a murder?

Ans. Under certain circumstances, where there is positive evidence to connect the accused with the crime, murder charges may be framed. A person may be tried and convicted for murder even if no corpse has been found. In this context reliance may be placed upon judgments of the Supreme Court reported as:

1. *Suresh Chander Bahri* v. *State of Bihar,* 1995 Supp (1) SCC (Cri) 60.
2. *Ram Gulam Chaudhary* v. *State of Bihar,* (2001) 8 SCC 311: AIR 2001 SC 2842: 2001 AIR SCW 3802.

Q.258. Is there any difference in the evidentiary value of a handwriting expert and a fingerprint expert?

Ans. Yes, there is a definite difference between the evidentiary value of a handwriting and fingerprint expert. The science of identification by thumb impressions is now an exact science and does not leave margin for mistake or doubt, whereas it is not so for handwriting analysis.

In fact, the Supreme Court in *Bhagwan Kaur* v. *Maharaj Krishan Sharma*, (1973) 4 SCC 46: AIR 1973 SC 1346: 1973 Cr LJ 1143, had held that the evidence of a handwriting expert, unlike that of a fingerprint expert, is generally of frail character. Moreover with the passage of time, handwriting and signature changes. The Punjab and Haryana High Court in the case of *Mohan Sarup* v. *Rajeshwar Sarup*, 1997 (1) PLR 336, had also observed that the science of handwriting is not exact and that handwriting experts generally toe the line of the party who summons them.

Q.259. Can a FIR be registered on the basis of a telegram?

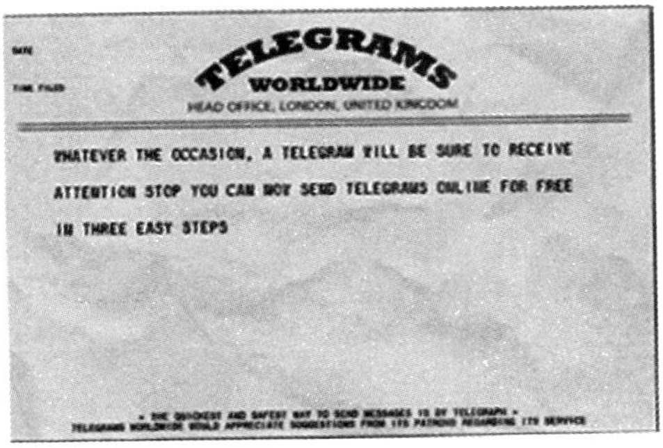

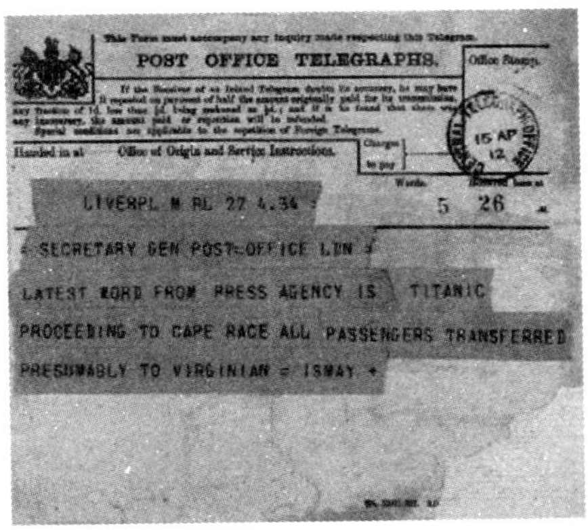

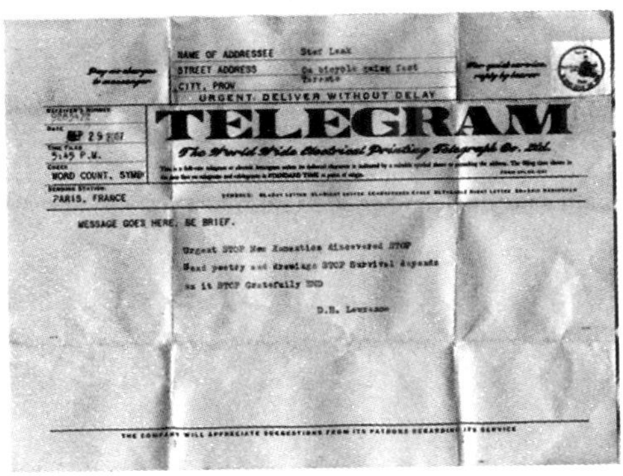

Ans. Various High Courts have given conflicting views on whether a case should be registered on the basis of a telegram. As a telegram does not satisfy the tests of sections 154 of the Cr P.C. and is not an oral statement reduced into writing, read over, admitted to be correct and signed by the informant, yet the Supreme Court in the case of *Wilayat Khan* v. *State,* AIR 1953 SC 122: 1953 Cr LJ 662: ILR 1953 1All 189 had held that the original telegram which was thumb-marked by the sender could very well form the basis of a FIR.

Q.260. Whether the right of private defence can be weighed in golden scales?

Ans. The general principle with regard to the right of private defence is that it is a defensive right. It is neither a right of aggression nor of reprisal. Moreover, the injury which is inflicted by the person exercising the right should commensurate with the injury with which he is threatened but at the same time it is difficult to expect from the person exercising the right in good faith to weigh with golden scales what maximum amount of physical force is necessary to keep within the right and every reasonable allowance will have to be made for the *bona fide* defence. In *Subramani* v. *State of Tamil Nadu,* (2002) 7 SCC 210: AIR 2002 SC 2980: 2002 AIR SCW 3488 the Supreme Court has said that in the exercise of the right of private defence only such force may be used as may be necessary but it is equally well-settled that at a time when a person is faced with immediate peril of life and limb of himself or other, he is not expected to weigh in golden scales the precise force needed to repel the danger. [Also: *Yogendra Murarji* v. *State of Gujarat,* (1980) 2 SCC 218: AIR 1980 SC 660: 1980 Cr LJ 459].

Q.261. What is the effect of non-examination of the complaint, who lodged FIR in a murder case, if he is given up by the prosecution as having been won over?

Ans. In *Hukam Singh* v. *State of Rajasthan,* (2000) 7 SCC 490: 2000 AIR SCW 4416: 2001 Cr LJ 511 the Supreme Court has said that the prosecution is entitled to skip witnesses who are not likely to support the prosecution version. Similarly, in *Krishna Mochi* v. *State of Bihar,* 2002 SCC (Cri) 1220: AIR 2002 SC 1965: 2002 Cr LJ 2645, the Supreme Court has observed that non-examination of the informant cannot in any manner affect the prosecution case and that if the FIR is not proved due to non-examination of the informant, it would not be a ground for acquittal of the accused as the case would depend upon the evidence led by the prosecution. The court repelled the contention of appellant's counsel that as informant was not examined, as such the first information report cannot be used as substantive evidence. It was observed, "It is matter of common experience that in recent times there has been sharp decline of ethical values in public life even in developed countries much less developing one, like ours, where the ratio of decline is higher. Even in ordinary cases, witnesses are not inclined to depose or their evidence is not found to be credible by courts for manifold reasons. One of the reasons may be that they do not have courage to depose against an accused because of threats to their life, more so when the offenders are habitual criminals or high-ups in the Government or close to powers, which may be political, economic or other powers including muscle power. .... These days when crime is looming large and humanity is suffering and society is so much affected thereby, duties and responsibilities of the courts have become much more. **Now the maxim "let hundred guilty persons be acquitted, but not a single innocent be convicted" is, in practice, changing world over and courts have been compelled to accept that "society suffers by wrong convictions and it equally suffers by wrong acquittals"** I find this Court in recent times has conscientiously taken notice of these facts from time to time. In the case *Inder Singh* v. *State (Delhi Administration),* AIR 1978 SC 1091: 1978 Cr LJ 766: (1978) 4 SCC 161, Krishna Iyer, J. laid down that "Proof beyond reasonable doubt is a guideline, not a fetish and guilty man cannot get away with it because truth suffers some infirmity when projected through human processes." In the case of *State of Uttar Pradesh* v. *Anil Singh,* AIR 1988 SC 1998: 1989 Cr LJ 88: JT 1988 (3) SC 491, it was held that **a Judge does not preside over a criminal trial merely to see that no innocent man is punished. A Judge also presides to see that a guilty man does not escape. One is as important as the other. Both are public duties which the Judge has to perform.** In the case of *State of West Bengal* v. *Orilal Jaiswal,* (1994) 1 SCC 73: AIR 1994 SC 1418: 1994 Cr LJ 2104, it was held that Justice cannot be made sterile on the plea that it is better to let hundred guilty escape than punish an innocent. Letting guilty escape is not doing justice, according to law. In the case of *Mohan Singh* v. *State of Madhya Pradesh,* (1999) 1 SCR 276: AIR 1999 SC 883: 1999 AIR SCW 553, it was held that the courts have been removing chaff from the grain. It has to disperse the suspicious cloud and dust out the smear of dust as all these things clog the very truth. So long chaff, cloud and dust remains, the criminals are clothed with this protective layer to receive the benefit of doubt. So it is a solemn duty of the courts, not to merely conclude and leave the case the moment suspicions are created. It is onerous duty of the court, within permissible limit to find out the truth. It means, on one hand no innocent man should be punished but on the other hand to see no person committing an offence should get scot free. If in spite of such effort suspicion is not dissolved, it remains writ at large, benefit of doubt has to be credited to the accused. Thus, in the present case where there was more or less a caste war between haves and have nots, gruesome murder of 35 persons of one community in which several persons were injured, great commotion in the locality, people became panicky as the accused persons were members of MCC, which is a very violent organisation, even if the complicity of the accused is proved by credible evidence of one or two witnesses, it would not be unsafe to convict an accused, rather a duty is enjoined upon the court not to acquit an accused on this ground alone unless the prosecution case is otherwise found to be untrustworthy. It is well settled that in a criminal trial credible evidence of even a solitary witness can form basis of conviction and that of even half a dozen witnesses may not form such a basis unless their evidence is found to be trustworthy inasmuch as what matters in the matter of appreciation of evidence of witnesses is not the number of witnesses, but the quality of their evidence. Thus, I do not find any substance in the submission of the learned counsel appearing on behalf of the appellants on this count."

Q.262. A person was convicted and sentenced to 10 years and was also fined Rs. 1 lakh for possessing 100 kg of poppy husk. During trial, he remained on bail. Whether in appeal, the sentence of imprisonment can be suspended in view the bar created by sections 32A and 37 of the Narcotic Drugs and Psychotropic Act?

Ans. The Supreme Court in *Dadu* alias *Tulsidas* v. *State of Maharashtra,* (2000) 8 SCC 437: AIR 2000 SC 3203: 2000 AIR SCW 3711 has declared section 32A of the Narcotic Drugs and Psychotropic Substances Act as unconstitutional by holding that "(1) section 32A does not in any way affect the powers of the authorities to grant parole; (2) It is unconstitutional to the extent it takes away the right of the court to suspend the sentence of a convict under the Act; (3) Nevertheless, a sentence awarded under the Act can be suspended by the appellate court only and strictly subject to the conditions spelt out in section 37 of the Act as dealt with in this judgment."

The Punjab and Haryana High Court, in *Piara Singh* v. *State of Punjab,* 2001 (1) RCR (Cri) 675, also ordered release of the offender on bail in a case under the Narcotic Drugs and Psychotropic Substances Act, by suspending his sentence.

Q.263. In a criminal complaint alleging medical negligence, the complainant did not produce hospital records. Subsequently, an application was moved under section 311, Cr. P.C for re-examination of the witness and for tendering the said documents. Please advise.

Ans. The court has been given wide powers under section 311, Cr. P.C. to recall or re-examine any person already examined if his evidence appears to the court to be essential for just decision of the case. This power can be exercised by the court at any stage of the trial. Such an application should be allowed because the production of documents and recalling/re-examining of witness would not cause any prejudice to the accused as he would get full opportunity to cross-examine.

In *P. Chhaganlal Daga* v. *M. Sanjay Shaw,* (2003) 11 SCC 486, the Supreme Court observed that the power to receive evidence in exercise of section 311 Cr.P.C. of the Court could be exercised even if evidence on both sides is closed and such jurisdiction of the Court is directed by exigency of situation and fair play. The only factor which should govern the Court in exercise of power under section 311 should be whether such material is essential for the just decision of the case.

Q.264. Three persons were convicted in a murder case. One of them, for the first time, pleaded before the Supreme Court that he was a juvenile at the time of murder and was entitled to the benefit of Juvenile Justice Act. Please guide.

Ans. As per section 7A of the Juvenile Justice (Care and Protection of Children) Act, 2002 (as amended in 2006) claim of juvenility may be raised at any stage before any court even after final disposal of the case. Such claim shall be determined as per the Act, even if the accused is no longer a juvenile on or before the data of commencement of the said Act but was a juvenile on the date of occurrence of the alleged offence. The Supreme Court in *Hari Ram* v. *State of Rajasthan,* (2009) 13 SCC 211 and in *Mohan Mali* v. *State of Madhya Pradesh,* (2010) 6 SCC 669: 2010 Cr LJ 2849: AIR 2010 SC 1790 has held that an accused can raise the plea of Juvenility for the first time in Supreme Court and claim benefits applicable to juvenile offenders. However, the procedure as provided under section 7A of the Act *ibid* will have to be followed by the court by making an inquiry by taking such evidence as may be necessary to determine the age of such person. The Supreme Court dealt with the point thus:

> "Section 64 of the 2000 Act deals with a situation where a juvenile in conflict with law is already undergoing sentence at the commencement of the Act, and the same reads as follows:—"Juvenile in conflict with law undergoing sentence at commencement of this Act.—In any area in which this Act is brought into force, the State Government shall direct that a juvenile in conflict with law who is undergoing any sentence of imprisonment at the commencement of this Act, shall, in lieu of undergoing such sentence, be sent to a special home or be kept in fit institution in such manner as the State Government thinks fit for the remainder of the period of the sentence; and the provisions of this Act shall apply to the juvenile as if he had been ordered by the Board to be sent to such special home or institution or, as the case may be, ordered to be kept under protective care under sub-section (2) of section 16 of this Act

"The said provision has to be read along with sections 7A and 20 of the 2000 Act, together with rule 98 of the 2007 Rules, which deals with disposed of cases of juveniles in conflict with law, and provides as follows:"Disposed of cases of juveniles in conflict with law. - The State Government or as the case may be the Board may, either suo motu or on an application made for the purpose, review the case of a person or a juvenile in conflict with law, determine his juvenility in terms of the provisions contained in the Act and rule 12 of these rules and pass an appropriate order in the interest of the juvenile in conflict with law under section 64 of the Act, for the immediate release of the juvenile in conflict with law whose period of detention or imprisonment has exceeded the maximum period provided in section 15 of the said Act"

"In the facts of this case, we are faced with a situation where the juvenile, Dhanna Lal, had already been tried along with adults and had been convicted under section 302/34, 326/34 and 324/34 IPC and was sentenced to life imprisonment, out of which he has already undergone about 9 years of the sentence. Rule 98 of the 2007 Rules, in our view, squarely applies to Appellant No.2 Dhanna Lal's case. His case is to be considered not only for grant of bail, but also for release in terms of the said Rule, since he has completed more than the maximum period of sentence as provided under section 15 of the 2000 Act."

Q.265. In a murder case, both the eye witnesses were declared hostile. As there was no other evidence against the accused, they were acquitted. What action against such witnesses is possible?

Ans. It is generally observed that witnesses, while supportive of the prosecution case at the investigation stage, do not support the case during trial by taking a complete U-turn. As a result the courts, in the absence of any other admissible evidence, have no option but to acquit the accused. This practice has become a menace in the criminal judicial system in our country which needs to be curbed. Although the trial court has power under section 344 Cr.P.C. to punish such witnesses summarily, after giving notice and giving reasonable opportunity of showing cause as to why he should not be punished for the offence of perjury, yet it is being seen that the trial courts are generally not taking any action against such witnesses. The Supreme Court in *Mahla Vinod Kumar* v. *State of Madhya Pradesh,* (2008) 8 SCC 34 has observed that this provision should be used effectively and frequently to stop the menace of perjury. In this case, the Supreme Court has laid down the following three conditions for exercising powers under section 344, Cr. P.C.:

(i) The court at the time of delivery of judgment or final order must express an opinion to the effect that the witness has given false evidence or fabricated such evidence before it (*i.e.,* court).

(ii) The court must come to the conclusion that in the interest of justice the witness concerned should be punished summarily by it for the offence which appears to have been committed by the witness.

(iii) The witness must be given reasonable opportunity of showing cause as to why he should not be punished for the offence of perjury.

85. Character Verification for a Government Job

Q.266. A person was selected as a police constable. During character verification it was revealed that he was earlier tried, though acquitted, in a criminal case for causing grievous hurt. Whether he can be denied appointment?

Ans. No, he cannot be denied appointment, since he did not suffer from 'moral turpitude'. Moral turpitude is an expression which is used in legal as well as social parlance to describe conduct which is inherently base, vile, depraved or having a connection showing depravity, as held by the Punjab and Haryana High Court in *Parvesh* v. *State of Haryana*, 2009 (4) RCR (Cri) 469 (P&H).

86. Ransom

Q.267. A seven years old boy was kidnapped for ransom. The police nabbed the culprit and recovered the child. Can the culprit be punished on the basis of child's statement?

Ans. The accused can be convicted for the offence of kidnapping for ransom punishable under section 364A of the IPC which provides for maximum punishment of death or imprisonment for life besides fine. A child of seven years is a competent witness and his evidence can be relied upon by the court if he is able to give rational answers to the questions put by the court to test his sense of understanding. Reference may be made to a Supreme Court judgment in *Shyam Babu* v. *State of Haryana,* (2008) 15 SCC 418.

87. Rioting and grievious hurt

Q.268. Eight persons were booked for offences under section 326/148/149, IPC. The court acquitted them of rioting under section 148 but convicted them for causing grievous hurt punishable under section 326 read with section 149, IPC. Please guide.

Ans. The offence of rioting must occur when members are charged with causing injuries as the common object of the unlawful assembly. Therefore, an accused person who has been expressly charged for the offence punishable under section 148 IPC (*i.e.* for rioting) and has been acquitted thereunder, cannot be legally convicted for the offence punishable under section 326, IPC read with section 149 IPC.

[(1) *Mahadev Sharma* v. *State of Bihar*, AIR 1966 SC 302: (1965) 2 SCWR 688: (1996) 1 SCR 189 (2) [*Md. Ankoor* v. *P.P.*, 2010 (1) RCR (Cri) 917].

88. Embezzlement – Bank's recovery

Q.269. If the Bank uses a guarantors' Fixed Deposit Receipts to recover its overdue amount from the borrower, can the manager be prosecuted under section 409 /422/426 IPC?

Ans. No. The Bank is entitled to recover its overdue amount from the borrower by appropriating deposits of the guarantors. If a complaint is filed against the Bank, the High Court may be approached to quash such proceedings under section 482 Criminal Procedure Code in view of law laid down by the Supreme Court in *M.N. Ojha* v. *Alok Kumar Srivastav*, (2009) 9 SCC 682: AIR 2010 SC 201: 2009 AIR SCW 5848.

The Court ruled: "It is the case of the complainant in his complaint that the first appellant should have appròpriated the hypothecated goods first and only thereafter steps could have been taken for recovery of the balance amount if any from the guarantors. It was alleged that the Branch Manager in conspiracy with the brother of the borrower who is none other than an employee of the bank allowed the operation of the account till the things became "bad to worse". According to him, the Branch Manager conspired with the borrower and committed criminal breach of trust. Repeated assertions have been made in the complaint that all the accused persons in conspiracy with each other have diverted huge bank money in a fraudulent manner for their own benefit. Surprisingly enough neither the borrower nor his brother with whom the bank officers are alleged to have colluded is arrayed as accused. The complainant in his complaint freely used choicest expressions such as fraud, collusion, conspiracy and cheating etc." but did not make any concrete allegations against the appellants suggesting commission of any offence. That a plain reading of the complaint and taking the allegations and averments made therein to be true on their face value do not reveal the commission of any offence whatsoever by the appellants who were only taking steps to realize the amount due to the bank from the borrower and in the process encashed the FDRs offered by the guarantors as security for the discharge of the loan. What is the crime they have committed even if they did not proceed against the hypothecated properties before realizing the FDRs offered by guarantors? Where is the misappropriation of money? Whom did they cheat?

In our considered view, criminal law has been set in motion by the complainant to harass the bank officers needlessly and to wreak personal vengeance in order to bring them under pressure not to further prosecute the proceedings already initiated by the appellants against the complainant on behalf of the bank."

89. Medical Jurisprudence & Ballistics

[Answers based on Modi's Medical Jurisprudence & Toxicology]

Q.270. Is there any difference between anti-mortem and post-mortem abrasions?

Ans. "Abrasions caused during life time appear as bleeding surfaces or scratches, and are within a day or two covered with reddish-brown crust or scabs owing to coagulation of the blood or serum. They generally heal in about four to seven days without leaving permanent scars. Abrasions produced after death, mostly seen over bony prominences are dark-brown and parchment-like in appearance, and look like abrasions caused during life, but they are distinguished by the complete absence of bleeding and injection of vessels in the underlying tissues."

Q.271. What are the distinguishing features of incised, punctured and lacerated wounds in fights which are a regular feature of life?

Ans. "An incise or slash wound is always broader than the edge of the weapon causing it owing to the detraction of the divided tissues. It is somewhat spindle-shaped and gaping, its length being greater than its width and depth.

Stabs are penetrating wounds, when passing through the tissues, they enter a cavity of the body, such as the thorax or abdomen. These wounds are produced by a long piercing or stabbing instrument, such as a pin, needle, knife, scissors, bayonet, spear, dagger, pickaxe, arrow, etc. The point of instrument may be sharp or blunt.

A stab wound caused by a sharp, pointed and cutting instrument has clean-cut edges, which are almost parallel but slightly curved to each other.

Lacerated wounds are tears produced by blows from blunt objections and missiles, by violent falls on hard projecting surfaces, by machinery and railway accidents, by the wheels of a vehicle causing a grinding compression by their weight resulting in avulsion of the skin. They can also be caused by the claws, teeth or horns of animals. These wounds do not generally correspond in shape or size to the weapon producing them. Their edges are torn, jagged, irregular and swollen or contused."

Q.272. What is the general fatal-time period in cases of death by suffocation?

Ans."Death occurs on an average from four to five minutes, after complete withdrawal of air from the lungs, although cases have occurred in which death was almost instantaneous when the windpipe was blocked by a foreign body. Recovery may occur if treated within four minutes."

Q. 273. What are the distinguishing high points between different kinds of wounds suffered by a victim of fatal injuries?

Ans."In case of death occurring from wounds, the question is often raised as to whether they were the result of suicide, homicide or accident. The answer is not always easy, but it can be given to some extent by a medical practitioner, by noting the following points:—

(1) The situation and character of the wounds.

(2) The number, direction and extent of the wounds.

(3) The condition of the locality, the surroundings of the wounded person and the circumstances of the injury."

Q. 274. Is there any difference between suicidal and homicidal wounds?

Ans."Suicidal wounds are usually on the front or on the sides of the body, and affect the vital organs. They are usually incised, punctured, or gunshot wounds. Suicidal incised wounds are generally situated on the front of the body in easily accessible position, especially, on the throat, chest, or wrist.

Incised and punctured wounds situated on the back or in such a position as cannot be easily reached by a suicide, are homicidal, though a suicidal may sometimes produce wounds on himself which may have the appearance of being homicidal. Incised wounds are on the nose, ears and genitals are usually homicidal, and are inflicted on account of jealousy or revenge in case of adultery.

Defence wounds like cuts on the fingers and palms are produced during attempts by the injured person to seize the weapon in order to instinctively defend himself and are, therefore, indicative of homicide."

Q. 275. Whether the direction, number and extent of wounds throw any light on the type of the wound?

Ans."Several injuries on the body, if they are deep and extensive, are as a rule, homicidal if we except accidents from falls, motor cars and other vehicles. In India, murderers select a heavy cutting instrument such as a gandasa (chopper), banka, khurpi, kulhari (axe) sword, etc, and inflict several deadly wounds on the head, cutting the skull bones and exposing the brain tissue, or on the neck cutting the larynx, oesophagus, large blood vessels, vertebrae and even the spinal cord. They are not generally satisfied by inflicting only one wound, but inflict several mortal wounds, and sometimes hack the body so much that the head is either severed altogether from the trunk, or remains, connected to it by a mere tag of skin. In addition to these, several wounds are usually inflicted on the trunk and limbs."

Q. 276. What are the features of a reliable post-mortem report?

Ans."A post-mortem report should be drawn by Civil Assistant Surgeons and counter-signed by District Medical Officer. Whenever reasonably possible, the Medical Officers should give a definite opinion about the cause of death. Ideally, such report should be as complete as possible, concise and clear. It should be forwarded to the Superintendent of Police as soon as possible, but not later than two days. In one of the reported cases, the Magistrate had to recall for proper examination of a medical officer whose evidence was vitiated by use of the words 'probably'. Thus in every cause of the death, efforts should be made to root out vagueness of any kind."

Q. 277. What is the co-relation between different kinds of wounds and the distance fired at from the fire-arm?

Ans. "If a firearm is discharged very close to the body or in actual contact, subcutaneous tissues over an area of two or three inches around the wound of entrance are lacerated and the surrounding skin is usually scorched and blackened by smoke and tattoed with unburnt grains of gunpowder or smokeless propellant powder. The adjacent hairs are singed, and the clothes covering the part are burnt by the flame.

Blackening is found, if a firearm like a shotgun is discharged from a distance of not more than three feet and a revolver or pistol discharged within about two feet. In the absence of powder residue no distinction can be made between one distant shot and another, as far as distance is concerned. Scorching in the case of the latter firearms is observed within a few inches, while some evidence of scorching in the case of shotguns may be found even at one to three feet."

90. Miscellaneous

Q.278. Whether a "divorced" wife is entitled to maintenance under section 125 of Criminal Procedure Code ?

Ans. A 'divorced' wife is entitled to maintenance under section 125 of Criminal Procedure Code till such time she is remarried. The word `wife' has been defined in *Explanation* (b) to section 125(1) of the Cr.P.C. as follows:—

> "(B) 'wife' includes a woman who has been divorced by, or has obtained a divorce from, her husband and has not remarried"

In *Vimala (K)* v. *Veeraswamy*, (1991) 2 SCC 375: 1991 AIR SCW 754, a three-Judge Bench of the Supreme Court held that section 125 is meant to achieve a social purpose and the object is to prevent vagrancy and destitution. Explaining the meaning of the word 'wife' the Court held: (SCC p. 378, para 3)

> "3..... the object is to prevent vagrancy and destitution. It provides a speedy remedy for the supply of food, clothing and shelter to the deserted wife. When an attempt is made by the husband to negative the claim of the neglected wife depicting her as a kept-mistress on the specious plea that he was already married, the court would insist on strict proof of the earlier marriage. **The term `wife' in section 125 of the Code of Criminal Procedure, includes a woman who has been divorced by a husband or who has obtained a divorce from her husband and has not remarried.** The woman not having the legal status of a wife is thus brought within the inclusive definition of the term `wife' consistent with the objective. However, under the law a second wife whose marriage is void on account of the survival of the first marriage is not a legally wedded wife, and is, therefore, not entitled to maintenance under this provision."

Again, in *Savitaben Somabhat Bhatiya* v. *State of Gujarat*, (2005) 3 SC 636: AIR 2005 SC 1809: 2005 AIR SCW 1601, the Supreme Court held that however desirable it may be to take note of the plight of an unfortunate woman, who unwittingly enters into wedlock with a married man, there is no scope to include a woman not lawfully married within the expression of 'wife'. The Bench held that this inadequacy in law can be amended only by the Legislature.

Q. 279. Whether a woman living in a "domestic relationship" with a man is entitled to maintenance under the Protection of Women from Domestic Violence Act, 2005.

Ans. Section 2(a) of the Protection of Women from Domestic Violence Act, 2005 reads:"2 (a) 'aggrieved person' means any woman who is, or has been, in a domestic relationship with the respondent and who alleges to have been subjected to any act of domestic violence by the respondent:—

Section 2 (f) states:

> "2(f) 'domestic relationship' means a relationship between two persons who live or have, at any point of time, lived together in a shared household, when they are related by consanguinity, marriage, or through a relationship

in the nature of marriage, adoption or are family members living together as a joint family.

Section 2(s) states:

> "2(s) 'shared household' means a household where the person aggrieved lives or at any stage has lived in a domestic relationship either singly or along with the respondent and includes such a household whether owned or tenanted either jointly by the aggrieved person and the respondent, or owned or tenanted by either of them in respect of which either the aggrieved person or the respondent or both jointly or singly have any right, title, interest or equity and includes such a household which may belong to the joint family of which the respondent is a member, irrespective of whether the respondent or the aggrieved person has any right, title or interest in the shared household."

Section 3(a) states that an act will constitute domestic violence in case it—

> "harms or injures or endangers the health, safety, life, limb or well-being, whether mental or physical, of the aggrieved person or tends to do so and includes causing physical abuse, sexual abuse, verbal and emotional abuse and economic abuse;"

The expression "economic abuse" has been defined to include:

> "3. (iv) (a) deprivation of all or any economic or financial resources to which the aggrieved person is entitled under any law or custom whether payable under an order of a court or otherwise or which the aggrieved person requires out of necessity including, but not limited to, household necessities for the aggrieved person and her children, if any, stridhan, property, jointly or separately owned by the aggrieved person, payment of rental related to the shared household and maintenance"

An aggrieved person under the Act can approach the Magistrate under section 12 for the relief mentioned in section 12(2). Under section 20(1)(d) the Magistrate can grant maintenance while disposing of the application under section 12(1). Section 26(1) provides that the relief mentioned in section 20 may also be sought in any legal proceeding, before a civil court, family court or a criminal court.

In *D. Velusamy* v. *D. Patchaiammal*, (2010) 10 SCC 469: AIR 2011 SC 479: 2010 AIR SCW 6731, the Supreme Court has explained in detail the meaning of "domestic relationship". Further, the Court has explained the phrase "a relationship in the nature of marriage" after discussing the American law on the subject. The law on the subject has been declared thus, "Some countries in the world recognize common law marriages. A common law marriage, sometimes called *de facto* marriage, or informal marriage is recognized in some countries as a marriage though no legally recognized marriage ceremony is performed or civil marriage contract is entered into or the marriage registered in a civil registry (see details on Google).

"In our opinion a `relationship in the nature of marriage' is akin to a common law marriage. Common law marriages require that although not being formally married:—

(a) The couple must hold themselves out to society as being akin to spouses.

(b) They must be of legal age to marry.

(c) They must be otherwise qualified to enter into a legal marriage, including being unmarried.

(d) They must have voluntarily cohabited and held themselves out to the world as being akin to spouses for a significant period of time.

(see 'Common Law Marriage' in Wikipedia on Google)

"In our opinion a `relationship in the nature of marriage' under the 2005 Act must also fulfill the above requirements, and in addition the parties must have lived together in a `shared household' as defined in section 2(s) of the Act. Merely spending weekends together or a one night stand would not make it a `domestic relationship'. In our opinion not all live in relationships will amount to a relationship in the nature of marriage to get the benefit of the Act of 2005. To get such benefit the conditions mentioned by us above must be satisfied, and this has to be proved by evidence. If a man has a `keep' whom he maintains financially and uses mainly for sexual purpose and/or as a servant it would not, in our opinion, be a relationship in the nature of marriage. No doubt the view we are taking would exclude many women who have had a live in relationship from the benefit of the 2005 Act, but then it is not for this Court to legislate or amend the law. Parliament has used the expression `relationship in the nature of marriage' and not `live in relationship'. The Court in the grab of interpretation cannot change the language of the statute. In feudal society sexual relationship between man and woman outside marriage was totally taboo and regarded with disgust and horror, as depicted in Leo Tolstoy's novel `Anna Karenina', Gustave Flaubert's novel `Madame Bovary' and the novels of the great Bengali writer Sharat Chandra Chattopadhyaya. However, Indian society is changing, and this change has been reflected and recognized by Parliament by enacting "The Protection of Women from Domestic Violence Act, 2005."

Q. 280. What is "surrogacy"? Is surrogacy an offence? Can a 'surrogate' mother rent her womb to produce a child for his 'biological' parents?

Ans. Surrogacy is a well known method of reproduction whereby a woman agrees to become pregnant for the purpose of gestating and giving birth to a child she will not raise but hand over to a contracted party. She may be the child's genetic mother (the more traditional form for surrogacy) or she may be, as a gestational carrier, carry the pregnancy to delivery after having been implanted with an embryo. In some cases surrogacy is the only available option for parents who wish to have a child that is biologically related to them.

The word "surrogate", from Latin "subrogare", means "appointed to act in the place of". The intended parent(s) is the individual or couple who intends to rear the child after its birth.

In "traditional surrogacy" (also known as the Straight method) the surrogate is pregnant with her own biological child, but this child was conceived with the intention of relinquishing the child to be raised by others; by the biological father and possibly his spouse or partner, either male or female. The child may be conceived *via* home artificial insemination using fresh or frozen sperm or impregnated *via* IUI (intrauterine insemination), or ICI (intra cervical insemination) which is performed at a fertility clinic.

In "gestational surrogacy" (also know as the Host method) the surrogate becomes pregnant *via* embryo transfer with a child of which she is not the biological mother. She may have made an arrangement to relinquish it to the biological mother or father to raise, or to a parent who is themselves unrelated to the child (*e.g.* because the child was conceived using egg donation, germ donation or is the result of a donated embryo). The surrogate mother may be called the gestational carrier.

"Altruistic surrogacy" is a situation where the surrogate receives no financial reward for her pregnancy or the relinquishment of the child (although usually all expenses related to the pregnancy and birth are paid by the intended parents such as medical expenses, maternity clothing, and other related expenses).

"Commercial surrogacy" is a form of surrogacy in which a gestational carrier is paid to carry a child to maturity in her womb and is usually resorted to by well off infertile couples who can afford the cost involved or people who save and borrow in order to complete their dream of being parents. This medical procedure is legal in several countries including in India where due to excellent medical infrastructure, high international demand and ready availability of poor surrogates it is reaching industry proportions. Commercial surrogacy is sometimes referred to by the emotionally charged and potentially offensive terms "wombs for rent", "outsourced pregnancies" or "baby farms".

Intended parents may arrange a surrogate pregnancy because a woman who intends to parent is infertile in such a way that she cannot carry a pregnancy to term. Examples include a woman who has had a hysterectomy, has a uterine malformation, has had recurrent pregnancy loss or has a healthy condition that makes it dangerous for her to be pregnant. A female intending parent may also be fertile and healthy, but unwilling to undergo pregnancy.

Alternatively, the intended parent may be a single male or a male homosexual couple. Surrogates may be relatives, friends, or previous strangers. Many surrogate arrangements are made through agencies that help match up intended parents with women who want to be surrogates for a fee. The agencies often help manage the complex medical and legal aspects involved. Surrogacy arrangements can also be made independently. [Reliance: *Baby Manji Yamada (minor)* v. *Union of India*, (2008) 13 SCC 518: AIR 2009 SC 84: 2008 AIR SCW 6964].

Q.281. What is the remedy for protection of human and civil rights violation of a child? Where can a complaint be lodged, if human and civil rights of a child are violated?

Ans. An aggrieved person may approach The National Commission for Protection of Child Rights (NCPCR), set up under the Commissions for

Protection of Child Rights Act, 2005, to protect, promote and defend child rights in the country.

One of the Core Mandates of the Commission is to inquire into complaints of violations of child rights. The Commission is also required to take ***suo moto*** cognizance of serious cases of violation of child rights and to examine factors that inhibit the enjoyment of rights of children. The functions of the Commission as laid out in section 13 of the Act are as follows:—

1. The Commission shall perform all or any of the following functions, namely:—
   a. Examine and review the safeguards provided by or under any law for the time being in force for the protection of child rights and recommend measures for their effective implementation
   b. Present to the Central Government, annually and at such other intervals, as the Commission may deem fit, Reports upon the working of those safeguards
   c. Inquire into violation of child rights and recommend initiation of proceedings in such cases
   d. Examine all factors that inhibit the enjoyment of rights of children affected by terrorism, communal violence, riots, natural disasters, domestic violence, HIV/ AIDS, trafficking, maltreatment, torture and exploitation, pornography, and prostitution and recommend appropriate remedial measures
   e. Look into matters relating to children in need of special care and protection, including children in distress, marginalised and disadvantaged children, children in conflict with law, juveniles, children without family and children of prisoners and recommend appropriate remedial measures
   f. Study treaties and other international instruments and undertake periodic review of existing policies, programmes, and other activities on child rights and make recommendations for their effective implementation in the best interest of children
   g. Undertake and promote research in the field of child rights
   h. Spread child rights literacy among various sections of society and promote awareness of the safeguards available for protection of these rights through publications, media, seminars and other available means
   i. Inspect or cause to be inspected any juvenile custodial home or any other place of residence or institution meant for children, under the control of the Central Government or any State Government or any other authority including any institution run by a social organization, where children are detained or lodged for the purpose of treatment, reformation or protection and take up with these authorities for remedial action, if found necessary
   j. Inquire into complaints and take *suo moto* notice of matters related to:

i. Deprivation and violation of child rights

ii. Non implementation of laws providing for protection and development of children

iii. Non compliance of policy decisions, guidelines or instructions aimed at mitigating hardships to and ensuring welfare of the children and to provide relief to such children or take up the issues arising out of such matters with appropriate authorities

k. Such other functions as it may consider necessary for the promotion of child rights and any other matter incidental to the above functions.

Q.282. Can a married woman claim right of residence in a property, belonging to her mother-in-law and/or father-in-law, in which her husband has no share.

Ans. In *Vimlaben Ajitbhai Patel* v. *Vatslaben Ashokbhai Patel*, (2008) 4 SCC 649: AIR 2008 SC 2675: 2008 AIR SCW 4475, the Supreme Court observed:

"26. We may notice that in *Balwant Kaur* v. *Chanan Singh*, (2000) 6 SCC 310: AIR 2000 SC 1908: 2000 AIR SCW 1518, this Court reiterated the said principle in the following words:—"21. This provision clearly indicates that if the widowed daughter-in-law is a destitute and has no earnings of her own or other property and if she has nothing to fall back upon for maintenance on the estate of her husband or father or mother or from the estate of her son or daughter, if any, then she can fall back upon the estate of her father-in-law. This provision also indicates that in case of a widowed daughter-in-law of the family if she has no income of her own or no estate of her husband to fall back upon for maintenance, then she can legitimately claim maintenance from her father or mother. On the facts of the present case, therefore, it has to be held that Appellant 1, who was a destitute widowed daughter of the testator and who was staying with him and was being maintained by him in his lifetime, had nothing to fall back upon so far as her deceased husband's estate was concerned and she had no estate of her own. Consequently, as per section 19(1)(a) she could claim maintenance from the estate of her father even during her father's lifetime. This was a pre-existing right of the widowed daughter qua testator's estate in his own lifetime and this right which was tried to be crystallised in the Will in her favour after his demise fell squarely within the provisions of section 22(2) of the Maintenance Act."

"27. The Domestic Violence Act provides for a higher right in favour of a wife. She not only acquires a right to be maintained but also thereunder acquires a right of residence. The right of residence is a higher right. The said right as per the legislation extends to joint properties in which the husband has a share."

"28. Interpreting the provisions of the Domestic Violence Act this Court in *S.R. Batra* v. *Taruna Batra*, (2007) 3 SCC 169: AIR 2007 SC 1118: 2007 AIR SCW 1088, held that a married woman could not claim a right of residence in the property belonging to her mother-in-law, stating:

"17. There is no such law in India like the British Matrimonial Homes Act, 1967, and in any case, the rights which may be available under any law can only be as against the husband and not against the father-in- law or mother-in-law.

"18. Here, the house in question belongs to the mother- in-law of Smt Taruna Batra and it does not belong to her husband Amit Batra. Hence, Smt Taruna Batra cannot claim any right to live in the said house.

"19. Appellant 2, the mother-in-law of Smt Taruna Batra has stated that she had taken a loan for acquiring the house and it is not a joint family property. We see no reason to disbelieve this statement."

Thus a married woman may claim her right of shared accommodation only against her husband and not against her in-laws.

Q.283. What considerations should normally weigh with the courts for granting bail?

Ans. In *Jayendra Saraswathi Swamigal* v. *State of Tamil Nadu*, (2005) 2 SCC 13: AIR 2005 SC 716: 2005 AIR SCW 323, the Supreme Court held as under: "The considerations which normally weigh with the Court in granting bail in non-bailable offences have been explained by this Court in *State* v. *Capt. Jagjit Singh*, AIR 1962 SC 253: 1962 (1) SCJ 408: (1962) 3 SCR 622 and *Gurcharan Singh* v. *State (Delhi Admn.)*, AIR 1978 SC 179: 1978 Cr LJ 129: (1978) 1 SCC 118 and basically they are

- the nature and seriousness of the offence;
- the character of the evidence;
- circumstances which are peculiar to the accused;
- a reasonable possibility of the presence of the accused not being secured at the trial;
- reasonable apprehension of witnesses being tampered with;
- the larger interest of the public or the State; and
- other similar factors which may be relevant in the facts and circumstances of the case."

Q.284. What considerations should normally weigh with the courts for cancellation of bail?

Ans. In *Jayendra Saraswathi Swamigal* v. *State of Tamil Nadu*, (2005) 2 SCC 13: AIR 2005 SC 716: 2005 AIR SCW 323, the Supreme Court cited with approval the following observations made in *Raghubir Singh* v. *State of Bihar*, (1986) 4 SCC 481: AIR 1987 SC 149: 1987 Cr LJ 157:

".....The order for release on bail may however be cancelled under section 437(5) or section 439(2). Generally, the grounds for cancellation of bail, are—

- interference or attempt to interfere with the due course of administration of justice, or
- evasion or attempt to evade the course of justice,

- The due administration of justice may be interfered with by intimidating or suborning witnesses, by interfering with investigation, by creating or causing disappearance of evidence etc.
- The course of justice may be evaded or attempted to be evaded by leaving the country or going underground or otherwise placing himself beyond the reach of the sureties.
- He may abuse the liberty granted to him by indulging in similar or other unlawful acts.
- Where bail has been granted under the proviso to section 167(2) for the default of the prosecution in not completing the investigation in 60 days, after the defect is cured by the filing of a charge- sheet, the prosecution may seek to have the bail cancelled on the ground that there are reasonable grounds to believe that the accused has committed a non-bailable offence and that it is necessary to arrest him and commit him to custody. In the last mentioned case, one would expect very strong grounds indeed. "

Q.285. Can a case under 498A IPC be transferred from one town to another in the same district?

Ans. There is no blanket ban for the court to transfer a case from one place to another. An appropriate order may be passed depending upon facts and circumstances of each case. In *Jyoti Mishra* v. *Dhananjaya Mishra,* Transfer Petition (Crl.) Nos. 94-95 of 2010, decided on 27-08-2010, the Supreme Court refused transfer of a criminal case from one State to another [Andhra Pradesh to Madhya Pradesh] by observing: "Having regard to the consequences of non-appearance of the accused in a criminal trial, we are loath to entertain the petitioner's prayer for transfer. In a criminal proceeding, the right of the accused to a fair trial and a proper opportunity to defend himself cannot be ignored for the convenience of the complainant simply because she happens to be the estranged wife."

One may apply to the concerned District & Sessions Judge for transfer of case by pleading available grounds for transfer.

Q.286. What is 'Plea Bargaining' and its effect in India?

Ans. "Plea bargaining" means pre-trial negotiations between the prosecution and the accused. Normally, the accused agrees to plead guilty in exchange for certain concessions by the prosecutor. "Plea bargaining" is an alternative method to deal with criminal cases. This concept is very popular in USA. The Law Commission recommended introduction of "Plea barginaing" in 142nd, 154th and 177th reports. Further, the Report of the Committee on the reform of criminal justice system, 2000 under the Chairmanship of Justice (Dr) Malimath stated that the experience of United States was an evidence of plea bargaining being a means for the disposal of accumulated cases and expediting the delivery of criminal justice.

Based on these recommendations, the concept of plea bargaining was introduced in India Criminal Justice System in the year 2005 by means of

Criminal Law (Amendment) Act, 2005. By this amendment, a new Chapter XXI A has been introduced in the Code of Criminal Procedure.

A Division Bench of the Gujarat High Court observed in *State of Gujarat* v. *Natwar Harchandji Thakor*, (2005) Cr LJ 2957: 2005 (1) GCD 749 Guj: 2005 (1) Guj LR 709 that, "The very object of law is to provide easy, cheap and expeditious justice by resolution of disputes, including the trial of criminal cases and considering the present realistic profile of the pendency and delay in disposal in the administration of law and justice, fundamental reforms are inevitable. There should not be anything static. It can thus be said that it is really a measure and redressal and it shall add a new dimension in the realm of judicial reforms."

Q.287. Which are the cases in which the 'plea bargaining' is applicable in India?

Ans. The cases in which plea bargaining is applicable have been enumerated in section 265A of Criminal Procedure Code which reads:

> "*265A. Application of the Chapter.*—(1) This Chapter shall apply in respect of an accused against whom—
>
> (a) the report has been forwarded by the officer in charge of the police station under section 173 alleging therein that an offence appears to have been committed by him other than an offence for which the punishment of death or of imprisonment for life or of imprisonment for a term exceeding seven years has been provided under the law for the time being in force; or
>
> (b) a Magistrate has taken cognizance of an offence on complaint, other than an offence for which the punishment of death or of imprisonment for life or of imprisonment for a term exceeding seven years, has been provided under the law for the time being in force, and after examining complainant and witnesses under section 200, issued the process under section 204, but does not apply where such offence affects the socio-economic condition of the country or has been committed against a woman, or a child below the age of fourteen years.

(2) For the purposes of sub-section (1), the Central Government shall, by notification, determine the offences under the law for the time being in force which shall be the offences affecting the socio-economic condition of the country."

Q.288. What is the procedure for effecting a 'plea bargain'.

Ans. The procedure involves filing an application before an appropriate Court as laid down in section 265B of Criminal Procedure Code which reads:

> "*265B. Application for plea bargaining.*—(1) A person accused of an offence may file an application for plea bargaining in the Court in which such offence is pending for trial.
>
> (2) The application under sub-section (1) shall contain a brief description of the case relating to which the application is filed including the offence to

which the case relates and shall be accompanied by an affidavit sworn by the accused stating therein that he has voluntarily preferred, after understanding the nature and extent of punishment provided under the law for the offence, the plea bargaining in his case and that he has not previously been convicted by a Court in a case in which he had been charged with the same offence.

(3) After receiving the application under sub-section (1), the Court shall issue notice to the Public Prosecutor or the complainant of the case, as the case may be, and to the accused to appear on the date fixed for the case.

(4) When the Public Prosecutor or the complainant of the case, as the case may be, and the accused appear on the date fixed under sub-section (3), the Court shall examine the accused in camera, where the other party in the case shall not be present, to satisfy itself that the accused has filed the application voluntarily and where—

(a) the Court is satisfied that the application has been filed by the accused voluntarily, it shall provide time to the Public Prosecutor or the complainant of the case, as the case may be, and the accused to work out a mutually satisfactory disposition of the case which may include giving to the victim by the accused the compensation and other expenses during the case and thereafter fix the date for further hearing of the case;

(b) the Court finds that the application has been filed involuntarily by the accused or he has previously been convicted by a Court in a case in which he had been charged with the same offence, it shall proceed further in accordance with the provisions of this Code from the stage such application has been filed under sub-section (1)."

Q. 289. What is legal position for curbing ragging in educational institutions?

Ans. In pursuant of order dated 27-11-2006 passed by the Supreme Court in SLP No (s) 24295 of 2006 *University of Kerala* v. *Council, Principals' Colleges*, a Committee was constituted by the Central Government under the Chairmanship of Shri R.K. Raghavan (former Director, CBI) to look into the issue of ragging and suggest means of prevention of ragging in educational institutions. On the basis of recommendations made by this Committee, the following directives were issued by the Supreme Court on 16 May, 2007 to all the educational institutions for necessary implementation:

(1) The punishment to be meted out has to be exemplary and justifiably harsh to act as a deterrent against recurrence of such incidents.

(2) Every single incident of ragging where the victim or his parent/guardian or the Head of institution is not satisfied with the institutional arrangement for action, a First Information Report (FIR) must be filed without exception by the institutional authorities with the local police authorities. Any failure on the part of the institutional authority or negligence or deliberate delay in lodging the FIR with the local police shall be construed to be an act of culpable negligence on the part of the institutional authority. If any victim or his parent/guardian of ragging intends to file FIR directly with the police,

that will not absolve the institutional authority from the requirement of filing the FIR.

(3) Courts should make an effort to ensure that cases involving ragging are taken up on a priority basis to send the correct message that ragging is not only to be discourageous but also to be dealt with sternness.

(4) In addition, the court directed the possibility of introducing in the educational curriculum a subject relating to ragging shall be explored by the National Council of Educational Research and Training (NCERT) and the respective State Council of Educational Research and Training (SCERT). This aspect can be included in the teaching of the subjects "Human Rights".

(5) In the prospectus to be issued for admission by educational institutions, it shall be clearly stipulated that in case the applicant for admission is found to have indulged in ragging in the past or if it is noticed later that he has indulged in ragging, admission may be refused or he shall be expelled from the educational institution.

(6) The Central Government and the State Governments shall launch a programme giving wide publicity to the menace of ragging and the consequences which follow in case any student is detected to have been involved in ragging.

(7) It shall be the collective responsibility of the authorities and functionaries of the concerned institution and their role shall also be open to scrutiny for the purpose of finding out whether they have taken effective steps for preventing ragging and in case of their failure, action can be taken; for example, denial of any grant-in-aid or assistance from the State Governments.

(8) Anti-ragging committees and squads shall be forthwith formed by the institutions and it shall be the job of the committee or the squad, as the case may be, to see that the Committee's recommendations, particularly those noted above, are observed without exception and if it is noticed that there is any deviation, the same shall be forthwith brought to the notice of this Court.

(9) The Committee constituted pursuant to the order of this Court shall continue to monitor the functioning of the anti-ragging committees and the squads to be formed. They shall also monitor the implementation of the recommendations to which reference has been made above.

SECTION III
Landmark Indian Supreme Court Judgements

IMPORTANT NOTE

DISCLAIMER

This section contains important and chosen extracts from landmark Judgements of the Supreme Court. It is clarified that the serial numbers of the paragraphs and their sequencing order, is not as per certified copies of the Judgements or the reports of various law journals. The authors have made compilation of extracts relevant for this work. The authors or the publisher do not vouch for any errors, grammatical or otherwise, and the same are regretted. The readers are requested to send their feed-back to the authors at goelsudershan@gmail.com OR ravisodhi28@gmail.com

CHAPTER 1

CRIME AGAINST WOMEN AND CHILDREN

Bachpan Bachao Andolan v. *Union of India*, (2011) 5 SCC 1

Background: This case addresses the vital issues of flourishing businesses in women and child trafficking and evolves strategies for combating sexual exploitation. It culminates with directions regarding child care and protection. It touches upon the deplorable condition of women and children and deals with Supersession of Immoral Trafficking Act, Geneva Convention on Immoral Trafficking of Women and Children, 1956, Right of Children to Free and Compulsory Education Act, 2009, Juvenile Justice Authority, Central Adoption Resource Agency (CARA), National Child Labour Project (NCLP) for rehabilitation of child labourers and Schemes for working children in need of care and protection. The Court directed the Central Government to file a comprehensive affidavit of compliance. The Court decided to deal with the menace of child exploitation systematically by issuing appropriate directions.

Verdict: "We plan to deal with the problem of children's exploitation systematically. In this order we are limiting our directions regarding children working in the Indian Circuses. Consequently, we direct:

(i) In order to implement the fundamental right of the children under Article 21A, it is imperative that the Central Government must issue suitable notifications prohibiting the employment of children in circuses within two months from today.

(ii) The respondents are directed to conduct simultaneous raids in all the circuses to liberate the children and check the violation of fundamental rights of the children. The rescued children be kept in the Care and Protective Homes till they attain the age of 18 years.

(iii) The respondents are also directed to talk to the parents of the children and in case they are willing to take their children back to their homes, they may be directed to do so after proper verification.

(iv) The respondents are directed to frame proper scheme of rehabilitation of rescued children from circuses."

Other aspects:

"It is submitted that India is home to 19% of world's children. More than one-third of the country's population around 440 million is below 18 years. India's children are India's future. They are the harbingers of growth, potential fulfilment, change, dynamism, innovation, creativity. It is necessary that for a healthy future, we must protect, educate and develop the child population so that their citizenry is productive. Resources must be invested in children proportionate to their huge population. As far as the total expenditure on children in 2005- 2006 is concerned, it was 3.86% and in 2006-2007 it was increased to 4.91%. It is highly inadequate looking at the population of children.

"In a report submitted by the Ministry of Women and Child Development, 40% of India's children have been declared to be vulnerable or experiencing difficult circumstances. They are entitled to special protection under Articles 14, 15, 16, 17, 21, 23 and 24 of the Constitution. The concerns of child and the paradigm of child rights have been addressed suitably in various international conventions and standards on child protection including the UN Convention on the Rights of the Child (UNCRC), 1989, the UN Standard Minimum Rules for the Administration of Juvenile Justice (the Beijing Rules), 1985, the UN Rules for the Protection of Juveniles Deprived of their Liberty, 1990, the Hague Convention on Inter Country Adoption, 1993. India has ratified the UN Convention on the Rights of the Child in 1992. The Convention inter alia prescribes standards to be adhered by all state parties in securing the best interest of the child.

"Trafficking in women and children has become an increasingly lucrative business especially since the risk of being prosecuted is vey low. Women and children do not usually come to the brothels on their own will, but are brought through highly systematic, organized and illegal trafficking networks run by experienced individuals who buy, transport and sell children into prostitution. Traffickers tend to work in groups and children being trafficked often change hands to ensure that neither the trafficker nor the child gets caught during transit. Different groups of traffickers include gang members, police, pimps and even politicians, all working as a nexus. Trafficking networks are well organized and have linkages both within the country and in the neighbouring countries. Most traffickers are men. The role of women in this business is restricted to recruitment at the brothels.

The Suppression of Immoral Trafficking Act was enacted after the Geneva Convention on Immoral Trafficking of Women and Children was signed by India in 1956. In order to have data on the success of rehabilitation strategies, delivery points in rehabilitation strategy would have to be strengthened as would be seen in the later parts of this report.

Submissions/Suggestions

1. "It is submitted that a trafficker never blows the gaff. It is done in silence and quiet. It becomes necessary to involve police authorities by means of acute sensitization to a realm of illegality. Therefore, there has to be a special initiative taken by police with reference to children. The Central Government has evolved the national plan of action to combat trafficking and commercial sexual exploitation of women and children in 1998. It is submitted that there has now been a very careful realization that the plan for rescue and rehabilitation must be through a conceptual map. The said map gives a very

good indication of the initiatives and possibly its positive and negative outcomes. Learned Solicitor General submitted that a trafficked child can be brought before the Magistrate under two circumstances:

(a) when the raid/search or removal takes place by a police action under section 15 of the ITPA or when the Magistrate herself/himself passes rescue orders;

(b) the trafficked child can also be brought before the Magistrate as an accused under section 8A and 8B of the ITPA.

2. "The following directions are necessary:—

(a) Every Magistrate before whom a child is brought must be conscious of the provisions of the Juvenile Justice (Care and Protection of Children) Act, 2000;

(b) He must find out whether the child is below the age of 18 years;

(c) If it is so, he cannot be accused of an offence under section 7 or 8 of ITPA;

(d) The child will then have to be protected under Juvenile Justice Authority;

(e) The Magistrate has a responsibility to ascertain and confirm that the person produced before her or him is a child by accurate medical examination;

(f) The definition of a child in section 2K means a juvenile or a child as a person who has not completed 18 years of age;

(g) Once the age test passed under section 17(2) establishes that the child is a child/minor less than 18 years of age, the Magistrate/Sessions Judge while framing charges must also take into account whether any offences have been committed under sections 342, 366, 366A, 366B, 367, 368, 370, 371, 372, 373, 375 and if so, he or she must also frame charges additionally;

(h) The child should be considered as a child in the protection of the Child Welfare Act.

(i) The child should be handed over to the Child Welfare Committee to take care of the child. The performance of the Child Welfare Committees must be reviewed by the High Court with a committee of not less than three Hon'ble Judges and two psychiatrists;

(j) A child must not be charged with any offence under the ITPA or IPC;

(k) A minor trafficked victim must be classified as a child in need of care and protection. Further, the Magistrate must also order for intermediate custody of minor under section 17(3) of the ITPA, 1956;

(l) There should not be any joint proceedings of a juvenile and a person who is not a juvenile on account of section 18 of the Juvenile Justice (Care and Protection) Act, 2002;

(m) It is necessary that Courts must be directed that the same lawyer must not represent the trafficker as well as the trafficked minor;

(n) Evidence of child should be taken in camera. Courts must protect the dignity of children. The children's best interest should be the priority."

3. "Learned Solicitor General also gave suggestions as under:

Child-line services are provided for children in distress

These should be catalogued and there should be a central registry which will provide information about the status of the child-line services at the local level. It should be the District Magistrate who must be responsible for the effective running of the child-line service. All District Magistrates in the country must post on the website their child-line service number and must give effective publicity to the services available and invite members of civil society to report any child in distress at numbers.

Shishu Griha to promote in-country adoption

Details of the working of the said scheme need to be collected and a database must be maintained in respect of orphans/abandoned/destitute infants or children upto 6 years. The adoptive parents must be obliged to give reports to the District Judge who will in turn examine whether the adoptive parents have taken care of the child failing which adequate court-monitored measures may be necessary.

Schemes for working children in need of care and protection

This scheme is very important. Children who are engaged as domestic labour, working at roadside dhabas and mechanic shops have to be rescued and a bridge education has to be provided including vocational training.

This must be undertaken again by identifiable points of responsibility. It is necessary that an Executive Magistrate must be allocated a certain area to be covered where children are rescued. This should be undertaken by a District Magistrate dividing his district in suitable divisions where such Executive Magistrates can rescue working children. They need to be rehabilitated. It is important that rescue will be effective only when there is scope for rehabilitation. It should not happen that in the name of rehabilitation children are put in detention homes or remand homes. That would be an act of cruelty."

4. "Learned Solicitor General further gave suggestions including Pilot Project to combat the trafficking of women and children for commercial sexual exploitation as under:

Pilot Project to combat the trafficking of women and children for commercial sexual exploitation:

This is a source and destination area for providing care and protection to trafficked and sexually abused women and children. Components of the scheme include networking with law enforcement agencies, rescue operation, temporary shelter for the victims, repatriation to hometown and legal services, etc.

Central Adoption Resource Agency (CARA)

It is an autonomous body under the Ministry of Women and Child Development to promote in-country adoption and regulate inter-country adoption. CARA also helps both Indian and foreign agencies involved in adoption of Indian children to function within a regulated framework, so that such children are adopted legally through recognised agencies and no exploitation takes place.

National Child Labour Project (NCLP) for rehabilitation of child labourers

Under the Scheme, project societies at the district level are fully funded for opening up of Special Schools/Rehabilitation centers to provide non-formal education, vocational training, supplementary nutrition, stipends, etc. to children withdrawn from employment.

The most outstanding feature of this scheme which needs to be implemented on a full-time and firm basis is the government civil society partnership. This will involve active involvement of the voluntary sector, research and training institutions, law college students, advocacy groups and the corporate sector. It should be the duty of the Health Secretary of each state government including under the chairmanship of the Health Secretary, Government of India to have a blueprint for implementing the Government - Civil Society initiative. It is necessary that there must be a 6- monthly strategy plan which must be prepared by the state government and also by the central government in this regard.

The ICPS programmes are now brought under one umbrella and are as follows:

(a) Care, support and rehabilitation services through child-line;

(b) Open shelters for children in need in urban/semi-urban areas;

(c) Family based non-institutional care through sponsorship, foster care, adoption and aftercare."

The provisions of the Right of Children to Free and Compulsory Education Act, 2009 are material. By virtue of section 3 of the Act, every child of the age of 6-14 years shall have a right to free and compulsory education in a neighbourhood school till completion of elementary education. The Central Government has notified the Act in the Gazette on 27th August, 2009 and the Act has been brought into force with effect from 1st April, 2010. It may also be noted that Chapter 6 of the Act has special provisions for protection of the right of children. The National Commission for Protection of Child Rights has already been constituted. The said Commission now receives a statutory status by virtue of this Act. In view of the performance of the present National Commission for Protection of Child Rights, which has taken pioneering efforts, it is expected that on a close interface between the National Commission for Protection of Child Rights, the State Governments and the Ministry of Women and Child Development, positive outcomes should actually be worked out.

It is, therefore, necessary that a coordinated effort must be made by the three agencies, namely, the Commission, the Ministry and the State Governments. Learned Solicitor General submitted that the recommendations be implemented by the concerned agencies. In the State/Union Territory, the responsibility must be cast either on the Chief Secretary or a Secretary In-charge of Children, Women and Family Welfare. It would be open to the State Government in appropriate cases to nominate a special officer for the said purpose not lower than the rank of a Secretary to the State Government. Each State must issue a circular effectively indicating how the recommendations will be implemented.

CHAPTER 2

BIGAMY

The Second Wife as "Aggrieved Person"

A. Subash Babu v. *State of Andhra Pradesh*, (2011) 7 SCC 616

Meaning of the phrase "aggrieved person" expanded so as to entitle a woman, with whom a second marriage is contracted by suppressing fact of former marriage, to make a complaint of bigamy under section 494.

Section 494 IPC introduces monogamy which is essentially voluntary union of life of one man with one woman to the exclusion of all others. It enacts that neither party must have a spouse living at the time of marriage .... In post vedic India a King could take and generally used to have more than one wife. Section 4, of Hindu Marriage Act nullifies and supersedes such practice all over India, among the Hindus. Section 494 is intended to achieve laudable object of monogamy. This object can be achieved only by expanding the meaning of the phrase "aggrieved person."

Background: In a landmark verdict, for the first time, the Supreme Court has held that a woman, with whom a second marriage is contracted by suppressing fact of former marriage, is an "aggrieved person" for purposes of section 198 Cr.P.C. and would be entitled to maintain a criminal complaint of bigamy under sections 494 and 495 IPC.

The Legal Imperative: If the woman with whom the second marriage is performed by concealment of former marriage is entitled to file a complaint for commission of offence under section 495 IPC, there is no reason why she would not be entitled to file complaint under section 494 IPC more particularly when section 495 IPC is extension and part and parcel of section 494 IPC.

"For variety of reasons the first wife may not choose to file complaint against her husband *e.g.* when she is assured of re-union by her husband, when husband assures to snap the tie of second marriage etc. Non-filing of the complaint under section 494 IPC by first wife does not mean that the offence is wiped out and monogamy sought to be achieved by means of section 494 IPC merely remains in statute book. Having regard to the scope, purpose, context and object of enacting section 494 IPC and also the prevailing practices in the society sought to be curbed by section 494 IPC, there is no manner of doubt that the complainant should be an aggrieved person. Section 198(1)(c) of the Criminal Procedure Code, amongst other things, provides that where the person aggrieved by an offence under section 494 or section 495 IPC is the wife, complaint on her behalf may also be filed by her father, mother, sister, son, daughter etc. or with the leave of the Court, by any other person related to her by blood, marriage or adoption.

> "In *Gopal Lal* v. *State of Rajasthan,* (1979) 2 SCC 170: AIR 1979 SC 713: 1979 Cr LJ 652 this Court has ruled that in order to attract the provisions of section 494 IPC both the marriages of the accused must be valid in the sense that the necessary ceremonies required by the personal law governing the parties must have been duly performed.
>
> "...... Though the law specifically does not cast obligation on either party to seek declaration of nullity of marriage and it may be open to the parties even without recourse to the Court to treat the marriage as a nullity, such a course is neither prudent nor intended and a declaration in terms of section 11 of the Hindu Marriage Act will have to be asked for, for the purpose of precaution and/or record. Therefore, until the declaration contemplated by section 11 of the Hindu Marriage Act is made by a competent Court, the woman with whom second marriage is solemnized continues to be the wife within the meaning of section 494 IPC and would be entitled to maintain a complaint against her husband.
>
> " ...... Section 494 does not restrict right of filing complaint to the first wife and there is no reason to read the said section in a restricted manner as is suggested by the learned Counsel for the appellant. Section 494 does not say that the complaint for commission of offence under the said section can be filed only by wife living and not by the woman with whom subsequent marriage takes place during the lifetime of the wife living and which marriage is void by reason of its taking place during the life of such wife. The complaint can also be filed by the person with whom second marriage takes place which is void by reason of its taking place during the life of first wife.
>
> "The offence mentioned in section 495 IPC is an aggravated form of bigamy provided in section 494 IPC. The circumstance of aggravation is the concealment of the fact of the former marriage to the person with whom the second marriage is contracted. Since the offence under section 495 IPC is in essence bigamy, it follows that all the elements necessary to constitute that offence must be present here also. A married man who by passing himself off as unmarried induces an innocent woman to become, as she thinks his wife, but in reality his mistress, commits one of the grossest forms of frauds known to law and therefore severe punishment is provided in section 495 IPC.
>
> "Section 495 begins with the words "whoever commits the offence defined in the last preceding section......"; The reference to section 494 IPC in section 495 IPC makes it clear that section 495 IPC is extension of section 494 IPC and part and parcel of it. The concealment spoken of in section 495 IPC would be from the woman with whom the subsequent marriage is performed. Therefore, the wife with whom the subsequent marriage is contracted after concealment of former marriage would also be entitled to

lodge complaint for commission of offence punishable under section 495 IPC. Where second wife alleges that the accused husband had married her according to Hindu rites despite the fact that he was already married to another lady and the factum of the first marriage was concealed from her, the second wife would be an aggrieved person within the meaning of section 198 Cr. P.C.

"For all these reasons, it is held that the woman with whom second marriage is contracted by suppressing the fact of former marriage would be entitled to maintain complaint against her husband under sections 494 and 495 IPC."

CHAPTER 3
LAW OF PERSONAL LIBERTY AND ANTICIPATORY BAIL

"Just as the Liberty is precious to an individual, so is the society's interest in maintenance of peace, law and order. Both are equally important."

–Justice Dalvir Bhandari

Siddharam Satlingappa Mhetre v. *State of Maharashtra*, (2011) 1 SCC 694: AIR 2011 SC 312: AIR 2011 SC (Criminal) 308

Section 438 CrPC – discretion of court to grant or refuse anticipatory bail – manner of exercise of – factors to be taken into consideration – arrest.

> "The society has a vital interest in grant or refusal of bail because every criminal offence is the offence against the State. The order granting or refusing bail must reflect perfect balance between the conflicting interests, namely, sanctity of individual liberty and the interest of the society. The law of bails dovetails two conflicting interests namely, on the one hand, the requirements of shielding the society from the hazards of those committing crimes and potentiality of repeating the same crime while on bail and on the other hand absolute adherence of the fundamental principle of criminal jurisprudence regarding presumption of innocence of an accused until he is found guilty and the sanctity of individual liberty."

Relevance and importance of personal liberty

1. All human beings are born with some unalienable rights like life, liberty and pursuit of happiness. The importance of these natural rights can be found in the fact that these are fundamental for their proper existence and no other right can be enjoyed without the presence of right to life and liberty. Life bereft of liberty would be without honour and dignity and it would lose all significance and meaning and the life itself would not be worth living. That is why "liberty" is called the very quintessence of a civilized existence.

2. Origin of "liberty" can be traced in the ancient Greek civilization. The Greeks distinguished between the liberty of the group and the liberty of the individual. In 431 B.C., an Athenian statesman described that the concept of liberty was the outcome of two notions, firstly, protection of group from attack and secondly, the ambition of the group to realize itself as fully as possible through the self-realization of the individual by way of human reason. Greeks assigned the duty of protecting their liberties to the State. According to

Aristotle, as the state was a means to fulfil certain fundamental needs of human nature and was a means for development of individuals' personality in association of fellow citizens so it was natural and necessary to man. Plato found his "republic" as the best source for the achievement of the self-realization of the people.

3. Chambers' Twentieth Century Dictionary defines "liberty" as

> "Freedom to do as one pleases, the unrestrained employment of natural rights, power of free chance, privileges, exemption, relaxation of restraint, the bounds within which certain privileges are enjoyed, freedom of speech and action beyond ordinary civility."

4. It is very difficult to define the "liberty". It has many facets and meanings. The philosophers and moralists have praised freedom and liberty but this term is difficult to define because it does not resist any interpretation. The term "liberty" may be defined as the affirmation by an individual or group of his or its own essence. It needs the presence of three factors, firstly, harmonious balance of personality, secondly, the absence of restraint upon the exercise of that affirmation and thirdly, organization of opportunities for the exercise of a continuous initiative.

5. "Liberty" may be defined as a power of acting according to the determinations of the will. According to Harold Laski, "liberty" was essentially an absence of restraints and John Stuart Mill viewed that "all restraint qua restraint is an evil." In the words of Jonathon Edwards, the meaning of "liberty" and freedom is:

> "Power, opportunity or advantage that anyone has to do as he pleases, or, in other words, his being free from hindrance or impediment in the way of doing, or conducting in any respect, as he wills."

6. It can be found that "liberty" generally means the prevention of restraints and providing such opportunities, the denial of which would result in frustration and ultimately disorder. Restraints on man's liberty are laid down by power used through absolute discretion, which when used in this manner brings an end to "liberty" and freedom is lost. At the same time "liberty" without restraints would mean liberty won by one and lost by another. So "liberty" means doing of anything one desires but subject to the desire of others.

7. As John Emerich Edward Dalberg in his monograph Essays on Freedom and Power wrote that Liberty is one of the most essential requirements of the modern man. It is said to be the delicate fruit of a mature civilization.

8. Harold J. Laski in his monumental work in Liberty in the Modern State observed that liberty always demands a limitation on political authority. Power as such when uncontrolled is always the natural enemy of freedom.

9. Roscoe Pound, an eminent and one of the greatest American Law Professors aptly observed in his book The Development of Constitutional Guarantee of Liberty that:

"whatever, `liberty' may mean today, the liberty is guaranteed by our bills of rights, is a reservation to the individual of certain fundamental reasonable expectations involved in life in civilized society and a freedom from arbitrary and unreasonable exercise of the power and authority of those who are designated or chosen in a politically organized society to adjust that society to individuals."

10. *Blackstone in Commentaries on the Laws of England,* Vol. I, p. 134 aptly observed that"

"Personal liberty consists in the power of locomotion, of changing situation or moving one's person to whatsoever place one's own inclination may direct, without imprisonment or restraint unless by due process of law."

11. Dicey, a distinguished English author, in his treatise on Constitutional Law observed that:

"Personal liberty, as understood in England, means in substance a person's right not to be subjected to imprisonment, arrest, or other physical coercion in any manner that does not admit of legal justification." [*Dicey on Constitutional Law,* 9th Edn., pp. 207-08]."

According to him, it is the negative right of not being subjected to any form of physical restraint or coercion that constitutes the essence of personal liberty and not mere freedom to move to any part of the Indian territory. In ordinary language personal liberty means liberty relating to or concerning the person or body of the individual, and personal liberty in this sense is the antithesis of physical restraint or coercion.

12. An eminent English Judge, Lord Alfred Denning, observed:

"By personal freedom I mean freedom of every law abiding citizen to think what he will, to say what he will, and to go where he will on his lawful occasion without hindrance from any person.... It must be matched, of course, with social security by which I mean the peace and good order of the community in which we live."

13. The Fundamental Rights represent the basic values enriched by the people of this country. The aim behind having elementary right of the individual such as the Right to Life and Liberty is not fulfilled as desired by the framers of the Constitution. It is to preserve and protect certain basic human rights against interference by the state. The inclusion of a Chapter in Constitution is in accordance with the trends of modern democratic thought. The object is to ensure the inviolability of certain essential rights against political vicissitudes.

14. The Framers of the Indian Constitution followed the American model in adopting and incorporating the Fundamental Rights for the people of India. The American Constitution provides that no person shall be deprived of his life, liberty, or property without due process of law. The due process clause not only protects the property but also life and liberty, similarly Article 21 of the Indian Constitution asserts the importance of life and liberty.

15. Life and personal liberty are the most prized possessions of an individual. The inner urge for freedom is a natural phenomenon of every human being. Respect for life, liberty and property is not merely a norm or a policy of the State but an essential requirement of any civilized society.

16. After dealing with the concept of life and liberty under the Indian Constitution, we would like to have the brief survey of other countries to ascertain how life and liberty has been protected in other countries.

UNITED KINGDOM

17. Life and personal liberty has been given prime importance in the United Kingdom. It was in 1215 that the people of England revolted against King John and enforced their rights, first time the King had acknowledged that there were certain rights of the subject called Magna Carta 1215. In 1628 the petition of rights was presented to King Charles-I which was the 1st step in the transfer of Sovereignty from the King to Parliament. It was passed as the Bill of Rights 1689.

18. Right to life is the most fundamental of all human rights and any decision affecting human right or which may put an individual's life at risk must call for the most anxious scrutiny. See: *Bugdaycay* v. *Secretary of State for the Home Department,* (1987) 1 All ER 940. The sanctity of human life is probably the most fundamental of the human social values. It is recognized in all civilized societies and their legal system and by the internationally recognized statements of human rights. [*Pretty* v. *Director of Public Prosecutions,* (2002) 1 All ER 1].

U.S.A.

19. The importance of personal liberty is reflected in the Fifth Amendment to the Constitution of U.S.A. which declares as under:

> "No person shall be deprived of his life, liberty or property, without due process of law."

(The 'due process' clause was adopted in section 1(a) of the Canadian Bill of Rights Act, 1960. In the Canada Act, 1982, this expression has been substituted by 'the principles of fundamental justice' [section 7].

20. The Fourteenth Amendment imposes similar limitation on the State authorities. These two provisions are conveniently referred to as the 'due process clauses'. Under the above clauses the American Judiciary claims to declare a law as bad, if it is not in accordance with 'due process', even though the legislation may be within the competence of the Legislature concerned. Due process as conveniently understood means procedural regularity and fairness. (*Constitutional Interpretation by Craig R. Ducat,* 8th Edn., 2002, p. 475.).

WEST GERMANY

21. Article 2(2) of the West German Constitution (1948) declares:

> "Everyone shall have the right to life and physical inviolability. The freedom of the individual shall be inviolable. These rights may be interfered with only on the basis of the legal order."

Though the freedom of life and liberty guaranteed by the above Article may be restricted, such restriction will be valid only if it is in conformity with the 'legal order' (or 'pursuant to a law, according to official translation). Being a basic right, the freedom guaranteed by Article 2(2) is binding on the legislative, administrative and judicial organs of the State [Article 1(3)]. This gives the individual the rights to challenge the validity of a law or an executive act violative of the freedom of the person by a constitutional complaint to the Federal Constitutional Court, under Article 93. Procedural guarantee is given by Articles 103(1) and 104. Article 104(1)-2(2) provides:

"(1) The freedom of the individual may be restricted only on the basis of a formal law and only with due regard to the forms prescribed therein.........

(2) Only the Judge shall decide on the admissibility and continued deprivation of liberty."

22. These provisions correspond to Article 21 of our Constitution and the court is empowered to set a man to liberty if it appears that he has been imprisoned without the authority of a formal law or in contravention of the procedure prescribed there.

JAPAN

23. Article XXXI of the Japanese Constitution of 1946 says:

> "No person shall be deprived of life or liberty nor shall any other criminal penalty be imposed, except according to procedure established by law."

This article is similar to Article 21 of our Constitution save that it includes other criminal penalties, such as fine or forfeiture within its ambit.

CANADA

24. Section 1(1) of the Canadian Bill of Rights Act, 1960, adopted the 'Due Process' Clause from the American Constitution. But the difference in the Canadian set-up was due to the fact that this Act was not a constitutional instrument to impose a direct limitation on the Legislature but only a statute for interpretation of Canadian status, which, again, could be excluded from the purview of the Act of 1960, in particular cases, by an express declaration made by the Canadian Parliament itself (section 2). The result was obvious: The Canadian Supreme Court in *R.* v. *Curr,* (1972) SCR 889 held that the Canadian Court would not import 'substantive reasonableness' into section 1(a), because of the unsalutary experience of substantive due process in the U.S.A.; and that as to 'procedural reasonableness', section 1(a) of the Bill of Rights Act only referred to 'the legal processes recognized by Parliament and the Courts in Canada'. The result was that in Canada, the 'due process clause' lost its utility as an instrument of judicial review of legislation and it came to mean practically the same thing as whatever the Legislature prescribes, - much the same as 'procedure established by law' in Article 21 of the Constitution of India, as interpreted in A.K. Gopalan (*supra*).

INTERNATIONAL CHARTERS

Universal Declaration, 1948.

25. Article 3 of the Universal Declaration says:

> "Everyone has the right to life, liberty and security of person."

Article 9 provides:

> "No one shall be subjected to arbitrary arrest, detention or exile."

Article 10 says:

> "Everyone is entitled in full equality to a fair and public hearing by an independent and impartial tribunal, in the determination of his rights and obligations and of any criminal charge against him." [As to its legal effect, see *M.* v. *Organisation Belge*, (1972) 45 Inter LR 446 (447, 451, et. Sq.)]

Covenant on Civil and Political Rights (1966)

26. Article 9 (1) says:

> "Everyone has the right to liberty and security of person. No one shall be subjected to arbitrary arrest or detention. No one shall be deprived of his liberty except on such grounds and in accordance with such procedure as are established by law."

European Convention for the Protection of Human Rights and Fundamental Freedoms, 1950.

27. This Convention contains a most elaborate and detailed codification of the rights and safeguards for the protection of life and personal liberty against arbitrary invasion.

28. In every civilized democratic country, liberty is considered to be the most precious human right of every person. The Law Commission of India in its 177th Report under the heading 'Introduction to the doctrine of arrest' has described as follows:

> "Liberty is the most precious of all the human rights. It has been the founding faith of the human race for more than 200 years. Both the American Declaration of Independence, 1776 and the French Declaration of the Rights of Man and the Citizen, 1789, spoke of liberty being one of the natural and inalienable rights of man. The universal declaration of human rights adopted by the general assembly on United Nations on December 10, 1948 contains several articles designed to protect and promote the liberty of individual. So does the international covenant on civil and political rights, 1996. Above all, Article 21 of the Constitution of India proclaims that no one shall be deprived of his right to personal liberty except in accordance with the procedure prescribed by law. Even Article 20(1) & (2) and Article 22 are born out of a concern for human liberty. As it is often said, 'one realizes the value of liberty only when he is deprived of it.' Liberty, along ;;with equality is the most fundamental of human rights and the fundamental freedoms guaranteed by the Constitution. Of equal importance is the maintenance of peace, law and order in the society. Unless, there is peace, no real progress

is possible. Societal peace lends stability and security to the polity. It provides the necessary conditions for growth, whether it is in the economic sphere or in the scientific and technological spheres."

29. Just as the Liberty is precious to an individual, so is the society's interest in maintenance of peace, law and order. Both are equally important.

30. It is a matter of common knowledge that a large number of under-trials are languishing in jail for a long time even for allegedly committing very minor offences. This is because section 438 Cr.P.C. has not been allowed its full play. The Constitution Bench in Sibbia's case (supra) clearly mentioned that section 438 Cr.P.C. is extraordinary because it was incorporated in the Code of Criminal Procedure, 1973 and before that other provisions for grant of bail were sections 437 and 439 Cr.P.C. It is not extraordinary in the sense that it should be invoked only in exceptional or rare cases. Some courts of smaller strength have erroneously observed that section 438 Cr.P.C. should be invoked only in exceptional or rare cases. Those orders are contrary to the law laid down by the judgment of the Constitution Bench in Sibbia's case (supra). According to the report of the National Police Commission, the power of arrest is grossly abused and clearly violates the personal liberty of the people, as enshrined under Article 21 of the Constitution, then the courts need to take serious notice of it. *When conviction rate is admittedly less than 10%, then the police should be slow in arresting the accused.* The courts considering the bail application should try to maintain fine balance between the societal interest vis-'-vis personal liberty while adhering to the fundamental principle of criminal jurisprudence that the accused is presumed to be innocent till he is found guilty by the competent court.

31. It is imperative for the courts to carefully and with meticulous precision evaluate the facts of the case. The discretion must be exercised on the basis of the available material and the facts of the particular case. In cases where the court is of the considered view that the accused has joined investigation and he is fully cooperating with the investigating agency and is not likely to abscond, in that event, custodial interrogation should be avoided.

32. A great ignominy, humiliation and disgrace is attached to the arrest. Arrest leads to many serious consequences not only for the accused but for the entire family and at times for the entire community. Most people do not make any distinction between arrest at a pre-conviction stage or post-conviction stage.

Grant of bail for limited period is contrary to the legislative intention and law declared by the Constitution Bench

32. In pursuance to the order of the Court of Sessions or the High Court, once the accused is released on bail by the trial court, then it would be unreasonable to compel the accused to surrender before the trial court and again apply for regular bail.

33. The court must bear in mind that at times the applicant would approach the court for grant of anticipatory bail on mere apprehension of being arrested

on accusation of having committed a non-bailable offence. In fact, the investigating or concerned agency may not otherwise arrest that applicant who has applied for anticipatory bail but just because he makes an application before the court and gets the relief from the court for a limited period and thereafter he has to surrender before the trial court and only thereafter his bail application can be considered and life of anticipatory bail comes to an end. This may lead to disastrous and unfortunate consequences. The applicant who may not have otherwise lost his liberty loses it because he chose to file application of anticipatory bail on mere apprehension of being arrested on accusation of having committed a non-bailable offence. No arrest should be made because it is lawful for the police officer to do so. The existence of power to arrest is one thing and the justification for the exercise of it is quite another. The police officer must be able to justify the arrest apart from his power to do so. This finding of the said judgment (supra) is contrary to the legislative intention and law which has been declared by a Constitution Bench of this court in *Sibbia's* case (supra).

34. The validity of the restrictions imposed by the Apex Court, namely, that the accused released on anticipatory bail must submit himself to custody and only thereafter can apply for regular bail. This is contrary to the basic intention and spirit of section 438 Cr.P.C. It is also contrary to Article 21 of the Constitution. The test of fairness and reasonableness is implicit under Article 21 of the Constitution of India. Directing the accused to surrender to custody after the limited period amounts to deprivation of his personal liberty.

35. It is a settled legal position crystallized by the Constitution Bench of this court in Sibbia's case (supra) that the courts should not impose restrictions on the ambit and scope of section 438 Cr.P.C. which are not envisaged by the Legislature. The court cannot rewrite the provision of the statute in the garb of interpreting it.

36. It is unreasonable to lay down strict, inflexible and rigid rules for exercise of such discretion by limiting the period of which an order under this section could be granted.

37. The Apex Court in Salauddin's case (supra) held that anticipatory bail should be granted only for a limited period and on the expiry of that duration it should be left to the regular court to deal with the matter is not the correct view. The reasons quoted in the said judgment is that anticipatory bail is granted at a stage when an investigation is incomplete and the court is not informed about the nature of evidence against the alleged offender. The said reason would not be right as the restriction is not seen in the enactment and bail orders by the High Court and Sessions Court are granted under sections 437 and 439 also at such stages and they are granted till the trial.

38. The view expressed by this Court in all the above referred judgments have to be reviewed and once the anticipatory bail is granted then the protection should ordinarily be available till the end of the trial unless the interim protection by way of the grant of anticipatory bail is curtailed when the anticipatory bail granted by the court is cancelled by the court on finding

fresh material or circumstances or on the ground of abuse of the indulgence by the accused.

SCOPE AND AMBIT OF ANTICIPATORY BAIL

39. A good deal of misunderstanding with regard to the ambit and scope of section 438 Cr.P.C. could have been avoided in case the Constitution Bench decision of this court in Sibbia's case (supra) was correctly understood, appreciated and applied. This Court in the *Sibbia's* case (*supra*) laid down the following principles with regard to anticipatory bail:

(a) Section 438(1) is to be interpreted in light of Article 21 of the Constitution of India.

(b) Filing of FIR is not a condition precedent to exercise of power under section 438.

(c) Order under section 438 would not affect the right of police to conduct investigation.

(d) Conditions mentioned in section 437 cannot be read into section 438.

(e) Although the power to release on anticipatory bail can be described as of an "extraordinary" character this would "not justify the conclusion that the power must be exercised in exceptional cases only." Powers are discretionary to be exercised in light of the circumstances of each case.

(f) Initial order can be passed without notice to the Public Prosecutor. Thereafter, notice must be issued forthwith and question ought to be re-examined after hearing. Such ad interim order must conform to requirements of the section and suitable conditions should be imposed on the applicant.

40. The Law Commission in July 2002 has severely criticized the police of our country for the arbitrary use of power of arrest which, the Commission said, is the result of the vast discretionary powers conferred upon them by this Code. The Commission expressed concern that there is no internal mechanism within the police department to prevent misuse of law in this manner and the stark reality that complaint lodged in this regard does not bring any result. The Commission intends to suggest amendments in the Criminal Procedure Code and has invited suggestions from various quarters. Reference is made in this Article to the 41st Report of the Law Commission wherein the Commission saw 'no justification' to require a person to submit to custody, remain in prison for some days and then apply for bail even when there are reasonable grounds for holding that the person accused of an offence is not likely to abscond or otherwise misuse his liberty. Discretionary power to order anticipatory bail is required to be exercised keeping in mind these sentiments and spirit of the judgments of this court in *Sibbia's* case (*supra*) and *Joginder Kumar* v. *State of Uttar Pradesh,* (1994) 4 SCC 260: AIR 1994 SC 1349: 1994 Cr LJ 1981.

Relevant consideration for exercise of the power

41. No inflexible guidelines or straitjacket formula can be provided for grant or refusal of anticipatory bail. We are clearly of the view that no attempt

should be made to provide rigid and inflexible guidelines in this respect because all circumstances and situations of future cannot be clearly visualized for the grant or refusal of anticipatory bail. In consonance with the legislative intention the grant or refusal of anticipatory bail should necessarily depend on facts and circumstances of each case. As aptly observed in the Constitution Bench decision in *Sibbia's* case (*supra*) that the High Court or the Court of Sessions to exercise their jurisdiction under section 438 Cr.P.C. by a wise and careful use of their discretion which by their long training and experience they are ideally suited to do. In any event, this is the legislative mandate which we are bound to respect and honour.

42. The following factors and parameters can be taken into consideration while dealing with the anticipatory bail:—

i. The nature and gravity of the accusation and the exact role of the accused must be properly comprehended before arrest is made;

ii. The antecedents of the applicant including the fact as to whether the accused has previously undergone imprisonment on conviction by a Court in respect of any cognizable offence;

iii. The possibility of the applicant to flee from justice; iv. The possibility of the accused's likelihood to repeat similar or the other offences.

v. Where the accusations have been made only with the object of injuring or humiliating the applicant by arresting him or her.

vi. Impact of grant of anticipatory bail particularly in cases of large magnitude affecting a very large number of people.

vii. The courts must evaluate the entire available material against the accused very carefully. The court must also clearly comprehend the exact role of the accused in the case. The cases in which accused is implicated with the help of sections 34 and 149 of the Indian Penal Code, the court should consider with even greater care and caution because over implication in the cases is a matter of common knowledge and concern;

viii. While considering the prayer for grant of anticipatory bail, a balance has to be struck between two factors namely, no prejudice should be caused to the free, fair and full investigation and there should be prevention of harassment, humiliation and unjustified detention of the accused;

ix. The court to consider reasonable apprehension of tampering of the witness or apprehension of threat to the complainant;

x. Frivolity in prosecution should always be considered and it is only the element of genuineness that shall have to be considered in the matter of grant of bail and in the event of there being some doubt as to the genuineness of the prosecution, in the normal course of events, the accused is entitled to an order of bail.

43. The arrest should be the last option and it should be restricted to those exceptional cases where arresting the accused is imperative in the facts and circumstances of that case. The court must carefully examine the entire available record and particularly the allegations which have been directly

attributed to the accused and these allegations are corroborated by other material and circumstances on record.

44. These are some of the factors which should be taken into consideration while deciding the anticipatory bail applications. These factors are by no means exhaustive but they are only illustrative in nature because it is difficult to clearly visualize all situations and circumstances in which a person may pray for anticipatory bail. If a wise discretion is exercised by the concerned judge, after consideration of entire material on record then most of the grievances in favour of grant of or refusal of bail will be taken care of. The legislature in its wisdom has entrusted the power to exercise this jurisdiction only to the judges of the superior courts. In consonance with the legislative intention we should accept the fact that the discretion would be properly exercised. In any event, the option of approaching the superior court against the court of Sessions or the High Court is always available.

Irrational and Indiscriminate arrest are gross violation of human rights

45. In *Joginder Kumar's* case (*supra*), a three Judge Bench of this Court has referred to the 3rd report of the National Police Commission, in which it is mentioned that the quality of arrests by the Police in India mentioned power of arrest as one of the chief sources of corruption in the police. The report suggested that, by and large, nearly 60% of the arrests were either unnecessary or unjustified and that such unjustified police action accounted for 43.2% of the expenditure of the jails.

46. In case, the State considers the following suggestions in proper perspective then perhaps it may not be necessary to curtail the personal liberty of the accused in a routine manner. These suggestions are only illustrative and not exhaustive.

(1) Direct the accused to join investigation and only when the accused does not cooperate with the investigating agency, then only the accused be arrested.

(2) Seize either the passport or such other related documents, such as, the title deeds of properties or the Fixed Deposit Receipts/Share Certificates of the accused.

(3) Direct the accused to execute bonds;

(4) The accused may be directed to furnish sureties of number of persons which according to the prosecution are necessary in view of the facts of the particular case.

(5) The accused be directed to furnish undertaking that he would not visit the place where the witnesses reside so that the possibility of tampering of evidence or otherwise influencing the course of justice can be avoided.

(6) Bank accounts be frozen for small duration during investigation.

47. In case the arrest is imperative, according to the facts of the case, in that event, the arresting officer must clearly record the reasons for the arrest of the accused before the arrest in the case diary, but in exceptional cases where it

becomes imperative to arrest the accused immediately, the reasons be recorded in the case diary immediately after the arrest is made without loss of any time so that the court has an opportunity to properly consider the case for grant or refusal of bail in the light of reasons recorded by the arresting officer.

48. In view of the clear declaration of law laid down by the Constitution Bench in *Sibbia's* case (supra), it would not be proper to limit the life of anticipatory bail. When the court observed that the anticipatory bail is for limited duration and thereafter the accused should apply to the regular court for bail, that means the life of section 438 Cr.P.C. would come to an end after that limited duration. This limitation has not been envisaged by the legislature. The Constitution Bench in *Sibbia's* case (supra) clearly observed that it is not necessary to re-write section 438 Cr.P.C. Therefore, in view of the clear declaration of the law by the Constitution Bench, the life of the order under section 438 Cr.P.C. granting bail cannot be curtailed.

49. The ratio of the judgment of the Constitution Bench in Sibbia's case (supra) perhaps was not brought to the notice of their Lordships who had decided the cases of *Salauddin Abdulsamad Shaikh* v. *State of Maharashtra*, AIR 1996 SC 1042: 1996 Cr LJ 1368; *K.L. Verma* v. *State*, (1998) 9 SCC 348; *Adri Dharan Das* v. *State of West Bengal*, (2005) 4 SCC 303: 2005 AIR SCW 1013 and *Sunita Devi* v. *State of Bihar*, AIR 2005 SC 498: (2005) 1 SCC 608.

50. In *Naresh Kumar Yadav* v. *Ravindra Kumar*, (2008) 1 SCC 632: AIR 2008 SC 218: 2007 AIR SCW 6617, a two-Judge Bench of this Court observed & quote the power exercisable under section 438 Cr.P.C. is somewhat extraordinary in character and it should be exercised only in exceptional cases. This approach is contrary to the legislative intention and the Constitution Bench's decision in *Sibbia's* case (supra).

51. We deem it appropriate to reiterate and assert that discretion vested in the court in all matters should be exercised with care and circumspection depending upon the facts and circumstances justifying its exercise. Similarly, the discretion vested with the court under section 438 Cr.P.C. should also be exercised with caution and prudence. It is unnecessary to travel beyond it and subject to the wide power and discretion conferred by the legislature to a rigorous code of self-imposed limitations.

52. In the instant case there is a direct judgment of the Constitution Bench of this court in *Sibbia's* case (*supra*) dealing with exactly the same issue regarding ambit, scope and object of the concept of anticipatory bail enumerated under section 438 Cr.P.C. The controversy is no longer *res integra*. We are clearly bound to follow the said judgment of the Constitution Bench. The judicial discipline obliges us to follow the said judgment in letter and spirit.

CHAPTER 4

CRIMES AGAINST SCHEDULED CASTES AND SCHEDULED TRIBES – NEED FOR SPECIAL PROTECTION

Kailas v. *State of Maharashtra*, (2011) 1 SCC 793: AIR 2011 SC 598: 2011 (2) AIR Bom R 207

Background: This case is living manifestation of the perverted male concept reflected in the age old saying:

"woman, dog and walnut tree. The more you beat them, the better they be"

It brings to light a case where a young woman Nanda Bai aged 25 years belonging to Bhil Tribe (Scheduled Tribe) in Maharashtra, was beaten with fists and kind and stripped and paraded naked in village by the Accused.

The Verdict

1. The victim was a young tribal woman 25 years of age who got paraded in naked condition on the village road in broad day light while being beaten and abused by the accused herein. The offence is shameful, shocking and outrageous.

2. Thus it is the Constitution of India which is keeping us together despite all our tremendous diversity, because the Constitution gives equal respect to all communities, sects, lingual and ethnic groups, etc. in the country. The Constitution guarantees to all citizens freedom of speech (Article 19), freedom of religion (Article 25), equality (Articles 14 to 17), liberty (Article 21), etc.

3. However, giving formal equality to all groups or communities in India would not result in genuine equality. The historically disadvantaged groups must be given special protection and help so that they can be uplifted from their poverty and low social status. It is for this reason that special provisions have been made in our Constitution in Articles 15(4), 15(5), 16(4), 16(4A), 46, etc. for the upliftment of these groups. Among these disadvantaged groups, the most disadvantaged and marginalized in India are the Adivasis (STs), who, as already mentioned, are the descendants of the original inhabitants of India, and are the most marginalized and living in terrible poverty with high rates of illiteracy, disease, early mortality etc. Their plight has been described by this Court in *Samatha* v. *State of Andhra Pradesh*, AIR 1997 SC 3297: 1997 AIR SCW 3361: 1997 (2) SCJ 539 (*vide* paragraphs 12 to 15). Hence, it is the duty of all people who love our country to see that no harm is done to the Scheduled

Tribes and that they are given all help to bring them up in their economic and social status, since they have been victimized for thousands of years by terrible oppression and atrocities. The mentality of our countrymen towards these tribals must change, and they must be given the respect they deserve as the original inhabitants of India.

Various Aspects

4. Since India is a country of great diversity, it is absolutely essential if we wish to keep our country united to have tolerance and equal respect for all communities and sects. It was due to the wisdom of our founding fathers that we have a Constitution which is secular in character, and which caters to the tremendous diversity in our country.

5. The injustice done to the tribal people of India is a shameful chapter in our country's history. The tribals were called 'rakshas' (demons), 'asuras', and what not. They were slaughtered in large numbers, and the survivors and their descendants were degraded, humiliated, and all kinds of atrocities inflicted on them for centuries. They were deprived of their lands, and pushed into forests and hills where they eke out a miserable existence of poverty, illiteracy, disease, etc. And now efforts are being made by some people to deprive them even of their forest and hill land where they are living, and the forest produce on which they survive.

6. The well known example of the injustice to the tribals is the story of Eklavya in the Adiparva of the Mahabharat. Eklavya wanted to learn archery, but Dronacharya refused to teach him, regarding him as low born. Eklavya then built a statue of Dronacharya and practiced archery before the statue. He would have perhaps become a better archer than Arjun, but since Arjun was Dronacharya's favourite pupil Dronacharya told Eklavya to cut off his right thumb and give it to him as 'guru dakshina' (gift to the teacher given traditionally by the student after his study is complete). In his simplicity Eklavya did what he was told.

7. This was a shameful act on the part of Dronacharya. He had not even taught Eklavya, so what right had he to demand 'guru dakshina', and that too of the right thumb of Eklavya so that the latter may not become a better archer than his favourite pupil Arjun?

8. Despite this horrible oppression on them, the tribals of India have generally (though not invariably) retained a higher level of ethics than the non-tribals in our country. They normally do not cheat, tell lies, and do other misdeeds which many non-tribals do. They are generally superior in character to the non-tribals. It is time now to undo the historical injustice to them.

CHAPTER 5

CHILD PROTECTION

Childline India Foundation v. *Allan John Waters,* (2011) 6 SCC 261: 2011 Cr LJ 2305: 2011 AIR SCW 1966

Constitutional and Statutory Safeguards for Children - Happy and healthy childhood free from abuse and exploitation:

Background: In October 2001, Ms. Maharukh Adenwala brought to the notice of the Bombay High Court that same children living at Anchorage shelters had complained about sexual abuse and sought the courts actual intervention.

The Verdict

1. Article 45 has provided that the State shall endeavor to provide early childhood care and education for all the children until they complete the age of fourteen years. This Directive Principle signifies that it is not only confined to primary education, but extends to free education whatever it may be upto the age of 14 years. Article 45 is supplementary to Article 24 on the ground that when the child is not to be employed before the age of 14 years, he is to be kept occupied in some educational institutions. It is suggested that Article 24 in turn supplements the clauses (e) and (f) of Article 39, thus ensuring distributive justice to children in the matter of education. Virtually, Article 45 recognizes the importance of dignity and personality of the child and directs the State to provide free and compulsory education for the children upto the age of 14 years.

2. The above analysis shows our Constitution provides several measures to protect our children. It obligates both Central, State & Union territories to protect them from the evils, provide free and good education and make them good citizens of this country. Several legislations and directions of this Court are there to safeguard their intent. But these are to be properly implemented and monitored. We hope and trust that all the authorities concerned through various responsible NGOs implement the same for better future of these children.

3. Under these circumstances, the impugned judgment of the High Court acquitting all the accused in respect of charges leveled against them is set aside and we restore the conviction and sentence passed by the trial Judge.

The Various Aspects

4. ...... Childline India Foundation and Ms. Maharukh Adenwala have been closely associated with the present case right from its inception. Childline

India Foundation as a *de facto* complainant and intervenor and Ms. Maharukh Adenwala as PW-2.

5. In October, 2001, when it was brought to the notice of Ms. Maharukh Adenwala that some children living at the Anchorage Shelters had complained about sexual abuse, she immediately brought this to the notice of the High Court of Bombay and obtained necessary orders. She along with the representatives of Childline lodged a complaint at Cuffe Parade Police Station about the unlawful activities at Anchorage Shelters. Since the police officers of Cuffe Parade Police Station refused to investigate the said complaint under the pretext that the matter is *sub judice* and pending before the High Court, she recorded the statements of some of the victims and placed it before the High Court seeking direction for the police to investigate into the complaint filed by the Childline.

6. It is unfortunate that respect for womanhood in our country is on the decline and cases of molestation and rape are steadily growing. Decency and morality in public and social life can be protected only if courts deal strictly with those who violate the social norms.

Constitutional provisions relating to children

7. Children are the greatest gift to humanity. The sexual abuse of children is one of the most heinous crimes. It is an appalling violation of their trust, an ugly breach of our commitment to protect the innocent. There are special safeguards in the Constitution that apply specifically to children. The Constitution has envisaged a happy and healthy childhood for children which is free from abuse and exploitation. Article 15(3) of the Constitution has provided the State with the power to make special provisions for women and children. Article 21A of the Constitution mandates that every child in India shall be entitled to free and compulsory education upto the age of 14 years. The word 'life' in the context of Article 21 of the Constitution has been found to include 'education' and accordingly this Court has implied that 'right to education' is in fact a fundamental right.

8. Article 23 of the Constitution prohibits traffic in human beings, beggars and other similar forms of forced labour and exploitation. Although this article does not specifically speak of children, yet it is applied to them and is more relevant in their context because children are the most vulnerable section of the society. It is a known fact that many children are exploited because of their poverty. They are deprived of education, made to do all sorts of work injurious to their health and personality. Article 24 expressly provides that no child below the age of 14 years shall be employed to work in any factory or mine or engaged in any hazardous employment. This Court has issued elaborate guidelines on this issue.

9. The Directive Principles of State Policy embodied in the Constitution of India provides policy of protection of children with a self- imposing direction towards securing the health and strength of workers, particularly, to see that the children of tender age are not abused, nor they are forced by economic necessity to enter into avocations unsuited to their strength.

CHAPTER 6

CRIMES AGAINST WOMEN BY POLICE – CUSTODIAL VIOLENCE OR DEATH

Mehboob Batcha v. *State,* (2011) 7 SCC 45

".....they should have been charged for murder and awarded death sentence, as murder by policemen in police custody is in our opinion in the category of rarest of rare cases deserving death sentence..."

Background: Nandagopal was illegally detained by the police on charges of theft. He died as a result of beating by policemen who also gang raped his wife Padmini in the most barbaric manner.

1. We have held in *Satya Narain Tiwari* v. *State of Uttar Pradesh,* JT 2010 (12) SC 154 and in *Sukhdev Singh* v. *State of Punjab,* SLP (Criminal) No. 8917 of 2010 decided on 12-11-2010 that crimes against women are not ordinary crimes committed in a fit of anger or for property. They are social crimes. They disrupt the entire social fabric, and hence they call for harsh punishment.

2. The horrendous manner in which Padmini was treated by policemen was shocking and atrocious, and calls for no mercy.

The Verdict:

3. We are surprised that the accused were not charged under section 302 IPC and instead the Courts below treated the death of Nandagopal as suicide. In fact they should have been charged under that provision and awarded death sentence, as murder by policemen in police custody is in our opinion in the category of rarest of rare cases deserving death sentence, but surprisingly no charge under section 302 IPC was framed against any of the accused. We are constrained to say that both the trial Court and High Court have failed in their duty in this connection. The entire incident took place within the premises of Annamalai Nagar police station and the accused deserve no mercy.

> "In the normal course, we could have issued notice of enhancement of sentence, but as no charge under section 302 IPC was framed, we cannot straightaway record conviction under that provision and enhance the punishment.

> [Authors' *Comment: The Supreme Court has condemned the trial court and High Court for failing in their duty; but failed to discharge its constitutional duty in passing appropriate orders by exercising powers vested under article 142 of the*

Constitution of India. Not framing a charge under section 302 was at best a technical error which could be corrected by remanding the case to trial court. – Perhaps the court realized its mistake and therefore, when a similar situation arose again, the Court in State of Uttar Pradesh v. *Alok Verma*, (2011) 8 SCC 434 *(decided after about six months), issued notice for enhancement of sentence proposing death penalty].*

4. Before parting with this case, we once again reiterate that custodial violence in police custody is in violation of this Court's directive in *D.K. Basu* v. *State of West Bengal*, (1997) 1 SCC 416: AIR 1997 SC 610: 1997 AIR SCW 233 and we give a warning to all policemen in the country that this will not be tolerated. The graphic description of the barbaric conduct of the accused in this case shocks our conscience. Policemen must learn how to behave as public servants in a democratic country, and not as oppressors of the people.

5. Let a copy of this order be sent to Home Secretary and Director General of Police of all States and Union Territories, who shall circulate the same to all police officers up to the level of S.H.O. with a directive that they must follow the directions given by this Court in *D.K. Basu's* case (*supra*), and that custodial violence shall entail harsh punishment."

6. In D.K. Basu's case this Court observed: ....

"Custodial violence, including torture and death in the lock-ups, strikes a blow at the rule of law, which demands that the powers of the executive should not only be derived from law but also that the same should be limited by law. Custodial violence is a matter of concern.It is aggravated by the fact that it is committed by persons who are supposed to be the protectors of the citizens. It is committed under the shield of uniform and authority in the four walls of a police station or lock-up, the victim being totally helpless. The protection of an individual from torture and abuse by the police and other law-enforcing officers is a matter of deep concern in a free society.In spite of the constitutional and statutory provisions aimed at safeguarding the personal liberty and life of a citizen, growing incidence of torture and deaths in police custody has been a disturbing factor. Experience shows that worst violations of human rights take place during the course of investigation, when the police with a *Mehboob Batcha* v. *State Rep.*, By Supdt. of Police on 29 March, 2011 Indian Kanoon -http://indiankanoon.org/doc/421778/5 view to secure evidence or confession often resorts to third-degree methods including torture and adopts techniques of screening arrest by either not recording the arrest or describing the deprivation of liberty merely as a prolonged interrogation. A reading of the morning newspapers almost everyday carrying reports of dehumanising torture, assault, rape and death in custody of police or other governmental agencies is indeed depressing. The increasing incidence of torture and death in custody has assumed such alarming proportions that it is affecting the credibility of the rule of law and the administration of criminal justice system. The community rightly feels perturbed. Society's cry for justice becomes louder. Custodial death is perhaps one of the worst crimes in a civilized society governed by the rule of law. The rights inherent in Articles 21 and 22(1) of the Constitution require to be jealously and scrupulously protected. We cannot wish away the problem. Any form of torture or cruel, inhuman or degrading treatment would fall within the inhibition of Article 21 of the Constitution, whether it occurs during investigation, interrogation or otherwise. If the functionaries of the Government become law-breakers, it is bound to breed contempt for law and would encourage lawlessness and every man would have the tendency to become law unto himself thereby leading to anarchism. No civilized nation can permit that to happen. Does a citizen shed off his fundamental right to life, the moment a policeman arrests him? Can the right to life of a citizen be put in abeyance on his arrest? These questions touch the spinal cord of human rights' jurisprudence. The answer, indeed, has to be an emphatic `No'".

CHAPTER 7

REHABILITATION OF SEX WORKERS

Budhadev Karmaskar v. *State of West Bengal*, (2011) 10 SCC 277: AIR 2011 SC 2636: 2011 AIR SCW 5233

Criminal Appeal No 135 of 2010 – Order dated 15 September, 2011

Sex workers rehabilitation panel constituted by Supreme Court – proper functioning – Art 21

Background

1. The Supreme Court emphasised the impending need to address the problems of sex workers. It opined that the task was Herculean and required long and patient effects. It recognized the need for awareness that sex workers were not bad girls but victims of poverty and circumstances.

Facts

2. The Supreme Court, while hearing the criminal appeal, felt the need to separately deal with the problems of sex workers and therefore continued the case by treating it as a Public Interest Litigation. The Court passed several orders from time to time in search of a solution for providing a life of dignity to the sex workers by giving them some technical skills through which they can earn their livelihood instead of by selling their bodies. The word 'life' in Article 21 of the Constitution was interpreted so as to mean a life of dignity, and not just an animal life.

3. The Court set up a panel for examining the problems and appointed Mr. Pradip Ghosh, Senior Advocate, as its Chairman. Earlier, the Court had out that the problem of sex workers cannot be resolved in a very short time and will require long, patient effort. In the language of the Court, "Our initial aim was to create awareness in the public that sex workers are not bad girls, but they are in this profession due to poverty. No girl would ordinarily enjoy this kind of work, but she is compelled to do it for sheer survival. Most sex workers come from poor families, they are subjected to ill treatment by the owners of the brothels, they are often beaten, not given proper food or medical treatment, and made to do this degrading work. Probably much of the money paid by their customers is taken away by others."

4. The Court noticed the panel's efforts in these words: "We are happy to note that the Panel has set about its task in right earnest, and is considering ways and means to implement our ideas so that the sex workers can get some technical training through which they can earn their livelihood and thus lead

a life of dignity which is guaranteed by Article 21 of the Constitution of India. In the Third Interim Report the Panel has prayed for the following:

(a) An appropriate order directing the State Governments and the Local Authorities to issue Ration Cards to the sex workers treating them as persons in special category and relaxing the rigours of the Rules/ requirements regarding the verification of their address and without mentioning their profession in the Card;

(b) An appropriate order be made directing the Central Government and the Election Commission to issue Voter's Identity Cards to the sex workers in relaxation of the rules/requirements in that behalf and without insisting on strict proof of their address/profession and without specifying their profession on the face of the Card;

(c) An order be made directing the Central Government and the State Governments to ensure that the admission of the children of sex workers in appropriate classes in the Government schools and Government sponsored schools and the schools run by the Municipal and District level authorities is not hampered in any way, because of their impaired social status.

(d) An appropriate order be made directing the Central Government to suitably alter and widen the UJWALA Scheme within a period of six months as directed by order dated 24-8-2011 (vide paragraph 26 of the said order) made in this matter.

(e) An order or direction be made to the effect that the amount paid or to be paid by the Central Government, State Governments and the Union Territories to the Secretary General of this Hon'ble Court as directed by order dated 24-8-2011, be deposited in the Bank Account of the Panel in the UCO Bank Supreme Court Compound Branch, in the name of "Panel Appointed by Supreme Court in Criminal Appeal No. 135/2011" to be operated jointly by the Chairman of the Panel Mr. Pradip Ghosh and Mr. Jayant Bhusan, a member of the Panel, in terms of the order dated 24-8-2011.

(f) Such appropriate orders as may be deemed fit and proper be made, for compliance by the Central Government of the earlier order made by the Hon'ble Court on 24-8-2011 with regard to office accommodation, secretarial staff assistance and furnishing the office with necessary infrastructure and to furnish report of compliance in this Hon'ble Court within a period to be fixed by the Hon'ble Court.

THE VERDICT

5. We are of the opinion that the suggestions of the Panel are good suggestions. Sex workers face great difficulty in getting ration cards, voter's identity cards or in opening bank accounts, etc. We are of the opinion that the authorities should see to it that sex workers do not face these difficulties as they are also citizens of India and have the same fundamental rights as others.

6. We, therefore, recommend that the suggestions made by the Panel in its Third Interim Report (which has been quoted above) shall be seriously taken into consideration by the Central Government, the State Governments and other

authorities and hence all efforts shall be made to implement these suggestions expeditiously. If there is any difficulty in implementing them, then on the next date we should be told about such difficulty.

7. From a perusal of the UJWALA Scheme it appears that the Central Government has scheme only for rescued trafficked women but no scheme for those sex workers who voluntarily want to leave the sex trade. In our opinion, proper effective scheme should be prepared for such women also. In this connection, we would like to say that the Central Government scheme has placed a condition that the rescued sex workers must stay in a corrective home in order to get technical training. In our opinion, no such condition should be imposed as many sex workers are reluctant to stay in these corrective homes which they consider as virtual prison."

Various aspects

8. This is a case of brutal murder of a sex worker. Sex workers are also human beings and no one has a right to assault or murder them. A person becomes a prostitute not because she enjoys it but because of poverty. Society must have sympathy towards the sex workers and must not look down upon them. They are also entitled to a life of dignity in view of Article 21 of the Constitution. In the novels and stories of the great Bengali Writer Sharat Chand Chattopadhyaya, many prostitutes have been shown to be women of very high character, *e.g.*, Rajyalakshmi in 'Shrikant', Chandramukhi in 'Devdas' etc.

9. The plight of prostitutes has been depicted by the great Urdu poet Sahir Ludhianvi in his poem 'Chakle' which has been sung in the Hindi film Pyasa "Jineh Naaz Hai Hind Per wo kahan hain"(simplified version of the verse 'Sana Khwan- e-taqdees-e-Mashrik Kahan Hain'). We may also refer to the character Sonya Marmelodov in Dostoyevsky's famous novel 'Crime and Punishment'. Sonya is depicted as a girl who sacrifices her body to earn some bread for her impoverished family. Reference may also be made to Amrapali, who was a contemporary of Lord Buddha. .... the prostitutes also have a right to live with dignity under Article 21 of the Constitution of India since they are also human beings and their problems also need to be addressed.

10. As already observed by us, a woman is compelled to indulge in prostitution not for pleasure but because of abject poverty. If such a woman is granted opportunity to avail some technical or vocational training, she would be able to earn her livelihood by such vocational training and skill instead of by selling her body. Hence, we direct the Central and the State Governments to prepare schemes for giving technical/vocational training to sex workers and sexually abused women in all cities in India. The schemes should mention in detail who will give the technical/vocational training and in what manner they can be rehabilitated and settled by offering them employment. For instance, if a technical training is for some craft like sewing garments, etc. then some arrangements should also be made for providing a market for such garments, otherwise they will remain unsold and unused, and consequently the women will not be able to feed herself."

CHAPTER 8

DOMESTIC VIOLENCE – PROTECTION OF WOMEN FROM DOMESTIC VIOLENCE ACT, 2005

Sandhya Manoj Wankhade v. *Manoj Bhimrao Wankhade*, (2011) 3 SCC 650

Background

This is a significant judgement interpreting the term "relative" of husband so as also to include his "female" relatives like his sister or mother. The judgment has widened the scope of the term "relative" of a husband against whom an aggrieved wife may lodge complaint.

This Appeal was directed against the judgment and order dated 5th March, 2010, passed by the Nagpur Bench of the Bombay High Court in Crl. W.P. No. 588 of 2009, *inter alia*, directing the Appellant to vacate her matrimonial house and confirming the order of the Sessions Judge deleting the names of the other Respondents from the proceedings.

Submissions

1. Questioning the said judgment and order of the Nagpur Bench of the Bombay High Court, Mr. Garvesh Kabra, learned Advocate appearing for the Appellant, submitted that the High Court had erred in confirming the order of the learned Sessions Judge in regard to deletion of names of the Respondent Nos.2 and 3 from the proceedings, upon confirmation of the finding of the Sessions Judge that no female could be made a party to a petition under the Domestic Violence Act, 2005, since the expression "female" had not been included in the definition of "respondent" in the said Act.

2. Mr. Kabra submitted that it would be evident from a plain reading of the proviso to section 2(q) of the Domestic Violence Act, 2005, that a wife or a female living in a relationship in the nature of marriage can, not only file a complaint against her husband or male partner but also against relatives of the husband or male partner. The term "relative" not having been defined in the Act, it could not be said that it excluded females from its operation.

3. Mr. Satyajit A. Desai, learned Advocate appearing for the Respondents, on the other hand, defended the orders passed by the Sessions Judge and the High Court and urged that the term "relative" must be deemed to include within its ambit only male members of the husband's family or the family of

the male partner. Learned counsel submitted that when the expression "female" had not been specifically included within the definition of "respondent" in section 2(q) of the Domestic Violence Act, 2005, it has to be held that it was the intention of the legislature to exclude female members from the ambit thereof.

The Verdict

4. Having carefully considered the submissions made on behalf of the respective parties, we are unable to sustain the decisions, both of the learned Sessions Judge as also the High Court, in relation to the interpretation of the expression "respondent" in section 2(q) of the Domestic Violence Act, 2005. For the sake of reference, section 2(q) of the above-said Act is extracted hereinbelow:

> "2(q). "respondent" means any adult male person who is, or has been, in a domestic relationship with the aggrieved person and against whom the aggrieved person has sought any relief under this Act:
>
> Provided that an aggrieved wife or female living in a relationship in the nature of a marriage may also file a complaint against a relative of the husband or the male partner."

5. From the above definition it would be apparent that although section 2(q) defines a respondent to mean any adult male person, who is or has been in a domestic relationship with the aggrieved person, the proviso widens the scope of the said definition by including a relative of the husband or male partner within the scope of a complaint, which may be filed by an aggrieved wife or a female living in a relationship in the nature of a marriage.

6. It is true that the expression "female" has not been used in the proviso to section 2(q) also, but, on the other hand, if the Legislature intended to exclude females from the ambit of the complaint, which can be filed by an aggrieved wife, females would have been specifically excluded, instead of it being provided in the proviso that a complaint could also be filed against a relative of the husband or the male partner.

7. No restrictive meaning has been given to the expression "relative", nor has the said expression been specifically defined in the Domestic Violence Act, 2005, to make it specific to males only. In such circumstances, it is clear that the legislature never intended to exclude female relatives of the husband or male partner from the ambit of a complaint that can be made under the provisions of the Domestic Violence Act, 2005.

8. In our view, both the Sessions Judge and the High Court went wrong in holding otherwise, possibly being influenced by the definition of the expression "respondent" in the main body of section 2(q) of the aforesaid Act.

9. The Appeal, therefore, succeeds. The judgments and orders, both of the learned Sessions Judge, Amravati, dated 15th July, 2009 and the Nagpur Bench of the Bombay High Court dated 5th March, 2010, in Crl. Writ Petition No.588 of 2009 are set aside. Consequently, the trial Court shall also proceed against the said Respondent Nos. 2 and 3 on the complaint filed by the Appellant.

CHAPTER 9

WITNESS PROTECTION AND SUPPORT

[A] Cancellation of bail on the prayer of the victim/complainant.

Ravindra Pal Singh v. *Ajit Singh,* (2011) 4 SCC 238

Background

This is a case where keeping in view the serious nature of allegations, the Supreme Court cancelled the Bail granted under section 439 Cr. PC on a prayer by the victim/complainant. The complainant, after performing last rites of his son, went back to Dehradun where he filed a case against the police personnel recorded as FIR No. 101/2009 dated 6-7-2009 under sections 120 B, 364, 302, 201 IPC. Later, in July 2009, the investigation was handed over to the CBI, Lucknow.

The Verdict

10. We have considered the submissions made by the learned counsel. We are of the considered opinion that the allegations made against the respondents cannot be brushed aside at this stage. The CBI after investigation of the matter has already submitted the charge-sheet. According to the prosecution all the accused were involved in the fake encounter in which an innocent young man lost his life. The High Court also ought to have taken into consideration the serious nature of the allegations, the possibilities of undue influence being exerted on the witnesses for the prosecution at the instance of the police officials. In our opinion, the High Court committed serious error in granting bail to the respondents.

[B] Transfer of case on the prayer of the victim/complainant.

Vikas Kumar Roorkewal v. *State of Uttarakhand,* (2011) 2 SCC 178: AIR 2011 SC 726: 2011 AIR SCW 643

Background

1. The issue involved in this case was 'witness protection'. Transfer of the case was a tool employed by the Supreme Court as a safeguard against intimidation of key witnesses. The petitioner was an eye witness and a complainant to a high profile murder of an engineer and was facing real life threats to himself and his family.

The Verdict

2. From the averments made in the petition it is evident that the accused belong to powerful gang operating in U.P. from which State of Uttarakhand is carved out. The petitioner has been able to show the circumstances from which it can be reasonably inferred that it has become difficult for the witnesses to safely depose truth because of fear of being haunted by those against whom they have to depose. The reluctance of the witnesses to go to the court at Haridwar in spite of receipt of repeated summons is bound to hamper the course of justice. If such a situation is permitted to continue, it will pave way for anarchy, oppression, etc., resulting in breakdown of criminal justice system. In order to see that the incapacitation of the eye-witnesses is removed and justice triumphs, it has become necessary to grant the relief claimed in the instant petition. On the facts and in the circumstances of the case this Court is of the opinion that interest of justice would be served if transfer of the case from Haridwar to Delhi is ordered.

The Various Aspects

3. Because of the high profile of the accused involved in the murder of the deceased engineer, the Uttarakhand police was found to be incapable/ reluctant to investigate the crime. Therefore, the State of Uttar Pradesh had directed the Special Task Force along with Special Operation Group to investigate the murder and to arrest the accused. It may be mentioned that the Special Task Force along with Special Operation Group appointed to investigate the matter and to arrest the accused had conducted large number of raids. All the arrests were made by Special Task Force, Uttar Pradesh except one which was effected by the Uttarakhand police on the information of Special Task Force, Uttar Pradesh. Court, Haridwar (Uttarakhand) and by this time, one witness is already examined.

4. Grievance of the petitioner is that continuously threats are being administered to his family including him and other witnesses that they would meet the same fate as that of the deceased, if they dare to depose before the Court. The petitioner has mentioned that the first eye witness examined in the court, who was the driver of the deceased, has turned hostile because of the threats given to him and the learned Judge presiding over the trial could not do anything except being a passive spectator. The petitioner claims that he along with his wife was chased by the gang when they were enroute to Haridwar to appear before the court on May 25, 2007, and due to fear, they have not been able to appear before the court on several dates.

5. From the record of the case it is evident that several letters have been written and/or applications have been made by the petitioner making grievances about the threats administered to him and his family by the accomplices of the accused. However, it is an admitted position that no action, worth the name, is taken either by the SSP, Haridwar or by Government of Uttarakhand either to afford protection to the petitioner and his family or to thwart such threats made by the accused and/or their accomplices. It is relevant to notice that it was claimed by the prosecution that the driver of the

deceased was an eye-witness and it is the case of the petitioner that due to threats, he turned hostile. The fact that the driver had turned hostile is not in dispute. The fact that inspite of the receipt of several summons neither the petitioner nor his wife nor his family members nor other witnesses have been able to go to Haridwar to depose before the Court is not denied by the State Government. Therefore, this Court is inclined to accept the case of the petitioner that he and other witnesses have not been able to respond the summons only because of fear to their lives due to the threats administered by the accomplices of the accused. There is no manner of doubt that because of chasing of the petitioner and his relatives by the accomplices of the accused, they have not been able to attend the Court and tender evidence. If this situation continues then the prosecution would not be able to lead any evidence in such a brutal murder case and the accused will have to be acquitted. The record indicates that four accused have been already enlarged on bail but neither the police nor the State agency has taken any steps for the purpose of getting their bail order cancelled.

6. The learned counsel for the petitioner has placed reliance on a decision of this Court in *Himanshu Singh Sabharwal* v. *State of Madhya Pradesh,* (2008) 4 SCR 783: AIR 2008 SC 1943: 2008 AIR SCW 2206, where this Court in paragraphs 14 and 15 has observed as under:

> "14". "Witnesses" "as Benthem said: are the eyes and ears of justice. Hence, the importance and primacy of the quality of trial process. If the witness himself is incapacitated from acting as eyes and ears of justice, the trial gets putrefied and paralysed, and it no longer can constitute a fair trial. The incapacitation may be due to several factors like the witness being not in a position for reasons beyond control to speak the truth in the Court or due to negligence or ignorance or some corrupt collusion. Time has become ripe to act on account of numerous experiences faced by Courts on account of frequent turning of witnesses as hostile, either due to threats, coercion, lures and monetary considerations at the instance of those in power, their henchmen and hirelings, political clouts and patronage and innumerable other corrupt practices ingenuously adopted to smother and stifle truth and realities coming out to surface rendering truth and justice, to become ultimate casualties. Broader public and societal interests require that the victims of the crime who are not ordinarily parties to prosecution and the interests of State represented by their prosecuting agencies do not suffer even in slow process but irreversibly and irretrievably, which if allowed would undermine and destroy public confidence in the administration of justice, which may ultimately pave way for anarchy, oppression and injustice resulting in complete breakdown and collapse of the edifice of rule of law, enshrined and jealously guarded and protected by the Constitution. There comes the need for protecting the witness. Time has come when serious and undiluted thoughts are to be bestowed for protecting witnesses so that ultimate truth is presented before the Court and justice triumphs and the trial is not reduced to mockery. The State has a definite role to play in protecting the witnesses, to start with at least in sensitive cases involving

those in power, who has political patronage and could wield muscle and money power, to avert trial getting tainted and derailed and truth becoming a casualty. As a protector of its citizens it has to ensure that during a trial in Court the witness could safely depose truth without any fear of being haunted by those against whom he has deposed. Some legislative enactments like the Terrorist and Disruptive Activities (Prevention) Act, 1987 (in short the 'TADA Act') have taken note of the reluctance shown by witnesses to depose against dangerous criminals-terrorists. In a milder form also the reluctance and the hesitation of witnesses to depose against people with muscle power, money power or political power has become the order of the day. If ultimately truth is to be arrived at, the eyes and ears of justice have to be protected so that the interests of justice do not get incapacitated in the sense of making the proceedings before Courts mere mock trials as are usually seen in movies.

15. Legislative measures to emphasise prohibition against tampering with witness, victim or informant have become the imminent and inevitable need of the day. Conducts which illegitimately affect the presentation of evidence in proceedings before the Courts have to be seriously and sternly dealt with. There should not be any undue anxiety to only protect the interest of the accused. That would be unfair as noted above to the needs of the society. On the contrary, the efforts should be to ensure fair trial where the accused and the prosecution both get a fair deal. Public interest in the proper administration of justice must be given as much importance if not more, as the interests of the individual accused. In this courts have a vital role to play".

7. Above judgment clearly enunciates the importance of witness in criminal trial. This is a case of murder of a Superintending Engineer. There is no manner of doubt that brutal assault was mounted on him which resulted into his death. The son of the deceased is seeking transfer of proceedings on ground of coercion and threat to the witnesses as well as doubtful sincerity of the investigating agency and prosecuting agency. In effective cross-examination by public prosecutor of the driver who resiled from the statement made during investigation speaks volumes about the sincerity/effectiveness of the prosecuting agency. The necessity of fair trial hardly needs emphasis. The State has a definite role to play in protecting the witnesses, to start with at least in sensitive cases. The learned Judge has failed to take participatory role in the trial. He was not expected to act like a mere tape recorder to record whatever has been stated by the witnesses. Section 311 of the Code and section 165 of the Evidence Act confers vast and wide powers on Court to elicit all necessary materials by playing an active role in the evidence collecting process. However, the record does not indicate that the learned Judge presiding the trial had exercised powers under section 165 of the Evidence Act which is in a way complimentary to his other powers. It is true that there must be reasonable apprehension on the part of the party to a case that justice may not be done and mere allegation that there is apprehension that justice will not be done cannot be the basis for transfer. However, there is no manner of doubt that the

reasonable apprehension that there would be failure of justice and acquittal of the accused only because the witnesses are threatened is made out by the petitioner.

8. This Court, on various occasions, had opportunity to discuss the importance of fair trial in Criminal Justice System and various circumstances in which a trial can be transferred to dispense fair and impartial justice. It would be advantageous to notice a few decisions of this Court with regard to the scope of section 406 of Code of Criminal Procedure. In *Gurcharan Dass Chadha* v. *State of Rajasthan*, AIR 1966 SC 1418: (1972) 1 SCWR 824: (1966) 2 SCR 678, this Court held as under:

> "A case is transferred if there is a reasonable apprehension on the part of a party to a case that justice will not be done. A petitioner is not required to demonstrate that justice will inevitably fail. He is entitled to a transfer if he shows circumstances from which it can be inferred that he entertains an apprehension and that it is reasonable in the circumstances alleged. It is one of the principles of the administration of justice that justice should not only be done but it should be seen to be done. However, a mere allegation that there is apprehension that justice will not be done in a given case does not suffice. The Court has further to see whether apprehension is reasonable or not. To judge the reasonableness of the apprehension the state of the mind of the person who entertains the apprehension is no doubt relevant but that is not all. The apprehension must not only be entertained, but must appear to the court to be a reasonable apprehension".

9. In *Maneka Sanjay Gandhi* v. *Rani Jethmalani*, (1979) 4 SCC 167: AIR 1979 SC 468: 1979 Cr LJ 458, this Court has observed as under:

> "Assurance of a fair trial is the first imperative of the dispensation of justice and the central criterion for the court to consider when a motion for transfer is made is not the hypersensitivity or relative convenience of a party or easy availability of legal services or like mini-grievances. Something more substantial, more compelling, more imperilling, from the point of view of public justice and its attendant environment, is necessitous if the Court is to exercise its power of transfer. This is the cardinal principle although the circumstances may be myriad and vary from case to case. We have to test the petitioner's grounds on this touchstone bearing in mind the rule that normally the complainant has the right to choose any court having jurisdiction and the accused cannot dictate where the case against him should be tried. Even so, the process of justice should not harass the parties and from that angle the court may weigh the circumstances".

10. In *K. Anbazhagan* v. *Superintendent of Police*, (2004) 3 SCC 767: 2003 AIR SCW 6468: 2004 Cr LJ 583, this Court held as under:

> "Free and fair trial is *sine qua non* of Article 21 of the Constitution. It is trite law that justice should not only be done but it should be seen to have been done. If the criminal trial is not free and fair and not free from bias, judicial fairness and the criminal justice system would be at stake shaking the confidence of the public in the system and woe would be the rule of law. It

is important to note that in such a case the question is not whether the petitioner is actually biased but the question is whether the circumstances are such that there is a reasonable apprehension in the mind of the petitioner."

11. In *Abdul Nazar Madani* v. *State of Tamil Nadu,* (2000) 6 SCC 204: 2000 AIR SCW 2425: 2000 Cr LJ 3480, this Court observed as under:

> "The purpose of criminal trial is to dispense fair and impartial justice uninfluenced by extraneous considerations. When it is shown that public confidence in the fairness of a trial would be seriously undermined, any party can seek the transfer of a case within the State under section 407 and anywhere in the country under section 406 Cr.P.C. The apprehension of not getting a fair and impartial inquiry or trial is required to be reasonable and not imaginary, based upon conjectures and surmises. If it appears that the dispensation of criminal justice is not possible impartially and objectively and without any bias before any court or even at any place, the appropriate court may transfer the case to another court where it feels that holding of fair and proper trial is conducive. No universal or hard-and-fast rules can be prescribed for deciding a transfer petition which has always to be decided on the basis of the facts of each case. Convenience of the parties including the witness to be produced at the trial is also a relevant consideration for deciding the transfer petition. The convenience of the parties does not necessarily mean the convenience of the petitioners alone who approached the court on misconceived notions of apprehension. Convenience for the purposes of transfer means the convenience of the prosecution, other accused, the witnesses and the larger interest of the society."

CHAPTER 10

WILD LIFE (PROTECTION) ACT, 1972 – POWER OF FORFEITURE

"Any power of forfeiture conferred upon the executive authorities merely on suspicion or accusation may amount to depriving a person of his property without authority of law."

Principal Chief Conservator of Forests v. *J.K. Johnson,* (2011) 10 SCC 794

Background

1. The significant issue involved in this case is as to whether a specified officer is empowered under section 54(1) of the Wild Life (Protection) Act, 1972 to compound offences on payment of composition money by a person suspected to have committed offence as per the Act.

The Verdict

2. In view of the above, the order passed by the Conservator of Forests, Nizamabad for forfeiture of the vehicle and two rifles to the state government is *de hors* the provisions of the 1972 Act and unsustainable. The High Court has rightly set aside such illegal order. However, the Single Judge was not right in his order dated March 29, 2005 in directing the respondents therein (present appellants) to release the vehicle and rifles. The Division Bench also erred in maintaining the above direction. Since the items were seized in exercise of the power under section 50(1)(c), the seized property has to be dealt with by the Magistrate under section 50(4) of the 1972 Act. The respondent nos. 1 to 3 must accordingly apply to the concerned Magistrate for the return of seized items who obviously will consider such application according to law.

3. We hold, as we must, that a specified officer empowered under section 54(1) of the 1972 Act as substituted by Act 16 of 2003 to compound offences, has no power, competence or authority to order forfeiture of the seized items on composition of the offence by a person who is suspected to have committed offence against the Act. Our answer to the question framed at the outset is in the negative.

The Various Aspects

4. Now, we have to see whether section 54(2) of the 1972 Act, after its amendment by Act 16 of 2003, empowers the specified officer to order forfeiture

of the property, in respect of the offences against the Act suspected to have been committed by such person, on composition of such offence. In other words, whether in the absence of any specific provision in section 54(2) that the property seized shall be released, the specified officer empowered to compound offences is authorized to order forfeiture of the seized property and not return the property to the person from whom it has been seized.

5. Section 54(2) of the 1972 Act, prior to the amendment by Act 16 of 2003, authorized the empowered officer, on payment of value of the property liable to be forfeited, to release the seized property, other than the government property. The provision underwent changes w.e.f. April 1, 2003 and the provision for release of the seized property has been deleted. Does the provision in new section 54(2) authorize the empowered officer to order forfeiture of the seized property to the state government? We think not. In the first place, by deletion of such expression, it cannot be said that the Parliament intended to confer power on the specified officer to order forfeiture of the seized property which is nothing but one form of penalty in the context of the 1972 Act. Had the Parliament intended to do so, it would have made an express provision in that regard. Such conferment of power of penalty upon the specified officer cannot be read by implication in section 54(2). Secondly, any power of forfeiture conferred upon Executive authority merely on suspicion or accusation may amount to depriving a person of his property without authority of law. Such power cannot be readily read by relying on the Statement of Objects and Reasons (Act 16 of 2003) without any express provision in the statute.

CHAPTER 11

DNA FINGERPRINTING – ESTABLISHMENT OF IDENTITY OF DEAD BODY

Nithari Missing Children (Murders) Case – *Surendra Koli* v. *State of Uttar Pradesh,* (2011) 4 SCC 80: AIR 2011 SC 970: 2011 Cr LJ 3137

US law referred – Supreme Court of Florida – *Thomas Mitchel Overton* v. *State of Florida*

Background

1. The killings by the appellant Surendra Koli are horrifying and barbaric. He used a definite methodology in committing these murders. He would see small girls passing by the house, and taking advantage of their weakness lure them inside the house [No. D-5, Sector 31, Nithari Village, Noida]. There he would strangulate them and after killing them he tried to have sex with the body and would then cut off their body parts and eat them. Some parts of the body were disposed of by throwing them in the passage gallery and drain (nala) beside the house. House No. D-5, Sector 31 had become a virtual slaughter house, where innocent children were regularly butchered. Thereby the issue of DNA finger printing acquired a front seat for establishing the identify of a dead body.

The Verdict regarding DNA

The DNA test of Rimpa by CDFD, a pioneer institute in Hyderabad matched with that of blood of her parents and brother. The Doctors at AIIMS have put the parts of the deceased girls which have been recovered by the Doctors of AIIMS together. These bodies have been recovered in the presence of the Doctors of AIIMS at the pointing out by the accused Surendra Koli. Thus, recovery is admissible under section 27 of the Evidence Act.

On the facts of the case we see no reason to interfere with the findings of the trial court and the High Court that the appellant Surendra Koli is guilty of murdering Rimpa Haldar. Both Courts have gone into the evidence in great detail and we have perused the same. The appellant appears to be a serial killer, and these cases in our opinion fall within the category of rarest of the rare cases as laid down in *Bachan Singh* v. *State of Punjab*, 1982 SCC 689 which has been subsequently followed in *Atbir* v. *Government of NCT of Delhi*, (2010) 9 SCC 1: AIR 2010 SC 3477: 2010 AIR SCW 5461.

CHAPTER 12

MERCY KILLING - LAW OF EUTHANASIA AND RIGHT OF SUICIDE

Aruna Ramchandra Shanbaug v. *Union of India,* (2011) 4 SCC 454: AIR 2011 SC 1290: 2011 AIR SCW 1625

Euthanasia – Legal Position In Other Countries - Legal Issues : Active and Passive Euthanasia

Background

1. This case triggered off the legal debate on EUTHANASIA in India. Under the Indian law, abetment of suicide and its attempt are both offences under sections 306 and 309 IPC. The Constitution Bench in *Gian Kaur* v. *State of Punjab,* (1996) 2 SCC 648: AIR 1996 SC 946: 1996 Cr LJ 1660 held both euthanasia and assisted suicide illegal in India. The legal position differs the world over. There has also been a worldwide debate over active and passive euthanasia, the terms 'Brain Death', 'PVS (permanent vegetative state)' etc. This case takes these issues head on and culls out a middle path.

The Verdict

2. There is no statutory provision in our country as to the legal procedure for withdrawing life support to a person in PVS or who is otherwise incompetent to take a decision in this connection. We agree with Mr. Andhyarujina that passive euthanasia should be permitted in our country in certain situations, and we disagree with the learned Attorney General that it should never be permitted. Hence, following the technique used in Vishakha's case (supra), we are laying down the law in this connection which will continue to be the law until Parliament makes a law on the subject.

(i) A decision has to be taken to discontinue life support either by the parents or the spouse or other close relatives, or in the absence of any of them, such a decision can be taken even by a person or a body of persons acting as a next friend. It can also be taken by the doctors attending the patient. However, the decision should be taken bona fide in the best interest of the patient.

(ii) even if a decision is taken by the near relatives or doctors or next friend to withdraw life support, such a decision requires approval from the High Court concerned as laid down in Airedale case.[Airedale *N.H.S.Trust* v. *Bland,* 1993 AC 789: (1993) 1 All ER 821 (CA and HL).

3. In our opinion, if we leave it solely to the patient's relatives or to the doctors or next friend to decide whether to withdraw the life support of an incompetent person there is always a risk in our country that this may be misused by some unscrupulous persons who wish to inherit or otherwise grab the property of the patient. Considering the low ethical levels prevailing in our society today and the rampant commercialization and corruption, we cannot rule out the possibility that unscrupulous persons with the help of some unscrupulous doctors may fabricate material to show that it is a terminal case with no chance of recovery. There are doctors and doctors. While many doctors are upright, there are others who can do anything for money (see George Bernard Shaw's play 'The Doctors Dilemma'). The commercialization of our society has crossed all limits. Hence we have to guard against the potential of misuse (see Robin Cook's novel 'Coma'). In our opinion, while giving great weight to the wishes of the parents, spouse, or other close relatives or next friend of the incompetent patient and also giving due weight to the opinion of the attending doctors, we cannot leave it entirely to their discretion whether to discontinue the life support or not. We agree with the decision of the Lord Keith in *Airedale's* case (*supra*) that the approval of the High Court should be taken in this connection. This is in the interest of the protection of the patient, protection of the doctors, relative and next friend, and for reassurance of the patient's family as well as the public. This is also in consonance with the doctrine of *parens patriae* which is a well known principle of law.

4. In our opinion, it is the High Court under Article 226 of the Constitution which can grant approval for withdrawal of life support to such an incompetent person. .... No doubt, the ordinary practice in our High Courts since the time of framing of the Constitution in 1950 is that petitions filed under Article 226 of the Constitution pray for a writ of the kind referred to in the provision. However, from the very language of the Article 226, and as explained by the above decisions, a petition can also be made to the High Court under Article 226 of the Constitution praying for an order or direction, and not for any writ. Hence, in our opinion, Article 226 gives abundant power to the High Court to pass suitable orders on the application filed by the near relatives or next friend or the doctors/hospital staff praying for permission to withdraw the life support to an incompetent person of the kind above mentioned.

Procedure as per the verdict

5. When such an application is filed, the Chief Justice of the High Court should forthwith constitute a Bench of at least two Judges who should decide to grant approval or not. Before doing so the Bench should seek the opinion of a committee of three reputed doctors to be nominated by the Bench after consulting such medical authorities/medical practitioners as it may deem fit. Preferably one of the three doctors should be a neurologist, one should be a psychiatrist, and the third a physician. For this purpose a panel of doctors in every city may be prepared by the High Court in consultation with the State Government/Union Territory and their fees for this purpose may be fixed.

6. The committee of three doctors nominated by the Bench should carefully examine the patient and also consult the record of the patient as well as taking the views of the hospital staff and submit its report to the High Court Bench. Simultaneously with appointing the committee of doctors, the High Court Bench shall also issue notice to the State and close relatives *e.g.* parents, spouse, brothers/sisters etc. of the patient, and in their absence his/her next friend, and supply a copy of the report of the doctor's committee to them as soon as it is available. After hearing them, the High Court bench should give its verdict. The above procedure should be followed all over India until Parliament makes legislation on this subject.

7. The High Court should give its decision speedily at the earliest, since delay in the matter may result in causing great mental agony to the relatives and persons close to the patient. The High Court should give its decision assigning specific reasons in accordance with the principle of 'best interest of the patient' laid down by the House of Lords in *Airedale's* case (*supra*). The views of the near relatives and committee of doctors should be given due weight by the High Court before pronouncing a final verdict which shall not be summary in nature.

The Various Aspects: (Including World Position)

8. Coming now to the legal issues in this case, it may be noted that euthanasia is of two types : active and passive. Active euthanasia entails the use of lethal substances or forces to kill a person e.g. a lethal injection given to a person with terminal cancer who is in terrible agony. Passive euthanasia entails withholding of medical treatment for continuance of life, *e.g.* withholding of antibiotics where without giving it a patient is likely to die, or removing the heart lung machine, from a patient in coma.

9. The general legal position all over the world seems to be that while active euthanasia is illegal unless there is legislation permitting it, passive euthanasia is legal even without legislation provided certain conditions and safeguards are maintained.

Legislation in some countries relating to euthanasia or physician assisted death.

Netherlands

10. Euthanasia in the Netherlands is regulated by the "Termination of Life on Request and Assisted Suicide (Review Procedures) Act", 2002. It states that euthanasia and physician-assisted suicide are not punishable if the attending physician acts in accordance with the criteria of due care. These criteria concern the patient's request, the patient's suffering (unbearable and hopeless), the information provided to the patient, the presence of reasonable alternatives, consultation of another physician and the applied method of ending life. To demonstrate their compliance, the Act requires physicians to report euthanasia to a review committee.

11. Euthanasia remains a criminal offense in cases not meeting the law's specific conditions, with the exception of several situations that are not subject

to the restrictions of the law at all, because they are considered normal medical practice. These are:

- stopping or not starting a medically useless (futile) treatment
- stopping or not starting a treatment at the patient's request
- speeding up death as a side-effect of treatment necessary for alleviating serious suffering

Switzerland

12. Switzerland has an unusual position on assisted suicide: it is legally permitted and can be performed by non-physicians. However, euthanasia is illegal, the difference between assisted suicide and euthanasia being that while in the former the patient administers the lethal injection himself, in the latter a doctor or some other person administers it.

13. Article 115 of the Swiss penal code, which came into effect in 1942 (having been approved in 1937), considers assisting suicide a crime if, and only if, the motive is selfish. The code does not give physicians a special status in assisting suicide; although, they are most likely to have access to suitable drugs. Ethical guidelines have cautioned physicians against prescribing deadly drugs.

Switzerland seems to be the only country in which the law limits the circumstances in which assisted suicide is a crime, thereby decriminalising it in other cases, without requiring the involvement of a physician. Consequently, non-physicians have participated in assisted suicide. However, legally, active euthanasia e.g. administering a lethal injection by a doctor or some other person to a patient is illegal in Switzerland (unlike in Holland where it is legal under certain conditions). The Swiss law is unique because (1) the recipient need not be a Swiss national, and (2) a physician need not be involved. Many persons from other countries, especially Germany, go to Switzerland to undergo euthanasia.

Belgium

14. Belgium became the second country in Europe after Netherlands to legalize the practice of euthanasia in September 2002. The Belgian law sets out conditions under which suicide can be practised without giving doctors a licence to kill. Patients wishing to end their own lives must be conscious when the demand is made and repeat their request for euthanasia. They have to be under "constant and unbearable physical or psychological pain" resulting from an accident or incurable illness. The law gives patients the right to receive ongoing treatment with painkillers — the authorities have to pay to ensure that poor or isolated patients do not ask to die because they do not have money for such treatment. Unlike the Dutch legislation, minors cannot seek assistance to die. In the case of someone who is not in the terminal stages of illness, a third medical opinion must be sought. Every mercy killing case will have to be filed at a special commission to decide if the doctors in charge are following the regulations.

UK, Spain, Austria, Italy, Germany, France, etc.

15. In none of these countries is euthanasia or physician assisted death legal. In January 2011 the French Senate defeated by a 170-142 vote a bill seeking to legalize euthanasia. In England, in May 2006 a bill allowing physician assisted suicide, was blocked, and never became law.

United States of America

16. Active Euthanasia is illegal in all states in USA, but physician assisted dying is legal in the states of Oregon, Washington and Montana. As already pointed out above, the difference between euthanasia and physician assisted suicide lies in who administers the lethal medication. In the former, the physician or someone else administers it, while in the latter the patient himself does so, though on the advice of the doctor.

Oregon

17. Oregon was the first state in U.S.A. to legalize physician assisted death. The Oregon legislature enacted the Oregon Death with Dignity Act, in 1997. Under the Death With Dignity Act, a person who sought physician-assisted suicide would have to meet certain criteria:

- He must be an Oregon resident, at least 18 years old, and must have decision making capacity.
- The person must be terminally ill, having six months or less to live.
- The person must make one written and two oral requests for medication to end his/her life, the written one substantially in the form provided in the Act, signed, dated, witnessed by two persons in the presence of the patient who attest that the person is capable, acting voluntarily and not being coerced to sign the request. There are stringent qualifications as to who may act as a witness.
- The patient's decision must be an 'informed' one, and the attending physician is obligated to provide the patient with information about the diagnosis, prognosis, potential risks, and probable consequences of taking the prescribed medication, and alternatives, including, but not limited to comfort care, hospice care and pain control. Another physician must confirm the diagnosis, the patient's decision making capacity, and voluntariness of the patient's decisions.
- Counselling has to be provided if the patient is suffering from depression or a mental disorder which may impact his judgment.
- There has to be a waiting period of 15 days, next of kin have to be notified, and State authorities have to be informed.
- The patient can rescind his decision at any time

18. In response to concerns that patients with depression may seek to end their lives, the 1999 amendment provides that the attending physician must determine that the patient does not have 'depression causing impaired judgment' before prescribing the medication. Under the law, a person who met all requirements could receive a prescription of a barbiturate that would be

sufficient to cause death. However, the lethal injection must be administered by the patient himself, and physicians are prohibited from administering it. The landmark case to declare that the practice of euthanasia by doctors to help their patients shall not be taken into cognizance was *Gonzalez* v. *Oregon*, 546 US 243 (2005).

Washington

19. Washington was the second state in U.S.A. which allowed the practice of physician assisted death in the year 2008 by passing the Washington Death with Dignity Act, 2008.

Montana:

20. Montana was the third state (after Oregon and Washington) in U.S.A. to legalize physician assisted deaths, but this was done by the State judiciary and not the legislature. On December 31, 2009, the Montana Supreme Court delivered its verdict in the case of Baxter v. Montana permitting physicians to prescribe lethal indication. The court held that there was "nothing in Montana Supreme Court precedent or Montana statutes indicating that physician aid in dying is against public policy."

Other States in USA

21. In no other State in USA is euthanasia or physician assisted death legal. Michigan banned euthanasia and assisted suicide in 1993, after Dr. Kevorkian (who became known as 'doctor death') began encouraging and assisting in suicides. He was convicted in 1999 for an assisted suicide displayed on television, his medical licence cancelled, and he spent 8 years in jail.

22. In 1999 the State of Texas enacted the Texas Futile Care Law which entitles Texas hospitals and doctors, in some situations, to withdraw life support measures, such as mechanical respiration, from terminally ill patient when such treatment is considered futile and inappropriate. However, Texas has not legalized euthanasia or physician assisted death. In California, though 75 of people support physician assisted death, the issue is highly controversial in the State legislature. Forty States in USA have enacted laws which explicitly make it a crime to provide another with the means of taking his or her life.

23. In 1977 California legalized living wills, and other States soon followed suit. A living will (also known as advance directive or advance decision) is an instruction given by an individual while conscious specifying what action should be taken in the event he/she is unable to make a decision due to illness or incapacity, and appoints a person to take such decisions on his/her behalf. It may include a directive to withdraw life support on certain eventualities.

Canada

24. In Canada, physician-assisted suicide is illegal vide section 241(b) of the Criminal Code of Canada. The leading decision of the Canadian Supreme Court in this connection is *Sue Rodriguez* v. *British Columbia (Attorney General)*, (1993) 3 SCR 519. Rodriguez, a woman of 43, was diagnosed with

Amyotrophic Lateral Sclerosis (ALS), and requested the Canadian Supreme Court to allow someone to aid her in ending her life. Her condition was deteriorating rapidly, and the doctors told her that she would soon lose the ability to swallow, speak, walk, and move her body without assistance. Thereafter she would lose her capacity to breathe without a respirator, to eat without a gastrotomy, and would eventually be confined to bed. Her life expectancy was 2 to 14 months.

25. The Canadian Supreme Court was deeply divided. By a 5 to 4 majority her plea was rejected. Justice Sopinka, speaking for the majority (which included Justices La Forest, Gonthier, Iacobucci and Major) observed:

> "Sanctity of life has been understood historically as excluding freedom of choice in the self infliction of death, and certainly in the involvement of others in carrying out that choice. At the very least, no new consensus has emerged in society opposing the right of the State to regulate the involvement of others in exercising power over individuals ending their lives".

26. There is a plethora of case law on the subject of the Courts all over the world relating to both active and passive euthanasia. It is not necessary to refer in detail to all the decisions of the Courts in the world on the subject of euthanasia or physically assisted dead (p.a.d.) but we think it appropriate to refer in detail to certain landmark decisions, which have laid down the law on the subject.

The Airedale case: [*Airedale NHS Trust* v. *Bland,* (1993) 1 All ER 821].

27. In the Airedale case decided by the House of Lords in the UK, the facts were that one Anthony Bland aged about 17 went to the Hillsborough Ground on 15th April 1989 to support the Liverpool Football Club. In the course of the disaster which occurred on that day, his lungs were crushed and punctured and the supply to his brain was interrupted. As a result, he suffered catastrophic and irreversible damage to the higher centres of the brain. For three years, he was in a condition known as 'persistent vegetative state (PVS). This state arises from the destruction of the cerebral cortex on account of prolonged deprivation of oxygen, and the cerebral cortex of Anthony had resolved into a watery mass. The cortex is that part of the brain which is the seat of cognitive function and sensory capacity. Anthony Bland could not see, hear or feel anything. He could not communicate in any way. His consciousness, which is an essential feature of an individual personality, had departed forever. However, his brain-stem, which controls the reflective functions of the body, in particular the heart beat, breathing and digestion, continued to operate. He was in persistent vegetative state (PVS) which is a recognized medical condition quite distinct from other conditions sometimes known as "irreversible coma", "the Guillain-Barre syndrome", "the locked-in syndrome" and "brain death".

28. The distinguishing characteristic of PVS is that the brain stem remains alive and functioning while the cortex has lost its function and activity. Thus the PVS patient continues to breathe unaided and his digestion continues to function. But although his eyes are open, he cannot see. He cannot hear.

Although capable of reflex movement, particularly in response to painful stimuli, the patient is incapable of voluntary movement and can feel no pain. He cannot taste or smell. He cannot speak or communicate in any way. He has no cognitive function and thus can feel no emotion, whether pleasure or distress. The absence of cerebral function is not a matter of surmise; it can be scientifically demonstrated. The space which the brain should occupy is full of watery fluid.

29. In order to maintain Mr. Bland in his condition, feeding and hydration were achieved by artificial means of a nasogastric tube while the excretory functions were regulated by a catheter and enemas. According to eminent medical opinion, there was no prospect whatsoever that he would ever make a recovery from his condition, but there was every likelihood that he would maintain this state of existence for many years to come provided the artificial means of medical care was continued. In this state of affairs the medical men in charge of Anthony Bland case took the view, which was supported by his parents, that no useful purpose would be served by continuing medical care, and that artificial feeding and other measures aimed at prolonging his existence should be stopped. Since however, there was a doubt as to whether this course might constitute a criminal offence, the hospital authorities sought a declaration from the British High Court to resolve these doubts. The declaration was granted by the Family Division of the High Court on 19-11-1992 and that judgment was affirmed by the Court of Appeal on 9-12-1992. A further appeal was made to the House of Lords which then decided the case.

30. The broad issued raised before the House of Lords in the Airedale case was "In what circumstances, if ever, can those having a duty to feed an invalid lawfully stop doing so"? In fact this is precisely the question raised in the present case of Aruna Shanbaug before us.

31. In *Airedale's* case (*supra*), Lord Keith of Kinkel, noted that it was unlawful to administer treatment to an adult who is conscious and of sound mind, without his consent. Such a person is completely at liberty to decline to undergo treatment, even if the result of his doing so will be that he will die. This extends to the situation where the person in anticipation of his entering into a condition such as PVS, gives clear instructions that in such an event he is not to be given medical care, including artificial feeding, designed to keep him alive.

32. It was held that if a person, due to accident or some other cause becomes unconscious and is thus not able to give or withhold consent to medical treatment, in that situation it is lawful for medical men to apply such treatment as in their informed opinion is in the best interests of the unconscious patient. That is what happened in the case of Anthony Bland when he was first dealt with by the emergency services and later taken to hospital.

US decisions

33. The two most significant cases of the U.S. Supreme Court that addressed the issue whether there was a federal constitutional right to assisted suicide arose from challenges to State laws banning physician assisted suicide brought by terminally ill patients and their physicians. These were *Washington* v. *Glucksberg,* 521 US 702 (1997); *Vacco* v. *Quill,* 521 US 793 (1997).

34. In Glucksberg's case, the U.S. Supreme Court held that the asserted right to assistance in committing suicide is not a fundamental liberty interest protected by the Due Process Clause of the Fourteenth Amendment. The Court observed (US p.725):

> "The decision to commit suicide with the assistance of another may be just as personal and profound as the decision to refuse unwanted medical treatment, but it has never enjoyed similar legal protection. Indeed the two acts are widely and reasonably regarded as quite distinct".

35. The Court went on to conclude that the Washington statute being challenged was rationally related to five legitimate government interest : protection of life, prevention of suicide, protection of ethical integrity of the medical profession, protection of vulnerable groups, and protection against the "slippery slope"; towards euthanasia. The Court then noted that perhaps the individual States were more suited to resolving or at least addressing the myriad concerns raised by both proponents and opponents of physician assisted suicide. The Court observed:

> "Throughout the Nation, Americans are engaged in an earnest and profound debate about the morality, legality and practicality of physician assisted suicide. Our holding permits this debate to continue, as it should in a democratic society".

36. In *Vacco's* case (*supra*) the U.S. Supreme Court again recognized the distinction between refusing life saving medical treatment and giving lethal medication. The Court disagreed with the view of the Second Circuit Federal Court that ending or refusing lifesaving medical treatment is nothing more nor less than assisted suicide. The Court held that:

> "...... The distinction between letting a patient die and making that patient die is important, logical, rational, and well established."

The Court held that the State of New York could validly ban the latter.

37. In *Cruzan* v. *Director, MDH,* 497 US 261 (1990) decided by the U.S. Supreme Court the majority opinion was delivered by the Chief Justice Rehnquist. In that case, the petitioner Nancy Cruzan sustained injuries in an automobile accident and lay in a Missouri State hospital in what has been referred to as a persistent vegetative state (PVS), a condition in which a person exhibits motor reflexes but evinces no indication of significant cognitive function. The state of Missouri was bearing the cost of her care. Her parents and co-guardians applied to the Court for permission to withdraw her artificial feeding and hydration equipment and allow her to die. While the trial Court granted the prayer, the State Supreme Court of Missouri reversed, holding that

under a statute in the State of Missouri it was necessary to prove by clear and convincing evidence that the incompetent person had wanted, while competent, withdrawal of life support treatment in such an eventuality. The only evidence led on that point was the alleged statement of Nancy Cruzan to a housemate about a year before the accident that she did not want life as a 'vegetable'. The State Supreme Court was of the view that this did not amount to saying that medical treatment or nutrition or hydration should be withdrawn.

38. Chief Justice Rehnquist delivering the opinion of the Court (in which Justices White, O'Connor, Scalia, and Kennedy, joined) in his judgment first noted the facts:—

> "On the night of January 11, 1983, Nancy Cruzan lost control of her car as she traveled down Elm Road in Jasper County, Missouri. The vehicle overturned, and Cruzan was discovered lying face down in a ditch without detectable respiratory or cardiac function. Paramedics were able to restore her breathing and heartbeat at the accident site, and she was transported to a hospital in an unconscious state. An attending neurosurgeon diagnosed her as having sustained probable cerebral contusions compounded by significant anoxia (lack of oxygen). The Missouri trial court in this case found that permanent brain damage generally results after 6 minutes in an anoxic state; it was estimated that Cruzan was deprived of oxygen from 12 to 14 minutes. She remained in a coma for approximately three weeks, and then progressed to an unconscious state in which she was able to orally ingest some nutrition. In order to ease feeding and further the recovery, surgeons implanted a gastrostomy feeding and hydration tube in Cruzan with the consent of her then husband. Subsequent rehabilitative efforts proved unavailing. She now lies in a Missouri state hospital in what is commonly referred to as a persistent vegetative state: generally, a condition in which a person exhibits motor reflexes but evinces no indications of significant cognitive function.The State of Missouri is bearing the cost of her care. [497 US 261, 267]
>
> After it had become apparent that Nancy Cruzan had virtually no chance of regaining her mental faculties, her parents asked hospital employees to terminate the artificial nutrition and hydration procedures. All agree that such a [497 US 261, 268] removal would cause her death. The employees refused to honor the request without court approval. The parents then sought and received authorization from the state trial court for termination."

While the trial Court allowed the petition the State Supreme Court of Missouri reversed. The US Supreme Court by majority affirmed the verdict of the State Supreme Court.

39. Chief Justice Rehnquist noted that in law even touching of one person by another without consent and without legal justification was a battery, and hence illegal. The notion of bodily integrity has been embodied in the requirement that informed consent is generally required for medical treatment. As observed by Justice Cardozo, while on the Court of Appeals of New York:

"Every human being of adult years and sound mind has a right to determine what shall be done with his own body, and a surgeon who performs an operation without his patient's consent commits an assault, for which he is liable in damages."

Vide Schloendorff v. *Society of New York Hospital,* 211 NY 125 (129-30, 105) N.E. 92 (93) (1914). Thus the informed consent doctrine has become firmly entrenched in American Tort Law. The logical corollary of the doctrine of informed consent is that the patient generally possesses the right not to consent, that is, to refuse treatment.

40. The question, however, arises in cases where the patient is unable to decide whether the treatment should continue or not *e.g.* if he is in coma or PVS. Who is to give consent to terminate the treatment in such a case? The learned Chief Justice referred to a large number of decisions of Courts in U.S.A. in this connection, often taking diverse approaches.

41. *In re Quinlan,* 70 NJ 10, 355 A. 2d 647, Karen Quinlan suffered severe brain damage as a result of anoxia, and entered into PVS. Her father sought judicial approval to disconnect her respirator. The New Jersey Supreme Court granted the prayer, holding that Karen had a right of privacy grounded in the U.S. Constitution to terminate treatment. The Court concluded that the way Karen's right to privacy could be exercised would be to allow her guardian and family to decide whether she would exercise it in the circumstances.

42. *In re Conroy,* 98 NJ 321, 486 A.2d 1209 (1985), however, the New Jersey Supreme Court, in a case of an 84 year old incompetent nursing home resident who had suffered irreversible mental and physical ailments, contrary to its decision in Quinlan's case, decided to base its decision on the common law right to self determination and informed consent. This right can be exercised by a surrogate decision maker when there was a clear evidence that the incompetent person would have exercised it. Where such evidence was lacking the Court held that an individual's right could still be invoked in certain circumstances under objective 'best interest' standards. Where no trustworthy evidence existed that the individual would have wanted to terminate treatment, and a person's suffering would make the administration of life sustaining treatment inhumane, a pure objective standard could be used to terminate the treatment. If none of these conditions obtained, it was best to err in favour of preserving life.

Law in India

43. In India abetment of suicide (section 306 Indian Penal Code) and attempt to suicide (section 309 of Indian Penal Code) are both criminal offences. This is in contrast to many countries such as USA where attempt to suicide is not a crime.

44. The Constitution Bench of the Indian Supreme Court in *Gian Kaur* v. *State of Punjab,* (1996) 2 SCC 648: AIR 1996 SC 946: 1996 Cr LJ 1660, held that both euthanasia and assisted suicide are not lawful in India. That decision overruled the earlier two Judge Bench decision of the Supreme Court in *P. Rathinam* v. *Union of India,* (1994) 3 SCC 394: AIR 1994 SC 1844: 1994 Cr LJ

1605. The Court held that the right to life under Article 21 of the Constitution does not include the right to die (vide para 33). In *Gian Kaur's* case (*supra*) the Supreme Court approved of the decision of the House of Lords in *Airedale's* case (*supra*), and observed that euthanasia could be made lawful only by legislation.

45. Sections 306 and 309 IPC read as under:

> "306. Abetment of suicide - If any person commits suicide, whoever abets the commission of such suicide, shall be punished with imprisonment of either description for a term which may extend to ten years, and shall also be liable to fine.
>
> "309. Attempt to commit suicide - Whoever attempts to commit suicide and does any act towards the commission of such offence, shall be punished with simple imprisonment for a term which may extend to one year or with fine, or with both".

46. We are of the opinion that although section 309 Indian Penal Code (attempt to commit suicide) has been held to be constitutionally valid in *Gian Kaur's* case (*supra*), the time has come when it should be deleted by Parliament as it has become anachronistic. A person attempts suicide in a depression, and hence he needs help, rather than punishment. We therefore recommend to Parliament to consider the feasibility of deleting section 309 from the Indian Penal Code.

47. It may be noted that in *Gian Kaur's* case (*supra*) although the Supreme Court has quoted with approval the view of the House of Lords in *Airedale's* case (supra), it has not clarified who can decide whether life support should be discontinued in the case of an incompetent person *e.g.* a person in coma or PVS. This vexed question has been arising often in India because there are a large number of cases where persons go into coma (due to an accident or some other reason) or for some other reason are unable to give consent, and then the question arises as to who should give consent for withdrawal of life support.

48. This is an extremely important question in India because of the unfortunate low level of ethical standards to which our society has descended, its raw and widespread commercialization, and the rampant corruption, and hence, the Court has to be very cautious that unscrupulous persons who wish to inherit the property of someone may not get him eliminated by some crooked method.

49. Also, since medical science is advancing fast, doctors must not declare a patient to be a hopeless case unless there appears to be no reasonable possibility of any improvement by some newly discovered medical method in the near future. In this connection we may refer to a recent news item which we have come across on the internet of an Arkansas man Terry Wallis, who was 19 years of age and newly married with a baby daughter when in 1984 his truck plunged through a guard rail, falling 25 feet. He went into coma in the crash in 1984, but after 24 years he has regained consciousness. This was perhaps because his brain spontaneously rewired itself by growing tiny new nerve connections to replace the ones sheared apart in the car crash. Probably

the nerve fibers from Terry Wallis' cells were severed but the cells themselves remained intact, unlike Terri Schiavo, whose brain cells had died (see Terri Schiavo's case on Google).

50. However, we make it clear that it is experts like medical practitioners who can decide whether there is any reasonable possibility of a new medical discovery which could enable such a patient to revive in the near future.

BRAIN DEATH

51. The term 'brain death' has developed various meanings. While initially, death could be defined as a cessation of breathing, or, more scientifically, a cessation of heart-beat, recent medical advances have made such definitions obsolete. In order to understand the nature and scope of brain death, it is worthwhile to look at how death was understood. Historically, as the oft-quoted definition in Black's Law Dictionary suggests, death was:

> "The cessation of life; the ceasing to exist; defined by physicians as a total stoppage of the circulation of the blood, and a cessation of the animal and vital functions consequent thereon, such as respiration, pulsation, etc. " [Black's Law Dictionary,488(4th Ed).

This definition saw its echo in numerous other texts and legal case law. This includes many American precedents - such as *Schmidt* v. *Pierce*, 344 S.W.2d 120 (133) (Mo. 1961) and *Sanger* v. *Butler*, 101 SW 459 (462) (Tex. Civ. App. 1907). The Encyclopaedic Dictionary, among others, gives the following definitions of death: 'The state of being dead; the act or state of dying; the state or condition of the dead.' The Century Dictionary defines death as 'cessation of life; that state of a being, animal or vegetable, in which there is a total and permanent cessation of all the vital functions".

52. When this situation is reached, it is possible to assume that the person is dead, even though he or she, through mechanical stimulation, may be able to breathe, his or her heart might be able to beat, and he or she may be able to take some form of nourishment. It is important, thus, that it be medically proved that a situation where any human functioning would be impossible should have been reached for there to be a declaration of brain death—situations where a person is in a persistent vegetative state but can support breathing, cardiac functions, and digestion without any mechanical aid are necessarily those that will not come within the ambit of brain death.

53. In legal terms, the question of death would naturally assume significance as death has a set of legal consequences as well. As per the definition in the American Uniform Definition of Death Act, 1980, an individual who "sustain[s] . . . irreversible cessation of all functions of the entire brain, including the brain stem, is dead". This stage, thus, is reached at a situation where not only consciousness, but every other aspect of life regulated from the brain can no longer be so regulated.

54. In the case of 'euthanasia', however, the situation is slightly different. In these cases, it is believed, that a determination of when it would be right or fair to disallow resuscitation of a person who is incapable of expressing his or her consent to a termination of his or her life depends on two circumstances:

(a) when a person is only kept alive mechanically, *i.e.* when not only consciousness is lost, but the person is only able to sustain involuntary functioning through advanced medical technology—such as the use of heart-lung machines, medical ventilators etc.

(b) when there is no plausible possibility of the person ever being able to come out of this stage. Medical "miracles"; are not unknown, but if a person has been at a stage where his life is only sustained through medical technology, and there has been no significant alteration in the person's condition for a long period of time—at least a few years—then there can be a fair case made out for passive euthanasia.

To extend this further, especially when a person is incapable of being able to give any consent, would amount to committing judicial murder.

55. In this connection we may refer to the Transplantation of Human Organs Act, 1994 enacted by the Indian Parliament. Section 2(d) of the Act states:

> "2. (d) 'brain-stem death' means the stage at which all functions of the brain-stem have permanently and irreversibly ceased and is so certified under sub-section (6) of section 3;"

Section 3(6) of the said Act states:

> "3. (6) Where any human organ is to be removed from the body of a person in the event of his brain-stem death, no such removal shall be undertaken unless such death is certified, in such form and in such manner and on satisfaction of such conditions and requirements as may be prescribed, by a Board of medical experts consisting of the following, namely:—
>
> (i) the registered medical practitioner, in charge of the hospital in which brain-stem death has occurred;
>
> (ii) an independent registered medical practitioner, being a specialist, to be nominated by the registered medical practitioner specified in clause (i), from the panel of names approved by the Appropriate Authority;
>
> (iii) a neurologist or a neurosurgeon to be nominated by the registered medical practitioner specified in clause (i), from the panel of names approved by the Appropriate Authority; and
>
> (iv) the registered medical practitioner treating the person whose brain-stem death has occurred";.

56. Although the above Act was only for the purpose of regulation of transplantation of human organs it throws some light on the meaning of brain death.

Doctrine of *Parens Patriae*

57. The doctrine of *Parens Patriae* (father of the country) had originated in British law as early as the 13th century. It implies that the King is the father of the country and is under obligation to look after the interest of those who are unable to look after themselves. The idea behind *Parens Patriae* is that if a citizen is in need of someone who can act as a parent who can make

decisions and take some other action, sometimes the State is best qualified to take on this role.

58. In *Heller* v. *DOE,* (509) US 312 Mr. Justice Kennedy speaking for the U.S. Supreme Court observed:

> "the State has a legitimate interest under its parens patriae powers in providing care to its citizens who are unable to care for themselves".

59. In our opinion, in the case of an incompetent person who is unable to take a decision whether to withdraw life support or not, it is the Court alone, as parens patriae, which ultimately must take this decision, though, no doubt, the views of the near relatives, next friend and doctors must be given due weight.

CHAPTER 13

ELECTRONIC EVIDENCE

Video-recording played in court room – *Aruna Ramachandra Shanbaug* v. *Union of India,* (2011) 4 SCC 454

Background: Replaying the second world war Nazi atrocities in a court room during the Nuremburg trials, the Indian Supreme Court followed the precedent and allowed the screening of CD depicting the condition of Aruna Shanbaug.

The precedent

On 2-3-2011, the matter was listed again before us and we first saw the screening of the CD submitted by the team of doctors along with their report. We had arranged for the screening of the CD in the Courtroom, so that all present in Court could see the condition of Aruna Shanbaug. For doing so, we have relied on the precedent of the *Nuremburg trials* in which a screening was done in the Courtroom of some of the Nazi atrocities during the Second World War.

CHAPTER 14

MAINTENANCE

Chanmuniya v. *Virendra Kumar Singh Kushwaha*, (2011) 1 SCC 141: AIR 2010 SC (Supp) 29

Background

The question arising for determination was whether 'living together' of a man and woman, without a valid marriage, would give rise to a presumption of marriage and entitle the woman to maintenance? A bench headed by Justice G.S. Singhvi referred the matter to a larger bench for considering the definition of 'wife' in section 125 CrPC. Whether a woman living in "live-in" relationship can be considered a 'wife' in view of similar law in America.

The Reference Order

1. We, therefore, request the Hon'ble Chief Justice to refer the following, amongst other, questions to be decided by a larger Bench. According to us, the questions are:

1. Whether the living together of a man and woman as husband and wife for a considerable period of time would raise the presumption of a valid marriage between them and whether such a presumption would entitle the woman to maintenance under section 125 Cr.P.C?
2. Whether strict proof of marriage is essential for a claim of maintenance under section 125 Cr.P.C. having regard to the provisions of Domestic Violence Act, 2005?
3. Whether a marriage performed according to customary rites and ceremonies, without strictly fulfilling the requisites of section 7(1) of the Hindu Marriage Act, 1955, or any other personal law would entitle the woman to maintenance under Section 125 Cr.P.C.?

2. We are of the opinion that a broad and expansive interpretation should be given to the term 'wife' to include even those cases where a man and woman have been living together as husband and wife for a reasonably long period of time, and strict proof of marriage should not be a pre-condition for maintenance under section 125 of the Cr.P.C, so as to fulfil the true spirit and essence of the beneficial provision of maintenance under section 125.

3. We also believe that such an interpretation would be a just application of the principles enshrined in the Preamble to our Constitution, namely, social justice and upholding the dignity of the individual.

The Various Aspects

4. One of the major issues which cropped up in the present case is whether or not presumption of a marriage arises when parties live together for a long time, thus giving rise to a claim of maintenance under section 125 Cr.P.C. In other words, the question is what is meant by 'wife' under section 125 of Criminal Procedure Code especially having regard to explanation under clause (b) of the section.

5. Thus, the question that arises is whether a man and woman living together for a long time, even without a valid marriage, would raise as in the present case, a presumption of a valid marriage entitling such a woman to maintenance.

6. On the question of presumption of marriage, we may usefully refer to a decision of the House of Lords rendered in *Piers* v. *Piers,* (1849) II HLC 331, in which their Lordships observed that the question of validity of a marriage cannot be tried like any other issue of fact independent of presumption. The Court held that law will presume in favour of marriage and such presumption could only be rebutted by strong and satisfactory evidence.

7. In *Lt. C.W. Campbell* v. *John A.G. Campbell,* (1867) Law Rep 2 HL 269, also known as the Breadalbane case, the House of Lords held that cohabitation, with the required repute, as husband and wife, was proof that the parties between themselves had mutually contracted the matrimonial relation. A relationship which may be adulterous at the beginning may become matrimonial by consent. This may be evidenced by habit and repute. In the instant case both the appellant and the first respondent were related and lived in the same house and by a social custom were treated as husband and wife. Their marriage was solemnized with Katha and Sindur. Therefore, following the ratio of the decisions of the House of Lords, this Court thinks there is a very strong presumption in favour of marriage. The House of Lords again observed in *Captain De Thoren* v. *The Attorney-General,* (1876) 1 AC 686, that the presumption of marriage is much stronger than a presumption in regard to other facts.

8. Again in *Sastry Velaider Aronegary* v. *Sembecutty Viagalie,* (1881) 6 AC 364, it was held that where a man and woman are proved to have lived together as man and wife, the law will presume, unless the contrary is clearly proved, that they were living together in consequence of a valid marriage, and not in a state of concubinage.

9. In India, the same principles have been followed in the case of *A. Dinohamy* v. *W.L. Balahamy,* AIR 1927 PC 185, in which the Privy Council laid down the general proposition that where a man and woman are proved to have lived together as man and wife, the law will presume, unless, the contrary is clearly proved, that they were living together in consequence of a valid marriage, and not in a state of concubinage.

10. In *Mohabbat Ali Khan* v. *Muhammad Ibrahim Khan,* AIR 1929 PC 135, the Privy Council has laid down that the law presumes in favour of marriage and

against concubinage when a man and woman have cohabited continuously for number of years.

11. In *Gokal Chand* v. *Parvin Kumari,* AIR 1952 SC 231: 1952 SCJ 331: 1952 SCR 825, this Court held that continuous co- habitation of man and woman as husband and wife may raise the presumption of marriage, but the presumption which may be drawn from long co- habitation is rebuttable and if there are circumstances which weaken and destroy that presumption, the Court cannot ignore them.

12. Further, in the case of *Badri Prasad* v. *Dy. Director of Consolidation,* (1978) 3 SCC 527: AIR 1978 SC 1557: 1978 All LJ 1010, the Supreme Court held that a strong presumption arises in favour of wedlock where the partners have lived together for a long spell as husband and wife. Although the presumption is rebuttable, a heavy burden lies on him who seeks to deprive the relationship of legal origin.

13. Again, in *Tulsa* v. *Durghatiya,* (2008) 4 SCC 520: 2008 AIR SCW 1148: AIR 2008 SC 1193, this Court held that where the partners lived together for a long spell as husband and wife, a presumption would arise in favour of a valid wedlock.

14. Sir James Fitz Stephen, who piloted the Criminal Procedure Code of 1872, a legal member of Viceroy's Council, described the object of section 125 of the Code (it was section 536 in 1872 Code) as a mode of preventing vagrancy or at least preventing its consequences.

15. Then came the 1898 Code in which the same provision was in Chapter XXXVI section 488 of the Code. The exact provision of section 488(1) of the 1898 Code runs as follows:

> "488. (1) If any person having sufficient means neglects or refuses to maintain his wife or his legitimate or illegitimate child unable to maintain itself, the District Magistrate, a Presidency Magistrate, a Sub-divisional Magistrate or a Magistrate of the first class may, upon proof of such neglect or refusal, order such person to make a monthly allowance for the maintenance of his wife or such child, at such monthly rate, not exceeding five hundred rupees in the whole as such Magistrate thinks fit, and to pay the same to such person as the Magistrate from time to time directs."

16. In *Jagir Kaur* v. *Jaswant Singh,* AIR 1963 SC 1521: (1963) 2 Cr LJ 413: (1964) 2 SCR 73: (1964) 1 SCJ 386, the Supreme Court observed with respect to Chapter XXXVI of Cr.P.C. of 1898 that provisions for maintenance of wives and children intend to serve a social purpose. Section 488 prescribes forums for a proceeding to enable a deserted wife or a helpless child, legitimate or illegitimate, to get urgent relief.

17. In *Nanak Chand* v. *Chandra Kishore Aggarwal,* (1969) 3 SCC 802: AIR 1970 SC 446: 1970 Cr LJ 522, the Supreme Court, discussing section 488 of the older CrPC, virtually came to the same conclusion that section 488 provides a summary remedy and is applicable to all persons belonging to any religion and has no relationship with the personal law of the parties.

18. In *Captain Ramesh Chander Kaushal* v. *Veena Kaushal,* AIR 1978 SC 1807: (1978) 4 SCC 70: 1978 Cr LJ 3, this Court held that section 125 is a reincarnation of section 488 of the Cr.P.C. of 1898 except for the fact that parents have also been brought into the category of persons entitled for maintenance. It observed that this provision is a measure of social justice specially enacted to protect, and inhibit neglect of women, children, old and infirm and falls within the constitutional sweep of article 15(3) reinforced by article 39. Speaking for the Bench Justice Krishna Iyer observed that. "We have no doubt that sections of statutes calling for construction by courts are not petrified print but vibrant words with social functions to fulfill. The brooding presence of the constitutional empathy for the weaker sections like women and children must inform interpretation if it is to have social relevance. So viewed, it is possible to be selective in picking out that interpretation out of two alternatives which advance the cause of the derelicts." (Para 9 on pages 1809-10)

19. Again in *Vimala (K)* v. *Veeraswamy (K),* (1991) 2 SCC 375: 1991 AIR SCW 754, a three-Judge Bench of this Court held that section 125 of the Code of 1973 is meant to achieve a social purpose and the object is to prevent vagrancy and destitution. Explaining the meaning of the word 'wife' the Court held:

> "The object is to prevent vagrancy and destitution. It provides a speedy remedy for the supply of food, clothing and shelter to the deserted wife. When an attempt is made by the husband to negative the claim of the neglected wife depicting her as a kept-mistress on the specious plea that he was already married, the court would insist on strict proof of the earlier marriage. The term `wife' in section 125 of the Code of Criminal Procedure, includes a woman who has been divorced by a husband or who has obtained a divorce from her husband and has not remarried. The woman not having the legal status of a wife is thus brought within the inclusive definition of the term `wife' consistent with the objective."

20. Thus, in those cases where a man, who lived with a woman for a long time and even though they may not have undergone legal necessities of a valid marriage, should be made liable to pay the woman maintenance if he deserts her. The man should not be allowed to benefit from the legal loopholes by enjoying the advantages of a *de facto* marriage without undertaking the duties and obligations. Any other interpretation would lead the woman to vagrancy and destitution, which the provision of maintenance in section 125 is meant to prevent.

21. The Committee on Reforms of Criminal Justice System, headed by Dr. Justice V.S. Malimath, in its report of 2003 opined that evidence regarding a man and woman living together for a reasonably long period should be sufficient to draw the presumption that the marriage was performed according to the customary rites of the parties. Thus, it recommended that the word 'wife' in section 125 Cr.P.C. should be amended to include a woman who was living with the man like his wife for a reasonably long period.

22. The Constitution Bench of this Court in *Mohammad Ahmed Khan* v. *Shah Bano Begum*, reported in (1985) 2 SCC 556: AIR 1985 SC 945: 1985 Cr LJ 875, considering the provision of section 125 of the 1973 Code, opined that the said provision is truly secular in character and is different from the personal law of the parties. The Court further held that such provisions are essentially of a prophylactic character and cut across the barriers of religion. The Court further held that the liability imposed by section 125 to maintain close relatives, who are indigent, is founded upon the individual's obligation to the society to prevent vagrancy and destitution.

23. In a subsequent decision, in *Dwarika Prasad Satpathy* v. *Bidyut Prava Dixit*, (1999) 7 SCC 675: AIR 1999 SC 3348: 1999 AIR SCW 3844, this Court held that the standard of proof of marriage in a section 125 proceeding is not as strict as is required in a trial for an offence under section 494 of IPC. The learned Judges explained the reason for the aforesaid finding by holding that an order passed in an application under section 125 does not really determine the rights and obligations of parties as the section is enacted with a view to provide a summary remedy to neglected wives to obtain maintenance. The learned Judges held that maintenance cannot be denied where there was some evidence on which conclusions of living together could be reached. (*See* para 9).

24. However, striking a different note, in *Yamunabai Anantrao Adhav* v. *Anantrao Shivram Adhav*, AIR 1988 SC 644: JT 1988 (1) SC 193, a two-Judge Bench of this Court held that an attempt to exclude altogether personal law of the parties in proceedings under section 125 is improper. The learned Judges also held that the expression 'wife' in section 125 of the Code should be interpreted to mean only a legally wedded wife.

25. Again in a subsequent decision of this Court in *Savitaben Somabhat Bhatiya* v. *State of Gujarat*, in AIR 2005 SC 1809: 2005 AIR SCW 1601: 2005 Cr LJ 2141, this Court held however desirable it may be to take note of plight of an unfortunate woman, who unwittingly enters into wedlock with a married man, there is no scope to include a woman not lawfully married within the expression of 'wife'. The Bench held that this inadequacy in law can be amended only by the Legislature. While coming to the aforesaid finding, the learned Judges relied on the decision in the *Yamunabai* case (supra).

26. We are inclined to take a broad view of the definition of 'wife' having regard to the social object of section 125 in the Code of 1973. However, sitting in a two-Judge Bench, we cannot, we are afraid, take a view contrary to the views expressed in the abovementioned two cases.

27. However, law in America has proceeded on a slightly different basis. The social obligation of a man entering into a live-in relationship with another woman, without the formalities of a marriage, came up for consideration in the American courts in the leading case of *Marvin* v. *Marvin*, (1976) 18 Cal 3d 660. In that context, a new expression of 'palimony' has been coined, which is a combination of 'pal' and 'alimony', by the famous divorce lawyer in the said case, Mr. Marvin Mitchelson.

28. In the *Marvin* case (*supra*), the plaintiff, Michelle Marvin, alleged that she and Lee Marvin entered into an oral agreement which provided that while "the parties lived together they would combine their efforts and earnings and would share equally any and all property accumulated as a result of their efforts whether individual or combined." The parties allegedly further agreed that Michelle would "render her services as a companion, homemaker, housekeeper and cook." Michelle sought a judicial declaration of her contract and property rights, and sought to impose a constructive trust upon one half of the property acquired during the course of the relationship. The Supreme Court of California held as follows:—

(1) The provisions of the Family Law Act do not govern the distribution of property acquired during a non-marital relationship; such a relationship remains subject solely to judicial decision.

(2) The courts should enforce express contracts between non-marital partners except to the extent that the contract is explicitly founded on the consideration of meretricious sexual services.

(3) In the absence of an express contract, the courts should inquire into the conduct of the parties to determine whether that conduct demonstrates an implied contract, agreement of partnership or joint venture, or some other tacit understanding between the parties. The courts may also employ the doctrine of 'quantum meruit', or equitable remedies such as constructive or resulting trusts, when warranted by the facts of the case.

29. Though in our country, law has not developed on the lines of the *Marvin* case (*supra*), but our social context also is fast changing, of which cognizance has to be taken by Courts in interpreting a statutory provision which has a pronounced social content like section 125 of the Code of 1973.

30. We think the larger Bench may consider also the provisions of the Protection of Women from Domestic Violence Act, 2005. This Act assigns a very broad and expansive definition to the term 'domestic abuse' to include within its purview even economic abuse. 'Economic abuse' has been defined very broadly in sub-explanation (iv) to *Explanation I* of section 3 of the said Act to include deprivation of financial and economic resources.

31. Further, section 20 of the Act allows the Magistrate to direct the respondent to pay monetary relief to the aggrieved person, who is the harassed woman, for expenses incurred and losses suffered by her, which may include, but is not limited to, maintenance under section 125 CrPC. [section 20(1)(d)].

32. Section 22 of the Act confers upon the Magistrate, the power to award compensation to the aggrieved person, in addition to other reliefs granted under the Act.

33. In terms of section 26 of the Act, these reliefs mentioned above can be sought in any legal proceeding, before a civil court, family court or a 19 criminal court, affecting the aggrieved person and the respondent.

34. Most significantly, the Act gives a very wide interpretation to the term 'domestic relationship' as to take it outside the confines of a marital

relationship, and even includes live-in relationships in the nature of marriage within the definition of 'domestic relationship' under section 2(f) of the Act. Therefore, women in live-in relationships are also entitled to all the reliefs given in the said Act.

35. We are thus of the opinion that if the abovementioned monetary relief and compensation can be awarded in cases of live-in relationships under the Act of 2005, they should also be allowed in a proceedings under section 125 of CrPC. It seems to us that the same view is confirmed by section 26 of the said Act of 2005.

36. We believe that in light of the constant change in social attitudes and values, which have been incorporated into the forward-looking Act of 2005, the same needs to be considered with respect to section 125 of CrPC and accordingly, a broad interpretation of the same should be taken.

CHAPTER 15

THE LAW OF SENTENCING – MITIGATING FACTORS FOR DEATH PENALTY

State of Maharashtra v. *Goraksha Ambaji Adsul,* (2011) 7 SCC 437: AIR 2011 SC 2689: 2011 Cr LJ 4286

Background:

1. The judgment reiterates the settled law of life imprisonment being the rule and death penalty, the exception in murder cases. It reaffirms the existence of 'rarest of rare' category to jointly a death sentence the presence of (mitigating) circumstances is also lucidly dealt within the ruling.

The Verdict

2. Awarding of death sentence amounts to taking away the life of an individual, which is the most valuable right available, whether viewed from the constitutional point of view or from the human rights point of view. The condition of providing special reasons for awarding death penalty is not to be construed linguistically but it is to satisfy the basic features of a reasoning supporting and making award of death penalty unquestionable. The circumstances and the manner of committing the crime should be such that it pricks the judicial conscience of the Court to the extent that the only and inevitable conclusion should be awarding of death penalty.

The Various Aspects

3. The principles governing the sentencing policy in our criminal jurisprudence have more or less been consistent, right from the pronouncement of the Constitution Bench judgment of this Court in the case of *Bachan Singh* v. *State of Punjab,* (1980) 2 SCC 684: AIR 1980 SC 898: 1980 Cr LJ 636. Awarding punishment is certainly an onerous function in the dispensation of criminal justice. The Court is expected to keep in mind the facts and circumstances of a case, the principles of law governing award of sentence, the legislative intent of special or general statute raised in the case and the impact of awarding punishment. These are the nuances which need to be examined by the Court with discernment and in depth. The legislative intent behind enacting section 354(3) of the CrPC clearly demonstrates the concern of the legislature for taking away a human life and imposing death penalty upon the accused. Concern for the dignity of the human life postulates resistance to taking a life through law's instrumentalities and that ought not to be done, save in the rarest of rare cases, unless the alternative option is unquestionably foreclosed. In exercise of

its discretion, the Court would also take into consideration the mitigating circumstances and their resultant effects.

4. The Constitution Bench judgment of this Court in the case of *Bachan Singh* (supra) has been summarized in paragraph 38 in the case of *Machhi Singh* v. *State of Punjab*, (1983) 3 SCC 470: AIR 1983 SC 957: 1983 Cr LJ 1457 and the following guidelines have been stated while considering the possibility of awarding sentence of death:

"(i) The extreme penalty of death need not be inflicted except in gravest cases of extreme culpability.

(ii) Before opting for the death penalty the circumstances of the 'offender' also required to be taken into consideration along with the circumstances of the 'Crime'.

(iii) Life imprisonment is the rule and death sentence is an exception, Death sentence must be imposed only when life imprisonment appears to be an altogether inadequate punishment having regard to the relevant circumstances of the crime, and provided, and only provided the option to impose sentence of imprisonment for life cannot be conscientiously exercised having regard to the nature and circumstances of the crime and all the relevant circumstances.

(iv) A balance-sheet of aggravating and mitigating circumstances has to be drawn up and in doing so the mitigating circumstances have to be accorded full weightage and a just balance has to be struck between the aggravating and the mitigating circumstances before the option is exercised."

5. The judgment in the case of *Bachan Singh* (supra), did not only state the above guidelines in some elaboration, but also specified the mitigating circumstances which could be considered by the Court while determining such serious issues and they are as follows:—

"206. .... 'Mitigating circumstances. - In the exercise of its discretion in the above cases, the court shall take into account the following circumstances:

(1) That the offence was committed under the influence of extreme mental or emotional disturbance.

(2) The age of the accused. If the accused is young or old, he shall not be sentenced to death.

(3) The probability that the accused would not commit criminal acts of violence as would constitute a continuing threat to society.

(4) The probability that the accused can be reformed and rehabilitated. The State shall by evidence prove that the accused does not satisfy the conditions (3) and (4) above.

(5) That in the facts and circumstances of the case the accused believed that he was morally justified in committing the offence.

(6) That the accused acted under the duress or domination of another person.

(7) That the condition of the accused showed that he was mentally defective and that the said defect impaired his capacity to appreciate the criminality of his conduct'."

6. This Court in *Santosh Kumar Satishbhushan Bariyar* v. *State of Maharashtra*, (2009) 6 SCC 498: 2010 AIR SCW 1130, also considered various doctrines, principles and factors which would be considered by the Courts while dealing with such cases. The Court discussed in some elaboration the applicability of doctrine of rehabilitation and the doctrine of prudence. While considering the application of the doctrine of rehabilitation and the extent of weightage to be given to the mitigating circumstances, it noticed the nature of the evidence and the background of the accused. The conviction in that case was entirely based upon the statement of the approver and was a case purely of circumstantial evidence. Thus, applying the doctrine of prudence, it noticed the fact that the accused were unemployed, young men in search of job and they were not criminals. In execution of a plan proposed by the appellant and accepted by others, they kidnapped a friend of theirs. The kidnapping was done with the motive of procuring ransom from his family but later they murdered him because of the fear of getting caught, and later cut the body into pieces and disposed it off at different places. One of the accused had turned approver and as already noticed, the conviction was primarily based upon the statement of the approver.

7. Basing its reasoning on the application of doctrine of prudence and the version put forward by the accused, the Court, while declining to award death penalty and only awarding life imprisonment, held as under (SCC pp. 551 & 559-60):

> "135. Right to life, in its barest of connotation would imply right to mere survival. In this form, right to life is the most fundamental of all rights. Consequently, a punishment which aims at taking away life is the gravest punishment. Capital punishment imposes a limitation on the essential content of the fundamental right to life, eliminating it irretrievably. We realize the absolute nature of this right, in the sense that it is a source of all other rights. Other rights may be limited, and may even be withdrawn and then granted again, but their ultimate limit is to be found in the preservation of the right to life. Right to life is the essential content of all rights under the Constitution. If life is taken away, all other rights cease to exist.
>
> *** *** ***
>
> 168. We must, however, add that in a case of this nature where the entire prosecution case revolves round the statement of an approver or dependent upon the circumstantial evidence, the prudence doctrine should be invoked. For the aforementioned purpose, at the stage of sentencing evaluation of evidence would not be permissible, the courts not only have to solely depend upon the findings arrived at for the purpose of recording a judgment of conviction, but also consider the matter keeping in view of evidences which have been brought on record on behalf of the parties and in particular the accused for imposition of a lesser punishment. A statement of approver in regard to the manner in which crime has been committed *vis-a-vis* the role played by the accused, on the one hand, and that of the approver, on the other, must be tested on the touchstone of the prudence doctrine

169. The accused persons were not criminals. They were friends. The deceased was said to have been selected because his father was rich. The motive, if any, was to collect some money. They were not professional killers. They have no criminal history. All were unemployed and were searching for jobs. Further if age of the accused was a relevant factor for the High Court for not imposing death penalty on Accused Nos. 2 and 3, the same standard should have been applied to the case of the appellant also who was only two years older and still a young man in age. Accused Nos. 2 and 3 were as much a part of the crime as the appellant. Though it is true, that it was he who allegedly proposed the idea of kidnapping, but at the same time it must not be forgotten that the said plan was only executed when all the persons involved gave their consent thereto.

*** *** ***

171. Section 354(3) of the Code of Criminal Procedure requires that when the conviction is for an offence punishable with death or in the alternative with imprisonment for life or imprisonment for a term of years, the judgment shall state the reasons for the sentence awarded, and in the case of sentence of death, the special reasons thereof. We do not think that the reasons assigned by the courts below disclose any special reason to uphold the death penalty. The discretion granted to the courts must be exercised very cautiously especially because of the irrevocable character of death penalty. Requirements of law to assign special reasons should not be construed to be an empty formality.

172. We have previously noted that the judicial principles for imposition of death penalty are far from being uniform. Without going into the merits and demerits of such discretion and subjectivity, we must nevertheless reiterate the basic principle, stated repeatedly by this Court, that life imprisonment is the rule and death penalty an exception. Each case must therefore be analyzed and the appropriateness of punishment determined on a case-by- case basis with death sentence not to be awarded save in the 'rarest of rare' case where reform is not possible. Keeping in mind at least this principle we do not think that any of the factors in the present case discussed above warrants the award of the death penalty. There are no special reasons to record the death penalty and the mitigating factors in the present case, discussed previously, are, in our opinion, sufficient to place it out of the 'rarest of rare' category.

8. The above principle, as supported by case illustrations, clearly depicts the various precepts which would govern the exercise of judicial discretion by the Courts within the parameters spelt out under section 354(3) of the Cr.P.C.

15A. Death penalty is justified in case of a gruesome murder – financial crisis of the accused is not a mitigating circumstance

State of Uttar Pradesh v. *Alok Verma*, (2011) 8 SCC 434: 2011 AIR SCW 6861

Importance: The Supreme Court issued notice to the accused proposing enhancement of sentence. (Earlier, in *Mehboob Batcha* v. *State*, (2011) 7 SCC 45, the Supreme Court had refrained from issuing notice despite observing that the accused deserved death sentence).

The Verdict: We cannot imagine a more ghastly act and, we are, prima facie, of the opinion that this falls in the category of rarest of rare cases in which death sentence should have been given. The trial court, no doubt, awarded death sentence to the respondent, but the High Court reduced it to life sentence by observing:—

> "... But on the other side, it is to be considered as to what were the circumstances under which the said murders were caused. Accused Alok Verma was postgraduate in Sociology, having failed in getting a job. It seems that due to financial crisis, he entered into the criminal world, due to which he had to go to jail. He had been away from his wife and children for a long time, and in these circumstances, he became pessimistic and began to suspect his wife's character. Advice of his wife to stay away from criminal activities he could not accept. In absence of alternative, in such circumstances, his wife's threat to disclose all of his wrong acts made the situation worse and resulted in occurrence of the incident which does not appear to be committed under any pre plan nor for any benefit, but has been caused due to hopelessness and doubts about the character of the wife wherein he was doubting that the children were not his. In the above circumstances considering the decision of the Hon'ble Supreme Court in *Prakash Dhawal Khairnath (Patil)* v. *State of Maharashtra,* AIR 2002 SC 340: 2002 Cr LJ 928: (2002) 2 SCC 35 and *State of Maharashtra* v. *Sandeep*, 2002 SCC (Cri) 281, the conclusion arrived is that the present case is not fit for death penalty."

Prima facie, we find the reasoning of the High Court to be strange. Merely because a person is in financial crisis does not mean that he is at liberty to commit ghastly and gruesome murders. It appears that the wife of the accused was of a noble character who tried to reform him, but the accused rather than being reformed committed these monstrous crimes. We fail to understand how the High Court could reduce the death sentence in these circumstances."

15B. Law of sentencing – requirement of reformatory approach for minor indiscretions.

Commissioner of Police v. *Sandeep Kumar,* (2011) 4 SCC 644

Background

1. In this visionary judgment the Supreme Court has reinforced the reformative mandate of law as opposed to its retributive aspect. It focuses on condoning minor indiscretions of the young in preference to branding them as criminals for the rest of their lives.

Facts

2. The respondent Sandeep Kumar applied for the post of Head Constable (Ministerial) in 1999. In the application form it was printed:

> "12(a) Have you ever been arrested, prosecuted kept under detention or bound down/fined, convicted by a court of law for any offence debarred/

disqualified by any Public Service Commission from appearing at its examination/selection or debarred from any Examination, rusticated by any university or any other education authority/Institution."

3. Against that column the respondent wrote: 'No', which was factually incorrect because he and some of his family members were involved in a criminal case being FIR 362 under section 325/34 IPC. This case was admittedly compromised on 18-1-1998 and the respondent and his family members were acquitted on 18-1-1998.

4. The respondent qualified in all the tests for selection to the post of temporary Head Constable (Ministerial). While filing his attestation forms on 03-04-2001, for the first time he disclosed that he had been involved in a criminal case with his tenant which, later on, had been compromised in 1998 and he had been acquitted. The authorities issued notice asking him to show cause why his candidature for the post should not be cancelled because he had concealed the fact of his involvement in the aforesaid criminal case and had made a wrong statement in his application form. The explanation offered by him was not accepted and his candidature was cancelled. The Court reversed.

The Verdict

5. Youth often commit indiscretions, which are often condoned. It is true that in the application form the respondent did not mention that he was involved in a criminal case under section 325/34 IPC. Probably he did not mention this out of fear that if he did so he would automatically be disqualified. At any event, it was not such a serious offence like murder, dacoity or rape, and hence a more lenient view should be taken in the matter. We respectfully agree with the Delhi High Court that the cancellation of his candidature was illegal, but we wish to give our own opinion in the matter.

The Reason

6. When the incident happened the respondent must have been about 20 years of age. At that age young people often commit indiscretions, and such indiscretions can often been condoned. After all, youth will be youth. They are not expected to behave in as mature a manner as older people. Hence, our approach should be to condone minor indiscretions made by young people rather than to brand them as criminals for the rest of their lives.

The precedent followed

7. In this connection, we may refer to the character 'Jean Valjean' in Victor Hugo's novel 'Les Miserables', in which for committing a minor offence of stealing a loaf of bread for his hungry family Jean Valjean was branded as a thief for his whole life. The modern approach should be to reform a person instead of branding him as a criminal all his life. We may also here refer to the case of Welsh students mentioned by Lord Denning in his book 'Due Process of Law'. It appears that some students of Wales were very enthusiastic about the Welsh language and they were upset because the radio programmes were being broadcast in the English language and not in Welsh. They came up

to London and invaded the High Court. They were found guilty of contempt of court and sentenced to prison for three months by the High Court Judge. They filed an appeal before the Court of Appeals. Allowing the appeal, Lord Denning observed:—

> "I come now to Mr. Watkin Powell's third point. He says that the sentences were excessive. I do not think they were excessive, at the time they were given and in the circumstances then existing. Here was a deliberate interference with the course of justice in a case which was no concern of theirs. It was necessary for the judge to show - and to show to all students everywhere - that this kind of thing cannot be tolerated. Let students demonstrate, if they please, for the causes in which they believe. Let them make their protests as they will. But they must do it by lawful means and not by unlawful. If they strike at the course of justice in this land - and I speak both for England and Wales - they strike at the roots of society itself, and they bring down that which protects them. It is only by the maintenance of law and order that they are privileged to be students and to study and live in peace. So let them support the law and not strike it down.
>
> But now what is to be done? The law has been vindicated by the sentences which the judge passed on Wednesday of last week. He has shown that law and order must be maintained, and will be maintained. But on this appeal, things are changed. These students here no longer defy the law. They have appealed to this court and shown respect for it. They have already served a week in prison. I do not think it necessary to keep them inside it any longer. These young people are no ordinary criminals. There is no violence, dishonesty or vice in them. On the contrary, there was much that we should applaud. They wish to do all they can to preserve the Welsh language. Well may they be proud of it. It is the language of the bards - of the poets and the singers - more melodious by far than our rough English tongue. On high authority, it should be equal in Wales with English. They have done wrong - very wrong - in going to the extreme they did. But, that having been shown, I think we can, and should, show mercy on them. We should permit them to go back to their studies, to their parents and continue the good course which they have so wrongly disturbed."
>
> [*Vide*: *Morris* v. *Crown Office*, (1970) 2 QB 114: (1970) 1 All ER 1079].

8. In our opinion, we should display the same wisdom as displayed by Lord Denning.

15C. Balancing sentence of fine versus imprisonment

K.A. Abbas H.S.A. v. *Sabu Joseph*, (2010) 6 SCC 230

Background:

1. The judgment addresses a sensitive aspect of penology as to whether for default of payment of compensation ordered under section 357(3) Cr. PC, could a default sentence be imposed in its place?

The Verdict

2. From the above line of cases, it becomes very clear, that, a sentence of imprisonment can be granted for default in payment of compensation awarded under section 357(3) of CrPC. The whole purpose of the provision is to accommodate the interests of the victims in the criminal justice system. Sometimes the situation becomes such that no purpose is served by keeping a person behind bars. Instead, directing the accused to pay an amount of compensation to the victim or affected party can ensure delivery of total justice. Therefore, this grant of compensation is sometimes in lieu of sending a person behind bars or in addition to a very light sentence of imprisonment. Hence on default of payment of this compensation, there must be a just recourse. Not imposing a sentence of imprisonment would mean allowing the accused to get away without paying the compensation and imposing another fine would be impractical as it would mean imposing a fine upon another fine and therefore would not ensure proper enforcement of the order of compensation. While passing an order under section 357(3), it is imperative for the courts to look at the ability and the capacity of the accused to pay the same amount as has been laid down by the cases above, otherwise the very purpose of granting an order of compensation would stand defeated.

3. section 421 of Cr.P.C. reads:—

"421. Warrant for levy of fine.

(1) When an offender has been sentenced to pay a fine the court passing the sentence makes action for the recovery of the fine in either or both of the following ways, that is to say, it may—

(a) Issue a warrant for the levy of the amount by attachment and sale of any movable property belonging to the offender

(b) Issue a warrant to the Collector of the district, authorizing him to realize the amount as arrears of land revenue from the movable or immovable property, or both of the defaulters;

Provided that, if the sentence directs that in default of payment of the fine, the offender shall be imprisoned, and if such offender has undergone the whole of such imprisonment in default, no court shall issue such warrant unless, for special reasons to be recorded in writing, it considers it necessary so to do, or unless it has made an order for the payment of expenses or compensation out of the fine under section 357.

(2) The State Government may make rules regulating the manner in which warrants under clause (a) of sub-section (1) are to be executed, and for the summary determination of any claims made by any person other than the offender in respect of any property attached in execution of such warrant.

(3) Where the court issues a warrant to the Collector under clause (b) of sub-section (1), the Collector shall realize the amount in accordance with the law relating to recovery of arrears of land revenue, as if such warrant were a certificate issued under such law:

Provided that no such warrant shall be executed by the arrest or detention in prison of the offender."

4. Section 431 of Cr.P.C. reads:—

> "431. Money ordered to be paid recoverable as a fine. Any money (other than a fine) payable by virtue of any order made under this Code, and the method of recovery of which is not otherwise expressly provided for, shall be recoverable as if it were a fine:
>
> Provided that section 421 shall, in its application to an order under section 359, by virtue of this section, be construed as if in the proviso to sub-section (1) of section 421, after the words and figures 'under section 357', the words and figures 'or an order for payment of costs under section 359' had been inserted."

5. Section 431 clearly provides that an order of compensation under section 357(3) will be recoverable in the same way as if it were a fine. Section 421 further provides the mode of recovery of a fine and the section clearly provides that a person can be imprisoned for non-payment of fine. Therefore, going by the provisions of the code, the intention of the legislature is clearly to ensure that mode of recovery of a fine and compensation is on the same footing. In light of the aforesaid reasoning, the contention of the accused that there can be no sentence of imprisonment for default in payment of compensation under section 357(3) should fail.

6. The Learned Counsel for the accused has placed reliance on the decision of this court in the case of *Ettappadan Ahammedakutty* v. *E.P. Abdullakeya* (Criminal Appeal No. 1013 of 2007), which reiterated the position taken by the Kerala High Court in a case reported in 2000 (2) KLT 349; wherein it was held that no sentence of imprisonment can be passed on default of paying compensation awarded under section 357(3). But in light of several decisions reiterating the opposite stand, this case needs to be viewed in isolation and cannot be taken to be against the established position preferred by the Supreme Court on this issue over a period of two decades."

Position in UK and Australia

7. A similar position is also prevalent in other countries. In the United Kingdom, section 82(3) of Magistrates' Courts Act, 1980 allows for a sentence of imprisonment for default in payment of a fine or any financial order. The section reds:—

> "Where on the occasion of the offender's conviction a magistrates' court does not issue a warrant of commitment for a default in paying any such sum as aforesaid or fix a term of imprisonment under the said section 77(2) which is to be served by him in the event of any such default, it shall not thereafter issue a warrant of commitment for any such default or for want of sufficient distress to satisfy such a sum unless:
>
> (a) he is already serving a sentence of custody for life, or a term of imprisonment, detention in a young offender institution, or detention under section 9 of the Criminal Justice Act, 1982; or
>
> (b) the court has since the conviction inquired into his means in his presence on at least one occasion."

8. In Australia, under section 4 of the Sentencing Act, 1997 the definition of 'fine' includes a compensation order. Procedure for enforcement of fines is provided for in section 47(7) of the Act and provides for a sentence of imprisonment on default in payment of fine.

The Various Aspects

9. The main question that requires to be considered and decided is, whether in default of payment of compensation ordered under section 357(3) of the CrPC, a default sentence can be imposed?

10. Let us now look at the relevant provisions and the decision of this court on which reliance is placed by learned counsel. section 357 of Cr.PC reads:

"357. Order to pay compensation.—

(1) When a court imposes a sentence of fine or a sentence (including a sentence of death) of which fine forms a part, the court may, when passing judgment order the whole or any part of the fine recovered to be applied-

(a) In defraying the expenses properly incurred in the prosecution,

(b) In the payment to any person of compensation for any loss or injury caused by the offence, when compensation is, in the opinion, of the court, recoverable by such person in a Civil Court;

(c) When, any person is convicted of any offence for having caused the death of another person or of having abetted the commission of shelf all offence, in paying in, compensation to the persons who are, under the Fatal Accidents Act, 1855 (13 of 1855) entitled to recover damages from the person sentenced for the loss resulting to them from such death;

(d) When any person is convicted of any offence which includes theft, criminal, misappropriation, criminal breach of trust or cheating, or of having dishonestly received or retained; or of having voluntarily assisted in disposing of stolen property knowing or having reason to believe the same to be stolen in compensating any bona fide purchaser of such property for the loss of the same if such property is restored to the possession of the person entitled thereto.

(2) If the fine is imposed in a case, which is subject to appeal, no such payment shall be made before the period allowed for presenting the appeal has elapsed, or if an appeal be presented, before the decision of the appeal.

(3) When a court imposes a sentence, of which fine does not form a part, the court may, when passing judgment order the accused person to pay, by way of compensation such amount as may be specified in the order to the person who has suffered any loss or injury by reason of the act for which the accused person his been so sentenced.

(4) An order under this section may also be made by all Appellate Court or by the High Court or Court of Session when exercising its powers of revision. (5) At the time of awarding compensation in any subsequent civil suit relating to the same matter, the court shall take into account any sum paid or recovered as compensation under this section.

11. Essentially the section empowers the courts, not to just impose a fine alone or fine along with the sentence of imprisonment, but also when the situation arises, direct the accused to pay compensation to the person who has suffered any loss or injury by reason of the act for which the accused person has been sentenced.

12. In *Balraj* v. *State of Uttar Pradesh,* AIR 1995 SC 1935: 1995 AIR SCW 2997: 1995 Cr LJ 3217, this court has held, that, section 357(3) Cr. P.C. provides for ordering of payment by way of compensation to the victim by the accused. It is an important provision and it must also be noted that power to award compensation is not ancillary to other sentences but it is in addition thereto.

13. In *Hari Kishan* v. *Sukhbir Singh,* AIR 1988 SC 2127: 1988 Rajdhani LR 527: (1988) 17 Reports 559, this court has observed that, sub-section (1) of section 357 provides power to award compensation to victims of the offence out of the sentence of fine imposed on accused. In this case, we are not concerned with sub-section (1). We are concerned only with sub-section (3). It is an important provision but Courts have seldom invoked it. Perhaps due to ignorance of the object of it. It empowers the Court to award compensation to victims while passing judgment of conviction. In addition to conviction, the Court may order the accused to pay some amount by way of compensation to victim who has suffered by the action of accused. It may be noted that this power of Courts to award compensation is not ancillary to other sentences but it is in addition thereto. This power was intended to do something to reassure the victim that he or she is not forgotten in the criminal justice system. It is a measure of responding appropriately to crime as well of reconciling the victim with the offender. It is, to some extent, a constructive approach to crimes. It is indeed a step forward in our criminal justice system. We, therefore, recommend to all Courts to exercise this power liberally so as to meet the ends of justice in a better way.

14. In *Dilip S. Dahanukar* v. *Kotak Mahindra Co. Ltd.,* (2007) 6 SCC 528: 2007 AIR SCW 2425: AIR 2007 SC (Supp) 1345, this court differentiated between fine and compensation, and while doing so, has stated that the distinction between sub-sections (1) and (3) of section 357 is apparent. Sub-section (1) provides for application of an amount of fine while imposing a sentence of which fine forms a part; whereas sub-section (3) calls for a situation where a Court imposes a sentence of which fine does not form a part of the sentence. The court further observed:—

> "Compensation is awarded towards sufferance of any loss or injury by reason of an act for which an accused person is sentenced. Although it provides for a criminal liability, the amount which has been awarded as compensation is considered to be recourse of the victim in the same manner which may be granted in a civil suit. ..... We must, however, observe that there exists a distinction between fine and compensation, although, in a way it seeks to achieve the same purpose. An amount of compensation can be directed to be recovered as a 'fine' but the legal fiction raised in relation to

recovery of fine only, it is in that sense `fine' stands on a higher footing than compensation awarded by the Court."

15. Moving over to the question, whether a default sentence can be imposed on default of payment of compensation, this court in the case of *Hari Singh* v. *Sukhbir Singh* and in *Balraj* v. *State of Uttar Pradesh,* has held that it was open to all courts in India to impose a sentence on default of payment of compensation under sub-section (3) of section 357. In *Hari Singh* v. *Sukhbir Singh,* (1988) 4 SCC 551, this court has noticed certain factors which require to be taken into consideration while passing an order under the section:—

"11. The payment by way of compensation must, however, be reasonable. What is reasonable, may depend upon the facts and circumstances of each case. The quantum of compensation may be determined by taking into account the nature of crime, the justness of claim by the victim and the ability of accused to pay. If there are more than one accused they may be asked to pay in equal terms unless their capacity to pay varies considerably. The payment may also vary depending upon the acts of each accused. Reasonable period for payment of compensation, if necessary by instalments, may also be given. The Court may enforce the order by imposing sentence in default."

CHAPTER 16

A DIVORCED MUSLIM WIFE'S MAINTENANCE RIGHTS UNDER MUSLIM WOMEN (PROTECTION OF RIGHTS ON DIVORCE) ACT, 1986 READ WITH SECTION 125 Cr PC

Shabana Bano v. *Imran Khan*, (2010) 1 SCC 666: AIR 2010 SC 305: 2010 Cr LJ 521

Background

1. Shah Bano, the appellant entered to a wedlock on 26.11.2001with Imran Khan as per Muslim rites. The appellant alleged cruelty and dowry demands by the husband. The question arose as to entitlement of maintenance under section 125 Cr.P.C. by a Muslim divorced wife, and if yes, the appropriate forum.

The Verdict

2. .... a Family Court established under the Family Act shall exclusively have jurisdiction to adjudicate upon the applications filed under section 125 of CrPC. The appellant's petition under section 125 of the Cr.P.C. would be maintainable before the Family Court as long as appellant does not remarry. The amount of maintenance to be awarded under section 125 of the Cr.P.C. cannot be restricted for the 'iddat' period only.

3. Cumulative reading of the relevant portions of judgments of this Court in *Danial Latifi* v. *Union of India*, (2001) 7 SCC 740: 2001 AIR SCW 3932: AIR 2001 SC 3958 and Iqbal Bano [(2007) 6 SCC (Cri) 258] would make it crystal clear that even a divorced Muslim woman would be entitled to claim maintenance from her divorced husband, as long as she does not remarry. This being a beneficial piece of legislation, the benefit thereof must accrue to the divorced Muslim women. It is held that even if a Muslim woman has been divorced, she would be entitled to claim maintenance from her husband under section 125 of the Cr.P.C. after the expiry of period of iddat also, as long as she does not remarry.

The various aspects

4. Appellant Shabana Bano was married to the respondent Imran Khan according to Muslim rites at Gwalior on 26-11-2001. According to the appellant, at the time of marriage, necessary household goods to be used by

the couple were given. However, despite this, the respondent-husband and his family members treated the appellant with cruelty and continued to demand more dowry. After some time, the appellant became pregnant and was taken to her parents' house by the respondent. The respondent threatened the appellant that in case his demand of dowry is not met by the appellant's parents, then she would not be taken back to her matrimonial home even after delivery.

5. The basic and foremost question that arises for consideration is whether a Muslim divorced wife would be entitled to receive the amount of maintenance from her divorced husband under section 125 of the Cr.P.C. and, if yes, then through which forum. Section 4 of the Muslim Women (Protection of Rights on Divorce) Act, 1986 (hereinafter referred to as 'Muslim Act') reads as under:

> "4. Order for payment of maintenance:—
>
> (1) Notwithstanding anything contained in the foregoing provisions of this Act or in any other law for the time being in force, where a Magistrate is satisfied that a divorced woman has not re-married and is not able to maintain herself after the iddat period, he may make an order directing such of her relatives as would be entitled to inherit her property on her death according to Muslim law to pay such reasonable and fair maintenance to her as he may determine fit and proper, having regard to the needs of the divorced woman, the standard of life enjoyed by her during her marriage and the means of such relatives and such maintenance shall be payable by such relatives in the proportions in which they would inherit her property and at such periods as he may specify in his order:
>
> Provided that where such divorced woman has children, the Magistrate shall order only such children to pay maintenance to her, and in the event of any such children being unable to pay such maintenance, the Magistrate shall order the parents of such divorced woman to pay maintenance to her;
>
> Provided further that if any of the parents is unable to pay his or her share of the maintenance ordered by the Magistrate on the ground of his or her not having the means to pay the same, the Magistrate may, on proof of such inability being furnished to him, order that the share of such relatives in the maintenance ordered by him be paid by such of the other relatives as may appear to the Magistrate to have the means of paying the same in such proportions as the Magistrate may think fit to order.
>
> (2) Where a divorced woman is unable to maintain herself and she has no relatives as mentioned in sub-section (1) or such relatives or any one of them have not enough means to pay the maintenance ordered by the Magistrate or the other relatives have not the means to pay the shares of those relatives whose shares have been ordered by the Magistrate to be paid by such other relatives under the second proviso to sub-section (1), the Magistrate may, by order, direct the State Wakf Board established under section 9 of the Wakf Act, 1954 (29 of 1954), or under any other law for the time being in force in a State, functioning in the area in which the woman resides, to pay such maintenance as determined by him under sub-section (1) or, as the case may

be, to pay the shares of such of the relatives who are unable to pay, at such periods as he may specify in his order."

6. Section 5 thereof deals with the option to be governed by the provisions of sections 125 to 128 of the CrPC. It appears that parties had not given any joint or separate application for being considered by the Court. Section 7 thereof deals with transitional provisions. Family Act, was enacted w.e.f. 14th September, 1984 with a view to promote conciliation in, and secure speedy settlement of, disputes relating to marriage and family affairs and for matters connected therewith. The purpose of enactment was essentially to set up family courts for the settlement of family disputes, emphasizing on conciliation and achieving socially desirable results and adherence to rigid rules of procedure and evidence should be eliminated. In other words, the purpose was for early settlement of family disputes.

7. The Act, *inter alia*, seeks to exclusively provide within jurisdiction of the family courts the matters relating to maintenance, including proceedings under Chapter IX of the Cr.P.C. Section 7 appearing in Chapter III of the Family Act deals with Jurisdiction. Relevant provisions thereof read as under:

"7. *Jurisdiction.*—(1) Subject to the other provisions of this Act, a Family Court shall—

(a) have and exercise all the jurisdiction exercisable by any district Court or any subordinate civil Court under any law for the time being in force in respect of suits and proceedings of the nature referred to in the Explanation; and

(b) be deemed, for the purposes of exercising such jurisdiction under such law, to be a district Court or, as the case may be, such subordinate civil Court for the area to which the jurisdiction of the Family Court extends.

Explanation.—The suits and proceedings referred to in this sub- section are suits and proceedings of the following nature, namely:—

(a), (b), (c), (d), (e) - ....

(f) a suit or proceeding for maintenance;

(g) ....."

8. Section 20 of the Family Act appearing in Chapter VI deals with overriding effect of the provisions of the Act. The said section reads as under:

"20. *Act to have overriding effect.*—The provisions of this Act shall have effect notwithstanding anything inconsistent therewith contained in any other law for the time being in force or in any instrument having effect by virtue of any law other than this Act."

A bare perusal of section 20 of the Family Act makes it crystal clear that the provisions of this Act shall have overriding effect on all other enactments in force dealing with this issue.

9. In our opinion, the point stands settled by judgment of this Court reported in *Danial Latifi* v. *Union of India*, (2001) 7 SCC 740: 2001 AIR SCW 3932: AIR 2001 SC 3958 pronounced by a Constitution Bench of this Court.

Paras 30, 31 and 32 thereof fully establish the said right of the appellant. The said paragraphs are reproduced hereinunder:

> "30. A comparison of these provisions with section 125 Cr.P.C. will make it clear that requirements provided in section 125 and the purpose, object and scope thereof being to prevent vagrancy by compelling those who can do so to support those who are unable to support themselves and who have a normal and legitimate claim to support are satisfied. If that is so, the argument of the petitioners that a different scheme being provided under the Act which is equally or more beneficial on the interpretation placed by us from the one provided under the Code of Criminal Procedure deprive them of their right, loses its significance. The object and scope of section 125 Cr.P.C. is to prevent vagrancy by compelling those who are under an obligation to support those who are unable to support themselves and that object being fulfilled, we find it difficult to accept the contention urged on behalf of the petitioners.
>
> 31. Even under the Act, the parties agreed that the provisions of section 125 Cr.P.C. would still be attracted and even otherwise, the Magistrate has been conferred with the power to make appropriate provision for maintenance and, therefore, what could be earlier granted by a Magistrate under section 125 Cr.P.C. would now be granted under the very Act itself. This being the position, the Act cannot be held to be unconstitutional.
>
> 32. As on the date the Act came into force the law applicable to Muslim divorced women is as declared by this Court in *Shah Bano's* case, (1985) 2 SCC 556: AIR 1985 SC 945: 1985 Cr LJ 875. In this case to find out the personal law of Muslims with regard to divorced women's rights, the starting point should be Shah Bano's case and not the original texts or any other material - all the more so when varying versions as to the authenticity of the source are shown to exist. Hence, we have refrained from referring to them in detail. That declaration was made after considering the Holy Quran, and other commentaries or other texts. When a Constitution Bench of this Court analysed Suras 241-242 of Chapter II of the Holy Quran and other relevant textual material, we do not think, it is open for us to re-examine that position and delve into a research to reach another conclusion. We respectfully abide by what has been stated therein. All that needs to be considered is whether in the Act specific deviation has been made from the personal laws as declared by this Court in Shah Bano's case without mutilating its underlying ratio. We have carefully analysed the same and come to the conclusion that the Act actually and in reality codifies what was stated in Shah Bano's case. The learned Solicitor General contended that what has been stated in the Objects and Reasons in Bill leading to the Act is a fact and that we should presume to be correct. We have analysed the facts and the law in Shah Bano's case and proceeded to find out the impact of the same on the Act. If the language of the Act is as we have stated, the mere fact that the Legislature took note of certain facts in enacting the law will not be of much materiality.

10. Judgment of this Court in *Iqbal Bano* v. *State of Uttar Pradesh*, (2007) 6 SCC 785: 2007 AIR SCW 3880: AIR 2007 SC 2215 whereby the provisions contained in section 125 of the Cr.P.C. have been aptly considered and the relevant portion of the order passed in *Iqbal Bano's* case reads as under:

> "10. Proceedings under section 125 Cr.P.C. are civil in nature. Even if the Court noticed that there was a divorced woman in the case in question, it was open to it to treat it as a petition under the Act considering the beneficial nature of the legislation. Proceedings under section 125 Cr.P.C. and claims made under the Act are tried by the same court."

CHAPTER 17

CIVIL REMEDIES AVAILABLE/CIVIL PROCEEDINGS PENDING

Joseph Salvaraj A. v. *State of Gujrat*, (2011) 7 SCC 59: AIR 2011 SC 2258: 2011 (3) Cur Cri R 113

Background

1. This case raises important issues of general public importance about invoking the criminal law machinery in 'disputes' which are essentially of civil nature. Would an FIR be an abuse of process of law in situations not warranting a criminal offence and should be quashed by the High Court at the very threshold?

The Verdict

2. It is necessary to draw a distinction between civil wrong and criminal wrong. The Supreme Court reiterated the law earlier laid down in *Devendra* v. *State of Uttar Pradesh*, (2009) 7 SCC 495, in which it was declared:

> "A distinction must be made between a civil wrong and a criminal wrong. When dispute between the parties constitute only a civil wrong and not a criminal wrong, the courts would not permit a person to be harassed although no case for taking cognizance of the offence has been made out."

The Various Aspects

3. Thus, from the general conspectus of the various sections under which the Appellant is being charged and is to be prosecuted would show that the same are not made out even prima facie from the complainant's FIR. Even if the charge-sheet had been filed, the learned Single Judge could have still examined whether the offences alleged to have been committed by the Appellant were prima facie made out from the complainant's FIR, charge-sheet, documents etc. or not.

4. In our opinion, the matter appears to be purely civil in nature. There appears to be no cheating or a dishonest inducement for the delivery of property or breach of trust by the Appellant. The present FIR is an abuse of process of law. The purely civil dispute, is sought to be given a colour of a criminal offence to wreak vengeance against the Appellant. It does not meet the strict standard of proof required to sustain a criminal accusation.

CHAPTER 18

PUBLIC TRIAL - SHIFTING OF COURT SITTING TO JAIL PREMISES

Mohd. Shahabuddin v. *State of Bihar,* (2010) 4 SCC 653

The Challenge

1. The Patna High Court decided to designate District Jail, Siwan as the place of sitting of Sessions Court and that of the Judicial Magistrate Ist Class for expeditious trial of cases pending against Md. Shahabuddin. The accused challenged the same bringing into sharp focus the issue of 'public trials' in our criminal justice system.

The Verdict

2. It will be clear from these decisions that the mandatory exclusion of the press and public to criminal trials in all cases violates the First Amendment to the United States Constitution. But if such exclusion is made by the trial Judge in the best interest of fairness to make that exclusion, it would not violate that constitutional right. On analysis of the provisions of law and the leading judgments which all in one voice say that in all civilized countries governed by the rule of law, all criminal trials have to be public trials where public and press have complete access.

3. Public access is essential if trial adjudication is to achieve the objective of maintaining public confidence in the administration of justice. Publicity is the authentic hallmark of judicial functioning distinct from administrative functioning. Open trial serves an important prophylactic purpose, providing an outlet for community concern, hostility, and emotion. Public trial restores the balance in cases when shocking crime occurs in the society. People have inherent distrust for the secret trials. One of the demands of the democratic society is that public should know what goes on in court while being told by the press or what happens there, to the end that the public may judge whether our system of criminal justice is fair and right. Criminal trial is a public event. What transpires is a public property. Therefore, I have no difficulty in concluding that open trial is the universal rule and must be scrupulously adhered to. The right to public trial has also been recognized under section 327 of the Code.

4. The importance of public trial in a democratic country governed by rule of law can hardly be over emphasized, but at the same time I cannot overlook

the fact that primary function of the judiciary is to do justice between the parties which bring their causes before it. Therefore, it is difficult to accede to the proposition that there cannot be any exception to the universal rule that all cases must be tried in open court. In a case of extraordinary nature, the universal rule of open trial may not be adhered to. This is the settled legal position crystallized by a three-Judge Bench of this court in Kehar Singh case (supra). The High Court looking to the exceptional and extraordinary circumstances can take such a decision and no personal hearing is warranted before taking such a decision.

5. I accept the main argument of the learned counsel of the appellant and reiterate that universal rule as recognized in all civilized countries governed by rule of law is that the criminal trial should be a public trial or open trial but in exceptional cases there can be deviation from the universal rule in the larger public interest. The case in hand would fall in the category of those extraordinary and exceptional cases where in the interest of justice it became imperative to shift the venue of the trials for the reasons stated in the preceding paragraphs."

Appellant's Submissions

6. Mr. Ram Jethmalani, learned senior counsel appearing for the appellant canvassed the following propositions of law:

(a) That in pending criminal cases of which cognizance had been taken and even evidence had been recorded can only be shifted to another venue by the trial court after satisfying the conditions laid down in section 9(6) of the Code.

(b) That the High Court's administrative power of creating a court is not applicable for transferring a case from one court to another. A new court with its own defined jurisdiction can be created for the public generally, or for specified class of cases generally but not for cases in which a particular citizen is involved. The High Court missed the significance of the word 'ordinarily' in section 9(6) of the Code.

(c) That the administrative power of the High Court can only be exercised where the principle of *audi alteram partem* does not apply. In all situations where an order affects the interests of a party in a pending case, this power is not available. That power can only be exercised under section 408 of the Code after hearing the affected parties. It is settled law that even administrative orders are subject to the rule of *audi alteram partem* and by not hearing the appellant before transferring of the venue of cases had led to infringement of the fundamental rights of the appellant under Articles 14 and 21 of the Constitution.

(d) That the administrative power is not available merely to expedite the trial of a particular case. Expedition is necessary for all cases. The High Court did not act in the interest of expedition but really for terrorizing witnesses into giving evidence which suited the prosecution.

(e) That the three notifications read together show that the action was taken by the State Government and the High Court has merely concurred with it. All the three notifications are thus without jurisdiction and void.

7. Mr. Jethmalani placed strong reliance on the observation of the US Supreme Court in *Richmond Newspapers, Inc. et al* v. *Commonwealth of Virginia* et al 65L Ed 2d 973: (1980) 448 US 555. One of the most conspicuous features of English justice, that all judicial trials are held in open court, to which the public have free access,........appears to have been the rule in England from time immemorial. This was mentioned by F. Pollock, The Expansion of the Common Law 31-32 (1904). [*See* also: E. Jenks, The Book of English Law 73-74 (6th ed 1967)].

8. The learned senior counsel for the appellant further relied upon the following passages of the *Richmond's* case (*supra*):

> 16.1 (Page 983) In some instances, the openness of trials was explicitly recognized as part of the fundamental law of the Colony. The 1677 Concessions and Agreements of West New Jersey, for example, provided:
>
> "That in all public courts of justice for trials of causes, civil or criminal, any person or persons, inhabitants of the said Province may freely come into, and attend the said courts, and hear and be present, at all or any such trials as shall be there had or passed, that justice may not be done in a corner nor in any covert manner." [Reprinted in Sources of Our Liberties 188 (R. Perry ed.1959). See also 1 B. Schwartz, The Bill of Rights: A Documentary History 129 (1971).]
>
> 18. (Page 985) Jeremy Bentham not only recognized the therapeutic value of open justice but regarded it as the keystone:
>
> "Without publicity, all other checks are insufficient: in comparison of publicity, all other checks are of small account. Recordation, appeal, whatever other institutions might present themselves in the character of checks, would be found to operate rather as cloaks than checks; as cloaks in reality, as checks only in appearance." [J. Bentham Rationale of Judicial Evidence 524 (1827)].
>
> 19. (Page 985) The early history of open trials in part reflects the widespread acknowledgment, long before there were behavioral scientists, that public trials had significant community therapeutic value.
>
> 20. (Pages 985-986) When a shocking crime occurs, a community reaction of outrage and public protest often follows. [See H. Weihofen, The Urge to Punish 130-131 (1956)]. Thereafter the open processes of justice serve an important prophylactic purpose, providing an outlet for community concern, hostility, and emotion. Without an awareness that society's responses to criminal conduct are underway, natural human reactions of outrage and protest are frustrated, and may manifest themselves in some form of vengeful "self-help", as indeed they did regularly in the activities of vigilante "committees" on our frontiers. "The accusation and conviction or acquittal, as much perhaps as the execution of punishment, operate to restore the imbalance which was created by the offense or public charge, to reaffirm the

temporarily lost feeling of security and, perhaps, to satisfy that latent 'urge to punish'." [Mueller, Problems Posed by Publicity to Crime and Criminal Proceedings, 110 U Pa L Rev 1, 6 (1961)].

21. (Page 987) From this unbroken, uncontradicted history, supported by reasons as valid today as in centuries past, we are bound to conclude that a presumption of openness inheres in the very nature of a criminal trial under our system of justice. This conclusion is hardly novel; without a direct holding on the issue, the Court has voiced its recognition of it in a variety of contexts over the years.

22. (Page 999) This Court too has persistently defended the public character of the trial process. In re Oliver established that the Due Process Clause of the Fourteenth Amendment forbids closed criminal trials. Noting the "universal rule against secret trials", 333 U.S. at 266, 92 L Ed 682, 68 S Ct 499, the Court held that: "In view of this nation's historic distrust of secret proceedings, their inherent dangers to freedom, and the universal requirement of our federal and state governments that criminal trials be public, the Fourteenth Amendment's guarantee that no one shall be deprived of his liberty without due process of law means, at least, that an accused cannot be thus sentenced to prison." [Id., at 273, 92 L Ed 682, 68 S Ct 499.]

23. (Page 1000) Tradition, contemporaneous state practice, and this Court's own decisions manifest a common understanding that "[a] trial is a public event. What transpires in the court room is public property." [*Craig* v. *Harney*, 331 US 367 (374): 91 L Ed 1546: 67 S Ct 1249 (1947).]

24. (Page 1000-1001) Publicity serves to advance several of the particular purposes of the trial (and, indeed, the judicial) process. Open trials play a fundamental role in furthering the efforts of our judicial system to assure the criminal defendant a fair and accurate adjudication of guilt or innocence. [See, *e.g.*, *Estes* v. *Texas*, 381 US 538 (539): 14 L Ed 2nd 543: 85 S Ct 1628]. But, as a feature of our governing system of justice, the trial process serves other, broadly political, interests, and public access advances these objectives as well. To that extent, trial access possesses specific structural significance.

25. (Page 1001) Secrecy is profoundly inimical to this demonstrative purpose of the trial process. Open trials assure the public that procedural rights are respected, and that justice is afforded equally. Closed trials breed suspicion of prejudice and arbitrariness, which in turn spawns disrespect for law. Public access is essential, therefore, if trial adjudication is to achieve the objective of maintaining public confidence in the administration of justice. [See *Gannett*, supra at 428-429: 61 L Ed 2d 608: 99 S Ct 2898 (Blackmum, J., concurring and dissenting).

26. (Page 1003) Shrewd legal observers have averred that:

"open examination of witnesses viva voce, in the presence of all mankind, is much more conducive to the clearing up of truth than the private and secret examination...where a witness may frequently depose that in private which he will be ashamed to testify in a public and solemn tribunal."

Other Aspects

9. The question regarding Article 21 of the Constitution was also dealt with by this Court in *Kehar Singh* v *State (Delhi Administration),* (1988) 3 SCC 609: AIR 1988 SC 1883: 1989 Cr LJ 1. The relevant para 23 of the judgment reads as under:

> "23. The next main contention advanced by the counsel for the appellants is about the nature of the trial. It was contended that under Article 21 of the Constitution a citizen has a right to an open public trial and as by changing the venue the trial was shifted to Tihar Jail, it could not be said to be an open public trial. Learned counsel also referred to certain orders passed by the trial court wherein it has been provided that representatives of the Press may be permitted to attend and while passing those orders the learned trial Judge had indicated that for security and other regulations it will be open to Jail authorities to regulate the entry or issue passes necessary for coming to the Court and on the basis of these circumstances and the situation as it was in Tihar Jail it was contended that the trial was not public and open and therefore on this ground the trial vitiates. It was also contended that provisions contained in section 327 Cr.P.C. clearly provides that a trial in a criminal case has to be public and open except if any part of the proceedings for some special reasons to be recorded by the trial court, could be in camera. It was contended that the High Court while exercising jurisdiction. under section 9(6) notified the place of trial as Tihar Jail, it indirectly did what the trial court could have done in respect of particular, part of the proceedings and the, High. Court has no jurisdiction under section 327 to order trial to be held in camera or private and in fact as the trial was shifted to Tihar Jail it ceased to be open and public trial. Learned counsel on this part of the contention referred to decisions from American Supreme Court and also from House of Lords. In fact, the argument advanced has been on the basis of the American decisions where the concept of open trial has developed in due course of time whereas so far as India is concerned here even before the Constitution our criminal practice always contemplated a trial which is open to public."

10. In this case, the Court dealt with section 327 Cr.P.C. which reads as under:

> "*327. Court to be open.*—(1) The place in which any. Criminal Court is held for the purpose of inquiring into or trying any offence shall be deemed to be an open Court, to which the public generally may have access, so far as the same can conveniently contain them:
>
> Provided that the Presiding Judge or Magistrate, may, if he thinks fit, of order at any stage of any inquiry into, or trial of, any particular case, that the public generally, or any particular person, shall not have access to, or be or remain in, the room or building used by the Court.
>
> (2) Notwithstanding anything contained in sub-section (1), the inquiry into and trial of rape or an offence under section 376, section 376A, section 376B, section 376C or section 376D of the Indian Penal Code shall be conducted in camera:

Provided that the presiding judge may, if he thinks fit, or on an application made by either of the parties, allow any particular per: son to have access to, or be or remains in, the room or building used by the court.

(3) Where any proceedings are held under sub-section (2) it shall not be lawful for any person to print or publish any matter in relation to any such proceedings, except with the previous permission of the court."

11. On analysis of section 327 Cr.P.C., this Court observed as under (Kehar Singh case, SCC p. 638, para 24):

> "24. .... So far as this country is concerned the law be very clear that as soon as a trial of a criminal case is held whatever may be the place it will be an open trial. The only thing that it is necessary for the appellant is to point out that in fact that it was not an open trial. It is not disputed that there is no material at all to suggest that any one who wanted to attend the trial was prevented from so doing or one who wanted to go into the Court room was not allowed to do so and in absence of any such material on actual facts all these legal arguments loses its significance. The authorities on which reliance were placed are being dealt with elsewhere in the judgment."

12. In the concurring judgment, Ray, J. has specifically dealt with this aspect of the case. On interpretation of section 327 Cr.P.C., the Court observed as under:

> ".......It is pertinent of mention that section 327 of the Cr.P.C. provides that any place in which any criminal court is held for the purpose of inquiring into or trying any offence shall be deemed to be an open court, to which the public generally may have access, so far as the same can conveniently contain them. The place of trial in Tihar Jail according to this provision is to be deemed to be an open court as the access of the public to it was not prohibited. Moreover, it has been submitted on behalf of the prosecution that there is nothing to show that the friends and relations of the accused or any other member of the public was prevented from having access to the place where trial was held. On the other hand, it has been stated that permission was granted to the friends and relations of the accused as well as to outsiders who wanted to have access to the court to see the proceedings subject, of course, to jail regulations. Section 2(p) Criminal Procedure Code defines places as including a house, building, tent, vehicle and vessel. So court can be held in a tent, vehicle, a vessel other than in court. Furthermore, the proviso to section 327 Criminal Procedure Code provides that the presiding Judge or Magistrate may also at any stage of trial by order restrict access of the public in general, or any particular person in particular in the room or building where the trial is held. In some cases trial of criminal case is held in court and some restrictions are imposed for security reason regarding entry into the court. Such restrictions do not detract from trial in open court. Section 327 proviso empowers the Presiding Judge or Magistrate to make order denying entry of public in court. No such order had been made in this case denying access of members of public to court."

13. Public trial is an important part of the judicial system and this court in *Kehar Singh's* case has ruled:

> "In open dispensation of justice, the people may see that the State is not misusing the State machinery like the Police, the Prosecutors and other public servants. The people may see that the accused is fairly dealt with and not unjustly condemned. There is yet another aspect. The courts like other institutions also belong to people. They are as much human institutions as any other. The other instruments and institutions of the State may survive by the power of the purse or might of the sword. But not the Courts. The Courts have no such means or power. The Courts could survive only by the strength of public confidence. The public confidence can be fostered by exposing Courts more and more to public gaze."

14. In *Adolph Dammerau* v. *Commonwealth of Virginia,* 3 Va App 285 (1986), the Court of Appeal ruled:

> "Rather, the surroundings and circumstances of each situation must be examined to determine if the public was inhibited from attending the trial so that 'freedom of access' was effectively denied."

15. This clearly shows that the approach of the court that there is no presumption that a trial in prison is not an open trial. In *The People* v. *Robert* England the Court 83 Cal. App. 4th 772 (2000) of Appeals of California held that reasonable restrictions, like security checks should be allowed. The court found:

> "In this case, the court did not close the trial to the public. Defendant argues only that it was more difficult for the public to attend because some people would be dissuaded from attending a proceeding held on prison grounds and some would resent having to identify themselves to prison officials to gain access to the grounds. Neither concern impacts defendant's right to a public trial."

16. As noted previously, because the courtroom was located outside the actual prison wires, there was little possibility that the public might come into contact with inmates or otherwise be exposed to prison activities. That some people might not want to go to a courtroom located on prison grounds is irrelevant to determining whether a trial was public. Other individuals might not want to go downtown to an urban courtroom, while others might not want to drive long distances in rural areas to attend a courtroom located in another town. These individual predilections do not make what is otherwise a public trial any less public. Nor does the fact that individuals have to identify themselves before entering prison grounds unlawfully curtail defendant's right to a public trial. Far more stringent security procedures have been permitted in other cases. Therefore, to hold that the appellant's right to a public trial has been denied the appellant has to prove more than mere shifting of the location of the trial.

17. Lord Wilberforce in *Malloch* v. *Aberdeen Corporation,* (1971) 1 WLR 1578 laid down a test for courts before it interfered in the decisions of administrative authorities on the ground of violation of audi alteram partem. He stated:

> "The appellant has first to show that his position was such that he had, in principle, a right to make representations before a decision against him was taken. But to show this is not necessarily enough, unless he can also show that if admitted to state his case he had a case of substance to make. A breach of procedure, whether called a failure of natural justice, or an essential administrative fault, cannot give him a remedy in the courts, unless behind it there is something of substance which has been lost by the failure. The court does not act in vain."

18. In the present case, it has been shown by the respondents that no one had been denied from attending or watching the trial. The appellant is being represented by 38 lawyers. Apart from is lawyers, the press and those who want to attend the trial or case had free access to remain present during the court proceedings.

19. Cooley, J. in his well known book Cooley's Constitutional Law, Vol. I, 8th Edn., at page 647 observed as under:

> "It is also requisite that the trial be public. By this is not meant that every person who sees fit shall in all cases be permitted to attend criminal trials; because there are may cases where, from the character of the charge and the nature of the evidence by which it is to be supported, the motives to attend the trial on the part of portions of the community would be of the worst character, and where a regard for public morals and public decency would require that at least the young be excluded from hearing and witnessing the evidences of human depravity which the trial must necessarily bring to light. The requirement of a public trial is for the benefit of the accused; that the public may see he is fairly dealt with and not unjustly condemned, and that the presence of interested spectators may keep his triers keenly alive to a sense of their responsibility into the importance of their functions; and the requirement is fairly observed if, without partiality of favouritism, a reasonable proportion of the public is suffered to attend, notwithstanding that those persons whose presence could be of no service to the accused, and who would only be drawn thither by a prurient curiosity, are excluded altogether."

20. Every criminal act is an offence against the society. The crime is a wrong done more to the society than to an individual. It involves a serious invasion of rights and liberties of some other person or persons. The people are, therefore, entitled to know whether the justice delivery system is adequate or inadequate. Whether it responds appropriately to the situation or it presents a pathetic picture. This is one aspect. The other aspect is still more fundamental. When the State representing the society seeks to prosecute a person, the State must do it openly.

21. In *Gannett Co. Inc.* v. *Danial A. DePasquale,* (1979) 443 US 368, the defendants were charged with murder and requested closure of the hearing of their motion to suppress allegedly involuntary confessions and physical evidence. The prosecution and the trial Judge agreed and said that closure was necessary. The public and the press were denied access to avoid adverse

publicity. The closure was also to ensure that the defendants' right to a fair trial was not jeopardized. The Supreme Court addressed to the question whether the public has an independent constitutional right of access to a pretrial judicial proceedings, even though the defendant, the prosecution, and the trial Judge had agreed that closure was necessary. Explaining that the right to a public trial is personal to the defendant, the Court held that the public and press do not have an independent right of access to pretrial proceedings under the Sixth Amendment.

22. Although the Court in Gannett held that no right of public access emanated from the sixth Amendment it did not decide whether a constitutional right of public access is guaranteed by the first amendment. This issue was discussed in great detail in *Richmond Newspaper* (supra). This case involved the closure of the court-room during the fourth attempt to try the accused for murder. The United States Supreme Court considered whether the public and press have a constitutional right of access to criminal trials under the first amendment. The Court held that the first and fourteenth amendments guarantee the public and press the right to attend criminal trials. But the *Richmond Newspapers* case (supra) still left the question as to whether the press and public could be excluded from trial when it may be in the best interest of fairness to make such an exclusion.

23. That question was considered in the *Globe Newspaper Co.* v. *Superior Court for the County of Norfolk,* (1982) 457 US 596: 73 L.Ed. 2d. 248 There the trial Judge excluded the press and public from the court room pursuant to a Massachusetts statute making closure mandatory in cases involving minor victims of sex crimes. The Court considered the constitutionality of the Massachusetts statute and held that the statute violated the first amendment because of its mandatory nature. But it was held that it would be open to the Court in any given case to deny public access to criminal trials on the ground of state's interest. Brennan, J., who delivered the opinion of the Court said (at 258-59):

> "We agree with appellee that the first interest - safeguarding the physical and psychological well-being of a minor - is a compelling one. But as compelling as that interest is, it does not justify a mandatory closure rule, for it is clear that the circumstances of the particular case may affect the significance of the interest. A trial court can determine on a case by case basis whether closure is necessary to protect the welfare of a minor victim. Among the factors to be weighed are the minor victim's age, psychological maturity and understanding, the nature of the crime, the desires of the victims, and the interests of parents and relatives. .... Such an approach ensures that the constitutional right of the press and public to gain access to criminal trials will not be restricted except where necessary to protect the State's interest."

CHAPTER 19

LAW PLACING BURDEN OF PROOF ON THE ACCUSED VALIDATED BEING NECESSARY TO MEET WITH THE MENACE OF LIQUOR ADULTERATION

Chandran @ Manichan v. *State of Kerala*, (2011) 5 SCC 161: AIR 2011 SC 1594: 2011 (2) Crimes 111

The High Points

1. Hooch tragedy causing 31 deaths and leaving 266 grievously hurt, 5 losing their eyesight – burden of proof – validity of law shifting burden of proof to accused

The Fact Sheet

2. Prosecution alleged that methyl alcohol which is a poisonous substance used to be brought from Karnataka and mixed with Ethyl alcohol. At times, this concoction was mixed with toddy and other essences resulting in a drink called Kalapani. The methyl alcohol used to be mixed with ethyl alcohol which was also illegally and illicitly procured in order to add potency to the drink so that larger number of people would purchase the same. These sales were made from the regularly licensed toddy shops and from other places. There was an organised gang, the main component of which was Chandran (accused No.7) who was a toddy contractor. His brothers, Manikantan (accused No.4) and Vinod Kumar (accused No.8) were deputies helping him. This group had servants like Balachandran (A-15), the Manager. Even their wives did not lag behind. There were laboratories, assistants and labourers. There were drivers and a fleet of vehicles which were used for importing methyl alcohol from Karnataka and then brought to the laboratories maintained by Chandran (A-7), Manikantan (A-4) and Vinod Kumar (A-8) where the mixing took place.

3. The prosecution alleged that the conspiracy was hatched in March, 2000 amongst all the accused and because of the criminal act on the part of the accused of mixing poisonous methyl spirit, death of as many as 31 persons was caused, and as many as 266 persons suffered grievous injuries while 5 persons lost their eye sight completely. All the accused persons were, therefore, charged with the offences under sections 302, 307, 326, 328, 201, 120B read with section 34 of the Indian Penal Code as also under section 55(a)(g)(h) and

(i), section 57A and section 58 of Abkari Act. On the basis of this charge, evidence of 270 witnesses was led. The accused abjured their guilt and claimed to be tried.

Departure from Settled Law

4. There was a gruesome liquor tragedy in Earnakulam district in the year 1982 resulting in loss of eye-sight and physical incapacity in case of several persons and, therefore, severe penalties were provided for those who were responsible for adulteration of liquor and its sale. These punishments were made further stringent by the Amendment Act No.12 of 1995. In short, the stringency was introduced in order to check the sale of spurious liquor. Section 57A of Act is the most relevant section for our purpose which the section reads as under:

Section "57A. For adulteration of liquor or intoxicating drug with noxious substances, etc.—

(1) whoever mixes or permits to be mixed any noxious substance or any substance which is likely to endanger human life or to cause grievous hurt to human beings, with any liquor or intoxicating drug shall, on conviction, be punishable—

(i) if, as a result of such act, grievous hurt is caused to any person, with imprisonment for a term which shall not be less than two years but which may extend to imprisonment for life, and with fine which may extend to fifty thousand rupees;

(ii) if, as a result of such act, death is caused to any person, with death or imprisonment for a term which shall not be less than three years but which may extend to imprisonment for life, and with fine which may extend to fifty thousand rupees;

(iii) in any other case, with imprisonment for a term which shall not be less than one year, but which may extend to ten years, and with fine which may extend to twenty-five thousand rupees.

Explanation.—for the purpose of this section and section 57B the expression 'grievous hurt' shall have the same meaning as in section 320 of the Indian Penal Code, 1860 (Central Act 45 of 1860).

(2) whoever omits to take reasonable precautions to prevent the mixing of any noxious substance or any substance which is likely to endanger human life or to cause grievous hurt to human beings, with any liquor or intoxicating drug shall, on conviction, punishable—

(i) if as a result of such omission, grievous hurt is caused to any person, with imprisonment for a term which shall not be less than two years but which may extend to imprisonment for life, and with fine which may extend to fifty thousand rupees;

(ii) if as a result of such omission, death is caused to any person, with imprisonment for a term which shall not be less than three years but which may extend to imprisonment for life, and with the fine which may extend to fifty thousand rupees;

(iii) in any other case, with imprisonment for a term which shall not be less than one year but which may extend to ten years, and with fine which may extend to twenty-five thousand rupees.

(3) whoever possesses any liquor or intoxicating drug in which any substance referred to in sub-section (1) is mixed, knowing that such substance is mixed with such liquor or intoxicating drug shall, on conviction, be punishable with imprisonment for a term which shall not be less than one year but may extend to ten years, and with fine which may extend to twenty-five thousand rupees.

(4) notwithstanding anything contained in the Code of Criminal Procedure, 1973 (Central Act 2 of 1974), no person accused or convicted of an offence under sub- section (1) or sub-section (3) shall, if in custody, be released on bail or on his own bond, unless—

(a) the prosecution has been given an opportunity to oppose the application for such release, and

(b) where the prosecution opposes the application, the Court is satisfied that there are reasonable grounds for believing that he is not guilty of such offence.

(5) notwithstanding anything contained in the Indian Evidence Act, 1872 (1 of 1872)—

(a) where a person is prosecuted for an offence under sub section (1) or sub-section (2) the burden of proving that he has not mixed or permitted to be mixed or, as the case may be, omitted to take reasonable precautions to prevent the mixing of, any substance referred to in that sub-section with any liquor or intoxicating drug shall be on him;

(b) where a person is prosecuted for an offence under sub-section (3) for being in possession of any liquor or intoxicating drug in which any substance referred to in sub-section (1) is mixed, the burden of proving that he did not know that such substance was mixed with such liquor or intoxicating drug shall be on him."

5. A plain reading of the section would mean that now the offence is not limited to the licence holders, but refers to anybody who mixes or permits to be mixed any noxious substance or any substance which is likely to endanger human life with any liquor. The section, therefore, is extremely general. In addition to the mixing or permitting to be mixed, sub-section (2) brings in the dragnet of the offence, a person who omits to take reasonable precaution to prevent the mixing of any noxious substance. It is significant to note that if, as a result of such act of mixing of the liquor with noxious or dangerous substance death is caused, the extreme penalty of death also is provided. Imprisonment provided is for a term not less than three years but which may extend to imprisonment for life as also with a fine of Rs. 50,000. Similar such penalties provided in sub-section 2(ii) and sub-section 2(iii) are also relevant providing for residuary cases. Section 3 is the punishment for possession of any liquor or intoxicating drug which is mixed with noxious substance or dangerous drug knowing it to be so. Sub-section (4) prohibits the bail and the

conditions for grant thereof. Sub-section (5) which is the most important section, puts the burden of proving that the accused has not mixed or permitted to be mixed or has not omitted to take reasonable precautions to prevent the mixing, is on the accused himself. Similarly, the burden would be on the accused to prove that while he was in possession of such liquor mixed with noxious or dangerous substance, he did not know that such substance was mixed with such liquor.

Role of *Mens Rea*

6. The question of intention bears no relevance to an offence under section 57A and equally of culpability or negligence. It is seen that mixing or permitting to mix noxious substance or any other substance with liquor or intoxicated drug or omission to take reasonable precaution or being in possession without knowledge of its adulteration for the purpose of unjust enrichment would be without any regard for loss of precious human lives or grievous hurt. The legislature has noted the inadequacy and deficiency in the existing law to meet the menace of adulteration of liquor etc. and provided for new offences and directed with mandatory language protection of the health and precious lives of innocent consumers. While interpreting the law, the court must be cognizant to the purpose of the law and respect the legislative animation and effectuate the law for social welfare. The legislature enacted deterrent social provisions to combat the degradation of human conduct. These special provisions are to some extent harsh and are a departure from normal criminal jurisprudence. But it is not uncommon in criminal statutes. It is a special mode to tackle new situations created by human proclivity to amass wealth at the alter of human lives. So it is not right to read down the law."

Challenge

7. The challenge was made on the basis of the Universal Declaration of Human Rights (UDHR) and the International Convention for Civil and Political Rights (ICCPR), to which India is a member which guarantees fundamental freedom and liberty to the accused. It was suggested that in criminal jurisprudence it was settled law that it was on the prosecution to prove all the ingredients of the offence with which the accused has been charged. It was suggested that sub-section (5) relieves the prosecution of its duty to prove its case beyond reasonable doubt which is incumbent under the Code and the Evidence Act and makes the accused to disprove the prosecution case. Thereby, the substantive provisions and the burden of proof not only violate the fundamental human rights but, also Fundamental Rights under Articles 20(3) and 14.

The Verdict

8. Coming to the burden of proof, the Court observed that though in civilized criminal jurisprudence the accused is presumed to be innocent unless he is found guilty and though the burden of proof always is on the prosecution to prove the offence beyond reasonable doubt yet the rule gets modulated with the march of time. The Court referred to the absolute right of the state to regulate production, transport, storage, possession and sale of

liquor or intoxicating drug and held that the accused did not have the absolute right to business or trade of liquor. The Court also referred to the prohibitions regarding mixing of noxious substance with liquor or possession thereof and further held that the State possessed the right to complete control on all kinds of intoxicants. The Court found that the regulation of sale of potable liquor prevents reckless propensity for adulterating liquor to make easy gain at the cost of health and precious life of consumer. The Court also noted the object of the Amendment Act which was to prevent recurrence of large scale deaths or grievous hurt to the consumers of adulterated liquor mixed with noxious substance. Referring to a judgment reported as *Salabiaku* v. *Grance,* [1988] 13 EHRR 379, the Court observed that the national legislature would be free to strip the trial Court of any genuine power of assessment and deprive the presumption of innocence of its substance, if the words 'according to law' were construed exclusively with reference to domestic law. It was held in that case that Article 6(2) of the Universal Declaration of Human Rights did not refer to presumption of fact or of law provided for in the criminal law with indifference. It requires States to confine them within reasonable limits which take into account the importance of that is at stake and maintain the rights of the defence. Providing exceptions or to place partial burden on the accused was not violative of universal declaration of human rights or even Convention on Civil or Political Rights.

While commenting on Article 20(3), this Court referred to *R.C. Cooper* v. *Union of India,* reported as (1970) 1 SCC 248: AIR 1970 SC 564: (1970) 2 SCA 37 as also *Kartar Singh* v. *State of Punjab,* (1994) 3 SCC 569: 1994 Cr LJ 3139: (1994) 2 SCR 375, where it was held that freedom could not last long unless it was coupled with order, freedom can never exist without order and both freedom and order may co-exist. It was observed that Liberty must be controlled in the interest of the society but the social interest must never be overbearing to justify total deprivation of individual liberty. It was then stated that liberty would not always be an absolute licence but must arm itself within the confines of law. In other words, there can be no liberty without social restraint. The Court also observed that the liberty of each citizen is borne of and must be subordinated to the liberty of the greatest number. The Court observed that common happiness is an end of the society, lest lawlessness and anarchy should tamper social wheel and harmony and powerful courses or forces would be at work to undermine social welfare and order. The Court then observed in paragraph 24 as under:

> "The State has the power to prohibit trade or business which are illegal, immoral or injurious to the health and welfare of the people. No one has the right to carry on any trade or occupation or business which is inherently vicious and pernicious and is condemned by all civilized societies. Equally no one could claim entitlement to carry on any trade or business or any activities which are criminal and immoral or in any articles of goods which are obnoxious and injurious to the safety and health of general public. There is no inherent right in crime. Prohibition of trade or business of noxious or dangerous substance or goods, by law is in the interest of social welfare."

CHAPTER 20

LEGAL MEANING OF "CONSENT" AND VALUE OF VICTIM'S STATEMENT IN RAPE CASES

State of Uttar Pradesh v. *Chhotey Lal,* (2011) 2 SCC 550 (Cri)

Background

1. The trial court convicted the accused for rape of a 17-years old girl. The High Court acquitted holding that the age could be 19-years and that absence of injury marks on her body indicated that she was habitual of sexual intercourse. The Supreme Court reversed explaining the concept of 'consent' and the value of prosecutrix's version.

Need of urgent steps to reform criminal justice system

2. We are constrained to observe that criminal justice system is not working in our country as it should. The police reforms have not taken place despite directions of this Court in the case of *Prakash Singh* v. *Union of India,* (2006) 8 SCC 1. We do not intend to say anything more in this regard since matter is being dealt with separately by a 3-Judge Bench.

3. The investigators hardly have professional orientation; they do not have modern *Prakash Singh* v. *Union of India,* (2006) 8 SCC 1: 2006 AIR SCW 5233 tools. On many occasions impartial investigation suffers because of political interference. The criminal trials are protracted because of non-appearance of official witnesses on time and the non-availability of the facilities for recording evidence by video conferencing. The public prosecutors have their limitations; the defence lawyers do not make themselves available and the court would be routinely informed about their pre-occupation with other matters; the courts remain over-burdened with the briefs listed on the day and they do not have adequate infrastructure. The adjournments thus become routine; the casualty is justice. It is imperative that the criminal cases relating to offences against the State, corruption, dowry death, domestic violence, sexual assault, financial fraud and cyber crimes are fast tracked and decided in a fixed time frame, preferably, of three years including the appeal provisions. It is high time that immediate and urgent steps are taken in amending the procedural and other laws to achieve the above objectives. We must remember that a strong and efficient criminal justice system is a guarantee to the rule of law and vibrant civil society.

The Verdict

Evidence of prosecutrix – importance and relevancy

4. ....the evidence of the prosecutrix needs to be analysed and examined carefully. But, before we do that, we state, as has been repeatedly stated by this Court, that a woman who is victim of sexual assault is not an accomplice to the crime. Her evidence cannot be tested with suspicion as that of an accomplice. As a matter of fact, the evidence of the prosecutrix is similar to the evidence of an injured complainant or witness. The testimony of prosecutrix, if found to be reliable, by itself, may be sufficient to convict the culprit and no corroboration of her evidence is necessary. In prosecutions of rape, the law does not require corroboration. The evidence of the prosecutrix may sustain a conviction. It is only by way of abundant caution that court may look for some corroboration so as to satisfy its conscience and rule out any false accusations.

Rape victim's predicament

5. The important thing that the court has to bear in mind is that what is lost by a rape victim is face. The victim loses value as a person. Ours is a conservative society and, therefore, a woman and more so a young unmarried woman will not put her reputation in peril by alleging falsely about forcible sexual assault. In examining the evidence of the prosecutrix the courts must be alive to the conditions prevalent in the Indian society and must not be swayed by beliefs in other countries. The courts must be sensitive and responsive to the plight of the female victim of sexual assault. Society's belief and value systems need to be kept uppermost in mind as rape is the worst form of woman's oppression. A forcible sexual assault brings in humiliation, feeling of disgust, tremendous embarrassment, sense of shame, trauma and lifelong emotional scar to a victim and it is, therefore, most unlikely of a woman, and more so by a young woman, roping in somebody falsely in the crime of rape. The stigma that attaches to the victim of rape in Indian society ordinarily rules out the leveling of false accusations. An Indian woman traditionally will not concoct an untruthful story and bring charges of rape for the purpose of blackmail, hatred, spite or revenge.

Determining age of a rape victim

6. We find ourselves in agreement with the view of the trial court regarding the age of the prosecutrix. The High Court conjectured that the age of the prosecutrix could be even 19 years. This appears to have been done by adding two years to the age opined by PW-5. There is no such rule much less an absolute one that two years have to be added to the age determined by a doctor. We are supported by a 3-Judge Bench decision of this Court in *State of Karnataka* v. *Bantara Sudhakara,* (2008) 11 SCC 38, wherein this Court stated as under:

> "Additionally, merely because the doctor's evidence showed that the victims belong to the age group of 14 to 16, to conclude that the two years' age has to be added to the upper age-limit is without any foundation."

7. Learned counsel for the respondent relied upon a decision of this Court in the case of *Mussauddin Ahmed* v. *State of Assam*, (2009) 14 SCC 541: AIR 2010 SC 3813: 2009 (3) Crimes 238 in support of his submission that the best evidence concerning the age of prosecutrix having been withheld, the finding of the High Court that the prosecutrix could be 19 years of age cannot be said to erroneous. In the present case, the brother of the prosecutrix has been examined as PW-1 and, therefore, it cannot be said that best evidence has been withheld. The decision of this Court in Mussauddin Ahmed has no application at all. In our view, the High Court fell in grave error in observing that the prosecutrix could be even 19 years of age at the time of alleged occurrence.

8. Be that as it may, in our view, clause Sixthly of section 375 IPC is not attracted since the prosecutrix has been found to be above 16 years (although below 18 years). In the facts of the case what is crucial to be considered is whether clause First or clause Secondly of section 375 IPC is attracted. The expressions 'against her Will' and 'without her consent' may overlap sometimes but surely the two expressions in clause First and clause Secondly have different connotation and dimension. The expression 'against her will' would ordinarily mean that the intercourse was done by a man with a woman despite her resistance and opposition. On the other hand, the expression 'without her consent' would comprehend an act of reason accompanied by deliberation.

The meaning of "consent" explained

9. The concept of 'consent' in the context of section 375 IPC has come up for consideration before this Court on more than one occasion. Before we deal with some of these decisions, reference to section 90 of the IPC may be relevant which reads as under:

> "*90. Consent known to be given under fear or misconception.*—A consent is not such a consent as it is intended by any section of this Code, if the consent is given by a person under fear of injury, or under a misconception of fact, and if the person doing the act knows, or has reason to believe, that the consent was given in consequence of such fear or misconception; or
>
> Consent of insane person.—if the consent is given by a person who, from unsoundness of mind, or intoxication, is unable to understand the nature and consequence of that to which he gives his consent; or
>
> Consent of child.—unless the contrary appears from the context, if the consent is given by a person who is under twelve years of age."

10. This Court in a long line of cases has given wider meaning to the word 'consent' in the context of sexual offences as explained in various judicial dictionaries. In *Jowitt's Dictionary of English Law* (2nd Edn.), Vol. 1 (1977) at p. 422 the word 'consent' has been explained as an act of reason accompanied with deliberation, the mind weighing, as in a balance, the good or evil on either side. It is further stated that consent supposes three things—a physical power, a mental power, and a free and serious use of them and if consent be obtained by intimidation, force, meditated imposition, circumvention, surprise,

or undue influence, it is to be treated as a delusion, and not as a deliberate and free act of the mind.

11. *Stroud's Judicial Dictionary* (4th Edn.), Vol. 1 (1971) at p. 555 explains the expression 'consent', *inter alia,* as under:

> "Every `consent' to an act, involves a submission; but it by no means follows that a mere submission involves consent," *e.g.* the mere submission of a girl to a carnal assault, she being in the power of a strong man, is not consent [per Coleridge J., *R.* v. *Day,* (1841) 9 C&P 722: 173 ER 1026]."

Stroud's Judicial Dictionary also refers to decision in the case of *Holman* v. *The Queen,* 1970 WAR 2 wherein it was stated:

> "But there does not necessarily have to be complete willingness to constitute consent. A woman's consent to intercourse may be hesitant, reluctant or grudging, but if she consciously permits it there is 'consent'."

12. In Words and Phrases, Permanent Edition, (Volume 8A) at pages 205-206, few American decisions wherein the word 'consent' has been considered and explained with regard to the law of rape have been referred. These are as follows:

> "In order to constitute 'rape', there need not be resistance to the utmost, and a woman who is assaulted need not resist to the point of risking being beaten into insensibility, and, if she resists to the point where further resistance would be useless or until her resistance is overcome by force or violence, submission thereafter is not 'consent'. [*People* v. *Mcilvain,* 55 Cal App 2d 322]."
>
> *** *** ***
>
> 'Consent', within Penal Law, ' 2010, defining rape, requires exercise of intelligence based on knowledge of its significance and moral quality and there must be a choice between resistance and assent. *People* v. *Pelvino,* (1926) 214 NYS 577.
>
> *** *** ***
>
> 'Consenting' as used in the law of rape means consent of the will and submission under the influence of fear or terror cannot amount to real consent. *Hallmark* v. *State,* 22 Okl Cr 422.
>
> *** *** ***
>
> Will is defined as wish, desire, pleasure, inclination, choice, the faculty of conscious, and especially of deliberate action. It is purely and solely a mental process to be ascertained, in a prosecution for rape, by what the prosecuting witness may have said or done. It being a mental process there is no other manner by which her will can be ascertained, and it must be left to the jury to determine that will by her acts and statements, as disclosed by the evidence. It is but natural, therefore, that in charging the jury upon the subject of rape, or assault with intent to commit rape, the courts should have almost universally, and, in many cases, exclusively, discussed 'consent' and resistance. There can be no better evidence of willingness is a condition or state of mind no better evidence of unwillingness than resistance. No

lexicographer recognizes 'consent' as a synonym of willingness, and it is apparent that they are not synonymous. It is equally apparent, on the other hand, that the true relation between the words is that willingness is a condition or state of mind and 'consent' one of the evidences of that condition. Likewise resistance is not a synonym of unwillingness, though it is an evidence thereof. In all cases, therefore, where the prosecuting witness has an intelligent will, the court should charge upon the elements of 'consent' and resistance as being proper elements from which the jury may infer either a favourable or an opposing will. It must, however, be recognized in all cases that the real test is whether the assault was committed against the will of the prosecuting witness. [*State* v. *Schwab*, 143 NE 29].

13. In *Uday* v. *State of Karnataka*, (2003) 4 SCC 46: AIR 2003 SC 1639: 2003 Cr LJ 1539, this Court put a word of caution that there is no straitjacket formula for determining whether consent given by the prosecutrix to sexual intercourse is voluntary, or whether it is given under a misconception of fact. The Court at SCC p. 57 stated: "In the ultimate analysis, the tests laid down by the courts provide at best guidance to the judicial mind while considering a question of consent, but the court must, in each case, consider the evidence before it and the surrounding circumstances, before reaching a conclusion, because each case has its own peculiar facts which may have a bearing on the question whether the consent was voluntary, or was given under a misconception of fact."